AWS Certified SysOps Administrator – Associate Guide

Your one-stop solution for passing the AWS SysOps
Administrator certification

Marko Sluga

BIRMINGHAM - MUMBAI

AWS Certified SysOps Administrator – Associate Guide

Commissioning Editor: Vijin Boricha
Acquisition Editor: Heramb Bhavsar
Content Development Editor: Abhishek Jadhav
Technical Editor: Prachi Sawant
Copy Editor: Safis Editing
Project Coordinator: Jagdish Prabhu
Proofreader: Safis Editing
Indexer: Pratik Shirodkar
Graphics: Tom Scaria
Production Coordinator: Aparna Bhagat

First published: January 2019

Production reference: 1280119

Published by Packt Publishing Ltd.
Livery Place
35 Livery Street
Birmingham
B3 2PB, UK.

ISBN 978-1-78899-077-6

www.packtpub.com

mapt.io

Mapt is an online digital library that gives you full access to over 5,000 books and videos, as well as industry leading tools, to help you plan your personal development and advance your career. For more information, please visit our website.

Why subscribe?

- Spend less time learning and more time coding with practical eBooks and videos from over 4,000 industry professionals

- Improve your learning with Skill Plans built especially for you

- Get a free eBook or video every month

- Mapt is fully searchable

- Copy and paste, print, and bookmark content

Packt.com

Did you know that Packt offers eBook versions of every book published, with PDF and ePub files available? You can upgrade to the eBook version at www.packt.com and as a print book customer, you are entitled to a discount on the eBook copy. Get in touch with us at customercare@packtpub.com for more details.

At www.packt.com, you can also read a collection of free technical articles, sign up for a range of free newsletters, and receive exclusive discounts and offers on Packt books and eBooks.

Contributors

About the author

Marko Sluga has had the opportunity to work in computing at a very exciting time and has been privileged enough to witness the rise of cloud computing in the last 20 years. Beginning his career as a service technician, he excelled at solving difficult problems. He worked his way up the IT food chain to work on servers, operating systems, virtualization, and the cloud. In the past, Marko has architected numerous cloud computing solutions and today works as a cloud technology consultant and an Authorized Amazon Instructor. He is AWS certified, holding the Architect, SysOps, and Developer Associate AWS certification, the DevOps and Architect Professional AWS certification, and the Security, Advanced Networking, and Big Data Specialty AWS certification.

About the reviewers

Ralph Parisi is an IT consultant, evangelist, and teacher. He has been working in the IT industry for over 20 years. His first career was in the broadcast television industry where he worked for WNYW as a post-production editor. Ralph has extensive knowledge of server operating systems, email, Active Directory, Group Policy, networking, and cloud architecture. Ralph has been certified as a Microsoft Certified Trainer, Citrix Certified Instructor, and Amazon Authorized Instructor. He holds the following certifications: AWS Certified Architect – Professional, AWS Certified SysOps Administrator – Associate, and AWS Certified Security – Specialty.

John Muia is an AWS Certified SysOps Administrator, with extensive experience in managing servers and IT infrastructure in the AWS cloud. He can effectively plan and calculate the total cost of ownership, and configure IT infrastructure that achieves high availability and performance. He has spent the last two years designing scalable, elastic, highly available, and secure system architectures and applications for customers in the cloud. He is proficient in the use of monitoring tools such as Grafana, Nagios, and CloudWatch.

Anthony Ngunjiri is a young Kenyan living and working in Nairobi. He was born in Kenya in 1990. Before venturing in information technology, he had an interest in aviation, and studied flight dispatch in 2014. He was a student at Zetech University studying for a diploma in Business and Information Technology. He graduated in 2018. He heard of AWS in 2016 when he started his practice, and he gained his AWS SysOps admin certification in 2017. He is currently preparing to become a certified AWS DevOps professional in April 2019.

Packt is searching for authors like you

If you're interested in becoming an author for Packt, please visit authors.packtpub.com and apply today. We have worked with thousands of developers and tech professionals, just like you, to help them share their insight with the global tech community. You can make a general application, apply for a specific hot topic that we are recruiting an author for, or submit your own idea.

Table of Contents

Preface

Before we begin, I would like to extend a warm welcome and congratulate you on your decision to embark on a journey to becoming an AWS Certified SysOps Administrator. This publication, the *AWS Certified SysOps Administrator – Associate Guide*, is designed to guide you through the process of learning about the services AWS offers and gives you the tools required to access, configure, and use of the AWS cloud computing environment as well as perform basic troubleshooting in the environment.

By reading through this book and trying out the practical examples that are outlined throughout, you will be able to gain valuable knowledge that can be put to use when you decide to attempt to take the AWS Certified SysOps Administrator exam. Taking an exam is no small feat and should be considered a learning process.

In general, this book is intended to familiarize the reader with the concept of cloud computing and the services offered by Amazon Web Services – currently, the market leader and *de facto* standard for public cloud computing services. The reader will learn about the technologies offered by Amazon Web Services that allow for the deployment and operation of modern, web-scale applications. Furthermore, particular attention will be given to those areas covered in the blueprint of the Amazon Web Services Certified SysOps Administrator-Associate exam, since the main purpose of this book is to prepare the reader with the information required to undertake and pass the aforementioned exam.

Who this book is for

This book is designed for system administrators, operators, and engineers who are looking to operate and maintain applications running on the AWS platform. While the book focuses on giving the reader the information required to pass the AWS Certified SysOps Administrator-Associate exam, it is also beneficial to keep the book close by in the workplace as a reference manual for understanding the common set of AWS services that a SysOps engineer works with on a daily basis.

What this book covers

Chapter 1, *Overview of AWS Certified SysOps Administrators and Associated Certification*, outlines the AWS Certified SysOps Administrator-Associate exam and highlights the critical aspects, knowledge areas, and services covered in the official Amazon blueprint that elaborates the scope of the aforementioned exam, the prerequisites for attending the exam, and the knowledge required to pass the exam.

Chapter 2, *The Fundamentals of Amazon Web Services*, begins with an explanation of what the cloud is and takes the reader through a brief journey of familiarizing them with the basic building blocks of Amazon Web Services. It highlights some of the critical aspects of how AWS works and provides an overview of AWS's core infrastructure.

Chapter 3, *Managing AWS Security with Identity and Access Management*, explains how AWS facilitates the provision of security, as one of the most critical aspects of IT operations and administration activities, through its Identity and Access Management (IAM) service. This service provides a very strong backbone for controlling the security of the user infrastructure. This chapter covers all the critical aspects of the IAM service and provides a proper understanding of the various features and functionalities of the IAM service.

Chapter 4, *Networking with the Virtual Private Cloud*, describes how you can create a Virtual Private Cloud and start building a secure network using a number of components of AWS Networking Services.

Chapter 5, *Managing Servers on AWS with Elastic Compute Cloud*, describes what EC2 is and how you can start provisioning servers with various Windows and Linux operating system flavors. It also describes how to connect and work with these servers. By the end of this chapter, readers should be able to work and manage EC2 instances. It also goes into various types of Elastic Block Storage, which is attached as a volume to EC2 instances.

Chapter 6, *Handling Server Traffic with Elastic Load Balancing*, describes different types of Elastic Load Balancing (ELB) and the step-by-step process for creating different types of ELB. It also elaborates on how ELB works and the critical aspects of the ELB service.

Chapter 7, *Understanding Simple Storage Service and Glacier*, provides an explanation of the Amazon Simple Storage Service (S3), Glacier, and CloudFront services. After elaborating on S3, this chapter explains the cheaper archival storage option, Glacier.

Chapter 8, *Understanding Content Distribution with CloudFront*, provides an overview of what CloudFront is and how it works, while also explaining a number of its critical features.

Chapter 9, *AWS Storage Options*, provides a brief description of various storage options available on AWS and touches on the AWS Storage Gateway service. It also provides an overview of AWS Snowball, which is a service that accelerates the transfer of large amounts of data into and out of AWS using physical storage appliances. It also provides a basic review of AWS Snowmobile, which is an exabyte-scale data transfer service used to move extremely large amounts of data to and from AWS.

Chapter 10, *Working with Route 53 Domain Name System*, affords an introduction to the Amazon Route 53 service and describes its various components.

Chapter 11, *Working with Relational Database Services*, provides an explanation of AWS Relational Database Services (AWS RDS). It covers the different types of engines supported by AWS RDS and how to efficiently and effectively create and manage RDS instances on AWS.

Chapter 12, *Introduction to ElastiCache*, provides an overview of ElastiCache and describes how you can use Redis and Memcached engine types.

Chapter 13, *Amazon DynamoDB – A NoSQL Database Service*, describes various components of DynamoDB and best practices for managing it.

Chapter 14, *Working with Simple Queue Service*, provides an overview of SQS (a distributed message queuing service) and describes a step-by-step process on how to create and manage it with the help of relevant examples.

Chapter 15, *Handling Messaging with SNS*, outlines the Simple Notification Service (SNS), which is a fully managed messaging service that can be used to send messages, alarms, and notifications to and from various AWS services, including Amazon RDS, CloudWatch, and S3, to other AWS services, such as SQS and Lambda.

Chapter 16, *Getting Started with Simple Workflow Service*, provides a basic understanding of the Simple Workflow Service and its various components, along with a brief description of how to use them.

Chapter 17, *Overview of AWS Lambda*, provides an overview of Lambda and describes how it runs code in response to events and automatically manages the compute resources required by that code.

Chapter 18, *Monitoring Resources with Amazon CloudWatch*, describes how you can use Amazon CloudWatch to collect and track a variety of resource metrics, collect and monitor log files, set alarms, and automatically react to changes in your AWS resources.

Chapter 19, *Understanding Elastic Beanstalk,* provides an introduction to Elastic Beanstalk and describes how to deploy and manage applications using the service.

Chapter 20, *Automation with CloudFormation Service,* provides an overview of the CloudFormation service, a service that helps you to describe and provision your AWS resources. A CloudFormation template provides a simpler and more efficient way to manage your resources on AWS.

Chapter 21, *Cloud Orchestration with OpsWorks,* provides an overview of the service and describes some of its critical components.

Chapter 22, *Exam Tips and Tricks,* provides detailed guidance on how you can prepare for the exam and provides tips and tricks on the topics covered in the book.

Chapter 23, *Mock Tests,* consists of two mock tests for readers to test their knowledge. It attempts to cover all the topics from the scope of the exam and challenges readers' understanding of the topics. Each mock test contains 60 questions. Readers should try to complete a mock test within 90 minutes.

To get the most out of this book

The knowledge that is required by readers in order to benefit from this book is as follows:

- A basic understanding of general cloud computing terminology and environments
- A basic understanding of networking, the OSI layers, and the IP stack
- A basic understanding of network function devices, such as routers, firewalls, load balancers, and content delivery networks
- A basic understanding of virtualization and server operating systems
- A basic understanding of user and security management
- A basic understanding of storage concepts (for example, object storage, block storage, and file storage)
- A basic understanding of database services
- A basic understanding of messaging in applications
- A basic understanding of serverless computing
- A basic understanding of automation and orchestration

In addition, a more in-depth understanding of the following topics will be beneficial:

- Designing applications for high availability and resilience
- Operating system scripting languages
- Database structures
- The JSON data format
- Programming languages and application design

Download the example code files

You can download the example code files for this book from your account at `www.packt.com`. If you purchased this book elsewhere, you can visit `www.packt.com/support` and register to have the files emailed directly to you.

You can download the code files by following these steps:

1. Log in or register at `www.packt.com`.
2. Select the **SUPPORT** tab.
3. Click on **Code Downloads & Errata**.
4. Enter the name of the book in the **Search** box and follow the onscreen instructions.

Once the file is downloaded, please make sure that you unzip or extract the folder using the latest version of:

- WinRAR/7-Zip for Windows
- Zipeg/iZip/UnRarX for Mac
- 7-Zip/PeaZip for Linux

The code bundle for the book is also hosted on GitHub at `https://github.com/PacktPublishing/AWS-Certified-SysOps-Administrator-Associate-Guide`. In case there's an update to the code, it will be updated on the existing GitHub repository.

We also have other code bundles from our rich catalog of books and videos available at `https://github.com/PacktPublishing/`. Check them out!

Download the color images

We also provide a PDF file that has color images of the screenshots/diagrams used in this book. You can download it here: `https://www.packtpub.com/sites/default/files/downloads/9781788990776_ColorImages.pdf`.

Conventions used

There are a number of text conventions used throughout this book.

`CodeInText`: Indicates code words in text, database table names, folder names, filenames, file extensions, pathnames, dummy URLs, user input, and Twitter handles. Here is an example: "Now, open the `index.html` file and edit the code to replace `https://yourimagelinkgoeshere` with your image link."

A block of code is set as follows:

```
<html>
<p>Everyone loves AWS!</p>
<p><a href="https://markocloud.com"><img
src="https://markocloud.com/wp-content/uploads/2016/02/markocloud-180.g
if" alt="" width="180" height="155" /></a></p>
</html>
```

Any command-line input or output is written as follows:

```
$ sudo file -s /dev/xvdb
```

Bold: Indicates a new term, an important word, or words that you see on screen. For example, words in menus or dialog boxes appear in the text like this. Here is an example: "To do so, we need to click on the bucket, select the **Management** tab, and click on **Add lifecycle rule**."

Warnings or important notes appear like this.

Tips and tricks appear like this.

Get in touch

Feedback from our readers is always welcome.

General feedback: If you have questions about any aspect of this book, mention the book title in the subject of your message and email us at customercare@packtpub.com.

Errata: Although we have taken every care to ensure the accuracy of our content, mistakes do happen. If you have found a mistake in this book, we would be grateful if you would report this to us. Please visit www.packt.com/submit-errata, selecting your book, clicking on the Errata Submission Form link, and entering the details.

Piracy: If you come across any illegal copies of our works in any form on the internet, we would be grateful if you would provide us with the location address or website name. Please contact us at copyright@packt.com with a link to the material.

If you are interested in becoming an author: If there is a topic that you have expertise in, and you are interested in either writing or contributing to a book, please visit authors.packtpub.com.

Reviews

Please leave a review. Once you have read and used this book, why not leave a review on the site that you purchased it from? Potential readers can then see and use your unbiased opinion to make purchase decisions, we at Packt can understand what you think about our products, and our authors can see your feedback on their book. Thank you!

For more information about Packt, please visit packt.com.

1
Overview of AWS Certified SysOps Administrators and Associated Certification

Before taking the exam, you should familiarize yourself with the knowledge requirements and the exam's structure to get a good understanding of the concepts that the exam is designed to test.

We will cover the exam's structure through the following topics:

- The exam's blueprint
- The exam's requirements
- The exam's structure
- The exam's scoring
- The knowledge domains
- The questions structure
- How to take the exam

The exam blueprint

For every certification, AWS delivers a blueprint that can be used as a reference tool to get an overview of the objectives and requirements of the exam. According to the blueprint for the AWS Certified SysOps Administrator – Associate exam. Taking and passing the exam will prove your technical ability to create and migrate resources, manage and operate them, and deliver highly available solutions in the cloud, as well as your ability to identify best practices and estimate costs.

The areas of knowledge that the exam is designed to test can be grouped into the following concepts:

- Deploying, managing, and operating systems and services on AWS
- Understanding how to select a service based on various requirements
- The ability to migrate an existing application to AWS
- Delivering scalability, high availability, and fault-tolerance
- Designing and securing the flow of data to and from AWS
- Identifying the appropriate use of AWS best practices
- Estimating AWS usage and utilizing operational cost-control mechanisms

The exam's requirements

As mentioned previously, you should consider passing the AWS Certified Systems Administrator exam as the end goal of this journey. Part of this journey is familiarizing yourself with the services AWS offers and being able to use them. You should also consider that an eligible candidate for this exam is required to have general knowledge of IT and experience with AWS in the following areas:

- General IT – 1-2 years' experience in a SysAdmin/SysOps role
- One or more years' hands-on experience operating production systems on AWS
- Hands-on experience with the AWS CLI and/or SDKs and/or API tools
- A good understanding of the practices of AWS architecting for the cloud
- An understanding of virtualization technology
- An understanding of monitoring and auditing systems
- Knowledge of networking concepts (DNS, TCP/IP, firewalls, and so on)
- An understanding of fundamental IT security concepts
- Hands-on experience of implementing security controls and compliance requirements
- The ability to collaborate across teams/company wide

I encourage you to fulfill as many of the hands-on experience requirements listed here, as your years of experience translate into real knowledge, and the learning that you can gain on the job is invaluable.

Although this experience with AWS is considered mandatory by AWS, you will still be able to take the exam, even if you have not completed all of the hands-on requirements. Perhaps you have only been assigned to run PoC or test/dev workloads in the cloud until you pass the exam and cannot fulfill the *running production workloads* requirement. If you have fulfilled most of the other requirements, and feel confident that you have a good grasp on the subjects discussed in this book, then you shouldn't worry.

In any case, this guide is designed to provide you with ample detailed content on each required subject and the ability to perform practical exercises by following this course at your own pace.

The exam's structure

The exam itself is has been designed in a multiple-choice, multiple-answer question format. There are approximately 70-80 questions in the exam, and you will have 130 minutes to complete them. The exam is available in English, Japanese, and Simplified Chinese, and you can also sign up for an online practice exam before taking the exam with a registered exam proctor. The registration fee for the actual exam is $150 USD and that of the practice exam is $20 USD. The exam questions come in three different formats:

- **Multiple choice**: You will need to select the option that provides the best answer to the question or select an answer that completes a statement. The question may come in the form of a graphic, where you will be able to point and click on the answer.
- **Multiple response**: You will need to select more than one option that best answers the question or completes a statement. Multiple response questions are limited to a maximum of four correct answers.
- **Sample directions**: You will read a statement or question and must select only the answer(s) that represent the most correct or logical response.

The scoring

Make sure that you take your time when answering the exam questions, since all of them are scored in full. That means that one incorrect answer for a multiple-response question will cause the entire question to be marked as not answered correctly, thus no points will be scored on the question at hand. Also, you should know that the exam pass/fail grade is not dependent on the number of correct answers, but is designed to give a score out of 1,000. The questions are considered to be of different levels of difficulty and, due to this, each question carries a different number of points that can be scored.

The passing score

The passing score itself is never released publicly and the only reference to the passing score is the community of test takers that have posted their pass/fail scores on various forums. The official stance of AWS is that the certification passing score is heavily dependent on the statistical analysis of multiple metrics that AWS receives from several sources. It is widely known that one of the initial sources for determining a passing score are existing AWS certified individuals who have access to technical previews and take the beta exams. The beta exams also determine which types of questions will be included in the final exam and the weight the questions will have. According to the results received from the beta, an initial pass level of the exam is usually selected by AWS.

The initial passing score for all AWS exams has historically been set as a wide range between 650 and 750 points out of a possible 1,000. The initial passing score has been heavily dependent on the type and difficulty of the exam itself; associate exams usually have a higher initial passing score, as the questions in the exam are considered to be less difficult than questions at the professional exam level. Upon release of the exam, the metrics received from the exam takers are also taken into account and the passing score of a particular AWS exam is adjusted periodically based on the live metrics from the exam takers. There have been reports of the passing score being even higher, so you should be aiming to prepare yourself to a confidence level that should ensure that you can answer at least 80% of the questions correctly.

The exam knowledge domains

There are several knowledge domains regarding questions, and the following breakdown will show you the topic measured by the exam and the extent to which they are represented as a percentage of all the questions. For instance, if you have 70 questions, you should expect to get 10 questions on monitoring and metrics, 10 on high availability, 8 on data management, and so on. The topics that are mentioned in the following breakdown do not constitute a full list, but rather, are summary that's intended for orientational purposes:

- **Domain 1: Monitoring metrics and managing cost – 15%**: The questions pertaining to domain 1 will allow AWS to assess your ability in monitoring availability and performance, cloud operations being issued, managing accounts and billing, following cost optimization best practices, and so on.

- **Domain 2: High availability and scaling – 15%**: This domain will assess your ability to implement scalable and elastic solutions based on certain scenarios, to deliver various levels of fault-tolerance based on the requirements outlined in the question that directly map to realistic business requirements, and so on.

- **Domain 3: Analysis of your AWS environment – 15%**: You should demonstrate your ability to optimize the environment to ensure maximum performance, to identify bottlenecks and issues, and so on. You will also be expected to be able to implement remedies depending on your application deployment and the AWS services being consumed.

- **Domain 4: Deployment and provisioning – 15%**: You should demonstrate your ability to build an environment and provision cloud resources in accordance with the AWS well-architected reference design. This domain is also highly focused on automation and delivering repeatable and reusable designs to your AWS environments.

- **Domain 5: Data management – 12%**: In domain 5, the ability to create and manage backups for different services is tested. Life cycling and enforcing compliance requirements is given a lot of weight, as is delivering disaster recovery processes.

- **Domain 6: Security – 15%**: Security is a very important – if not the most important – part of keeping AWS running smoothly. The questions in this domain will test your ability to implement and manage users, groups, roles and security policies, and access controls; to be able to prepare for a security assessment, your understanding of the shared responsibility model; and your understanding of the requirements for data integrity. You will also be quizzed on the features that are available for managing security on the AWS platform.

- **Domain 7.0: Networking – 13%**: The networking domain will test you on concepts that any individual with basic general IT knowledge should be able to demonstrate their knowledge of, such as the differentiation between LAN and WAN networks, the internet protocol addressing model, describing the functions of network function devices such as DNS, routers, NAT, firewalls, and so on. It will also test your ability to implement networking and connectivity features of AWS and configure services to allow for resolving computer names across a hybrid AWS and on-premises network.

The questions structure

At the end of this book, we will provide sample questions so that you can get familiar with the general structure of the exam questions and to provide guidance on determining the information that's vital to answer the questions correctly. For example, a question will start off with a detailed description of the company's size, the number of branch offices, and number of users, and will then lay out the requirements, such as the requirements for authentication from a centralized directory, requirements for connecting the branch offices like bandwidth or amount of data being transferred, and so on. Sometimes, it will take a bit of simple math, such as dividing the number of hours in a backup window with the throughput of the device provided in the question, and so on. We will also point out the explanation for the answers to the questions by providing excerpts from and links to the AWS documentation.

Taking the exam

Once you have finished this book and completed the practical exercises, my personal recommendation is to first determine whether you have the confidence that you will score at least 80% on the exam. To determine this, come back to this section and read the overview. Next, run through the practice questions in this book, as they will map quite well to the questions in the actual exam. After that, if you still need more assurance, take the practice exam.

Once you decide to take the exam, there are some general guidelines you should be aware of. First, make sure you arrive at least 15 minutes before your scheduled time. Plan to arrive even earlier if possible – I usually plan to be at the proctor about 30 minutes early. This is to avoid any eventuality en route to the testing center such as traffic or public transport delays. If you live in an area of traffic extremes, you should take that into consideration. Remember that this is an important day and you should not be subject to additional stress such as traffic when you have an AWS exam to worry about.

Once you have arrived, you will be signed in and you will need to put your possessions in a locker. The lockers in typical testing centers are designed to hold only your essentials, so avoid bringing a laptop bag or other bulkier items. Once you get to your exam station, you will need to accept the terms and conditions of the exam. The exam timer starts immediately after this. The terms and conditions page is not timed, so if you need a few seconds to take a deep breath before your exam or to clear your head, this is the time to do it. After the clock starts, make sure that you read all the questions carefully and follow the advice given in `Chapter 22`, *Example Tips and Tricks*.

You have the option of marking each question you are unsure of so that you can come back to it later. I highly recommend doing that, as you might come across a question with a similar topic as you progress through the questions and that might help you answer the original question. Once you come to the end and you submit your exam, you will take a quick satisfaction survey. Immediately after that, you will be shown a page with either a pass or a fail score. Soon after the exam result has been recorded, you will receive an email with a breakdown of scores across each domain. If you fail, this will help you focus on the necessary domains that you need to brush up on. And always remember: keep calm. Good luck!

2
The Fundamentals of Amazon Web Services

Amazon Web Services (**AWS**) was officially launched in 2006 by its parent company, Amazon. At that time, it was an online book store. The business saw an opportunity in the marketplace to deliver services based on in-house experience in building highly scalable web application services, which they were using for Amazon. The mid 2000s was a time when the first massive, web-scale applications were starting to really take off, and Amazon was running such a web application. They had also invested heavily in the underlying technologies, infrastructure, and data centers to run their application reliably, with the best possible response times on a global scale. Those data centers and the services to run them were, of course, designed to meet highly variable capacity requirements so that Amazon could be run. This variability was due to the nature of the business, where traffic to Amazon would increase dramatically whenever they were running any promotions or sales, or due to an increase in purchase traffic during the holiday season. For this reason, an enormous amount of standby capacity had to be designed so that the system could handle any kind of spikes in traffic. The business initially saw an opportunity to market this unused capacity to developers so that they could run their test environments. Overnight, word spread and demand increased, as not only were developers able to use the available capacity but also the tools and services that Amazon developed to make its own site highly available and resilient to any possible failure in the backend and traffic increase from the frontend. With the increase in demand, even more capacity was dedicated to the external tenants and Amazon Web Services as we know it today was born.

The following topics will be covered in this chapter:

- What is the AWS platform?
- The shared responsibility model
- Advantages of using AWS
- AWS Foundation Services
- AWS Platform Services
- Using Amazon Web Services
- Cloud native and serverless designs
- Choosing availability zones and regions

Technical requirements

A basic understanding of common IT terminology and practices is required for you to follow the content of this chapter.

What is the AWS platform?

Amazon Web Services essentially put the words **cloud** and **Infrastructure as a Service** (**IaaS**, in its abbreviated form) into the IT dictionary. I'm not implying that Amazon Web Services invented cloud computing, not at all! The creation of cloud computing is a multi-faceted story that took time and organic growth to become what it is today. I am simply implying that Amazon Web Services was the one that really made your typical enterprise start thinking of IT as services instead of investments.

Cloud computing can be broken down into three categories that define what kind of service is being consumed from the cloud, that is, **Infrastructure as a Service (IaaS)**, **Platform as a Service (PaaS)**, and **Software as a Service (SaaS)**. The following diagram illustrates the services that are offered by each service layer:

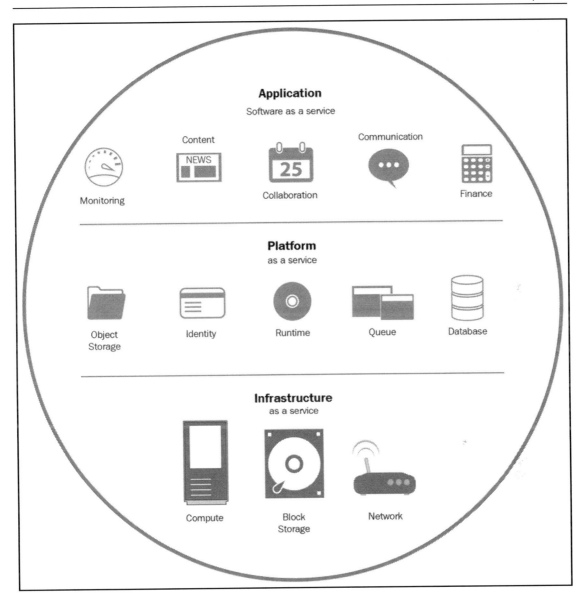

Infrastructure as a Service

Services that are consumed from IaaS offerings include compute services such as virtual machine instances, block storage, private network segments, and network function devices that allow for connectivity, such as routers, NAT, firewalls, and so on. These resources are fairly standard units of computing that are commonly found in any enterprise environment. Therefore, the value of IaaS is that a cloud computing tenant can mirror their environment completely in the cloud and use these services. This can be very useful in the following circumstances:

- When strict policies of low-level operating system access are required
- For solutions such as backup and disaster recovery
- For hybrid solutions between on-premise and cloud servers, and so on

The drawback of IaaS is that there will still be a lot of infrastructure work that needs to be done to bring an application to life. For instance, in IaaS, we get a fresh operating system that needs to be optimized, services and applications that need to be installed, patched, secured, and kept safe, as well as periodically updated and upgraded. This can bring a lot of overhead and complexity to deployment as the environment is extended into the cloud and more virtual machine instances, storage volumes, network environments, and so on will need to be maintained, secured, and operated by the enterprise itself. The highest level of IT knowledge is required to use and configure IaaS, but it does give us the most control over the resources we are configuring.

Platform as a Service

On the other hand, when the goal of using cloud computing is to reduce the infrastructure maintenance overhead, then PaaS can be considered as an option. The platform layer takes the complexity out of the equation, since the provider of the cloud service will be in charge of the operating system and the platform that provides the service. For instance, a development team is considering whether to install, maintain, and operate its own database platform or use a **Database as a Service** option such as the **Relational Database Service (RDS)** provided by Amazon Web Services.

In the case of building a database server, they can consume an IaaS virtual machine instance, install the database server, configure it with a database instance, and pass the connection details into the application. When using PaaS, they simply request the database instance to be created (this can be done via an API call) and the provider passes the connection details of the database instance back to the user as a reply to the initial request. As you can see, using PaaS can be a very effective way of using cloud computing services, as there is very little (if any) management overhead when provisioning, using, and releasing PaaS resources from the cloud. PaaS resources come in many forms including services such as the following:

- Highly available relational and NoSQL databases, database caching services
- Big data ingestion, processing, and warehousing solutions
- Scalable and durable web-accessible storage
- Services for message queuing, distribution, and delivery
- Serverless processing
- Analytics, transcoding, and searching
- Services for mobile and IoT
- Server management and automation tools

PaaS is also very effective when designing applications with a cloud-native approach, where applications are designed for the cloud and the most mundane tasks like updating, upgrading, and even some security tasks, are simply handed off to the cloud provider.

The SaaS layer represents the user domain where users come in and consume services straight from the cloud. No IT knowledge is usually required to use these applications and none or very little access to the underlying environment running the application is provided to the user.

The shared responsibility model

Once we begin consuming cloud resources, we need to be aware that we are operating our application on some kind of provider-managed infrastructure and that both parties have a different level of access to the environment.

The following diagram represents an overview of the shared responsibility model:

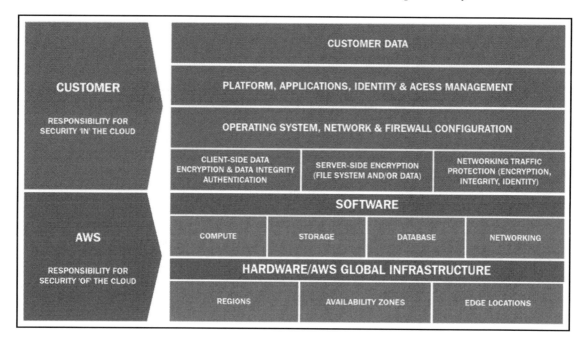

There are quite a few differences between the shared responsibilities depending on whether a customer is running an IaaS or a PaaS. For example, if the customer is using IaaS and running a virtual machine with a database instance on the cloud, the provider has access to and responsibility for securing the following:

- The underlying hardware in their data center
- The server and hypervisor where the VM instance is running
- The storage subsystem where the data volume is residing
- The physical network devices that connect the hypervisor to the internet
- The uplink to the internet and the uplinks between the data center and other provider locations

The customer has access to and responsibility for maintaining the following:

- Network and user access to the operating system (ports, users, keypairs, and so on)
- Updating and upgrading the operating system
- Installing, updating, and upgrading the database application
- Securing the database application running inside the operating system
- Securing access to the database application and the database instance
- Securing the customer data inside the database instance

In the case of a PaaS service with the same requirements, you must run a database in the cloud, where the customer has consumed a database instance that's been delivered by the cloud provider. The cloud provider will, of course, keep the same responsibilities for the infrastructure, but also take on some of the responsibilities for securing the following:

- Network and user access to the operating system (ports, users, keypairs, and so on)
- Updating and upgrading the operating system
- Installing, updating, and upgrading the database application
- Securing the database application running inside the operating system
- Securing access to the database application

The customer's responsibility is now reduced only to the following:

- Securing access to the database instance (when using additional user-generated credentials)
- Securing the customer data inside the database instances

The overall management footprint of the services being consumed in the cloud can be reduced dramatically when using PaaS. This usually means that the developers, SysOps, and architects can focus on building the application instead of focusing on building and maintaining infrastructure. PaaS is ideal for enterprises that strive for high agility, lean and effective development and DevOps teams, and overall high efficiency. On the other hand, PaaS has drawbacks when it comes to strict the control of data flows, high security requirements, regulatory and compliance, and so on.

The following diagram summarizes the difference between the IaaS and PaaS shared responsibility models:

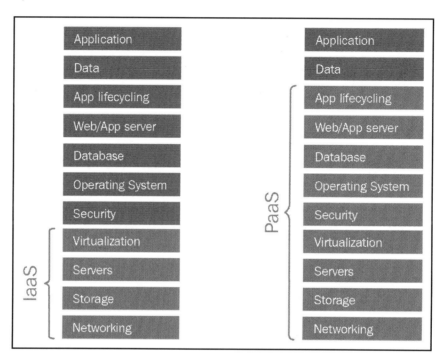

Advantages of using AWS

Any conversation about cloud computing will eventually lead to the question *"Why? What's the benefit and why should I be using cloud computing?"* There are multiple factors that contribute to cloud computing outperforming the traditional, on-premises data center-oriented approach to computing, but the following capabilities are the ones that are the most likely to make on-premises data centers a thing of the past:

- The ability to trade capital expenses for operational expenses when running IT
- The ability to use inexpensive compute units on demand
- Increased application delivery speed and agility
- Capacity matched to demand
- The ability to go global in minutes

Perhaps the most prominent advantage when using Amazon Web Services is the ability to deploy your services globally within minutes. Using scripts, templates or 3rd party tools, you can deploy your application to any region where AWS operates with simplicity and great velocity. AWS also offers its customers the ability to very simply synchronize their data across regions and deliver an application to a broad range of audiences with the lowest possible latency.

Secondly, the ability to trade in capital expenditures for operating expenditures is very important. AWS allows users to provision and consume resources on demand, whenever resources are needed, and to scale those resources dynamically. There is complete control from the user's end regarding when and how to use the platform, the services, and resources provided, and the user also has complete control over the way they pay for that consumption, giving them the ability to pay only for the exact amount of usage in the cloud. This is a very valuable proposition to any business, as the cost of computing and application delivery can be relative to the demand for the application, and thus the income the business receives from providing the application for its users.

There is also the ability to use very inexpensive units of computing compared to traditional data centers and compared to the on-demand cloud services on offer. AWS allows its customers to essentially bid on unused resources that are reserved to provide other customers with dynamically expandable capacity. The users bidding on the unused capacity have the ability to use the capacity they bid on until any other client bidding a higher price or paying the regular on-demand price requests that capacity. As a price bid jumps to a higher price or the on-demand price, the lower bidder is outbid and their resources are terminated in favor of the higher bidder. We will discuss the way this feature operates by looking at the **Elastic Cloud Compute** (**EC2**) spot instance marketplace in a later chapter.

Lastly, the ability to increase application delivery velocity and agility should not be overlooked. By utilizing a combination of DevOps approaches, agile methodologies, and using PaaS, any application development company can tune the performance of their development teams to deliver their applications in an increasingly fast manner. This allows them to quickly react to any new business requirements, changing market conditions, and other factors outside the business itself.

AWS Foundation Services

Amazon Web Services defines two service layers a bit more loosely than the standard IaaS and PaaS models. The underlying layer of AWS services is called AWS Foundation Services and includes all of the IaaS deliveries that AWS provides, as well as some services that fall squarely into the PaaS, and even SaaS layers of cloud computing. AWS Foundation Services can be divided into the following functional groups:

- Network services
- Compute services
- Storage services
- Security and identity services
- End user applications

Network services

Network services are sub-divided into different offerings that deliver services that allows for the complete management of our network infrastructure. Examples include the following service offerings:

- **Amazon Virtual Private Cloud (VPC)**: Delivers network management and connectivity features such as private network ranges, the ability to connect to the internet and use publicly routable IPs
- **AWS Direct Connect**: Allows for the creation of hybrid clouds with on-premise devices
- **Amazon Route 53**: Delivers DNS as a Service with an innovative API that can allow users to address the DNS service programmatically
- **Amazon CloudFront**: Delivers a highly efficient, scalable, and dynamic caching and CDN service
- **Amazon Elastic Load Balancing (ELB)**: Allows the delivery of de-coupling, scalability, and high availability to EC2 and other services:

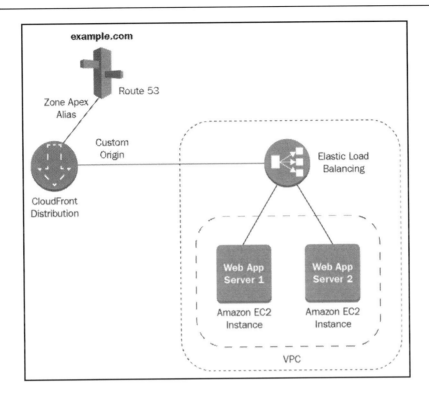

Compute services

Compute services are sub-divided into different offerings that deliver services that allow the execution of compute-oriented tasks in a variety of ways. Examples include the following service offerings:

- **Amazon Elastic Cloud Computing (EC2)**: Delivers a virtual machine instance provisioning and management environment for building highly scalable, custom applications running on a variety of operating systems
- **Amazon Elastic Container Service (ECS)**: Delivers the ability to provision and manage containerized applications in the cloud

- **Amazon Lambda**: Provides the serverless processing of functions and cloud-based computing workloads

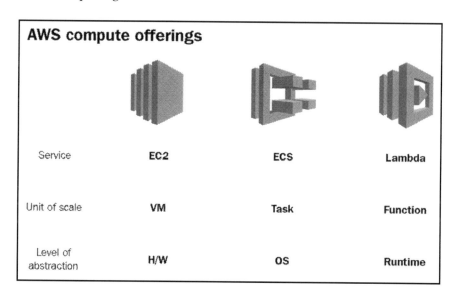

Storage services

Storage services are sub-divided into different offerings that deliver services that allow different methods for the storage and delivery of data. Examples include the following service offerings:

- **Amazon Elastic Block Storage (EBS)**: Allows virtual machine instances and containers to attach and use block storage volumes of different sizes with shared or provisioned performance
- **Amazon Elastic File System (EFS)**: Allows storing files in a standard network filesystem approach
- **Amazon Simple Storage Service (S3)**: Allows storing various static data via a standardized web-accessible platform
- **Amazon Glacier**: A data-archiving system that can be used to lifecycle data from S3 or as a standalone low-cost archiving solution
- **AWS Storage Gateway**: Allows connecting on-premises data with the AWS storage infrastructure

- **AWS Snow Family**: Provides data transfer services for physically moving one-time data from on-premises to the cloud at tera- and peta-byte scales

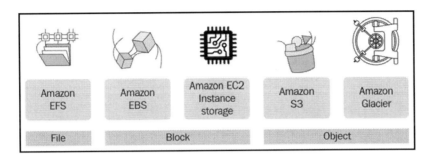

Security and identity services

Security and identity services are sub-divided into different tools that allow ease of identity management and secure our applications. Examples include the following service offerings:

- **Amazon Identity and Access Management (IAM)**: This allows user and system access management by assigning policies to users, groups and roles from within the account. It also offers features to allow for the integrated management, and federation of access from other AWS accounts and other directories.
- **Amazon Key Management Service (KMS)**: A managed service on AWS that allows users to easily manage the encryption keys being used in their AWS environment. It allows access in a programmatic manner to give developers the ability to automate the delivery of encryption credentials to applications running in AWS.
- **Amazon Cloud Hardware Security Module (CloudHSM)**: A cloud-enabled hardware security device that allows for the complete control of the encryption of data within applications running on AWS.
- **Amazon Inspector**: Allows a security assessment of applications running in AWS. Delivers a prioritized list of vulnerabilities and misconfigurations that allow developers and architects to design their application and the AWS services it depends on to the highest security standard and achieve compliance.

- **Amazon Web Application Firewall (WAF)**: Protects your web applications from external attacks using exploits and security vulnerabilities. WAF gives you complete control and visibility over the traffic being sent to your web instances and allows granular security policies to be designed to keep your web application secure and to prevent the overuse of resources due to malicious activity from the internet.

End user applications

End user applications are essentially different tools that offer services to end users, which can then be consumed from the cloud. Examples include the following service offerings:

- **Amazon WorkMail**: An enterprise-grade email and calendar tool in the cloud that has the ability to seamlessly integrate with multiple different email clients.
- **Amazon WorkDocs**: A cloud-based document creation, collaboration, and management environment with an extensible SDK.
- **Amazon WorkSpaces**: A managed cloud **virtual desktop infrastructure (VDI)** service, providing Windows and Linux desktops to users on a global basis. This helps simplify the way enterprises deliver desktop environments to their workforce.

AWS Platform Services

Platform Services provide users with *platform* and *software* options that allow developers to easily provision, deploy, and deliver services to their application without the typical infrastructure management overhead. AWS Platform Services can be divided into the following functional groups:

- Databases
- Management tools
- Analytics
- Application services
- Developer tools
- Mobile and IoT services

Databases

Database services are sub-divided into different offerings that deliver database services and allow for the acceleration of the delivery of data. Examples include the following service offerings:

- **Amazon Relational Database Service (RDS)**: A fully managed relational database service that allows for the seamless creation, management, and simple integration of Amazon Aurora, PostgreSQL, MySQL, MariaDB, Oracle, and Microsoft SQL Server databases into your AWS infrastructure
- **Amazon ElastiCache**: This provides the ability to run a Redis or Memcached-compatible in-memory data store that allows for the caching of various structured and unstructured data types
- **Amazon DynamoDB**: A fully managed **Not only SQL (NoSQL)** database service that delivers predictable and consistent performance at any scale
- **Amazon DynamoDB Accelerator (DAX)**: A fully managed caching service for DynamoDB that can lower the response times of the DynamoDB system from milliseconds to microseconds
- **Amazon RedShift**: A data warehousing and business intelligence solution that can handle petabyte-scale data with high performance and cost effectively

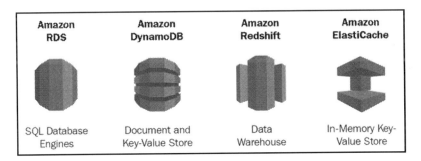

Management tools

The management services offer management of AWS cloud resources. Some also offer management of on premises resources. Examples include the following service offerings:

- **Amazon CloudWatch**: A fully managed monitoring service that stores metrics and logs from your environment and helps with diagnosing issues, understanding application load, and can deliver alerts to other services such as Amazon Auto Scaling, Lambda, and so on.

- **Amazon CloudTrail**: Allows for the logging and monitoring of API calls being issued to your AWS environment. It can record any changes in your infrastructure and deliver the data required for use in security and compliance processes.
- **AWS Config**: A feature that allows you to record the state and evaluate the configurations of your AWS resources.
- **AWS CloudFormation**: A template-based mechanism that allows you to create specification documents for your AWS instances and services and deploy them in an automated and repeatable manner. CloudFormation allows you to treat your infrastructure as code so that you can store, maintain, and deliver your infrastructure seamlessly from within your application life cycle environment.
- **AWS OpsWorks**: A configuration management service that allows you to easily deploy Chef or Puppet configuration management system instances and take control of and automate your infrastructure in the cloud and on-premises.

Analytics tools

Analytics tools are sub-divided into different offerings that deliver services, that can be consumed from the cloud or are able to perform analytics workloads. Examples include the following service offerings:

- **Amazon Kinesis**: A managed service that allows the real-time capturing, storing, and processing of streaming data at any scale with the flexibility of integration with any type of processing system.
- **Amazon Elastic Mapreduce (EMR)**: An environment for running cloud-based big data processing frameworks such as Hadoop, Apache Spark, HBase, Presto, Hive, Flink, and so on. It allows users to cost-effectively perform large-scale tasks such as log analysis, web indexing, financial analysis, data transformations, machine learning.
- **Amazon CloudSearch**: A managed service that provides the ease of integration of powerful search functionality into your application or website. It allows you to search in different languages and supports features such as autocomplete, ranking, and highlighting to deliver great results and enrich the user's experience.

Application services

Application services are sub-divided into different offerings that deliver services that can then be consumed by applications running in the cloud. Examples include the following service offerings:

- **Amazon API Gateway**: A fully managed service that allows creating, maintaining, and securing custom APIs at any scale. API Gateway can handle hundreds of thousands of concurrent API calls and can handle common tasks such as traffic management, monitoring, authorization and access control.
- **Amazon Elastic Transcoder**: A highly available and cost-effective media transcoding service in the cloud.
- **Amazon Simple Workflow Service (SWF)**: A tool that enables you to manage and control the state of your application or business logic in the cloud.

Developer tools

Developer tools help developers to easily cooperate and deploy applications in the cloud. Examples include the following service offerings:

- **AWS CodeCommit**: Allows you to store, maintain, and version your developer's code with a Git-based repository backend.
- **AWS CodeBuild**: A fully managed service that allows the simple implementation of continuous integration in your development process. This is done by enabling the automation of compiling, running, testing, and delivering packages that are ready to deploy.

- **AWS CodeDeploy**: A fully managed service that allows the deployment of your software packages to various cloud and on-premise systems:

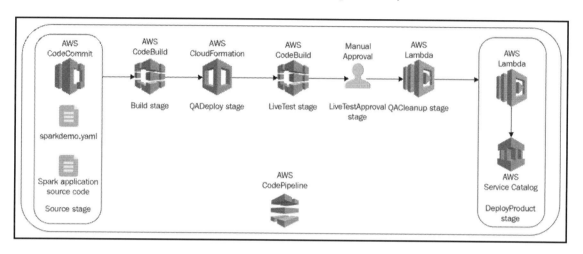

Mobile and IoT services

Mobile and IoT services help developers to easily create and deploy mobile and IoT applications in the cloud. Examples include the following service offerings:

- **AWS Pinpoint**: Allows developers and businesses to engage with their clients via various channels, such as email, SMS, and mobile push messages. It also provides analytics for client responses on top of those delivery channels.
- **AWS Device Farm**: Allows the cloud-enabled testing of mobile applications on fleets of AWS-based Amazon and iOS devices. This allows developers to test their applications at production scale before delivering them to their users.
- **AWS Cognito**: Allows developers to easily integrate signup and authentication services into their application and provides a hassle-free integration with web identity providers such as Amazon, Google, and Facebook.
- **AWS Internet of Things (IoT) Services**: Provides services and features that can be utilized by IoT developers such as Amazon FreeRTOS, a free real-time operating system that allows for the ease of programming IoT devices; AWS Greengrass, a service for messaging and caching that allows IoT devices to securely connect to your processing environment, IoT analytics services, security services.

Using AWS services

When the AWS environment was conceived, the initial requirement for the creation and consumption of resources was that they were simple, easy, and intuitive to consume, with no training required. If we look back to 2006-2007, the early years of AWS, this was very true. AWS had a simple design and the creation and consumption of the limited number of resources was relatively simple for anyone with an appropriate level of general IT knowledge so that they could come along and create resources with very little adjustment to the way AWS defined them. Nowadays, this is starting to become less and less true. Over the past decade or so, the AWS platform has evolved, seemingly at an exponential speed, to a point where it has so many services and so many offerings that you would be hard pressed to find anyone who would say that they clearly understand and are able to use the AWS platform with just the general IT knowledge that was needed back in the early days to operate the same environment. Even AWS itself now recommends that training be taken and whitepapers be read before you begin using the AWS infrastructure and the services and features it provides.

AWS Management Console

There are several ways to approach consuming resources and configuring services in AWS. The simplest and most intuitive way to access the AWS environment is through AWS Management Console. Before you begin using AWS Management Console, you will be required to create an account and log in to the console with your newly created account.

Simply browse to `https://aws.amazon.com/` and you will be presented with the home page of Amazon Web Services. Click on the **Create an AWS Account** button to begin the AWS account creation process:

On the next page, simply enter an email address that you would like to use with AWS as the root user, a password that meets the AWS complexity requirements, and the AWS account name that you would like to use. Your password must fulfill the following conditions:

- It must be eight characters long
- It must include any three out of the following: lowercase, uppercase, numbers, and special characters
- It must not be identical to your AWS account name:

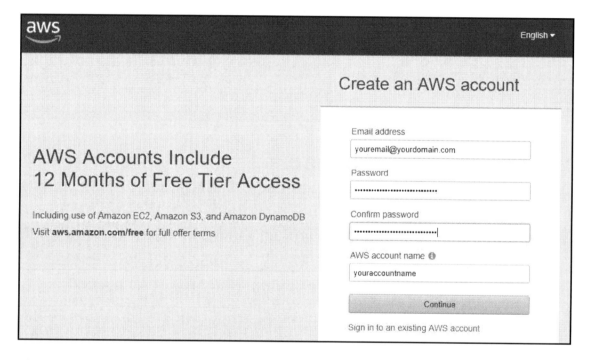

There are some general considerations regarding the email used for the initial user that is creating the AWS account. We will call this user the root user, as they have permission to the root and thus full control of the AWS account. Since the root user is tied to the email you enter on the signup page, this email will have complete access to the AWS account, including the ability to create and delete resources, view and modify billing data, and control the creation of IAM users, groups, and permission assignments. Make sure that you choose your email address wisely so that it is not tied to one individual. Instead, choose a new email address or an existing group that is in control of this account.

It is generally not recommended to use the AWS root user account for any day-to-day tasks. Once you have created your account, it is recommended that you create IAM users with the appropriate permissions so that you can manage all of the features of your account. After you have gained access with an IAM user, it is also recommended that you do the following:

- Delete the root user's access keys so that no programmatic access is allowed for that user.
- Create and activate an MFA token on your root account. This gives the root user two-factor authentication and will prevent unauthorized access to your account by third parties.
- Create individual IAM users for the rest of your team. The recommendation is that you do not assign any permissions to the users being created as you should create and use groups to assign permissions to your users.
- Apply an IAM password policy that complies with your enterprise password policy.

Store the MFA device and the password for the root user in a safe place and put a procedure in place that will allow authorized personnel to access those credentials in the event that you lose access to all of your administrative IAM users. We will guide you through the process of securing the root user and your account in Chapter 3, *Managing AWS Security with Identity and Access Management*.

It is also wise to put some kind of *breaking the glass policy* in place for the retrieval of these credentials. *Breaking the glass* refers to fire alarms that have an alarm activation button behind a small glass panel that is broken if we push the button. You should implement some kind of policy that will show *broken glass* when a user requests or uses the root user. This refers to any kind of digital trace, such as sending an email whenever the root user is logged in or any similar event that can be captured and put forward as evidence of use of the root account.

The steps to complete account signup are as follows:

1. Enter your contact details, address, and phone number
2. Agree to the AWS terms and conditions
3. Enter a credit card number for billing purposes

After you have completed the signup process, you will gain access to AWS Management Console. Along with the ability to manage your account, you will have the ability to search for services, and learn about AWS. Let's take a look at the structure of the console:

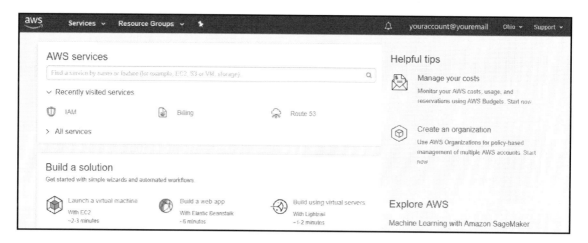

On the top bar, there are several pull-down menus:

- Services
- Resource groups
- A small bell symbol, representing alerts
- Your account name
- Region
- Support

Clicking on the **Services** pull-down menu will open the **Services** screen where you can either browse grouped services or choose the selector on the right to sort them from A to Z. You also have the ability to search for a specific service. There is also a history of your recently visited AWS services, which is on the left:

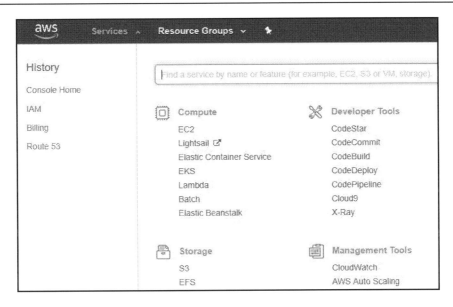

Clicking on **Resource Groups** will show a menu for dealing with resource groups. These allow you to tag and manage groups of instances and services all at once. You can add any resource to a resource group – this can span the entire region that the services and instances are deployed in. This can help in automating tasks such as patching, monitoring, and security operations. From the pull-down menu, you also have the ability to create a resource group, see your saved groups, and access the **Tag Editor**:

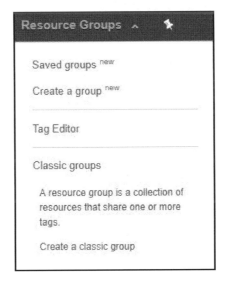

The little bell symbol that represents alerts will show the latest alerts and notifications regarding your account:

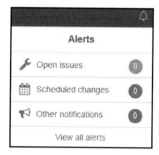

Clicking on your username will open a drop-down menu that will allow you to perform the following actions:

- Manage your own account
- Manage your organization's account (if not using root, your IAM user needs to be granted the permissions that allow organization management)
- Access your **Billing Dashboard** (if the IAM user has permissions)
- Manage your own security credentials (if IAM users are allowed to do so)
- **Switch Role** (if the IAM user has the ability to switch role to a role with different permissions)
- **Sign Out**:

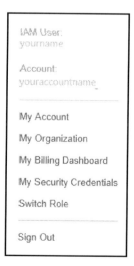

The region selector (which is set to Ohio in the following screenshot) allows you to select the region in which you would like to deploy your services. Selecting a region can be very important from different standpoints, possibly the most important being compliance with national regulations. Different countries and regions have different laws that have been put in place regarding sensitive and personal data and how the data is stored and handled. By choosing to deploy your services only in the region that is within the national or regional territory where the laws are applicable, you can ensure compliance with those regulations. You would also want to select a region based on the location of the majority of your users. This can help deliver better performance for your application with reduced latency and more available bandwidth to transfer data. At the time of writing, there are five North American regions, five Asian regions, four European regions, and one South American region, all of which are available to the typical user. US government entities are also able to choose the GovCloud region, which has specifics that are only available to them. Also, any registered business that has a license to operate within the Peoples Republic of China is also able to choose from several Chinese regions on top of the publicly available ones:

US East (N. Virginia)

US East (Ohio)

US West (N. California)

US West (Oregon)

Asia Pacific (Mumbai)

Asia Pacific (Seoul)

Asia Pacific (Singapore)

Asia Pacific (Sydney)

Asia Pacific (Tokyo)

Canada (Central)

EU (Frankfurt)

EU (Ireland)

EU (London)

EU (Paris)

South America (São Paulo)

Clicking on **Support** opens the **Support** pull-down menu, where we have the ability to access the following:

- **Support Center**: Here, we can open tickets with AWS in the event of technical issues
- **Forums**: Where we can get help and discuss features with our peers
- **Documentation**: A link to the AWS documentation
- **Training**: A link to the training resource with self-paced labs, online and classroom training
- **Other resources**: Other resources related to AWS

The body of the console is divided into the following parts:

- AWS services
- Build a solution
- Learn to build
- Helpful tips
- Explore AWS

The **AWS services** section has a **Search** functionality, and allows you to simply enter a common term such as database or messaging. From here, the search interface will show you suggestions that are based on your search, along with common services that are related to *database*, as shown in the following screenshot:

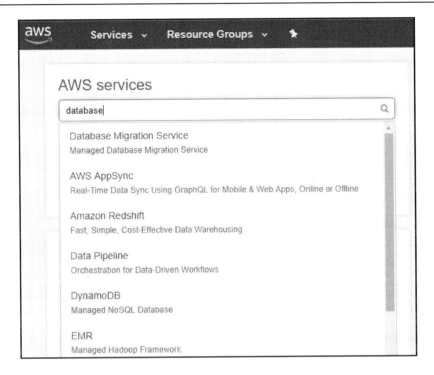

It is essentially a quicker way to access services compared to the **Services** pull-down menu.

The other sections are a good place to start if you are new to AWS and AWS Management Console. The **Learn to build** section will give you an introduction to how to create and use services and will provide you with tutorials, videos, self-paced labs, project guides, and documentation that you can use to get hands-on experience with AWS. The **Build a solution** section includes wizards and workflows that will guide you through the creation of common resources and service types, while **Helpful tips** and **Explore AWS** will give you helpful advice on a number of topics.

The AWS Command-Line Interface

Another way to access the AWS environment is through the AWS **Command-Line Interface (CLI)**. This is a powerful open source tool based on the AWS SDK for Python, which allows us to manage features of the AWS cloud straight from the Linux shell or Windows command line. The ability to use the CLI allows us to integrate the management of our AWS services with shell scripting such as Bash and PowerShell. This means that we can manage and automate our AWS infrastructure straight out of our instance operating systems with a standard shell script approach.

For instance, the AWS CLI can be used to provide existing configuration management or a continuous integration server so that you can access and manage the creation, deployment, scaling, and deletion of AWS instances and services from an on-premise location or from within the AWS environment. The AWS CLI can also be a powerful tool to use when doing proof of concept or development, since the ability to provision and configure AWS resources straight from the command line can make the process much faster. Saving CLI commands can make the process repeatable and immutable.

The AWS Software Development Kit

AWS also offers a **Software Development Kit (SDK)** that allows developers to seamlessly connect to the AWS environment from within their code and deliver AWS instances and services as part of the software code. Not only is the software able to be designed to run on AWS, but it can also provide the capability of software to self-provision services and instances whenever required. The AWS SDK is the right way to approach AWS service configuration when developers need a way to build their application with a cloud native or serverless approach. The SDK is available for a number of programming languages, including but not limited to Java, .NET, Python, Node.js, Ruby, PHP, Go, C++. Along with the standard SDKs, AWS also offers an SDK for mobile and IoT applications. The SDK empowers developers and DevOps teams with the ability to function as a self-contained unit that can fully manage all of their application requirements.

Cloud-native and serverless designs

When we talk about cloud-native applications, we are simply defining them as applications that are built to run on the cloud and have the ability to access the cloud environment they are running on in one way or another. This capability can allow an application to be self-managed and, among other factors, can allow it to do any or all of the following:

- Provision its own resources, such as instances, databases, storage, and networks
- Access services in the cloud, such as monitoring and enumerating services to determine its own state
- Have the ability to scale itself according to events or metrics that are retrieved from the cloud
- Manage other applications running in the cloud

On the other hand, applications that have been designed with a server less approach in mind are designed in a way that they consume no visible server instance resources, and all of their processing, data storage, databases, and other features are delivered from environments managed by AWS delivered completely transparently to us. This can be achieved with any application that has very spiky, short bursts of processing activity and mostly delivers a static web page to users. A static web page can be simply deployed in AWS S3 and served by a CloudFront distribution, which will make the static website accessible and highly available by design. Any kind of request that requires processing can be forwarded in one way or another to one or multiple AWS Lambda functions, which can then run that query on predefined processing functions that have been stored in S3 with the static content itself. Outputs of Lambda can be stored in DynamoDB, the contents of which can also be viewed from JavaScript, and embedded within the static website hosted on S3:

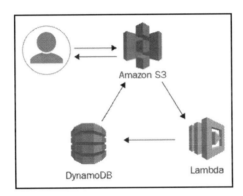

This is just one example of a serverless application. Not one server instance needs to be running for this website to function, but it can still provide both static and dynamic content. It can also be integrated with other services to provide authentication, access from mobile applications, monitoring and advanced triggering through SQS queues, SNS notifications or AWS SWF, and so on.

Choosing availability zones and regions

One of the most important aspects of running your application in an efficient and highly available manner is the correct selection of the location of your AWS services. AWS is designed to offer multiple facilities in several different regions so that it can provide both high availability of services within a single region and the ability for us to architect solutions that are distributed and replicated across different regions.

Based on the experience gained from running Amazon since the 90s, AWS has set out to create a world-class infrastructure architecture that is composed of the following components:

- Datacenter
- Availability zones
- Region

The lowest infrastructure component in the AWS architecture is the datacenter. A datacenter is essentially designed to hold raw compute, network, and storage capacity and to provide no redundancy to your applications at all. The AWS datacenter design has the following characteristics:

- Compute capacity: Between 50.000 – 80.000 servers
- Storage capacity: Approximately 11 petabytes per rack
- Network throughput: Up to 100 terabits per second
- Proprietary redundant network stack, delivered via multiple other device manufacturers
- Proprietary redundant network security stack:

Regional high availability

As we stated previously, each datacenters provide no redundancy, so multiple datacenters will be connected together and made into an availability zone. The connections between datacenters are low-latency layer 2 connections over metro links. An availability zone is thus geographically distributed across multiple facilities that are still close enough to provide low latency across the zone:

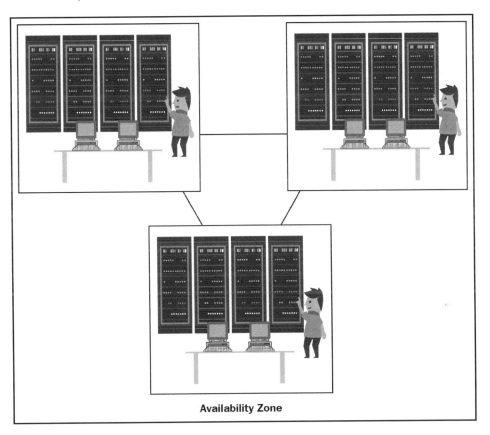

Availability Zone

The availability zone provides minimal support for redundancy. For instance, an EBS volume in an availability zone is redundantly placed on two different volume arrays in two different facilities. But even with features such as EBS volume redundancy, which traditionally might be considered as high availability, all the datacenters in an availability zone are connected in such a way that the whole availability zone is considered a one-fault isolation environment. Thus, if we want to achieve high availability within a region, we need to deploy our infrastructure to at least two availability zones.

The availability zones are also interconnected via low-latency network connections, although due to a wider geographical distribution of the availability zones themselves, we can expect to see a bit higher latency (usually within 5 ms) than within one availability zone (usually under 2 ms). This is a consideration that needs to be kept in mind when designing any application that is very sensitive to latency. However, as long as the traffic within a region does not traverse from the private network to the public network, it does not count toward our outgoing AWS transfer pricing:

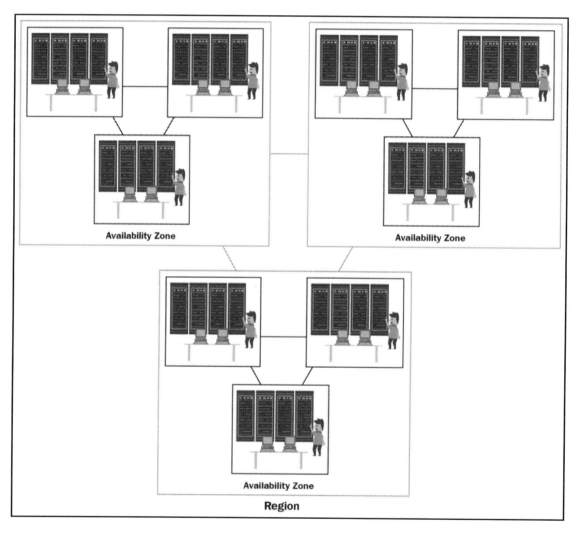

There are services, such as AWS S3, that will be automatically distributed across at least three availability zones to provide regional high availability. There are others where we can simply specify the requirement for increased regional redundancy, such as AWS RDS, where setting up a multi-availability zone RDS database will deploy two instances in two availability zones that are synchronously replicated. Then, there are services such as AWS EC2, where we can select the availability zone when we launch instances. Is it then up to us to correctly deploy and configure services so that they are fully redundant within a region.

Cross-regional high availability

When even higher availability is required to prevent an outage due to an AWS region failure, then we have to choose multiple regions to host our application. We can choose from a number of regions, and these have a geographical distribution that aligns well with the developed world's population density. The following map outlines the AWS regions that are currently in operation or under construction and will be online in the near future:

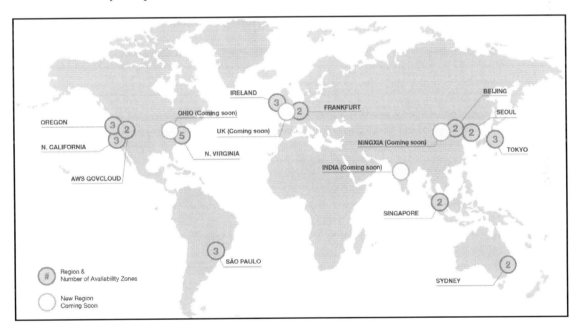

If we want to deploy our application across multiple regions, we need to consider the impact of such a decision. Within a region, the connections between datacenters and AZs are low latency, and are usually layer 2 links. Across regions, traffic is carried across a long-distance public Internet infrastructure. The following considerations need to be accounted for:

- **Latency**: We won't be able to maintain synchronous replication across multiple regions, since the latency between regions will be counted in tens to hundreds of milliseconds
- **Cost**: Since the traffic being sent out of a region traverses the internet, it will be counted as standard outgoing traffic and billed accordingly
- **Lack of built-in redundancy**: Only a selection of services are designed to provide built-in replication of data to multiple regions
- **Recovery from region failure**: You will need to design recovery and re-synchronization procedures for services that are deployed across multiple regions
- **Latency to your clients**: Choosing a region far from your clients or failing over to such a region will have an impact on the latency that's experienced by your end users

Edge locations

There are some ways to mitigate the latency your clients experience. You can generally improve the performance of your application delivery infrastructure by utilizing features such as the Route53 DNS system and CloudFront caching, as well as the CDN environment. Services that help with delivery to clients are delivered from **edge locations**. These are locations that are separate from the datacenters that the AWS availability zones reside in and are positioned closer to where traffic from end users is coming from. In some geographical locations, the edge locations are positioned close to where the AWS region exists so that the experience delivered to end users is close to what it would be if a region was located nearby. However, these services are optional and do carry a certain cost, so it is up to the system architect building the solution to evaluate whether the cost of running a service in an edge location will be beneficial and is a justified expense.

The following map shows the edge locations in relation to their closest regions:

Summary

Amazon Web Services provides a unified environment where cloud computing infrastructure, platform, and software services can be consumed by the end user. It enables us to be able to build an application by utilizing any combination of the AWS services on offer.

In this chapter, we learned how easy it is to create an AWS account and started using those services to build complex and powerful applications before making them available on the internet or on our internal network by using a VPN or Direct Connect uplink. AWS is a great environment when ease of management, the ability to provision quickly and globally, and financial constraints require us to build compute capacity from operating expenditures.

Although it is fairly simple to build applications on AWS, there are several challenges when using cloud computing systems as a standalone solution or as a hybrid model with an on-premises data center. First, there is the security concern, as we lose control of part of the system by delegating that control to the cloud provider. We looked at the shared security model and how it applies across infrastructure and platform as a service. Along with security, there is a real challenge to provide high availability, as some services within the cloud do not offer any intrinsic high availability, resilience, or backups. Because of this, we need to understand how to make each service highly available and build resilience and backups into our application.

We then took a quick glance at AWS regions, availability zones, and data centers to get a better overview of how AWS has designed its infrastructure to support the high availability of services. As we continue with this book, part of each chapter will also focus on making our services highly available and resilient.

Questions

1. What is the difference between Infrastructure as a Service and Platform as a Service?
2. Which layers is the cloud vendor responsible for when looking at Platform as a Service?
3. What are the most obvious advantages of using AWS?
4. List the five AWS Foundation service categories.
5. Define the three ways of accessing the AWS environment outlined in this book.
6. Essentially, what is a cloud-native application?
7. What is the difference between regions and availability zones?
8. Would running two virtual machine instances in two datacenters in one availability zone make your application highly available?

Further reading

- **Overview of the AWS Platform**: `https://docs.aws.amazon.com/aws-technical-content/latest/aws-overview/introduction.html`
- **Using the AWS CLI**: `https://docs.aws.amazon.com/lambda/latest/dg/setup-awscli.html`
- **AWS developer tools and SDKs**: `https://aws.amazon.com/tools/`
- **Cloud-native computing**: `https://aws.amazon.com/blogs/opensource/cloud-native-computing/`
- **AWS regions and AZs**: `https://docs.aws.amazon.com/AmazonRDS/latest/UserGuide/Concepts.RegionsAndAvailabilityZones.html`

3
Managing AWS Security with Identity and Access Management

In this chapter, we will be looking at the **Identity and Access Management (IAM)** component of AWS. We will learn how to design an environment that is secure and how to use IAM as an identity management tool for our virtual machine instances, as well as AWS services and platforms. We will also be looking at examples of how to manage IAM within the AWS console.

The following topics will be covered in this chapter:

- Overview of IAM
- Managing access with IAM
- Integration with external directories
- IAM best practices

Technical requirements

To follow along with the examples provided in this book, you will need to create an AWS account. Instructions on how to create the AWS account can be found in Chapter 2, *The Fundamentals of Amazon Web Services*.

Overview of Identity and Access Management

Identity and Access Management (IAM) is essentially a software as a service solution from AWS that provides the ability to create and manage identity objects and services within AWS. In this chapter, we will discuss how these can be applied to provide fine-grained access control to AWS resources and build authentication services for your applications that can use AWS IAM directly, or for the federation of access control for mobile applications with web identity providers and corporate directories. In this section, we will look at best practices for the following:

- Creating Users, Groups, and Roles, and assigning permissions
- Using **Multi-Factor Authentication (MFA)** for privileged users
- Using IAM roles to share access
- Restricting privileged access with conditions

Getting started with IAM

When starting out with AWS, the first security task is to secure the root user. We have outlined the procedure in `Chapter 2`, *The Fundamentals of Amazon Web Services*, in the section about the *AWS Management Console*. Before continuing, we will make sure our root account is secured by logging in to the AWS Management Console and navigating to `https://console.aws.amazon.com/iam/home`.

We should see a **Security Status** for our account and we should make sure all of the described statuses have a green check mark. When we first create the account, the security status will look like this:

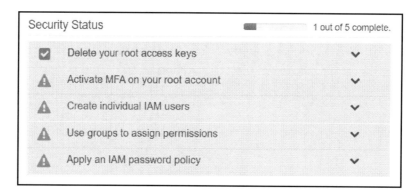

For all the missing check marks, please click on the chevron on the right to see the instructions on how to complete any of the missing tasks. Let's begin by activating **Multi-Factor Authentication (MFA)** for our root user account. In our example, we will be using Google Authenticator, which is one of the supported virtual MFA devices on Android devices and iPhones; however, Authy 2-Factor Authentication is also supported on both of these platforms, as well as Authenticator for Windows Phone. First, we will expand the **Activate MFA on your root account** task and click on **Manage MFA**:

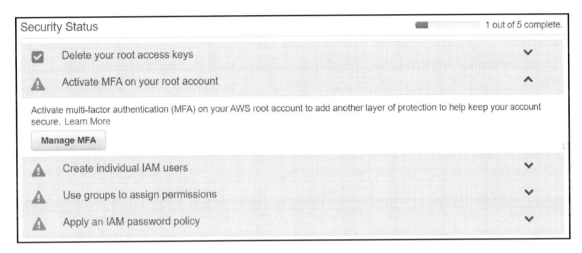

There will be a message warning you that the AWS best practice is to use IAM users with limited permissions. Since we are securing the root account, we will click on **Continue to Security Credentials**:

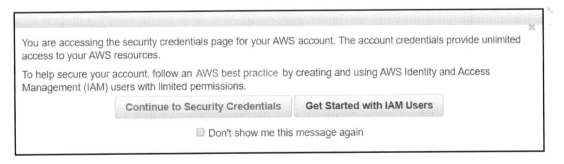

We now need to expand the **Multi-factor authentication (MFA)** task and click on **Activate MFA**:

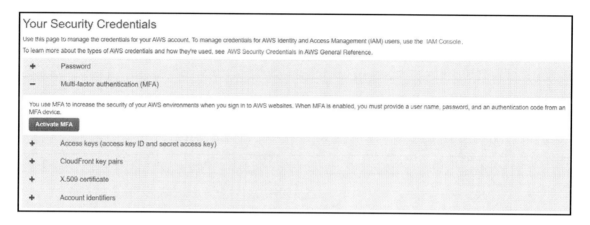

A window will pop up where you can select an MFA device. Since we are using Google Authenticator, we will select **A virtual MFA device**. If you have a supported hardware device, you should select the other option for **A hardware MFA device**. After selecting, press the **Next Step** button:

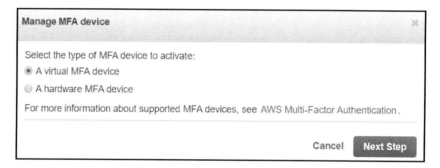

Press **Next Step** on the virtual MFA information screen:

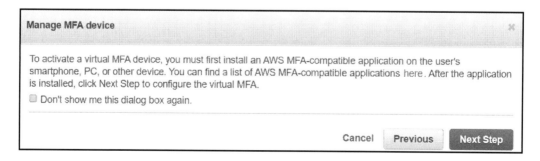

On the next screen, you will be presented with a QR code. Scan the QR code with Google Authenticator. When the account is successfully added, you will be presented with a time-rotating, six-digit, time-based, one-time password. You will need to enter two of those codes to verify the MFA and then press **Activate virtual MFA**:

Now that you have activated MFA, you will need to use the MFA code every time you log in with the root user. It is recommended that the MFA device for the root user be stored in a safe place and only retrieved in emergencies. If you happen to lose the MFA for your root account, you will still be able to recover your access via a recovery system, which will send you an email to the email registered as the root account user and then call the telephone number you used to register your account. Make sure you are also using a phone number that is secured against hostile takeovers such as SIM hacking, as this could be a way for the attacker to gain access to your root account. We will cover additional security in the *IAM best practices* of this chapter.

Heading back to our IAM Dashboard, we will see that two of five tasks have been completed, so we can open the **Create individual IAM users** task and click on **Manage Users**:

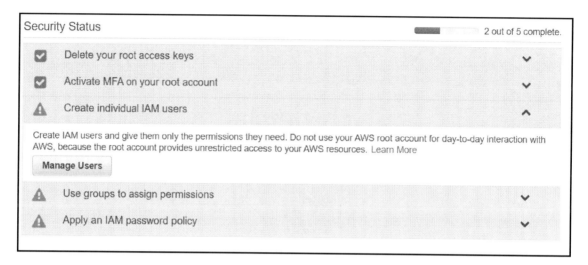

This will take us to the **Users** section of IAM, where we will now create a user by clicking on **Add user**:

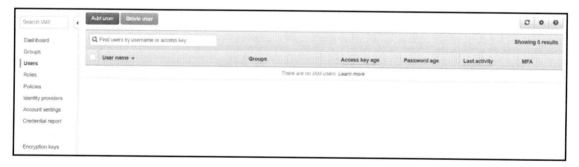

Here, we will be able to do the following:

- Give our user a user name; in this example, we called the user mynewuser
- Allow **Programmatic access** via access key ID and secret access key, which can be used with the AWS API, CLI, SDK, and any other development tools

- Allow **AWS Management Console access** via a browser with the user's username and password:
  - We are able to generate a random or our own password
  - We are also able to force the user to change the password on their next sign in

After we have completed this part, we will click on **Next: Permissions**:

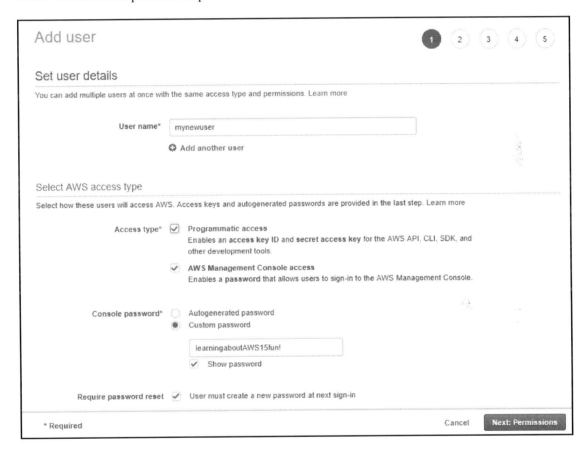

In the **Permissions** section, we can choose to do the following:

- **Add the user to a group**
- **Copy permissions from an existing user**
- **Attach an existing policies directly**

As per the best practices, we will be adding this user to a group, so we can continue with the **Create Group** task included in this section. You can also expand and explore **Set permissions boundary**. A permissions boundary is an advanced feature in which a user or a role can be limited in the maximum permissions that it can have. We will not be applying a permission boundary in our exercise:

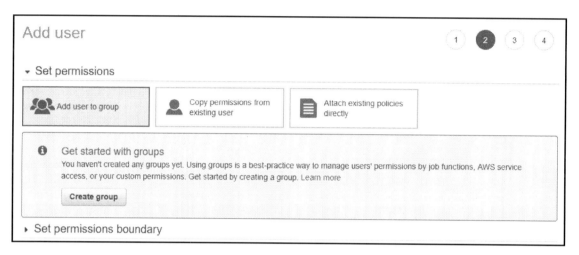

In the **Create group** section, we will create a group for the administrators and give it the default Administrative Permissions Policy name **AdministratorAccess**. We will click the **Create group** button and continue with the creation of our user:

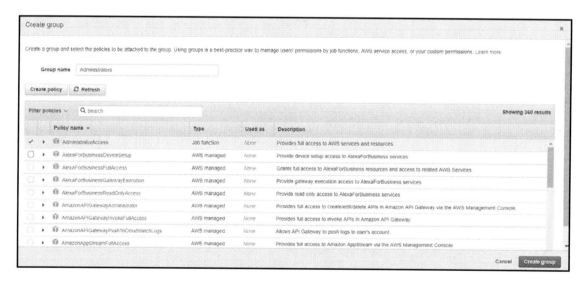

As you can see, after clicking **Create group** we are sent back to the **Create user** section, where we can now see that the newly created **Administrators** group is selected. Once selected, click on **Next: Tags**:

Next, we will be presented with a dialogue that will allow us to add tags. You can add up to 50 tags to the users to be able to identity them within your environment according to different attributes. You could add a tag with **key**: type and **value**: standard user or **key**: team and **value**: SysOps and so on. Once you have set the tags that you would like to add to the user simply click on **Next: Review**:

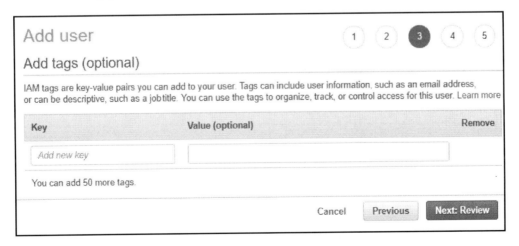

Finally we will be presented with a review screen where we will be able to review the configuration for our user before clicking on the **Create user** button at the bottom of the screen:

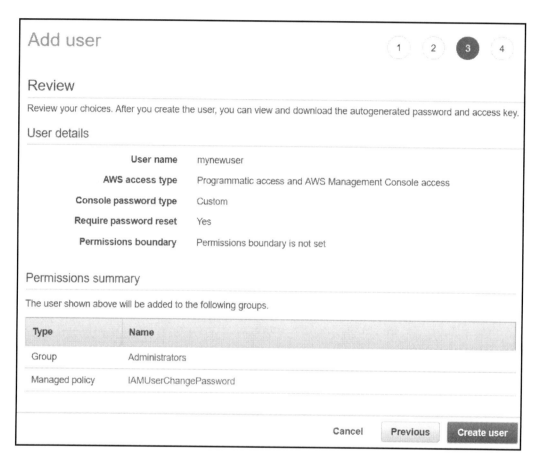

At this point, you will have the ability to download a CSV with the user's credentials or to display them in the browser. This is the only time the credentials will be displayed to the person creating the account as at any other time displaying credentials in IAM is not possible. If the credentials for a user account are lost, they will need to be disabled and re-created; for example, you will need to reset the password and/or recreate a new access key ID and secret access key. You can click the **Close** button once you are done with storing the credentials for your new user:

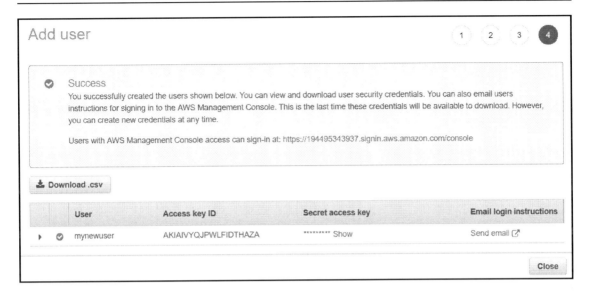

Checking the dashboard, you will now see that four out of five tasks have been completed as we have added an IAM user and created a group. We also assigned a security policy to the group, so the **Use groups to assign permissions** task was also completed at the same time. The last task left for us is **Apply an IAM password policy**; here, we will specify the password length and complexity to comply with AWS best practices.

Let's expand the **Apply an IAM password policy** section and click **Manage Password Policy**:

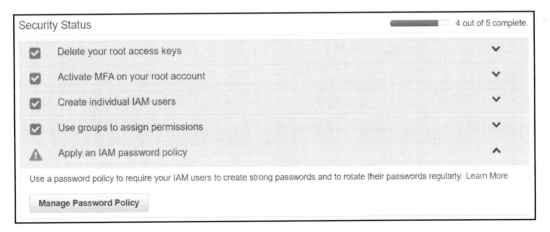

By managing the password policy, you will have the ability to enforce rules that comply with your enterprise security policy and AWS best practices. You can set the following attributes for your password policy:

- Set the minimum password length
- Require at least one uppercase or lowercase character, number, or special character
- Allow users to change their own passwords
- Enable password expiration after a number of days
- Prevent the reuse of passwords
- Enable administrative reset on expired passwords

All of the features listed here are standard enterprise features for password complexity and rotation, and your enterprise probably has an existing password policy that the AWS password policy can be made to comply with:

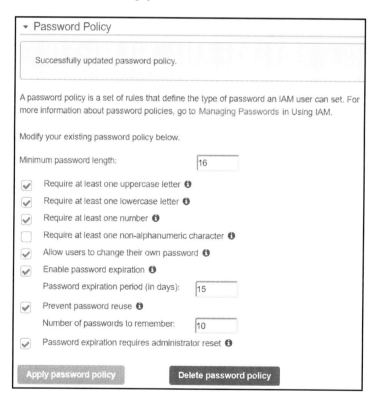

By clicking **Apply password policy**, you have completed the last task in the IAM Dashboard security overview and all check marks should be green:

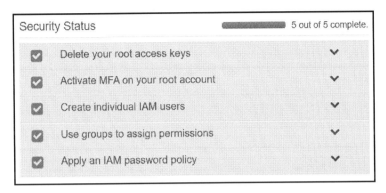

Managing access with IAM

There are three different identity entities in IAM that we will be taking a deeper look at in this chapter:

- **Users**: These are identifying objects that uniquely represent the person or service that is interacting with AWS. A user will always specify a username and then a credential that will be used with the username to authenticate the user.
- **Groups**: These are collections of IAM users that allow for the grouping of users with identical requirements into an entity that can be easily managed as a single entity. Any permissions set to the group will be automatically inherited by all the users in the group. It is a best practice of AWS to apply permissions to groups and then move users in and out of groups when their permission requirements change.

- **Roles**: These are identifying objects that help AWS identify the service's or a person's permissions when using AWS services. Contrary to users, roles do not identify a unique person or service and can be assumed by multiple entities at the same time. Roles are a way to temporarily acquire certain permissions that are beyond the usual scope of the permissions assigned to the user or a service. For example, you can allow users to assume a role when needing elevated or administrative access, or you can use roles to give virtual machine instances access to other AWS resources, such as S3 or DynamoDB, without having to hardcode security credentials into the instance itself.

Managing Users

In AWS, the combination of Users, Groups, and Roles can be used to build a model for role-based access for users and applications using AWS services. As we have already mentioned, a user in AWS represents an entity that needs to be uniquely identified within the AWS environment when interacting with AWS services and components. This entity can be a user, a service, a server, or any other uniquely identifiable initiator of a request to AWS services. We have the ability to create up to 5,000 users in IAM in our AWS account. To manage users, we will sign in to the AWS Management Console with the newly created user and navigate to the **Users** section of AWS IAM:

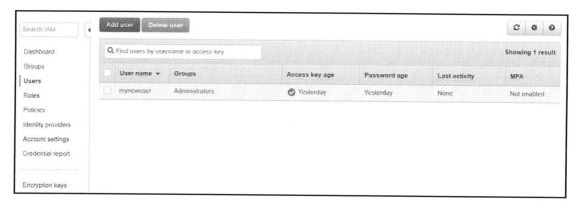

Here, we can click on the user and manage the user's properties. On the **Summary** page, we can see the policies attached to this user:

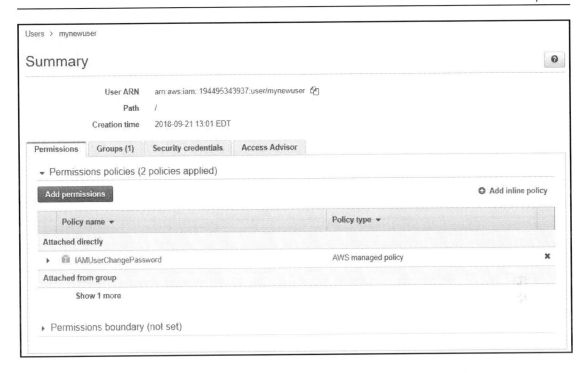

Since we chose to set a global password policy for all users to be able to change their own password, all users will automatically be assigned the default `IAMUserChangePassword` policy, which defines this permission. All other permissions are set via the group membership, which we can see if we click on **Groups**. Here, we are able to look at the group membership and add the user to other groups:

By clicking on **Security credentials**, we can manage the way this user authenticates to AWS, reset the console password, manage the MFA device, and inactivate and create new access key IDs and secret access keys. As we already explained, the credentials are visible to the administrators only upon creation:

Let's go ahead and rotate the user's access key by making the existing key inactive by clicking on **Make Inactive**, then clicking on **Create access key** to create a new one. Once we have done this, we can see two access key IDs in our console, one of them inactive and one of them active. A user can have multiple access keys assigned to them and all of those can be arbitrarily deactivated and reactivated if needed:

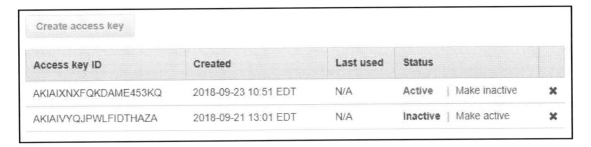

You are encouraged to explore the **Security Credentials** tab and perform all of the tasks that can be done in this section:

- Reset the user's management console password
- Add an MFA device to the user
- Manage access keys
- Optionally, you can test out a signing certificate or SSH key for this user if you have one

Managing Groups

To group the users together in pools that can be managed as one object, we use groups in AWS. We have the ability to create up to 300 groups in IAM in our AWS account. Let's go back to the management console and click on **Groups** in IAM:

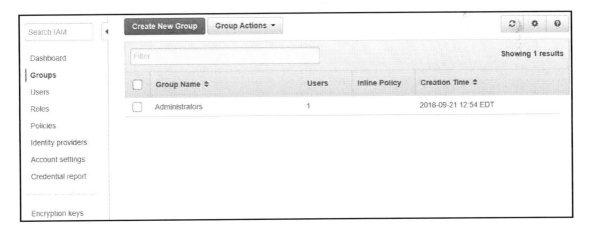

Now, open the **Administrators** group by clicking on its **Group Name**. You are presented with the **Access Advisor** tab where you can quickly see what kinds of permissions have been assigned to this group. You can see the **AdministratorAccess** policy is granting access to all of the AWS services. We will be looking at this policy in the *Managing Policies and Assigning Permissions* section of this chapter:

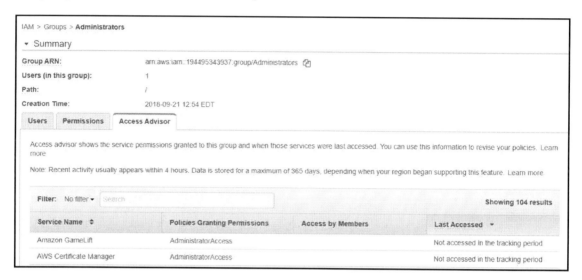

By clicking on the **Permissions** and **Users** tabs, we can assign other policies defining other permissions to the group and add or remove users from the group.

Managing Roles

When we create an AWS account, no roles are created initially, so by clicking on the **Roles** section in IAM, we will get the **Create Role** dialogue presented to us. A brief explanation is also presented that outlines a way roles can be used. As we already mentioned at the beginning of this chapter, roles are not used to identify a unique user or service, but are rather designed to allow multiple entities that require the same level of access to assume the role and present temporary credentials that allow access to the service for a limited time. We have the ability to create up to 1,000 roles in IAM in our AWS account.

Let's go ahead and create a role by clicking on the **Create role** button:

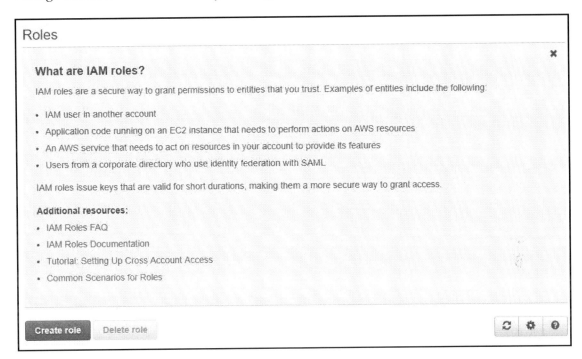

When creating a role, we have the ability to create the following roles:

- **AWS service roles**: These are assigned to AWS services so that they can access other AWS services without the need for storing credentials in the service itself. For instance, perhaps we have an EC2 instance running an application that needs to store session data in DynamoDB.
- **Another AWS account**: Cross-account roles can be used to grant access to services in our account to other AWS accounts. This can be used for sharing administrative roles in multiple accounts owned by one enterprise, giving access to an external auditing company also using AWS and granting permissions with any other entities with which we share services or data.

- **Web identity role**: We are able to create roles that grant access to users that are identified via a web identity such as Amazon, Amazon Cognito, Google, and Facebook, or other OpenID and SAML-compatible web identities.
- **SAML 2.0 federation**: Similarly to web identity, we can create roles that are assigned and grant access to users from our SAML 2.0-compatible corporate directories.

By selecting EC2 and clicking **Next: Permissions**, we will initiate the creation of a simple EC2 role that will allow EC2 instances that assume this role to have access to DynmoDB:

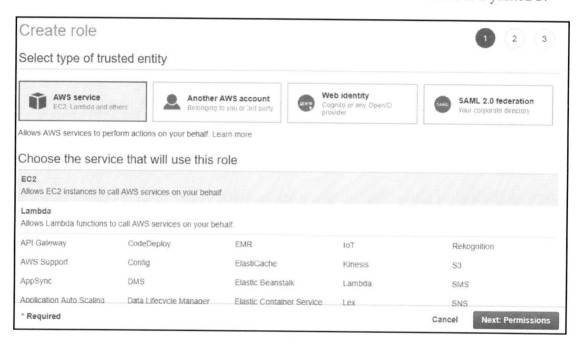

We will search for the DynamoDB roles and select the **AmazonDynamoDBFullAccess** policy, then press the **Next: Review** button:

The last step is to name the role and click **Create role**:

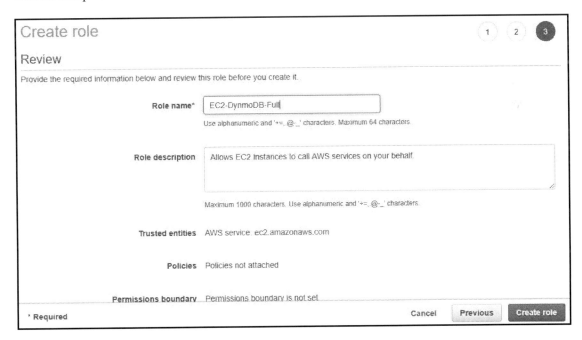

Types of credentials in AWS

Whenever a user or service is authenticating to AWS, they will need to present a certain credential, depending on the way the AWS environment is being accessed. There are several different types of credentials used in AWS:

- **User credentials**: By default, a user has none but can be assigned any of the following credentials:
    - **The AWS Management Console password**: This is only used to access the AWS Console from a browser.
    - **The access keys**: Both the access key ID and secret access key can be used to authenticate to AWS when using the AWS CLI or the SDK.
    - **An SSH key**: This can be used when accessing AWS CodeCommit and for general access to SSH consoles of servers on AWS.
- **Server credentials**: Servers can use X.509 Certificate authentication for SSL/TLS connections.
- **Role credentials**: When a user or service assumes a role, temporary security credentials are created and exchanged between the caller and the service being called. The credentials expire every hour by default but the value can also be set to anything between 15 minutes and 12 hours upon role assumption.
- **Temporary token credentials**: Security tokens issued by the AWS **Security Token Service (STS)** web service on AWS that enables the requesting and issuing of temporary, limited-privilege credentials for users within IAM or users authenticated by a federation with an external directory.

All of the credentials mentioned here can be managed and distributed securely and automatically within the AWS environment. This means we can easily automate the way we create, manage, and assign security permissions and grant access to our application running on AWS.

Managing policies and assigning permissions

Assigning permissions in AWS is done through policies. Policies are implemented as JSON objects that define the scope of actions that are able to be executed over AWS resources. A combination of policies and security principles will be looked at before the final permissions are determined by AWS, and those include the following:

- **Identity-based policies**: These are attached to users, groups, and roles.

- **Resource-based policies**: Policies can be attached directly to resources; for example, S3 bucket policies can control access to the S3 bucket.
- **Access control lists (ACLs)**: ACLs are also attached to certain resources, but unlike resource-based policies are use XML rather than JSON.
- **Organizations service control policies (SCP)**: We use SCPs to assign permissions boundaries to AWS organizations or **organizational units (OUs)**.

Policies have a certain structure, written in JSON, and are composed of two parts:

- Policy-wide information at the top of the document (optional)
- One or more policy statements (mandatory)

Statements include information about a single permission, so to define multiple permissions you can include multiple statements. When evaluating the final permission, a logical AND is applied across all statements. When evaluating multiple policies, a logical AND will be applied across all of those policies, meaning the most restrictive setting in all policies combined will become the effective set of permissions.

Let's take a look at a policy by navigating to the IAM service, selecting the **Policies** | **AdministrativeAccess** policy, and selecting the **{} JSON** button:

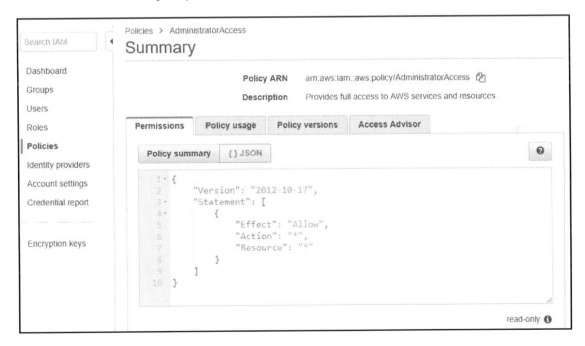

We can see that the version and one statement are included in this policy, and we can see that the effect of the statement is that it will **Allow** any action across all resources. The JSON policy can include all of the following attributes:

- **Version**: Here, we can specify the version of the policy language; in most cases, the latest 2012-10-17 version should be used.
- **Statement**: It is used as a container for statement elements:
    - **Sid**: An optional statement ID to differentiate between your statements
    - **Effect**: Allow or Deny
    - **Principal**: Should be the account, user, role, or federated user being assigned the permission
    - **Action**: A list of actions that the policy allows or denies
    - **Resource**: A list of resources to which the actions apply
    - **Condition (Optional)**: Specify the circumstances under which the policy grants permission

Integration with external directories

The AWS IAM service is offered as a simple way to build authentication into our application. But, there are some limitations as to what IAM can provide.

The typical limitations of IAM are soft limits. For instance, the number of users we can create in IAM is limited to 5,000, the number of groups to 300, and so on, and if our application is built for the web, we would also expect web-scale user numbers to be supported. When we talk about web-scale, we are talking about hundreds of thousands, millions, and potentially billions of users. To support large sets of individually authenticated users, IAM can be integrated with web identities, **Security Assertion Markup Language (SAML)**, and OpenID-compatible providers. There is built-in support for Amazon, Amazon Cognito, Google, and Facebook web identity providers, but any other compatible provider can be used as well. This can help us make use of the web identity provider's account management system to authenticate our users seamlessly and with very little effort. Upon authentication, the application can make use of the `AssumeRoleWithWebIdentity` call and allow the application to get permissions to access AWS web resources.

For example, you can build a mobile game that keeps track of scores in a DynamoDB database and game files in S3. To be able to access game files and record the score for each individual user, the application would assume the role, and then be able to enter a new high score straight into the DynamoDB table and access the S3 bucket to retrieve the game files. There is no need to store any credentials in the application, which is insecure:

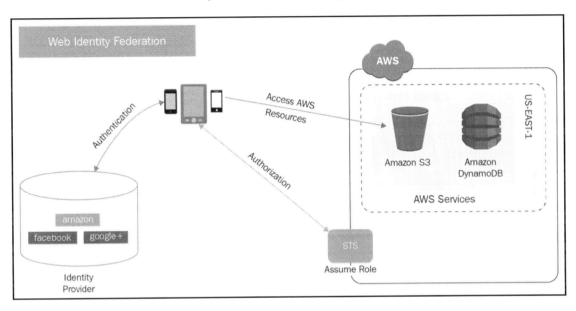

Another example of why we would need to use an external directory is when we are using an existing corporate directory with possibly millions of objects that have very complicated relationships. Since the directory already exists and the users are already used to the current authentication system, we can simply federate our corporate directory with IAM. This allows us to use our corporate directory to provide a single sign-on system that also allows access to the AWS services. The federated system can delegate the authentication to the corporate directory and then use the AWS STS service to issue temporary credentials that can be then passed along with every request to the AWS environment, enabling the user to be granted access to AWS.

Here is an example flow of authentication with AWS federated access with Active Directory:

1. The user authenticates against the **Active Directory Federated Service (ADFS)**.
2. Security Assertion Markup Language is used to issue an assertion back to the user's client.

3. The SAML assertion is sent to the **Security Token Service (STS)** to assume a role within IAM.

4. The STS responds to the user requesting federated access with temporary security credentials.

5. The user is granted federated access to the necessary AWS services as per the role permissions:

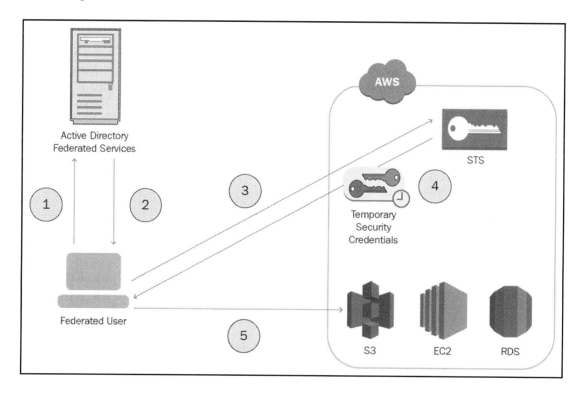

IAM best practices

In this chapter, we have covered some of the best practices that apply to AWS. At this point, I need to again stress the importance of securing your account and making sure that the root user is not being used for day-to-day tasks. The root credentials should be locked away in a secure place so that they are retrievable only in case of emergencies.

As a best practice, we want to create individual users so that these users can be uniquely identified when performing tasks within AWS and assign permissions to the users via group membership. Assigning permissions directly to users can lead to inconsistencies in access levels for users performing similar tasks. By adding permissions to groups, we can simplify the way permissions are delivered to large numbers of AWS users and apply permissions based on job role or service function, rather than configuring permissions individually.

Make sure to try and use AWS's predefined policies whenever possible. AWS has taken care of writing very well-designed JSON policies that apply exact access permission levels to resources, which can be used for various applications. Using the built-in policies makes it easier to manage access, as relying on custom policies can bring in difficulties when design and functional changes are needed in the application.

Another best practice is to ensure we are following the **least privilege approach** when assigning permissions. With the least privilege approach, we only assign the permissions required to complete a certain task. As an additional level of security, we can configure all our users and groups with a fairly basic set of permissions, then allow these users to assume roles that have elevated permissions.

For console and programmatic access, some other best practices should be considered:

- Configuring a strong password policy for your users; this will depend on any compliance or enterprise requirements but it is always a good practice to secure your passwords as much as you can
- Enabling multi-factor authentication for any privileged users
- Rotating credentials on a regular basis
- Removing any unnecessary credentials
- Do not share your access keys with anyone

For applications that run on Amazon EC2 instances and require access to other AWS resources, you should implement role-based access. The instance should have the permission to assume a role that gives it access and once started, that role will allow the application on the instance to securely access the resource without the need for storing credentials inside the application.

Roles can also be used to delegate permissions to users within the same account, to users from others accounts and to users authenticated by external directories. For instance, you can use roles to grant administrative access to your administrators, whose user accounts are initially set with very low permissions such as read-only. Only after they temporarily assume the role do they gain elevated access to the environment. All role assumptions can be monitored and tracked so any kind of unauthorized administrative access can be quickly identified and stopped. A second example is an external auditor, who can be given a cross-account role with read-only permissions in your AWS account. The auditor can simply use their existing user and assume the role to perform any task their role requires them to do.

Lastly, you need to monitor your AWS environment. You can simply implement monitoring of all the actions and API calls inside your AWS account by enabling CloudTrail on your account. The added value of logging all actions within your account is that you are able to have a detailed overview of how your resources are being used, who is doing what, and if any unauthorized actions are being attempted. Also, having a log of all the actions in your AWS account can be invaluable for auditing and compliance purposes. With CloudTrail, you can view, filter, and download the most recent 90 days of your account activity for all management events in supported AWS services free of charge. Since August 2017, AWS CloudTrail has been enabled by default for all customers and will provide visibility into the past seven days of account activity, without the need to configure a trail in the service to get started.

Summary

AWS Identity and Access Management is a complete and free tool provided by AWS that allows us to control security inside our AWS account, inside an application running on AWS, and for granting access to external entities. This built-in capability is very valuable when building applications and running services in AWS, and can help us relieve the burden of building and managing our own identity management system. By following the AWS IAM best practices, we also have the ability to highly secure our environment and use its features to build compliance and adhere to regulations that govern application security. If the soft limits of the IAM system are not sufficient to support the authentication needs of our application, we can integrate the IAM environment with corporate directories such as Active Directory and other SAML 2.0-compatible providers. We can also introduce web identity federation with Amazon, Cognito, Google, and Facebook when building web-scale applications with huge numbers of users. This can be especially useful for mobile applications and games. In the next chapter, we will use Virtual Private Cloud (VPC) to create our own private networking environment.

Questions

1. In what case would it be normal practice to keep using the root account for administrative tasks?
2. What is multi-factor authentication?
3. What kinds of features does the AWS IAM password policy provide?
4. What are the three main identity objects within IAM?
5. Can a user have more than one active access key assigned to their account?
6. A user has lost their secret access key and is asking the administrator to retrieve the existing secret access key for them. How can this be done?
7. You are looking to give an application running on EC2 access to S3. What is the best practice way to achieve that?
8. You are in charge of directory services in your enterprise and you have been given the task of granting everyone in your organization access to AWS. There are approximately 15000 users in your directory. What is the best way to approach authentication in AWS?
9. State true or false: Yesterday someone deleted a server that inadvertently had some important data on it. The owner of that server is requesting you identify the culprit. You explain that you did not configure CloudTrail on the account and that data is not available.

Further reading

- **The AWS Root User**: https://docs.aws.amazon.com/IAM/latest/UserGuide/id_root-user.html
- **AWS Security Credentials**: https://docs.aws.amazon.com/general/latest/gr/aws-security-credentials.html
- **IAM Service Limits**: https://docs.aws.amazon.com/IAM/latest/UserGuide/reference_iam-limits.html
- **IAM Policies and Permissions**: https://docs.aws.amazon.com/IAM/latest/UserGuide/access_policies.html
- **IAM Best Practices**: https://docs.aws.amazon.com/IAM/latest/UserGuide/id_root-user.html

4
Networking with the Virtual Private Cloud

When running **Infrastructure as a Service (IaaS)** in the cloud, the core requirement is that we have complete control of the network environment and connectivity to that environment. In AWS, we can use **Virtual Private Cloud (VPC)** to create our own private networking environment where we can define the security policies and routing to build a custom setup with complete control of the network traffic in the cloud.

The following topics will be covered in this chapter:

- VPC overview
- VPC subnets
- Connecting to on-premises resources
- VPC endpoints and AWS PrivateLink
- VPC peering
- Network security in the VPC
- Building a custom VPC

Technical requirements

To follow along with this topic, familiarity with general IT networking terminology will be required. Specifically, familiarity with local area networking, network address translation, network routing, network firewalls, **Internet Protocol Version 4 (IPv4)**, and the OSI layers is required.

VPC overview

Amazon VPC is designed to give us the ability to provision a logically isolated network within the AWS cloud. Once created, we have complete control over the networking environment. We can set up our own IP address ranges and subnets and configure routes and network gateways. Both IPv4 and IPv6 can be used in the VPC to access resources and applications. Once the VPC and connectivity options are created, we can spin up AWS **Elastic Compute Cloud (EC2)** or **Elastic Container Service (ECS)** instances inside public or private subnets. To control network security within the VPC, we can use security groups and network **access control lists (ACLs)**.

VPC subnets

Subnets in a VPC are created within the network that's defined in the VPC and are defined as **Classless Inter-Domain Routing (CIDR)** subset ranges within the VPC network. By default, addressing in the VPC uses the IPv4 protocol, but IPv6 can be configured separately. When defining the network with the CIDR, IP addresses are described as consisting of two groups of bits in the address – the network address and the host address. To define the number of bits used in the network address, we use / (slash) with a number. Let's look at an example:

- In an IP address where the first 16 bits represent the network address, we use a CIDR of /16
- The remaining 16 bits can be used for host addresses
- Since bits can be 0 or 1, we have 2 on the power of 16 available addresses
- A /16 network can thus support 65,536 hosts

The number of usable addresses is smaller than the theoretical maximum because of the following:

- The first (for example, `10.0.0.0`) host address is used for the network
- The last (for example, `10.0.255.255`) host address is used for broadcasting
- Some services are reserved by AWS – for instance, the internet gateway, DHCP service, and NAT gateway

Default VPC and default subnets

When creating an account in AWS, you will find that a default VPC has been created within each AWS Region. A default VPC is a quick-start option that allows you to use AWS without having to create your own VPC and define your own subnets. A default VPC will have subnets already created. You can launch EC2 instances into your default VPCs in all regions and use other services such as Elastic Load Balancing, Auto Scaling, and Amazon RDS in any default VPC. While a default VPC can help you get off the ground rapidly when running tests, **Proof of Concepts** (**PoC**), and demos, you should always consider building your own VPC according to your own requirements when it comes to production. For each region, the default VPCs that were created initially have the following characteristics:

- A default VPC has a `/16` IPv4 CIDR block (`172.31.0.0/16`) with up to 65,536 private IPv4 addresses
- A default VPC has a default security group and a default network ACL
- There are default subnets in each availability zone with a size of `/20` and up to 4,096 addresses per subnet
- Routing is created that allows all subnets to talk to each other
- An **internet gateway** (**IGW**) is created and a route to the IGW is created for internet traffic
- All subnets are considered public and public IPs are assigned automatically to all instances

Defining networks in a VPC

Within a VPC, we define a network and then we split the network down into one or several subnets. For instance, a network with the `10.0.0.0/16` address can have two `/17` subnets, where the first one has the `10.0.0.0/17` address with host addresses from `10.0.0.0` to `10.0.127.255` and the second subnet has the address `10.0.128.0/17` with host addresses of `10.0.128.0–10.0.255.255`. The following best practices should be followed when creating a VPC:

- Make sure to size the network appropriately so that it can support the correct number of both private and public subnets
- A `/16` network is usually recommended as it is the largest logical network that can be created and gives us the most flexibility with defining subnets
- Make sure to size your subnets correctly, as once the network and the subnets are defined, they cannot be changed
- Subnets of size `/24` or larger are usually recommended so that they can support the correct number of instance IP addresses
- Separate subnets into public and private according to the role of the services within the subnet
- Secure instances within the same group with the same security group
- Use ACLs to achieve granular control over network security and traffic flows

Public and private subnets

When we create subnets within the VPC network, we typically see subnets with IP addresses that are considered to be private IPs from ranges such as `10.0.0.0/16`, `172.16.0.0/16`, or `192.168.0.0/24`. This can sound confusing when we have a VPC with a network of `10.0.0.0/16` that has a public subnet with `10.0.0.0/24` and a private subnet with `10.0.1.0/24`. The only difference between public and private subnets is that a public subnet has the following properties:

- An IGW attached to it
- A route pointing to the internet gateway configured
- The ability to attach public or Elastic IPs to instances to make them accessible from the internet

Public IP addresses are addresses from AWS-controlled public IP address pools that are attached to the instance randomly whenever the instance is started. When an instance using a public IP address fails and is recreated or is shut down and then restarted, it will not maintain the same public IP address. However, an Elastic IP address is associated with your account and is persistent, so you have the ability to assign the Elastic IP to your instance to retain the address when it is shut down and restarted, or you can attach the same Elastic IP the failed instance was using to an instance that was recreated.

When we say the public or Elastic IP is attached to the instance, we mean that a virtual connection between the public or Elastic IP address and the instance has been created. From the instance itself, a user will see only the address from within the subnet assigned to the Ethernet adapter of the instance. However, we do have an option to see the public or Elastic IP address from the instance itself by looking at the instance metadata with the following command, which will return either the public or Elastic IP address associated with the instance:

```
curl http://169.254.169.254/latest/meta-data/public-ipv4
```

A private subnet is simply a subnet where no internet gateway is attached, thus no public or Elastic IPs can be assigned to the instances. A private subnet can still have outbound access to the internet via a **network address translation (NAT)** gateway or a NAT instance. A NAT gateway can be easily created within the VPC configuration and has the following features:

- Supports 5 GBps of bandwidth and automatically scales up to 45 GBps.
- Supports up to 55,000 simultaneous TCP, UDP, and ICMP connections to each unique destination.
- Can associate exactly one Elastic IP address with a NAT gateway – once created, it can not be dissociated.
- Cannot associate a security group with a NAT gateway – however, access can be controlled at the instance level with security groups.
- A NAT gateway has an automatically assigned private IP in your subnet that can be viewed in the AWS Management Console.
- NAT gateways do not support IPv6 traffic. In case of IPv6, an egress-only internet gateway can be used.

If any of the characteristics of the NAT instance do not suit your needs, you are able to spin up your own custom NAT instance. There are plenty of open source and commercial options available both online and from the AWS Marketplace for NAT instances.

You would want to build private subnets whenever there is a requirement for running services that are not directly accessible from the internet, such as application backends or database servers. For instance, a general security recommendation is that an RDS database be spun up in a private subnet due to the inherent security within.

Connecting to on-premises resources

Another option for running services in private subnets in the cloud is to extend your on-premise workloads to the cloud as hybrid or cloud-burst solutions. You are able to connect your subnets to your on-premise data center via a **Virtual Private network** (**VPN**) or an AWS Direct Connect link.

AWS VPN connectivity options

There are three VPN options for connecting to AWS:

- AWS managed VPN gateway
- AWS VPN CloudHub
- Using a VPN instance

An Amazon VPN gateway can be used as a simple, secure, and cost-effective solution when you need to quickly provision access to your AWS VPC subnets from your on-premise datacenter via a private link. For each VPN connection, two public tunnel endpoints are created to enable automatic failover from your gateway device:

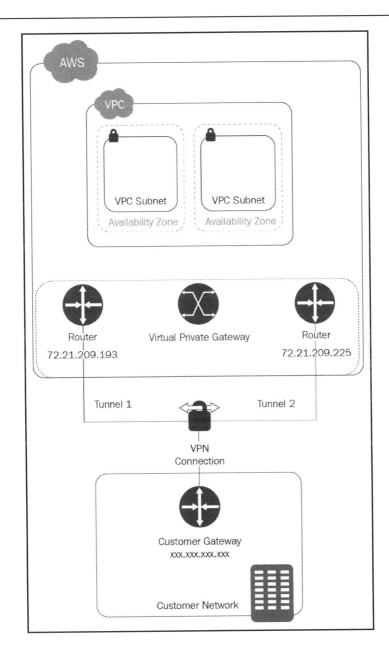

You can also connect to multiple remote sites from one AWS VPN gateway; however, no transient traffic can pass through a VPN gateway:

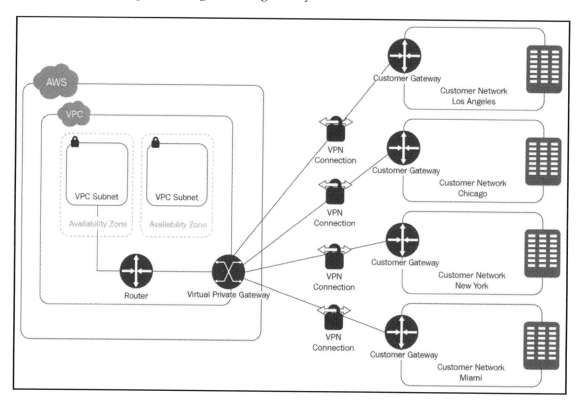

If transient traffic is required between your sites, AWS VPN CloudHub can be considered as a solution. The VPN CloudHub is designed with a hub-and-spoke model that you can use with or without a VPC. The AWS VPN CloudHub allows you to arbitrarily connect your AWS resources and on-premises data centers together:

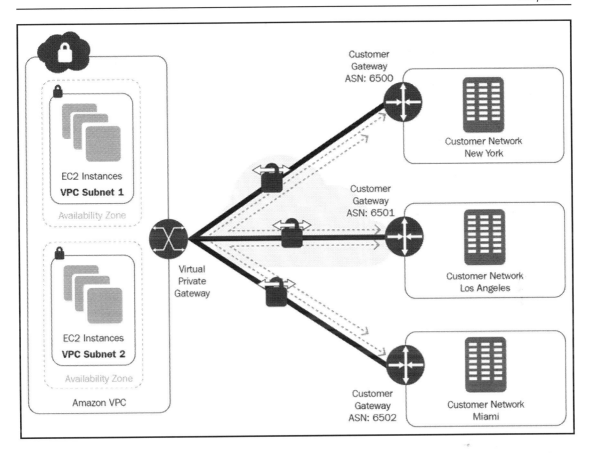

If neither of those options are satisfactory, then you can use a custom VPN instance that can be configured arbitrarily inside your environment. There are many open source and commercial options of VPN instances available on the internet and the AWS marketplace.

AWS Direct Connect

Sometimes, internet connectivity just isn't good enough. When a need for a reliable and fast private link is identified, AWS customers can choose AWS Direct Connect. AWS Direct Connect allows you to establish a dedicated network connection between your network and one of the AWS Direct Connect locations around the globe. Using private optical layer 2 links and 802.1q VLANs, AWS Direct Connect can be partitioned into multiple virtual interfaces for accessing multiple private subnets or public AWS services, such as S3, each over its own VLAN that makes sure that traffic is separated on layer 2. You can consider using AWS Direct Connect whenever there is a requirement for the following:

- Lower latency
- Higher bandwidth throughput
- A more consistent network experience
- Large amounts of data are being transferred daily between your on-premises environment and AWS
- Security and compliance requirements prevent the use of internet links

AWS Direct Connect can also save you money on transfer costs from AWS to your datacenter as it is much cheaper to transfer data through the Direct Connect link compared to transferring it over the internet. You can configure a lot of services to be directly accessible via the Direct Connect link by creating a public virtual interface for those services or by adding those services as VPC endpoints to the subnet you are connecting to.

VPC endpoints and AWS PrivateLink

When connecting from your VPC to other AWS resources with a public address (such as S3, DynamoDB, and others), this will inherently mean that we are traversing the router and entering the public IP space. Moving any data out of the VPC via the internet router will fall under the transfer-out charges and mean that any traffic traversing the internet router is getting charged, even if its final destination is another service within AWS. To avoid charges and increase the performance to the AWS resource that we are connecting to, we can create a VPC endpoint or use PrivateLink.

A VPC endpoint is a managed virtual connection from an AWS service that attaches to your VPC subnet and lets you communicate with that service on your private IP range. No transfer charges are applied to traffic being passed through the VPC endpoint as the traffic is contained within the private IP range of the VPC. The VPC endpoint is also inherently highly available and scalabe, meaning that there are several benefits to using VPC endpoints versus going through the internet to access these resources:

- AWS resources are directly available to private instances with no internet access
- There are no bandwidth limitations imposed by routing and NAT devices
- A lot of savings can be achieved due to no transfer costs

There are two types of endpoints available in AWS.

Gateway endpoints

A gateway endpoint is generated for a specific AWS supported service and is designed as a route within the VPC routing table. Any instance running within the VPC will need to consult the routing table to access the AWS service. At the time of writing, Amazon S3 and DynamoDB support gateway endpoints and will probably remain the only services to be supported in this way.

Interface endpoints – powered by AWS PrivateLink

An interface endpoint is represented as an elastic network interface attached to the VPC. The interface will be assigned a private IP address within the VPC and the service that is attached to an interface endpoint will be responding on that private IP address. Please consult the *VPC endpoints* link in the *Further reading* section of this chapter to get a full list of services as many more services are supported as an interface endpoint. This is because these are enabled by using AWS PrivateLink. PrivateLink provides the capability of attaching the ENI to the VPC and essentially allows the service to be accessible within your VPC subnet, so it is like having the AWS service delivered as a private solution to your application – like having your own little AWS:

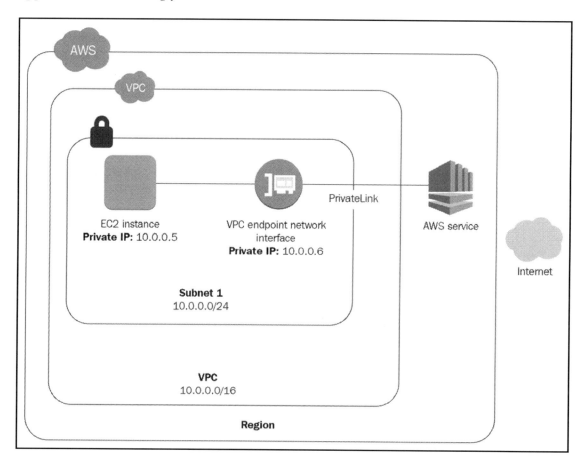

VPC peering connections

When we need to connect one VPC to other VPCs that we have created inside our environment, we can use VPC peering connections. A VPC peering connection is a networking connection between two VPCs that enables you to route traffic between them privately and have the ability to connect instances in private subnets within separate VPCs to communicate directly. AWS provides the ability to create VPC peering connections between our own VPCs or with a VPC in another AWS account. The VPC peering connections can be established within or across different AWS Regions. AWS uses existing, scalable network technologies with no single point of failure to enable VPC peering. When enabling VPC peering between regions, AWS will take care of the VPN connection between the locations and maintain redundant pathways for the traffic. Since the traffic between regions will pass over the internet, standard inter-region charges apply when using VPC peering between regions. No charges to traffic within a region are applied:

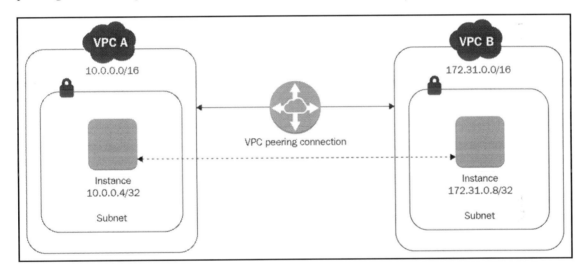

When setting up a VPC peering connection, we need to be aware of the limitations of VPC peering:

- It is not possible to peer VPC with overlapping IPv4 or IPv6 CIDR blocks
- Transitive peering is not supported – for example, peering A to B and B to C does not establish a link between A and C
- Unicast reverse path forwarding in VPC peering connections is not supported
- Tagging a VPC peering connection is only applied in the account or region in which you create them

Additionally, inter-region VPC peering connections have the following limitations:

- The peer VPC's security groups cannot be referenced in security groups that are created in the other VPC
- DNS resolution of hostnames that have both public and private IPs will only resolve public IPs when queried from the peered VPC
- Communication over IPv6 is not supported
- Communication over ClassicLink for EC2-Classic instances is not supported
- Jumbo frames are not supported across the inter-region VPC peering connection

Network security in the VPC

There are two ways to provide network security to instances running in a VPC, which are as follows:

- Security groups
- NACLs

Security groups

The first layer of defense for our instances is the security group. A security group always needs to be applied or created when we spawn a new instance in the AWS EC2 service. The security group acts like a personal stateful firewall sitting right in front of the instance and it provides stateful port filtering capabilities. For instance, when we start a Linux web server, we want to do the following:

- Access the console by establishing an SSH connection on port 22 with the system
- Accept connections on the HTTPS port 443 so secure communication without web server can be established
- Optionally, HTTP can be allowed on port 80

To allow access to this server, we would simply create a security group and add ports 22, 443, and, optionally, 80 as allowed ports for the TCP protocol from wherever we are communicating with the instance. Any instance that is a member of the security group will become accessible on the ports defined in the policy within the group. Any return traffic from the instance will also be allowed, no matter what the return port is, since the security group works in a stateful manner. By default, all ports are implicitly denied and we need to create an allow rule to open communication on a port and protocol.

Since one instance can be a member of multiple security groups, we can also separate the rules into several security groups, one allowing port 22, one allowing port 443, and one allowing port 80, and then arbitrarily assign these to instances that require them. If traffic is coming from other instances that are members of security groups, we can also simply specify the security group as a source for the traffic and allow communication in a very strict and easily manageable fashion.

Network ACLs or NACLs

The second layer of defense is our network ACLs. These are stateless network control mechanisms where each rule will have the ability to allow or deny traffic in exactly one direction. An ACL can be used to define strict rules on network access and provide protection at the network level. There are default, modifiable network ACLs in each VPC we create that are designed to allow all incoming and outgoing traffic to the network. In a similar way to how we assign security groups to instances, we can assign network ACLs to our VPCs. We can define multiple ACLs within our VPC; however, a subnet in a VPC can only be assigned one network ACL at a time. ACLs can be used to control traffic between subnets within one VPC as all traffic is initially allowed between subnets. Also, ACLs can be used when a certain set of IP addresses needs to be prevented from accessing our networks; for example, if we need to block certain geographies or a certain set of IPs that have been determined to be malicious.

The following diagram shows how security groups and network ACLs apply within a VPC:

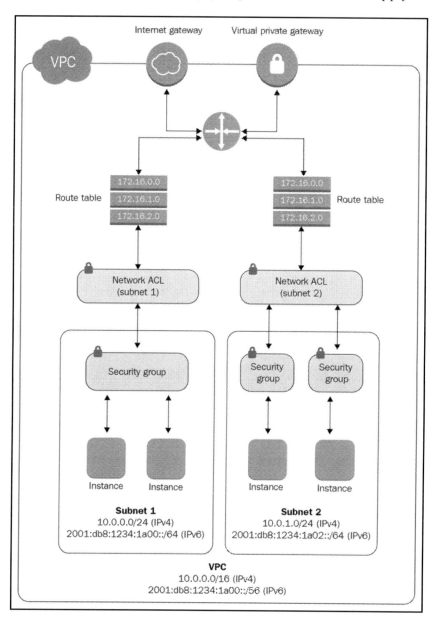

Building a custom VPC

When building a VPC according to your requirements, the first step would be to log in to the AWS console and choose the correct region. We have already discussed how to choose a region in Chapter 2, *The Fundamentals of Amazon Web Services*, under the *Choosing availability zones and regions* section. After logging in, we can search for VPC and select it. For ease of access to VPC management across regions, we can always remember the naming schema that AWS uses in their URL, which as the follows:

```
https://{region}.console.aws.amazon.com/vpc/home?region={region}
```

For example, the **US East (Ohio)** region is also referred to as **us-east-2**, so the URL for the Ohio region would be as follows:

```
https://us-east-2.console.aws.amazon.com/vpc/home?region=us-east-2
```

On the other hand, the **Asia Pacific (Singapore)** region is also referred to as **ap-southeast-1**, so the URL for Singapore would be as follows:

```
https://ap-southeast-1.console.aws.amazon.com/vpc/home?region=ap-southeast-1
```

This naming schema will be quite common across all AWS services.

On the **VPC Dashboard**, you will have the ability to enumerate **VPCs**, **Subnets**, **Route Tables**, **Internet Gateways**, and so on in all regions, no matter what region you have connected to. This allows us to get a quick overview of the numbers of VPC objects that are created in your whole AWS environment:

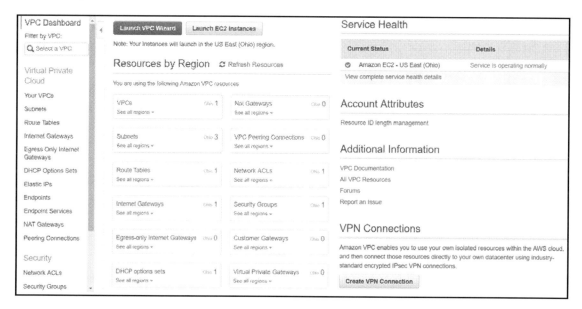

To create a VPC, we can either select the **Launch VPC Wizard** button or create a VPC manually by navigating to each of the sections and creating each VPC object separately. While the VPC wizard is nice and can cover most usage scenarios, it does offer limited configuration options:

- A /16 VPC with a single /24 public subnet
- A /16 VPC with one /24 public and one /24 private subnet connected to the internet via a NAT instance
- A /16 VPC with one /24 public and one /24 private subnet connected to on-premises via VPN
- A /16 VPC with a single /24 private subnet connected to on-premises via VPN:

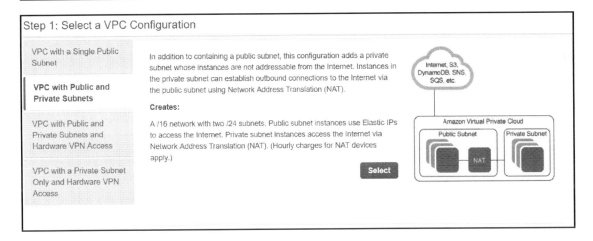

Although the VPC wizard will create all the required resources for us, we should consider building the VPC ourselves when we require more flexibility with the configuration. The following elements need to be planned and created for a VPC to function properly:

- VPC network CIDR with an IPv4 address range between /16 and /28
- An optional IPv6 block to be provided by Amazon
- Any requirement for a dedicated tenancy for the VPC
- The number and type of subnets and mapping of subnets to AZs
- The CIDRs for the subnets
- Number of public and private subnets
- NAT for private subnets
- Any special routing requirements
- The need for custom DNS, NTP, or NetBIOS settings
- The need for Elastic IPs
- Any needs for VPC endpoints
- Any VPC peering requirements
- VPN connectivity to on-premise or other locations
- Security considerations on NACL and security policy levels

All of these considerations will need to be determined and evaluated when building a custom VPC. This will ensure we have a plan that will allow for the creation of a compliant and reliable network architecture in the AWS cloud. To make your configuration even more reliable, you can consider building a CloudFormation template for your VPCs. We will discuss the concepts of CloudFormation and how to utilize it to build VPCs in one of the upcoming chapters of this book.

For now, let's focus on creating a VPC from the AWS Management Console. Let's navigate to the **VPC Dashboard** and select **Your VPCs**. You should notice that the URL to the **Your VPCs** section has an additional `#vpcs:` at the end to denote that part of the VPC Dashboard:

```
https://us-east-2.console.aws.amazon.com/vpc/home?region=us-east-2#vpcs:
```

Now, let's create a new VPC by clicking on **Create VPC**:

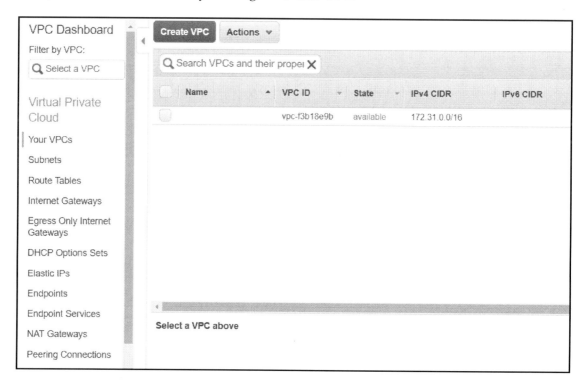

We will need to give our new VPC a name and a CIDR that we want to use within our VPC. We also have the option of selecting whether we would like to have an IPv6 CIDR added to the VPC and whether the VPC needs to have dedicated tenancy. For our purposes, we will leave these options at their defaults and click **Yes, Create**:

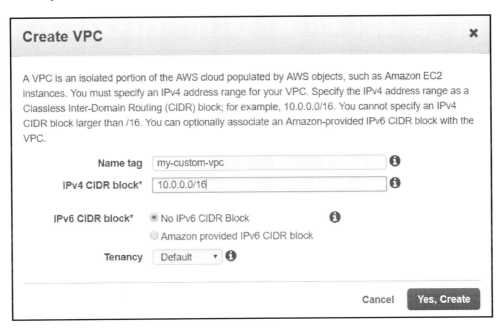

Once we have created the new VPC, we will need to create the subnets for the VPC. We need to navigate to the **Subnets** section of the **VPC Dashboard** and click on **Create subnet**. Once in the **Create Subnet** dialogue, we have the option to give the subnet a name and select the VPC in which we will be creating it. Please choose your newly created VPC here. Next, we will select the availability zone and create a new CIDR block for the subnet.

Please create four subnets in your desired region. Please make sure that two of the subnets are in availability zone a – in this example, the AZ is `us-east-2a` – and two in the availability zone b – in this example, that would be `us-east-2b`. Make sure you also assign non-overlapping IPv4 CIDR blocks to your AZs. In our example, we will create IP subnets (`10.0.1.0/24` and `10.0.2.0/24`) for two public subnets in AZs, that is, `us-east-2a` and `2us-east-b`, respectively and CIDRs `10.0.100.0/24` and `10.0.101.0/24` for two private subnets in AZs, `us-east-2a` and `us-east-2b`, respectively:

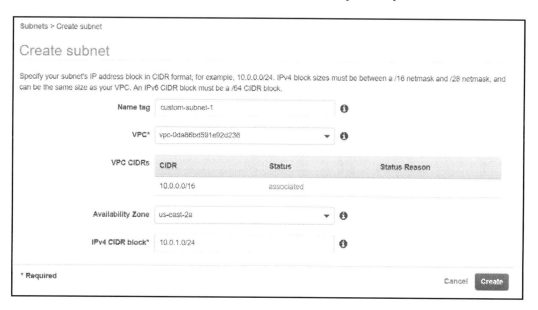

After completing the creation of our subnets, we need to create an **Internet Gateway** to support internet connectivity to the public subnets. We need to navigate to the **Internet Gateways** section of the **VPC Dashboard** and click the **Create internet gateway** button. Once in the **Create internet gateway** dialogue, we simply need to name our IGW and click **Create**:

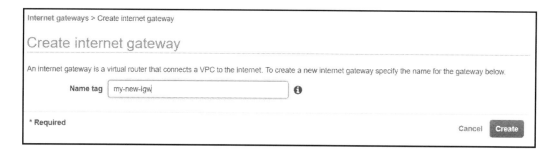

Once created, the IGW is detached. Now, we need to select the newly created IGW and attach it to our newly created VPC by clicking on **Actions** and selecting **Attach to VPC**:

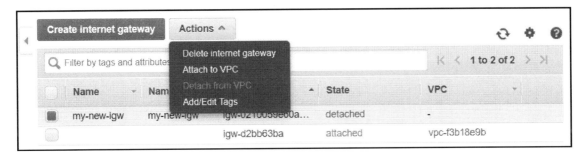

In the **Attach to VPC** dialogue, we select our VPC and click on **Attach**:

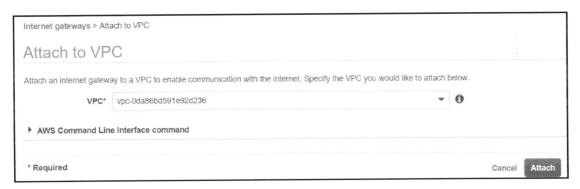

Now that we have attached the IGW to the VPC, we need to create a new route table so that our public subnets can have access to the internet. Navigate to the **Route Tables** section of the **VPC Dashboard** and select the route table that was created for your VPC. This route table is also called the **main** route table. It is predefined to allow all subnets within the 10.0.0.0/16 network to communicate with each other. All of the subnets that are created are associated with this route table by default.

Let's create a new route table by clicking on the **Create Route Table** button:

In the **Create Route Table** section, we need to give it a name and select our VPC, and then click **Yes, Create**:

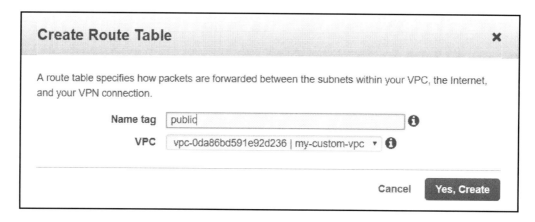

Once the route has been created, we need to allow access to the internet via this route. Select the newly created route, click on the **Routes** tab, click **Edit**, and then click **Add another route**. We need to select our IGW as the target and `0.0.0.0/0` for the destination – this denotes *all* routes and is the default CIDR for the internet. Click on the **Save** button to put the new setting into effect:

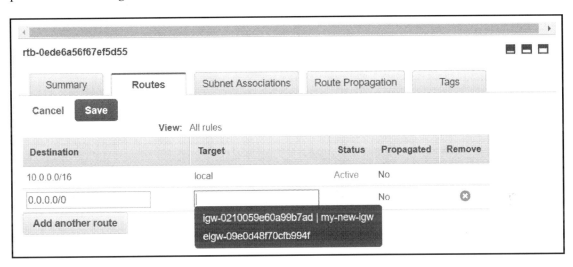

Now, we need to associate our public subnets with this newly created route table. Select the **Subnet Associations** tab and click **Edit**. Select the subnets you want to make public and click **Save**:

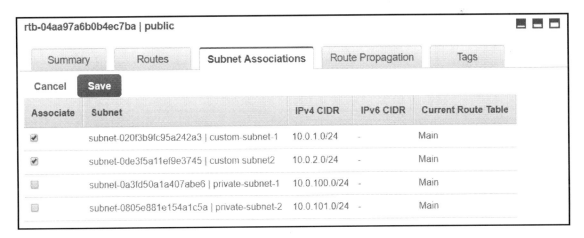

We will now make sure that the public subnets will get public IPs automatically assigned to the instances that we spin up in the public subnets. This is an optional step, but we will make use of this feature in our future exercises. Navigate to the **Subnets** section of the **VPC Dashboard**, select the first one of your public subnets, click on **Actions**, and click on **Modify auto-assign IP settings**. We should also note the other options when clicking on **Actions**. You can see that, here, you are able to edit the subnet associations and tags, delete the subnet, and also create a flow log. Flow logs are very important when diagnosing connectivity issues as they can show the connection results for all the packets going in and out to targets within our subnet. VPC Flow logs do not give any insight into the packet content so if deep packet analysis is required, we would need to use a third-party tool:

Select the check mark next to **Auto-assign IPv4** and click on **Save**. Make sure to repeat this step for the second public subnet:

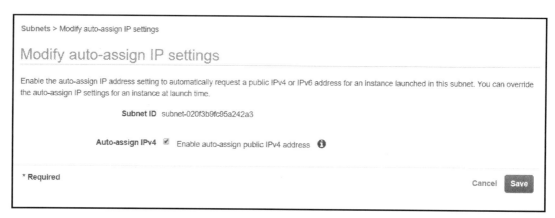

We have now created the basic setup for a custom VPC that will provide the ability to spin up instances in two separate availability zones and thus provide high availability to our application. We have also created a public and private subnet in each region allowing, for hiding services such as databases and application servers that don't need to be accessible from the internet. We have multiple other options within the VPC configuration and you should take a look at the other options in the VPC Dashboard. For example, take a look at the option to create a **DHCP options set**. Here, we have the ability to create a custom setup with a custom domain name and custom DNS, NTP, and NetBIOS servers:

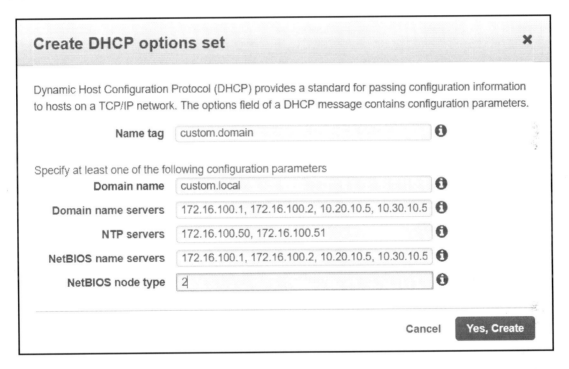

We also have the ability to allocate Elastic IPs if required in advance. When requiring an unchangeable IP address for any of our services, you can choose to allocate an Elastic IP for it. In the **Allocate new address** dialogue, we also have a nice feature that shows us the AWS CLI command for requesting a new EIP. Please note that, by default, all AWS accounts are limited to five Elastic IP addresses per region:

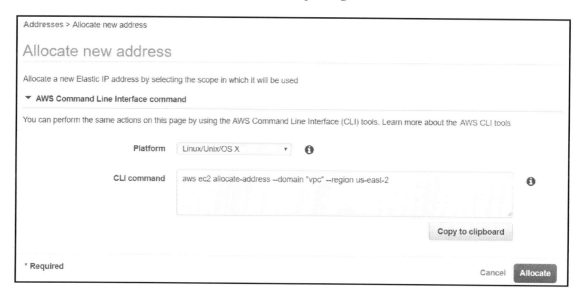

You can navigate to the **Endpoints** section to see how a service or other VPC endpoint can be created. Note the ease of configuring these features within the VPC Dashboard:

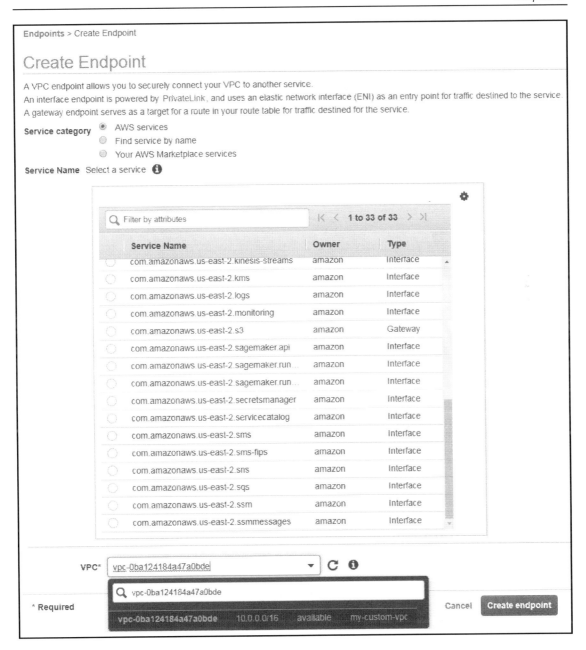

You are encouraged to explore all the features of the VPC endpoint at this stage and familiarize yourself with the options that the VPC Dashboard provides.

Managing ACLs and security policies

Two of the security features that are built into the VPCs are network ACLs and security groups. A detailed explanation on both can be found in this chapter, under the *Network security in the VPC* section. To configure network ACLs, we would navigate to the **Security** section of the **VPC Dashboard** and select **Network ACLs**. Here, we can create the network ACLs and modify existing ones. Select the network ACL that is associated with your VPC and explore the inbound and outbound rules and subnet associations. You can see that, by default, the ACL permits all inbound and outbound traffic and is associated with all your subnets.

To manage network traffic, you can create and associate custom NACLs with your subnets here:

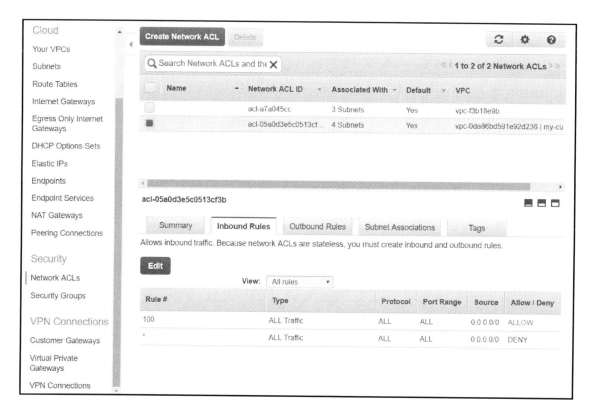

Next, let's navigate to the **Security Groups** section and select the security group that's associated with our VPC. Here, you can see that the security group allows only inbound traffic from itself, effectively denying all traffic to the instances associated with it. To allow traffic to instances, we will be creating new security groups when we spin up EC2 instances in `Chapter 5`, *Managing Servers on AWS with Elastic Compute Cloud*. Take your time to explore the **Security Groups** section and familiarize yourself with the options that are available:

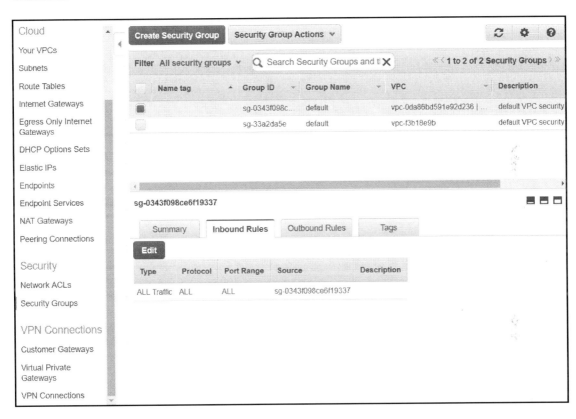

Summary

In this chapter, we have discussed the VPC networking concepts that are available in Amazon Web Services. We looked at the way networking is defined with CIDRs for the VPC network and the subnets contained within the VPC. We have also learned how to provide connectivity to the subnets via the internet gateway and on-premises connectivity options, and defined the difference between a public and private subnet. We also learned how to connect our VPC to other VPCs and services running in AWS by using endpoints and private links. Security is a very important component of networking and in this chapter we have learned how to use network access control lists and security groups to provide comprehensive security to instances running inside our VPC. The *Building a custom VPC* section outlined the steps that are needed to create a VPC. This ensures that you have a compliant networking environment running in AWS. In the next chapter, we will look into how we can manage servers on AWS using EC2.

Questions

1. What are the two layers of networks in the VPC?
2. What is a CIDR?
3. Which CIDR sizes can be assigned to the VPC?
4. What is the difference between a private and a public subnet?
5. What connectivity options does VPC provide for connecting to the internet and on-premises?
6. VPC A is peered to VPC B. VPC B is peered to VPC C. Can instances in VPC A reach instances in VPC C?
7. Your WEB application is running in a VPC. You have allowed inbound port 80 in the inbound policy of the network ACL and the inbound policy of the security group. Your application is still not responding. What could be the reason?

Further reading

- **AWS VPCs and Subnets**: https://docs.aws.amazon.com/vpc/latest/userguide/VPC_Subnets.html
- **AWS VPN Connections**: https://docs.aws.amazon.com/vpc/latest/userguide/vpn-connections.html
- **AWS Direct Connect**: https://docs.aws.amazon.com/aws-technical-content/latest/aws-vpc-connectivity-options/aws-direct-connect-network-to-amazon.html
- **VPC Peering Basics**: https://docs.aws.amazon.com/vpc/latest/peering/vpc-peering-basics.html
- **VPC endpoints**: https://docs.aws.amazon.com/vpc/latest/userguide/vpc-endpoints.html
- **AWS Network ACLs**: https://docs.aws.amazon.com/vpc/latest/userguide/vpc-network-acls.html
- **AWS Security Groups**: https://docs.aws.amazon.com/vpc/latest/userguide/VPC_SecurityGroups.html

5
Managing Servers on AWS with Elastic Compute Cloud

One of the core components of AWS is the **Elastic Compute Cloud (EC2)** service. It provides AWS users with the capability to create, run, and manage fleets of virtual machines in the cloud. When running a virtual machine in the AWS cloud we also call it a virtual machine instance or just simply *an instance*, since it is just one instance of many that have been run from the same virtual machine image.

The following topics will be covered in this chapter:

- EC2 overview
- Instance storage and EBS volumes
- Components of a virtual machine instance
- Connecting instances to the network
- EC2 high availability
- EC2 placement groups
- Configuring security groups for EC2 instances
- Building an EC2 instance in AWS

Technical requirements

To follow along with this topic, familiarity with general IT virtualization terminologies will be required. Specifically, you will need familiarity with running virtual machines on hypervisors, connecting virtual machines to the network, providing storage to virtual machines, and basic knowledge of the supporting technologies for achieving those tasks. Please refer to the GitHub repository for this chapter: `https://github.com/PacktPublishing/AWS-Certified-SysOps-Administrator-Associate-Guide/tree/master/Chapter05`.

EC2 overview

The AWS EC2 service provides the capability to use virtual machine instances in the AWS cloud. This service would fall squarely into the IaaS cloud category and is one of the basic services on which a lot of cloud PaaS and SaaS offerings are built. The EC2 service lets us run many versions of Windows and Linux based operating systems and gives us complete control of the operating system and its capabilities.

Virtualization types

There are two different virtualization types supported on EC2 that can deliver differing features and, in the past, differing performance to the visualized operating system and they are defined as the following:

- Fully visualized or **Hardware Virtual Machine** (**HVM**)
- VMs with some direct access to hardware or **paravirtual** (**PV**) machine

HVM are presented with a set of virtual resources (virtual CPU, disk, network, and GPU) and allow for a lot of flexibility when it comes to virtual computing as the instance is essentially fully decoupled from the hardware. That means it can operate on multiple different hardware profiles with no modification at all as the hardware is always presented as virtual devices.

In the past, PV was used to allow for better performance versus HVM due to its nature of allowing the guest operating system to access some underlying hardware and perform direct execution on the CPU, but the advances made in the way HVM operates and the virtualization extensions built into modern CPUs mean that the advantage is now irrelevant. Also, advanced services such as GPUs and enhanced network devices are not supported on PV instances. As there is no advantage to PV anymore, the newest EC2 instance types now only support the HVM virtualization instance type.

EC2 shared responsibility and availability

In line with the shared responsibility model that we discussed in Chapter 2, *The Fundamentals of Amazon Web Services*, AWS makes sure that the underlying host the virtual machine is running on is secure and available at least 99.99% of the time during a monthly billing cycle, as defined in the EC2 **Service Layer Agreement** (**SLA**). That means that the security and configuration of the operating system and any application running within the operating system is our responsibility.

The EC2 SLA also does not define the EC2 service as an inherently highly available service, meaning a failure within AWS can cause us to lose a particular EC2 instance which is expected within the scope of the way EC2 functions. What that means is that we need to ensure high availability of our infrastructure when running EC2 instances and configure them in a way that achieves the following:

- The data processed by the EC2 instances is stored securely and replicated
- The application running in an EC2 instance can be easily recovered or can withstand failure of an EC2 instance

EC2 instance pricing models

There are several pricing models defined in EC2 that allow us to use the resources in the most economical way possible while allowing AWS to achieve very high utilization of the EC2 environment as a whole, further giving Amazon the ability to provide competitive pricing for its services. The resources in the EC2 environment can be consumed according to the following pricing models:

- On-Demand Instances
- Reserved Instances
- Spot Instances
- Dedicated Instances
- Dedicated Hosts

On-Demand Instances

On-Demand Instances allow us to pay only for the compute capacity we use. The instances are charged by the hour or by the second depending on the instance type. There are no long-term commitments with On-Demand Instances; we simply launch an instance when needed and terminate it when not required any more. On-Demand Instances are great for any task that has an unpredictable or temporary workload, such as the following:

- Processing tasks from a variable source such as a message queue
- Running code execution in response to an event
- Covering temporary burst capacity requirements for EC2 clusters
- Developing and testing applications
- PoC deployments

Reserved Instances

While On-Demand Instances provide us with very high flexibility, Reserved Instances provide us with save costs for stable workloads that will run over time. We are able to create one or three year reservations for instances within our AWS account of the following types:

- **Standard Reserved Instances**: For stable, long-running tasks on one type of instance – can provide up to a 75% saving over the on-demand price of the instance
- **Convertible Reserved Instances**: For stable, long-running task where the instance type is projected to be converted to equal or larger capacity – provides up to a 54% saving
- **Scheduled Reserved Instances**: For scheduled tasks such as monthly billing

Reserved Instance pricing can be deployed on an availability zone or region scope and will be applied to all instances that match the reservation. For instance, if we have a reservation for an `m5.large` instance in the `us-east-1` region the pricing will be applied as long as an instance is running in any availability zone and any VPC within that region in our AWS account. Payments for Reserved Instances can be any of the following:

- **All Upfront**: Pay for all your instance hours at the start of the contract and run all of those instances for free. This option offers the biggest discount.
- **Partial Upfront**: Pay part of the cost upfront and then get the lowest discounted hourly price.
- **No Upfront**: Pay nothing upfront and get a discount on the hourly price of the instances.

There is also a reserved instance market where reservations can be traded after the purchase has been made but is no longer needed. This gives us the option to buy reservations for shorter terms and at even lower prices.

Spot Instances

To get even bigger discounts, you can look at the Spot Instance market. Spot Instances essentially run on available spare capacity that is provided to EC2 instances whenever they need to be scaled elastically. As you can imagine, at the scale AWS operates there is a huge requirement for spare capacity, meaning there are a lot of unused resources just waiting to be consumed in the AWS environment. AWS will let you use this environment by bidding on the price that you are willing to pay for your instances. You can save up to 90% off the instance price by running spot instances with one big caveat – Spot Instances can be terminated at any time. When the Spot Instance price increases the instance will be terminated within two minutes of the price increase. Spot prices can increase in the following scenarios:

- When there is more demand from users in the spot market
- When there is more demand from On-Demand Instances
- When there is an event such as a failure or scheduled maintenance that decreases the available spare capacity in the EC2 environment

EC2 will post a message of pending termination exactly 120 seconds before the instance is terminated into the instance metadata. Reading the metadata thus allows the instance to detect a pending termination and gracefully unload any remaining tasks it is currently running. Spot Instances are thus suitable only for tasks that are highly distributed across multiple instances and can handle sudden changes in the cluster size.

AWS now also offers *Sport Fleet* that can automate the usage of Spot Instances. Simply tell Spot Fleet how much capacity you need and fleet does the rest.

Dedicated Instances and Dedicated Hosts

While we have covered most of the use cases that can utilize shared computing resources within EC2, there are certain workloads that require us to run our instances on dedicated EC2 hardware. Dedicated Instances and hosts allow us to run EC2 compute resources on hardware that will not be shared with any other EC2 tenant. In the case of Dedicated Instances, we have the ability to use EC2 as we would On-Demand Instances, while Dedicated Hosts give us the ability to gain access to the hypervisor. Dedicated environments might be required in the following cases:

- The compliance and regulations require that virtual machines may not share hardware with other tenants

- The **bring your own licensing** (**BYOL**) scenarios that require use of our own licenses for operating systems and application
- The custom setups requiring access to the hypervisor

Components of a virtual machine instance

A virtual machine instance running in EC2 is always created from an **Amazon Machine Images** (**AMIs**) and the process of the creation of an EC2 instance is referred to as a launch. Whenever we launch an instance we also need to define the amount of CPU, memory, and disk attached to the instance and we define those characteristics using an EC2 instance type.

Amazon Machine Images (AMIs)

An AMI provides all the software required to launch an instance including the following:

- The boot sectors and disk layout
- The operating system
- The cloud-init components to configure your instance at launch
- Default block device mappings that define the volumes to be attached to the instance
- Launch permissions controlling who can run the instance
- Any optional applications
- Custom images that include user data

You can use a pre-existing AMI provided by Amazon or partners on the Amazon marketplace to launch your instances so can create and register your own AMIs. The simplest way of creating your own AMI is to launch a new instance, customize it, and then save your instance as a custom AMI.

AMIs are always created within a region, so you can only run EC2 instances from a specific image with a specific image ID within any availability zone of a region. If you need to use the same AMI in multiple regions, you can copy the particular AMI over to another region. The AMI in the new region will receive a new AMI ID. You can then run the same configuration in another region by specifying the copied AMI during launch. When you no longer require an AMI, you can de-register it; this will essentially delete the AMI and remove it from AWS. It is a good practice to de-register your old AMIs as they are stored on S3 so you will be charged for the consumed resources:

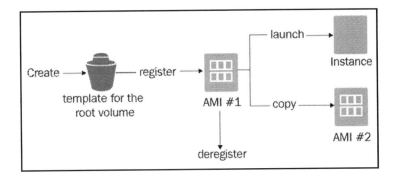

Amazon Linux AMI

AWS provides and maintains Amazon Linux 2 and the Amazon Linux AMIs, which are optimized to run on EC2. The features of the AMIs can be found at `https://docs.aws.amazon.com/AWSEC2/latest/UserGuide/AMIs.html`

Amazon EC2 instance types

After we have selected an image to run our EC2 instance, we also need to select the instance type. A selection of instance types optimized to fit different use cases are available on EC2 with varying combinations of CPU, memory, storage, and networking capabilities. Having such a variety gives us the flexibility to choose the appropriate mix of resources for our applications. For each instance type, we need to select an appropriate instance size that allows us to scale the resources to the requirements of the target workload but maintain the costs within our budget. Over-provisioning can cause costs to rise while under-provisioning can cause resource constraints within our application. Instance types come in five different types:

- General purpose
- Compute optimized
- Memory optimized
- Storage optimized
- Accelerated computing

The general purpose types come in two variants:

- T type or burstable instances that provide a baseline level of CPU performance with the ability to burst CPU usage at any time for as long as required
- M type with a good balance of compute, memory, and network resources

The burstable instances are useful when we have an application with spiky performance. Each burstable instance type comes with a predictable baseline of performance and can burst up over the baseline to either a limited or unlimited CPU usage (depending on the chose instance type). When choosing a limited T2 type the price will be constant and the CPU will be throttled by AWS once the allotted CPU time has been consumed by the instance. Unlimited T type instances will be allowed to burst as much as needed, but higher charges will apply if the instance's average CPU utilization exceeds the baseline of the instance.

The compute optimized C type instances are optimized for compute-intensive workloads and deliver very cost-effective high performance at a low price per compute ratio. They generally have half the memory per number of CPUs compared to M type instances.

The memory optimized instances come in two types:

- **R type**: Optimized for memory-intensive applications
- **X type**: Optimized for high-performance databases, in-memory databases, and other memory-intensive enterprise applications

The R type instances usually have double the memory to CPU compared to the M type instances of the same size, while the X type instances scale from 4 CPUs with 122 GB of memory to 128 CPUs and 3904 GB of memory.

The storage optimized instance types come in three different variants:

- H type instances leverage a balanced CPU and memory configuration and will allow the creation of up to 16 TB of HDD-based local storage with high disk throughput.
- I types are optimized for low latency and very high disk IOPS and feature the use of **non-volatile memory express** (**NVMe**) SSD-backed instance storage.
- D type instances are designed to deliver high disk throughput at low prices. We can configure up to 48 TB of HDD-based local storage for these instances.

The accelerated computing instances offer GPU and FPGA enhancements that can be used within our application and come in the following types:

- P type instances offer general purpose GPU acceleration
- G type instances are optimized for highly graphics-intensive applications
- F type instances offer customization hardware acceleration with **field programmable gate arrays (FPGAs)**

Instance types also sometimes come in generations and you will see that sometime you will be able to choose from multiple generations of the same type in the same region, whereas some type generations might not yet be available or not be available anymore in certain regions. Type generations are distinguished by the number next to the instance type, for instance M4 and M5, T2 and T3, or P2 and P3.

Instance store and EBS volumes

Once we have selected our instance AMI and type, we also need to consider the storage options for our instance. Some instance types come with a so-called instance store, while others are only compatible with volumes that are created with the **Elastic Block Storage (EBS)** service.

The root device

When we create and launch a new instance, the operating system is run off the so-called **root device**. When we select a certain instance type, it will specify whether it has some instance store or whether it is backed by EBS. This will determine where the root device will be deployed and what the characteristics, as far as the data persistence and performance of the root device, will be.

Amazon instance store

The Amazon instance store provides ephemeral block-level storage for EC2 instances. The storage is consumed from physical disks attached to the hypervisor and is ideal for the temporary storage of information that changes frequently, such as the operating system paging, buffers, caches, scratch, and other temporary data. It can also be used for data that is securely replicated across a cluster of instances, such as a distributed NoSQL database or Hadoop cluster.

The data written to the instance store volumes exist only while your instance is powered on. That means the data in the instance store will not survive in any of the following cases:

- The underlying disk subsystem fails
- The instance is stopped or the operating system is shut down
- The instance is terminated

The allotted storage from the instance store depends on the instance type and will be represented as one or more volumes (up to 24) that range in size from 4 GB on the smallest to 2 TB on the largest instance types. The instance store volumes are included in the price of the instance type, so we should make use of them whenever we are choosing an instance type that comes with an instance store volume.

Amazon EBS

With most instance types can use EBS as the volume storage mechanisms as the instance store volumes are not supported on all instance types. We can also use EBS when the instance store volume assigned to the instance type does not satisfy our requirements because of the following:

- Persistent storage that is highly available
- Storage that will survive reboots and instance failure
- Block volume sizes up to 16 TB

EBS volumes are delivered from a durable, block-level storage device and can be attached to one EC2 instance at a time. The EC2 instance that has the volume attached is able to store data persistently. Once stored, the data will survive any EC2 life cycles or EC2 instance failures. We also have the ability to detach the volume from the existing EC2 instance and attach it to another one. This makes it very simple to perform updates of the operating system with the ability to roll back in case of issues.

For example, a database server running on an EC2 instance stores the data to an EBS volume. When the need arises to update the operating system or the database platform, we can simply deploy a new instance with an updated operating system and an updated database platform. We transfer the configuration from the existing EC2 instance to the new one, power the existing instance down, and detach the volume. Next, we attach the volume to the newly created, updated EC2 instance and power it on. The instance is able to access the data on the attached volume and spin up the database since we have already transferred the configuration from the old one. We can now perform some tests on the newer instance and put it in production or revert to the old instance by powering the new one down, attaching the volume to the old one, and powering the old instance back on.

There are several different types of EBS volumes that we can use with our EC2 instances:

- **General Purpose SSD (gp2)**: General purpose SSD-backed disks with up to 10,000 IOPS, 160 MBps throughput, and a size of between 1 GB and 16 TB per volume
- **Provisioned IOPS SSD (io1)**: Performance optimized SSD-backed disks with up to 32,000 IOPS, 500 MBps throughput, and a size of between 4 GB and 16 TB per volume
- **Throughput Optimized HDD (st1)**: Throughput optimized magnetic disks with up to 500 IOPS, 500 MBps throughput, and a size of between 500 GB and 16 TB per volume
- **Cold HDD (sc1)**: Lowest cost magnetic disks with up to 250 IOPS, 250 MBps throughput, and a size of between 500 GB and 16 TB per volume

If the limitations of EBS volumes do not suffice, you have the ability to attach multiple volumes and create a **Redundant Array of Independent Disks** (**RAIDs**) across multiple volumes, although certain limitations do apply, for instance the maximum IOPS per instance using EBS volumes is limited to 80,000 and the maximum throughput per instance is 1,750 MBps.

EBS volumes are also designed to be highly available within an availability zone and adhere to the EC2 99.99% SLA. Each volume is replicated to two different physical devices within the same availability zone, so any disk failure or failure of the backend disk subsystem will not affect the EBS volume. Even though the EBS volumes are highly available within an availability zone, failures can occur that will bring the availability zone down and the EBS volumes with it. Also, there is no guarantee for data durability on an EBS volume, so make sure you protect the volumes with important data by either replicating the data to another instance in another availability zone with another EBS volume attached or snapshot the EBS volume.

Amazon EBS snapshots

By creating a snapshot, we are creating a point-in-time copy of the whole volume and storing it on the Amazon **Simple Storage Service (S3)**, which we will discuss in detail in Chapter 7, *Understanding Simple Storage Service and Glacier*. Snapshots are incremental copies of the EBS volume, meaning that only the blocks on the storage device that have changed since your most recent snapshot are stored to the snapshot. Although this sounds like a good way to perform traditional backups of an EC2 instances storage, we need to be aware that snapshots need to be integrated with a backup procedure, script, or backups software that sits within the instance and will commit all the outstanding I/O operations to disk before the snapshot is started. If there are any pending I/O operations that are left out of a snapshot, it could cause the data that's being copied to the snapshot to be of no use when we try to restore it.

Volume web console

To manage the volumes that we have created, we can look at the EC2 Management Console and select **Volumes** from the **Elastic Block Store** section in the menu. Here, we are able to see all of the volumes that we have created and manage their properties. We can also control the attachment of each volume to instances as we desire and we can also see a quick overview of the status of the volume. The status is derived from the automated status checks that AWS performs on the volume backends every 5 minutes, and the status can be any of the following:

- okay: The volume is operational and available for use
- warning: The volume is experiencing degraded performance due to an action or operation being performed against it, for instance creating a snapshot during high usage of the volume
- impaired: The volume is severely impacted in performance or is not available due to a failure in the backend of the EBS environment
- insufficient-data: This usually means that not enough health checks, have been performed to determine the state of the volume

The following is an example of the volume web console, and the data being displayed is for a 1 GB volume. If you would like to create a volume and attach it to a running instance, you can click the **Create Volume** button:

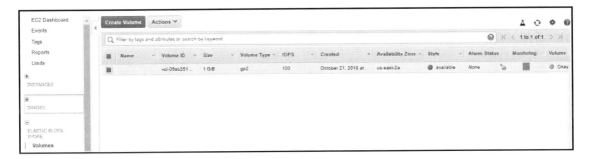

Connecting instances to the network

Once we have decided on the compute capacities of the instance, we need to select the network to connect the instance to. Instances are connected to the network by selecting the VPC and an appropriate subnet. We have taken a look at how to create a VPC in Chapter 4, *Networking with Virtual Private Cloud*. The selection of the VPC and subnet will determine the following:

- The private IP addressing of the instance
- The internet availability and public IP address of the instance
- The availability zone in which the instance will be started

An instance network connection details will be determined upon creation of the instance. A MAC address will be assigned to the primary network interface of the instance and the DHCP service within the VPC subnet will assign an IP address to the instance from its pool of IP addresses.

If we require more control over the networking configuration, we can use an additional **Elastic Network Interface** (**ENI**) to the EC2 instance. An additional ENI can be created and attached to an instance when the following conditions are satisfied:

- We need to attach an instance to multiple subnets
- We require an interface independent of instances life cycle
- We require a fixed MAC address due to licensing purposes
- We want to attach a specific Elastic IP to a specific private IP

For example, we have a specific instance that has some kind of software on it that is licensed to the MAC address of that instance. We wouldn't want to use the primary MAC because if the instance fails and we want to restore it from a snapshot or backup to a new instance, the metadata will not be maintained. This is when we can opt to use an ENI as the ENI can survive the instance failure and can be re-attached to the restored instance. The same applies to any kind of instance where we want to maintain a static relationship between an Elastic IP and an internal IP address, for example, a custom routing, NAT, or firewall instance within our environment.

EC2 high availability scenarios

There are several approaches to making our EC2 instances and the applications running on them highly available. The approach we take will be dependent on the SLA that we need to achieve in our application, that is, whenever it is higher than the SLA of the EC2 service. When we are designing applications, we should always be thinking of them as disposable objects that do not need to be protected, but that kind of approach is not possible with a lot of legacy and enterprise workloads being moved to the cloud. Thus when talking about high availability, we need to determine the following:

- Are our instances stateful or stateless?
- Are tasks being processed by our instances sticky or distributed?
- What does our SLA define as the percentage of high availability?
- What is the **Recovery Time Objective** (**RTO**) and **Recovery Point Objective** (**RPO**) when failures occur?

Stateful EC2 instance high availability

When our instances are stateful, we need to consider whether the tasks being processed can be distributed across the cluster and any data being received and stored is shareable across instances.

In the worst case, the stateful instances will also have stickiness in their application processing, meaning that one client request will need to be fully processed by one particular instance. When clients and instances need to have a strict relationship, the failure of an instance will cause the client or clients using this instance to lose their connection and possibly lose their data that has not been saved to a persistent disk capable of withstanding an instance failure. In this case, a traditional backup scenario needs to be implemented. Such an instance within AWS should be configured with an ELB volume for stateful data and both the instance and the ELB volume will need to have frequent snapshots created against them. The instance should also have an ENI attached to it if a strict MAC or IP relationship is required. You can also use the EC2 Auto Recovery service that can monitor your instance and automatically recover it with the same metadata of the instance that failed (bring it up with the same IP, MAC, ID, and so on) in the case of a hardware failure within AWS.

Stateless EC2 instance high availability

When our instances are stateless, it is very easy to make them highly available. The only thing that needs to be done is to create multiple instances in two or more availability zones in a region and put an **Elastic Load Balancer** (**ELB**) in front of them so that the requests being received from the clients (load) are evenly distributed across all instances.

EC2 placement groups

When you deploy a fleet of instances that are processing transactions in a distributed manner, you sometimes need to control the placement of the instances in the underlying architecture to allow for certain specific application requirements. You can use placement groups to control this behavior.

Cluster placement groups

You can use the cluster placement groups to group instances together in a configuration to allow for very low network latency. Cluster placement groups allow for the non-blocking, non-oversubscribed, fully bi-sectional nature of the connectivity, meaning that instances in a placement group will be able to utilize the full line rate of 10 GBps to talk to each other. To place instances in a cluster placement group, we need to start the instances at the same time.

Spread placement groups

When the requirement is to minimize the effect of a hardware failure on your application, you can use the spread placement groups. Any application with a small number of critical instances that should be kept separate from each other and made highly available can make use of this feature. To place the instances in a spread placement group, we need to start the instances at the same time.

Building an EC2 instance in AWS

Now, let's tie this all together and look at the process of building an EC2 instance:

1. First, we'll navigate to the **EC2 Dashboard** and click on the blue **Launch Instance** button:

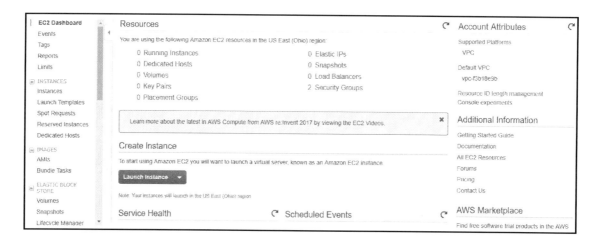

This opens the launch instance dialogue where we can search for and choose an AMI representing an operating system. From the quick start menu, we can select **My AMIs**, the **AWS Marketplace**, and the **Community AMIs**. For the sake of this demonstration, we'll run an **Amazon Linux AMI**:

2. Next, we can choose an instance type. We will select `t2.micro` as it is free-tier eligible, meaning that if you create a new AWS account, you can run over 700 hours of this type of instance each month for free for the first year:

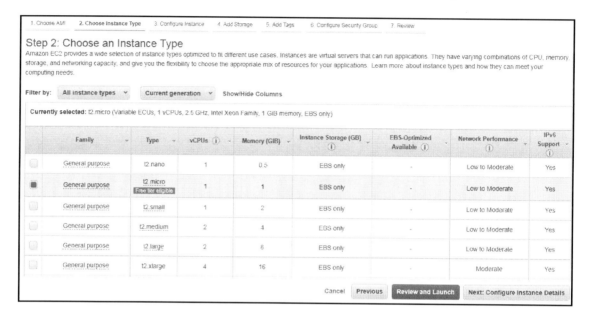

3. Next, we will configure the instance details. Here, we can choose the number of instances to run. If we need a fleet of instances, we can just choose any number up to our soft limit set by AWS. If we need to increase the soft limit for our account, we can contact AWS. We can also request spot instances straight out of this dialogue, but for the purpose of this demonstration, we will just run an On-Demand Instance.

We need to select a VPC and a subnet to connect the instance to the network. When building a highly available cluster you will need to repeat this operation multiple times so that you can put instances in more different subnets. You only need to do this if you're if building the cluster through the console.

Here, we also have the ability to give a role to the EC2 instance, determine the behavior on shutdown, and set up detailed CloudWatch monitoring, if required.

For the purposes of this demo, we will run one instance in the default VPC and put it in any default subnet:

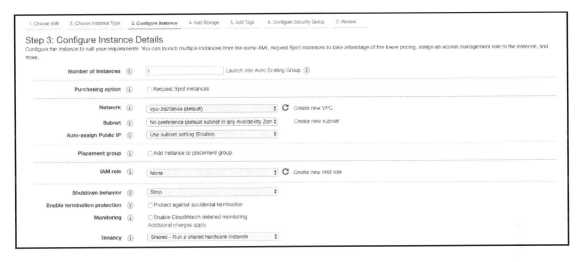

4. Next, we will add an additional EBS volume. We will choose an **EBS** volume and select how the volume will be represented in our operating system as either **/dev/xvdb** or **/dev/sdb** by selecting the device type:

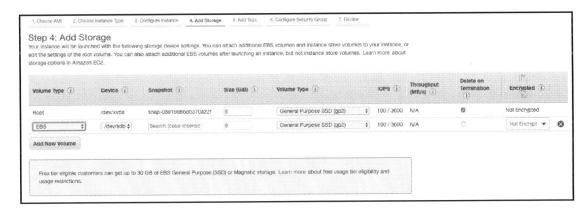

5. Next, we can add tags to the EC2 instance – tags help with the administration of EC2 instances. We can do advanced filtering on tags to help determine which application the instances belong to, for instance. Tags are represented as key:value pairs:

6. Now, we will create a security group. This security group will allow us to SSH into the instance from everywhere. Make sure you choose the type as **SSH** and enter 0.0.0.0/0 in the source:

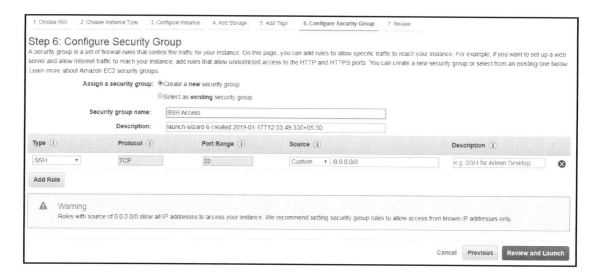

7. In the **Review Instance Launch** window, we will see a review of the instance creation parameters:

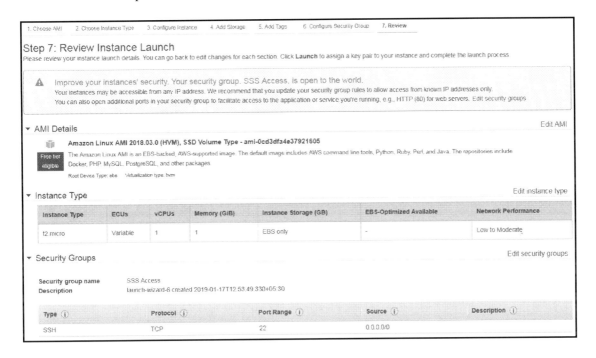

We will also need to choose an SSH key to log in to the instance. Password logins are not allowed to EC2 instances by default, so a SSH key is used to log in. If you have not created a key pair, you can create one, give it a name, and then download the key pair by pressing on the **Download Key Pair** button. Save it securely as this is your credential to authenticate to the EC2 instance:

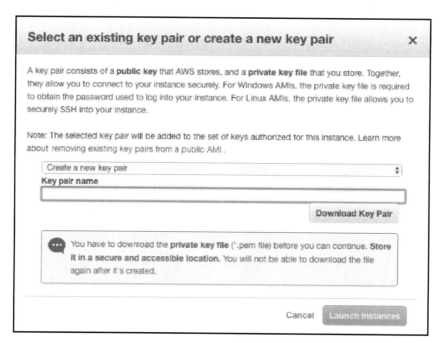

8. Once we launch the instance we will see a **Launch Status** window with an instance ID. We can click the instance ID and that will take us into the **EC2 Dashboard** under the **Instances** section:

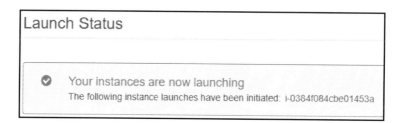

9. Under the **Instances** section, we will now see the instance. Record the IP address or DNS name assigned to the instance as we will use this to SSH into the instance and configure the secondary volume:

10. Now, log in to the instance with your favorite SSH client using the SSH key pair that you downloaded in this exercise. Please refer to the link named *Connecting to Your Linux Instance Using SSH* provided in the *Further reading* section of this chapter.

11. Once logged in, we can run the following command to see if there is any file structure on our secondary disk:

```
sudo file -s /dev/xvdb
```

If you have chosen /dev/sdb as your device please replace /dev/xvdb with /dev/sdb

```
[ec2-user@ip-172-31-32-189 ~]$ sudo file -s /dev/xvdb
/dev/xvdb: data
```

12. The result of the preceding command should be /dev/xvdb: data, meaning that there is no structure on this disk. Next, we will create a new partition by running the following command:

```
sudo mkfs -t ext4 /dev/xvdb
```

```
[ec2-user@ip-172-31-32-189 ~]$ sudo mkfs -t ext4 /dev/xvdb
mke2fs 1.43.5 (04-Aug-2017)
Creating filesystem with 8388608 4k blocks and 2097152 inodes
Filesystem UUID: 2adaf47e-bddf-4b14-bb33-b1a3ffa4194e
Superblock backups stored on blocks:
        32768, 98304, 163840, 229376, 294912, 819200, 884736, 1605632, 2654208,
        4096000, 7962624

Allocating group tables: done
Writing inode tables: done
Creating journal (65536 blocks): done
Writing superblocks and filesystem accounting information: done
```

13. Next, we will create a directory and mount it to our newly created volume. To create the volume, run the following command:

```
sudo mkdir /newvolume
```

14. To mount the column after it has been created, run the following command:

```
sudo mount /dev/xvdb /newvolume
```

Now that we have mounted the column, we can perform traditional disk operations such as traversing directories with `cd`, determining storage usage with `df`, and writing to the new volume:

```
[ec2-user@ip-172-31-32-189 ~]$ sudo mkdir /newvolume
[ec2-user@ip-172-31-32-189 ~]$ sudo mount /dev/xvdb /newvolume
[ec2-user@ip-172-31-32-189 ~]$ cd /newvolume
[ec2-user@ip-172-31-32-189 newvolume]$ df -h .
Filesystem      Size  Used Avail Use% Mounted on
/dev/xvdb        32G   49M   30G   1% /newvolume
```

If we need to restart the instance we can run the `sudo reboot` or `sudo init 6` commands from within the command line or we can log back in to the AWS Management Console and perform a reboot from the EC2 Dashboard. This is a good option when the instance is not accessible over the network for any application reason (perhaps we ran `ifdown` on the Ethernet interface or an application has a memory leak).

Once we don't require the instance anymore we can simply terminate the instance from the AWS Management Console.

Summary

EC2 is a service within AWS that allows us to run virtual machine instances. It allows us to control the type of operating system and set the amount of the instance CPU count, memory, and disk attached to the instances. Some instance types come with an instance store, which is included in the instance price, while others only support EBS. The EBS subsystem lets us create volumes that can survive instance life cycles and a loss of an instance and can be detached and attached arbitrarily to one instance at a time. To determine the availability zone and networking configuration, we put the instance into the VPC and select a subnet. When we have special requirements, an ENI can be used to persist the networking information independently of the instance. High availability should be configured for EC2 instances when required and placement groups can be used in special circumstances when we need to control how the cluster is placed. We also learned how to start an EC2 instance from the console. In next chapter, we'll handle server traffic with ELB.

Questions

1. What kind of objects does EC2 allow us to create?
2. Which layer of cloud computing does EC2 belong in?
3. What determines the maximum number of EC2 instances that we can run in our newly created account?
4. Which block storage type would you use for volumes that require persistence?
5. There is a requirement to create a volume with 20,000 IOPS that's a size of 30 TB – what would be the appropriate configuration for this volume?
6. How do we determine in which AZ the instance will run?
7. An application has a license tied to a MAC address. What can be used in AWS to prevent the machine from being arbitrarily assigned with MAC addresses?

Further reading

- **EC2 Supported Operating Systems**: https://aws.amazon.com/marketplace/b/2649367011
- **EC2 SLA**: https://aws.amazon.com/compute/sla/
- **Reserved Instance Pricing**: https://aws.amazon.com/ec2/pricing/reserved-instances/pricing/
- **EC2 AMIs**: https://docs.aws.amazon.com/AWSEC2/latest/UserGuide/AMIs.html
- **EC2 Instance Types**: https://aws.amazon.com/ec2/instance-types/
- **EC2 Instance Launch Commands**: https://docs.aws.amazon.com/AWSEC2/latest/UserGuide/user-data.html
- **Instance Store**: https://docs.aws.amazon.com/AWSEC2/latest/UserGuide/InstanceStorage.html
- **EBS Volume Types**: https://docs.aws.amazon.com/AWSEC2/latest/UserGuide/EBSVolumeTypes.html
- **EC2 Placement Groups**: https://docs.aws.amazon.com/AWSEC2/latest/UserGuide/placement-groups.html
- **Monitoting Volume Status**: https://docs.aws.amazon.com/AWSEC2/latest/UserGuide/monitoring-volume-status.html
- **Connecting to Your Linux Instance Using SSH**: https://docs.aws.amazon.com/AWSEC2/latest/UserGuide/AccessingInstancesLinux.html

6
Handling Server Traffic with Elastic Load Balancing

One of the key requirements of running highly available instances in the cloud is the ability to distribute traffic among a set of instances serving the same content. This can be achieved through load balancing. The AWS environment provides a load balancer as a service solution. We will look at the AWS **Elastic Load Balancing** (**ELB**) service and learn how to design and build an ELB deployment.

The following topics will be covered in this chapter:

- The AWS Elastic Load Balancing service
- Maintaining session state
- Building an ELB for EC2 instances

Technical requirements

To follow along with this topic, familiarity with running applications in a distributed environment will be required, specifically familiarity with load balancing technologies, delivering network load distribution to groups of servers, and a basic knowledge of the supporting technologies for achieving those tasks. Please refer to the GitHub link for this chapter `https://github.com/PacktPublishing/AWS-Certified-SysOps-Administrator-Associate-Guide/tree/master/Chapter06`.

The AWS Elastic Load Balancing service

The ELB service delivers the ability to balance the load of traffic from our users to either multiple instances or containers within our AWS environment. The service has the ability to automatically distribute incoming application traffic and allow integration with the EC2 Auto Scaling feature for scaling of resources that serve the responses to the traffic to meet user demands.

ELB helps an IT team to tune the instance capacity according to incoming application and network traffic across multiple availability zones within a region. This helps to deliver consistent application performance. ELB supports three types of load balancing that can meet various application requirements:

- Classic Load Balancer
- Application Load Balancer
- Network Load Balancer

Classic Load Balancer

This initial load balancer offering from AWS, which just used to be called ELB, has now been renamed the **Classic Load Balancer** (**CLB**). This is the simplest load balancer offering that can be found in AWS, but that does not mean that it is not powerful. The CLB is a highly available and secure load balancer that supports both IPv4 and IPv6, and both of them can load balance requests on the connection level. In some cases, it can also perform some load balancing on the request level with support for X-Forwarded HTTP headers and sticky sessions when we are using application cookies. It allows us to offload HTTPS traffic at the load balancer, thus reducing the work that needs to be done by our instances. As with any other service on AWS, it is fully integrated with CloudWatch metrics, from which we can extract real-time metrics and set it up with alarms that can integrate with Auto Scaling and other services.

Application Load Balancer

The next iteration of the ELB service came when AWS saw a requirement for some more advanced features for modern applications that could deliver even more flexibility of routing traffic based on layer 7 requests. The **Application Load Balancer** (**ALB**) was introduced to the layer 7 traffic shaping capability.

As with the CLB, the ALB is a highly available managed solution and provides the same features, but on top of the CLB features gives us the power of being able to target multiple backends that respond to different types of requests, including the following:

- Browser-based clients requesting `https://www.example.com` will get redirected to a set of frontend instances serving your website
- Mobile clients requesting `https://www.example.com` will get redirected to the mobile version of the website running on a separate set of frontend instances
- Browser-based clients requesting `https://www.example.com/partners/` will get redirected to the partner application running on the backend
- Remote servers accessing the partner application requiring API access on `https://www.example.com/partners/API/` will get redirected directly to the API service of your backend instances

The ALB is also able to connect to the following:

- Any reachable IP in the same VPC
- Any reachable IP within a peered VPC in the same region
- An EC2 instance connected to a VPC via ClassicLink
- An on-premises resource connected via VPN or an AWS Direct Connect connection

Network Load Balancer

The newest delivery from AWS is the **Network Load Balancer** (**NLB**). This highly available fully managed service was introduced to deliver a very high network throughput and very low latencies to client services at the network level. It can serve millions of requests per second and deliver consistent performance, even for very spiky application operating patterns. Since it works on the network layer, it cannot deliver any higher layer features, like those provided by the ALB, and it is tied to a specific static or Elastic IP address and a specific target availability zone – that is the trade off for the performance. We are, however, able to expose the requester's source address and that still gives us the ability to control session behavior within our backend.

Maintaining session state

By implementing load balancing and distributing the traffic to multiple instances running our application, we introduce better resiliency and higher availability, but, as a drawback, we also introduce complexity as far as maintaining session state is concerned. In a single server setup, the application can easily maintain the state of the application; since all connections are received by the server, the application has a complete picture of incoming requests. When we implement a load balancer, the load balancer receives the connections and forwards the requests to multiple servers running the application, causing each application part to only be able to see the traffic to itself. When a load balancer detects an instance with a high load, it will try to redirect the users to another instance and if we maintain the session state in the application, the new node would not be able to know the previous session state and would restart the session.

One way we can avoid this situation is by delegating the load balancer with session persistence by implementing sticky sessions. This allows the load balancer to always direct the user to the same server that created the application cookie. This allows us to use a distributed environment, but still maintain the session state within the application. The drawback is that the load on the servers will eventually become uneven, especially when we have sessions of different lengths. Also, a failure of one of the instances in the backend will inherently mean all its sessions will be reconnected, as the session state within the application on that instance is lost.

To mitigate the limitations of the sticky session approach, we should always strive to maintain the session state outside the application. In AWS, we can use an ElastiCache cluster or a DynamoDB table to record the session state. This way, all the instances in the target group of the load balancer can record session information in a highly available location that is accessible to all nodes. Any node receiving a connection can now consult the data in ElastiCache or DynamoDB and evaluate whether this is a new or an existing session, and if it is an existing session, what the state is at this time. This way, we can easily distribute the traffic over the instances evenly and survive any instance failures without affecting the clients.

Building an ELB for EC2 instances

Now that we have taken a look at our load balancer options, we will create a simple application on EC2 instances and present it through a CLB.

Prerequisite

Before we start, we need to spin up two instances running Amazon Linux and put them in two availability zones. This way, we will demonstrate how to make an application highly available:

1. We can follow the procedure to build an EC2 instance from the *Building an EC2 instance in AWS* section in `Chapter 5`, *Managing Servers on AWS with Elastic Compute Cloud*. Once created, we should see two instances running in two availability zones:

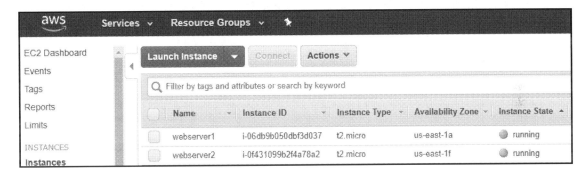

2. We will also create a new security group to open port `80` on those instances, as we will be serving a simple HTTP site to show the server's name in the response:

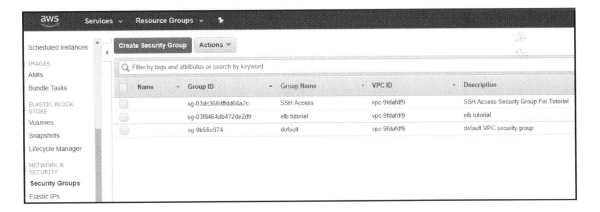

3. Choose **Create Security Group**, specify a name and description for the security group, and attach it to the VPC in which the instances are running. After you have created the security group, create a rule of type HTTP and source from anywhere:

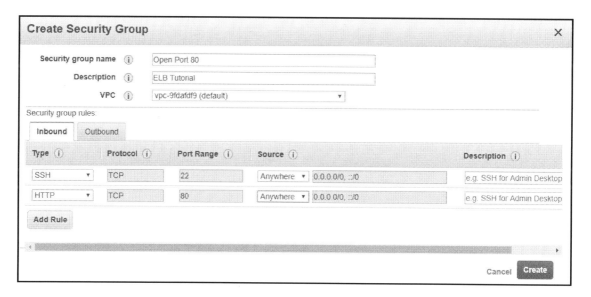

4. In the EC2 Management Console, select the **Instances** and choose **Actions** | **Networking** | **Change Security Groups**:

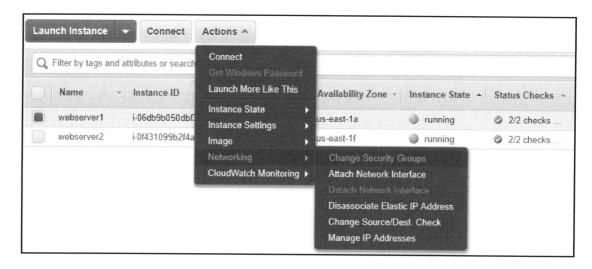

5. Select the newly created security group:

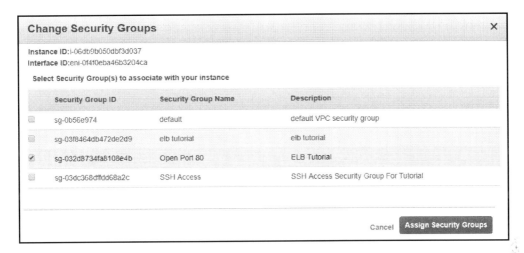

6. To verify the current security group associations of each instance, we can select the instance and check the **Security groups** section in the **Description**:

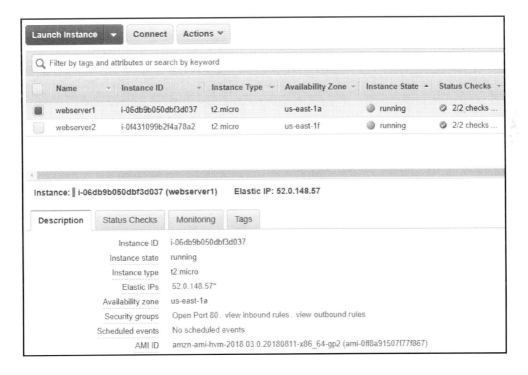

7. To create a simple HTTP response on port 80, we will connect to each instance and run a simple command on each of the servers. For webserver1, run the following command:

```
sudo su
nohup sh -c "mkdir test && cd test && echo '<html>Hello from
webserver1</html>' > index.html && python -m SimpleHTTPServer 80" &
```

The output for it should look like this:

```
[ec2-user@ip-172-31-23-162 ~]$ sudo su
[root@ip-172-31-23-162 ec2-user]# nohup sh -c "mkdir test && cd test && echo '<html>Hello from webserver1<
/html>' > index.html && python -m SimpleHTTPServer 80" &
[1] 2715
[root@ip-172-31-23-162 ec2-user]# nohup: ignoring input and appending output to 'nohup.out'
```

8. For webserver2, we just need to change the text to the following:

```
sudo su
nohup sh -c "mkdir test && cd test && echo '<html>Hello from
webserver2</html>' > index.html && python -m SimpleHTTPServer 80" &
```

And the result should look like this:

```
[ec2-user@ip-172-31-89-90 ~]$ sudo su
[root@ip-172-31-89-90 ec2-user]# nohup sh -c "mkdir test && cd test && echo '<html>Hello from webserver
2</html>' > index.html && python -m SimpleHTTPServer 80" &
[1] 2734
[root@ip-172-31-89-90 ec2-user]# nohup: ignoring input and appending output to 'nohup.out'
```

9. After we have completed the previous steps, browsing to the instance IP addresses should give us the following responses. This is on webserver1:

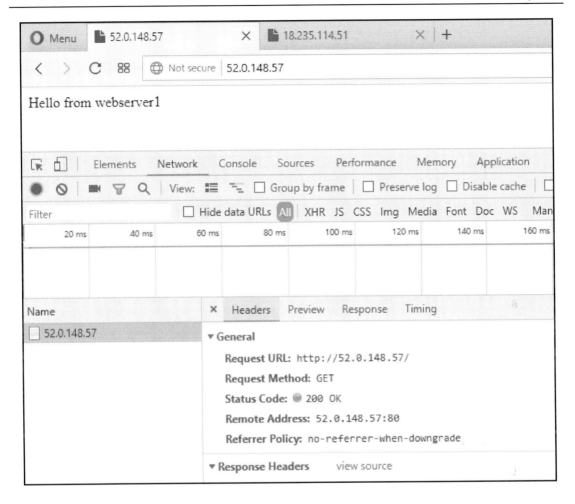

And this is on `webserver2`:

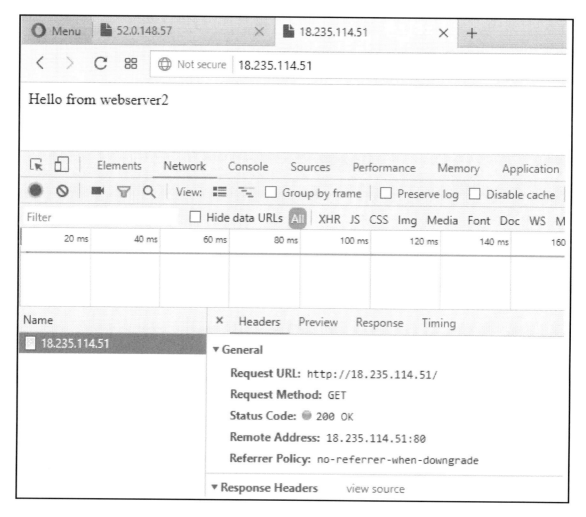

By setting up two instances with two different responses, we will be able to see the load balancer in action. When the load balancer chooses `webserver1`, it will respond with its name and when the content is served from `webserver2`, its name will be visible in the response. With this, we can be assured that the content is being delivered from two different servers in two different availability zones, and that our application is highly available.

Building the Load Balancer

Now that we have created the instances that will be serving the content, we need to create the load balancer:

1. We'll start off by going to the **EC2 Dasboard** and selecting **Load Balancers** from the menu. Next, press the **Create Load Balancer** button:

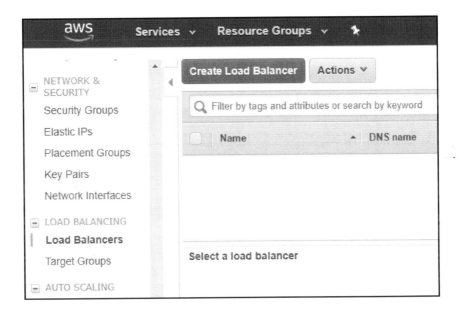

2. In the next window, we will select the **Classic Load Balancer** as the type of the load balancer. The service windows shows **PREVIOUS GENERATION**; that is essentially true, but as mentioned in the *The AWS Elastic Load Balancing service* section of this chapter, we can still use it whenever a simple load balancing solution is required.

Next, press the **Create** button:

Select load balancer type

Elastic Load Balancing supports three types of load balancers: Application Load Balancers, Network Load Balancers (new), and Classic Load Balancers. Choose the load balancer type that meets your needs. Learn more about which load balancer is right for you

Application Load Balancer

HTTP
HTTPS

Create

Choose an Application Load Balancer when you need a flexible feature set for your web applications with HTTP and HTTPS traffic. Operating at the request level, Application Load Balancers provide advanced routing and visibility features targeted at application architectures, including microservices and containers.

Learn more >

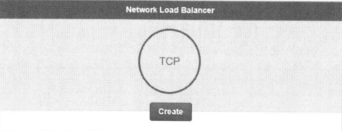

Network Load Balancer

TCP

Create

Choose a Network Load Balancer when you need ultra-high performance and static IP addresses for your application. Operating at the connection level, Network Load Balancers are capable of handling millions of requests per second while maintaining ultra-low latencies.

Learn more >

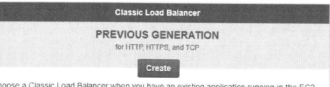

Classic Load Balancer

PREVIOUS GENERATION
for HTTP, HTTPS, and TCP

Create

Choose a Classic Load Balancer when you have an existing application running in the EC2-Classic network.

Learn more >

3. In the **Define Load Balancer Basic Configuration** window, we will need to define a name. The name needs to be unique within the region. By default, the load balancer will be internet-facing, meaning it will respond to the traffic on the internet. To make it internal, we can select the **Create an internal load balancer** check mark, which means it will only respond on an internal IP. Internal ELBs can be used to decouple parts of your application, such as the web and the backend tier, from communicating directly, with the ability to introduce separate scaling groups for each tier. If we want to select the availability zones and VPC we can select the **Enable Advanced VPC Configuration** check mark. In our case, this is not necessary, as we have deployed the instances in the default VPC. We will also need to select the IP protocol and port in the **Listener Configuration** section. In our case, we will use the HTTP listener, as we are exposing our application on port 80. We also need to select the correct two availability zones in the VPC that we used to spin up our EC2 instances. Next, we click on **Next: Assign Security Groups**:

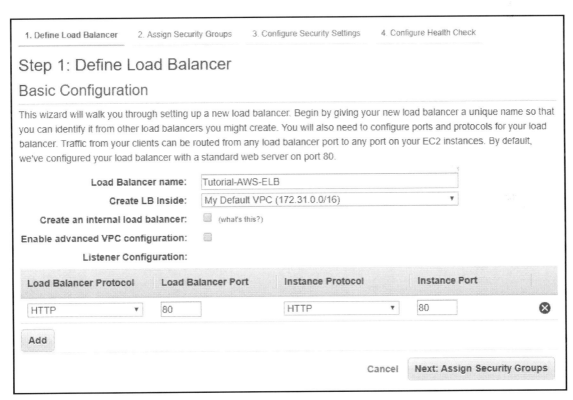

4. In the **Assign Security Groups** page, we need to configure the security group that will allow traffic to our load balancer. If you have already configured a security group that opens port 80, you can simply reuse the same security group by choosing **Select an existing security group** and then select the security group or create a new one, as shown in the following screenshot. Next, we click on **Next: Configure Security Settings**:

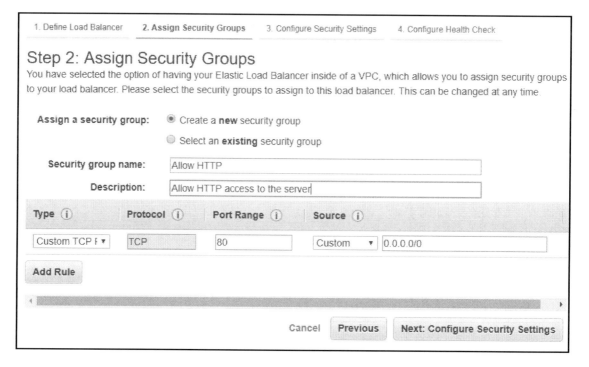

5. Since we are not creating an HTTPS listener, we will disregard the alert on the next page and choose **Next: Configure Health Checks**:

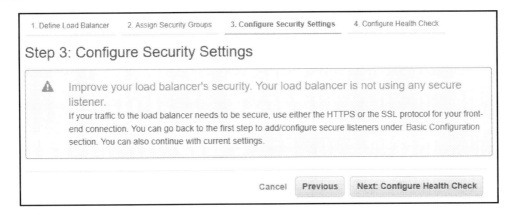

6. In the **Configure Health Check** section. A target group in a load balancer is used to group instances to which the traffic from a listener is directed. In our case, the instances are listening on port 80 and the protocol needs to be set as **HTTP**. If our application is running any other custom layer 4 connection mechanism, we can still load balance it by selecting the protocol as TCP instead. We can also select **SSL** or **HTTPS** in this section, and define health checks if we have a health check page that is on a specific path. At the end, we will choose **Next: Add EC2 Instances**:

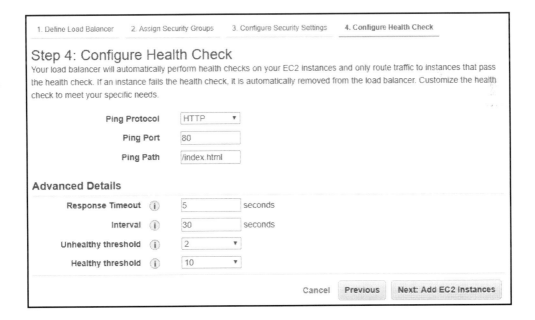

7. On the **Add EC2 instances** section, we can select the instances that will be part of our target group. You can also configure cross-zone load balancing and connection draining here. Once done, choose **Next: Add Tags**:

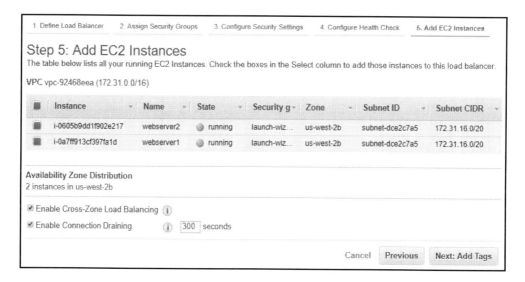

8. In the **Add Tags** section, we are able to apply key-value pairs that we can use to appropriately identify our load balancer. For instance, we can give it a key-value pair matching the instances, so they can be managed together, or we can add a key-value pair that will identify the load balancer uniquely. Once done, choose **Review and Create**:

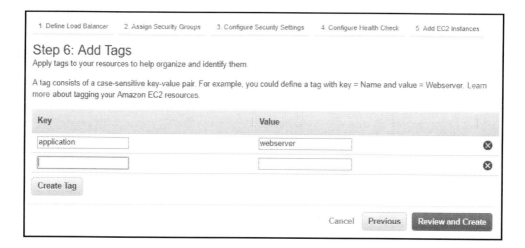

9. In the **Review** step, we will get presented with all the information that we have input in the previous steps. Once done reviewing, click on the **Create** button:

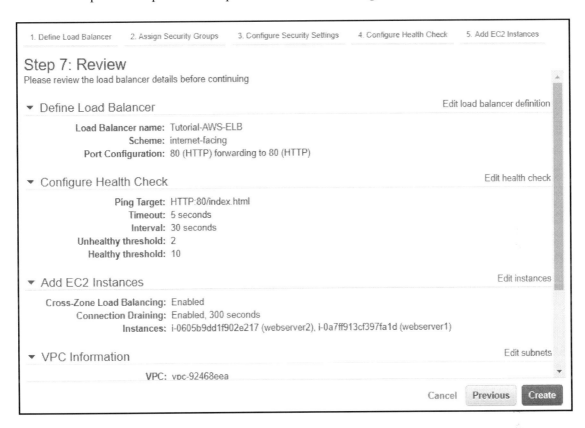

10. There will be a notification presented upon the load balancer creation; we can choose **Close** to exit from the dialog:

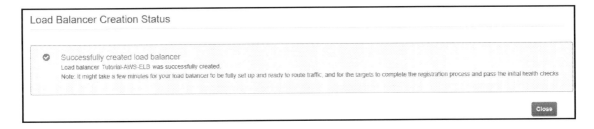

11. Now, we can browse back to the load balancing section in the EC2 Management Console and check our target group:

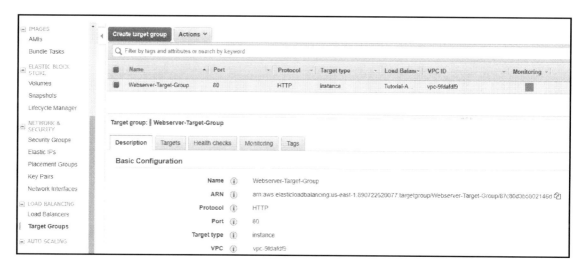

12. Before we try to access the application, we need to verify that our instances are ready. We can look at the targets and verify their status. The *initial* status means it is in the process of being registered, or it has already been added but the number of health checks is still at zero. As soon as we get a healthy response from the instance to the load balancer, the status will be changed to healthy:

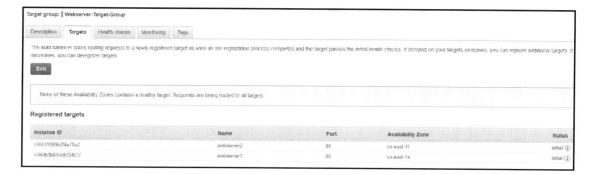

13. As soon as at least one instance is healthy, we can test our load balancer. The **Targets** tab is very useful, as it can also be used to identify an instance that has failed, or that has an unhealthy status when operating our application behind a load balancer:

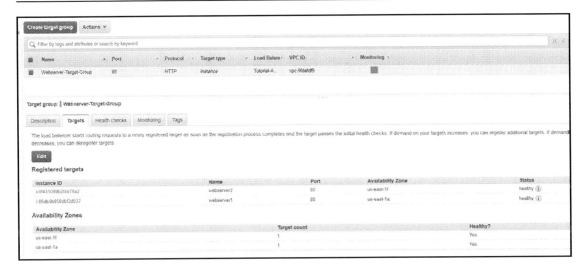

14. To test the load balancer, we need to go back to the EC2 Management Console and select the **Load Balancers** section. Choose the newly created load balancer and search for the DNS name in the **Description** tab. In our example, the DNS name is `Tutorial-AWS-ELB-1353523812.us-east-1.elb.amazonaws.com`:

Paste the DNS name into your web browser, which should display the same web page that is served by one of our servers. You should get two different responses, showing that the actual content is coming from `webserver1`:

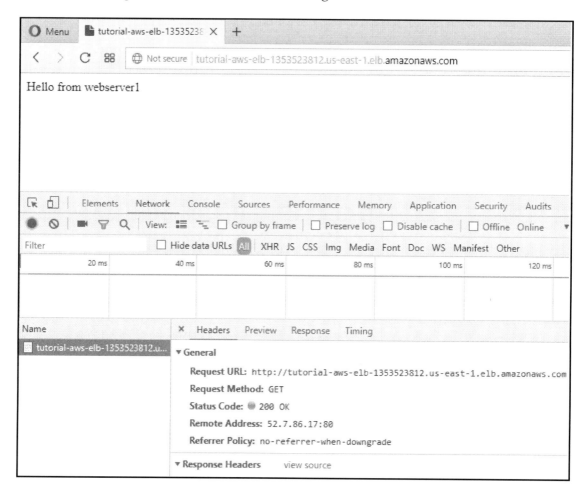

Or, you'll see this when the response is coming from `webserver2`:

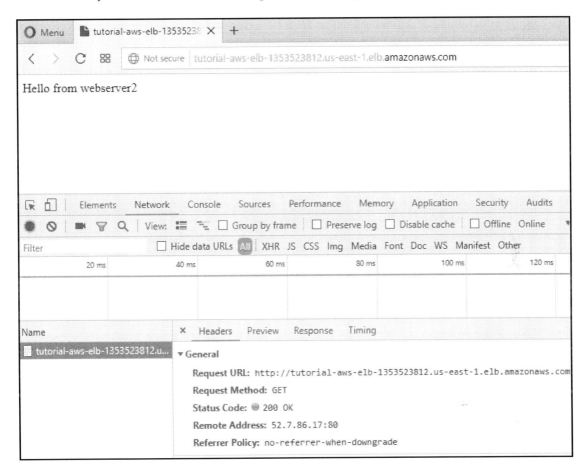

We now have a working application being served by the load balancer. As predicted, the response of the servers can identify each server and the application is highly available as it is being served by two instances from two different availability zones. In production, you would naturally serve the same content from both sites and that would enable your application to survive a failure of an availability zone, while maintaining the delivery of the application uninterrupted.

Deleting the highly available application

In every application life cycle, we sooner or later need to decommission resources. Deleting the load balancer will also stop the costs associated with the load balancer service, so if there is no requirement for a load balancer any more, you should delete it as soon as possible:

1. To delete a load balancer, select the checkbox in front of the load balancer, and then choose **Actions** | **Delete**:

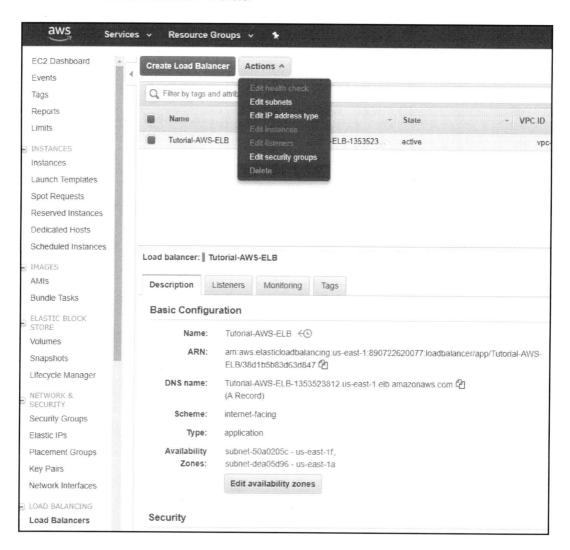

2. Deleting the load balancer does not affect the running instances and the target group, as they are still available. When decommissioning, we will also need to delete the **Target Group**. Select the checkbox next to the **Target Group**, and then choose **Actions** | **Delete**:

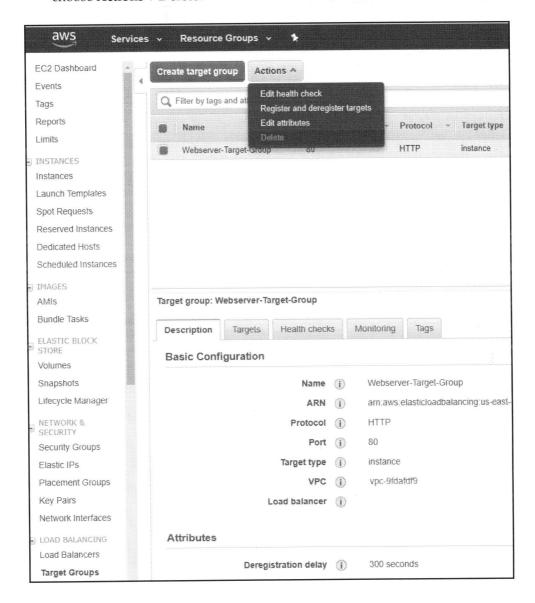

After you have deleted the load balancer and target groups, delete the instances by following the delete procedure outlined in the *Building an EC2 instance in AWS* section in `Chapter 5`, *Managing Servers on AWS with Elastic Compute Cloud*.

Summary

To make the applications running on Amazon EC2 highly available, we need to create a cluster of instances, run them in several availability zones, and provide access to the instances via a load balancer. There are three load balancer types available in AWS: the Application Load Balancer, the Network Load Balancer, and the Classic Load Balancer. Each of the load balancer types can be used for a certain type of application, and all load balancer types are deployed as managed services that are highly available. We took a look at building a load balancer and showing that the traffic was really distributed to multiple servers, and we learned how to decommission it because we pay for the existence of the load balancer and need to remove it when not needed to avoid incurring costs. In the next chapter, we will look into Amazon S3 service and how it is used to overcome the limitations of typical filesystems when storing millions or even billions of files.

Questions

1. What is the scope of operation of a load balancer service?
2. Which types of load balancers are supported in AWS?
3. We have an application that requires low latencies at scales of millions of connections. Which type of load balancer would you suggest?
4. An application requires mobile clients to be redirected to a special cluster running the mobile web design. Which type of load balancer would you suggest?
5. We need to perform cross-region load balancing. Which type of load balancer would you suggest?
6. After creating a Classic Load Balancer, what kind of group needs to be created?
7. Immediately after adding the instances to the load balancer, the website does not show on the browser. Why?

Further reading

- **Features of ELB**: https://aws.amazon.com/elasticloadbalancing/features

7
Understanding Simple Storage Service and Glacier

Storing data at scale can be a challenge for even the most advanced storage systems. Not only does it become quite difficult and expensive to store massive amounts of data, it can also become a hassle finding the right type of data storage solution for the right type of data. Imagine if there was a service that could overcome the limitations of typical filesystems when storing millions or even billions of files, that was unlimited in scale, allowed the data to be accessible via a standard protocol to anyone on the internet, and was cheap to use. There is one, the Amazon **Simple Storage Service (S3)**.

The following topics will be covered in this chapter:

- Overview of Amazon S3 and Glacier
- S3 storage classes
- S3 bucket restrictions and limitations
- S3 performance recommendations
- Amazon S3 and Glacier use cases
- Working with S3

Technical requirements

The key points of prerequisite knowledge in this chapter are understanding modern application storage requirements and basic knowledge of the inner workings of the HTTP server-client protocol. Please refer to the GitHub link for this chapter: `https://github.com/PacktPublishing/AWS-Certified-SysOps-Administrator-Associate-Guide/tree/master/Chapter07`.

Overview of Amazon S3 and Glacier

The Amazon S3 is a fully managed, highly available, autoscaled object/blob storage service that offers unlimited storage and **99.999999999% durability** of data within a 24/7/365 regimen. This means that **for every 10 million objects** stored, you can expect to **lose one object every 10,000 years**.

The S3 service is addressable via standard HTTP PUT, GET, and DELETE calls, and has the built-in ability to deliver files and content via standard web services to users. This means the service offers the ability to serve static websites directly from the S3 environment in a serverless fashion by simply hosting an index file in the storage location of the content. All S3 content is stored in buckets, which serve as logical containers for files and need to be unique across all of AWS.

Since the service hosts only static content that needs to be retrieved by the client before it can be presented (which is the standard way of operation for any HTTP service), there is no support for server-side execution on S3. However, even with this limitation, S3 gives developers the ability to use client-side execution with programming languages such as Node.js, JavaScript, and Angular, among others. Moreover, developers are also able to utilize the change notification system built into S3 to trigger functions and push data to other AWS services, due to an action over an object or bucket on S3.

While the ability to serve content might be the defining feature for some companies, others see benefit in the ability to store an unlimited amount of data and having the ability to only pay for the data while it is needed and stored. This is especially valuable for companies that run big data and machine learning workloads. S3 can allow for massive amounts of data to be ingested. Once ingested, the work can be performed by consuming the data from S3 and then delivering the results of the workload either to another S3 location or another data target. Once the process completes, the initially ingested data can easily be removed with a few simple commands.

Also notable is the ability to programmatically address storage. All commands for updating and retrieving data can be issued through a standard programmable API. This capability gives developers and enterprises the ability to come up with innovative ways to address common enterprise data workflow needs and deliver full data cycle automation.

Amazon S3 is the most widely supported object storage system available and Amazon, other vendors, and independent developers are continuously coming up with new ways to use S3. Each object in the S3 environment also has metadata that carries information about the object, the storage class it's sitting on, and also custom metadata that we can use to extend the capabilities of S3. This is one of the tools in the S3 arsenal that we can use to build innovative solutions on top of S3.

S3 storage classes

S3 can be divided into four distinct storage classes:

- **S3 Standard**: Provides the highest price per GB but lowest price per request
- **S3 Infrequent Access**: Provides a lower price per GB but has a higher price per request
- **S3 One Zone-Infrequent Access**: Provides a 20% saving over S3 IA by replicating only within one availability zone
- **S3 Reduced Redundancy Storage (RRS)**: A cheaper version of S3 providing 99.99% durability and 99.99% availability of objects
- **Glacier**: The cheapest per GB solution, intended for archiving and long-term storage

S3 Standard

The S3 Standard class is designed for general purpose object delivery. With its low latency response and highly scalable throughput capacity, it delivers the lowest price for any content that is frequently accessed. It offers the ability to encrypt data at rest with **Server Side Encryption** (**SSE**) and encryption of data in transit with SSL. The objects stored in the S3 standard class deliver 99.999999999% durability and 99.99% availability within a 24/7/365 regimen. The objects are replicated across three availability zones within one region or three facilities in two regions if the region only has 2 zones. The service is designed to self-correct disk errors, and can withstand a complete loss of data within one region.

The ability to self-correct errors is derived from having three pieces of data that can be compared. S3 maintains MD5 checksums of all objects stored on the S3 backend, which can be compared. If there is an error in one of the objects, then the MD5 checksum will be different than the other two. Now have a quorum with a majority of 2:1 that will define what the correct piece of data is and that can push a replication request for the object that is corrupted. Even though unrecoverable errors in data storage happen at a very small statistical scale - the ratio is about 10^{14} bits read successfully to reach one bit error - when you're working with billions of files stored across hundreds of thousands of disks, even a small statistical failure rate is not so insignificant at all.

S3 also supports the ability to replicate data to buckets in other regions, giving us the ability to protect the data even further, but there are of course cost implications for such replication as the data is transiting the internet and we will have to consider the cost of the traffic generated for replication.

S3 standard is our entry point when building a life cycle for our data, as it integrates seamlessly with the other storage classes in a policy that we can customize to our needs. For instance, we can keep the most recent, most frequently accessed or so-called *hot* data needed in our application in S3 for a certain time - perhaps 30 days - and after that time, we can set a life cycle policy that will move that data to S3 Infrequent Access as it becomes *cold*, meaning less frequently accessed.

S3 Infrequent Access

S3 **Infrequent Access (IA)** has the same characteristics as the S3 Standard tier, delivering high performance, low latency, and high durability, but is designed to provide a lower cost per GB of storage and a higher price per request for storage retrieval. The objects stored in S3 IA are retrievable directly, as with S3 Standard, but the storage system is designed for cold data that is unlikely to be accessed but should be deliverable with the same performance as the data in S3 Standard. This cold data storage facility allows us to take data from S3 and store it in a more efficient manner. Life cycling is also integrated into S3 IA, as we can define the data within IA to be life cycled off to Glacier once it is no longer needed to be accessible and ready for archiving, perhaps when it is 90 days old.

S3 One Zone-Infrequent Access

The S3 One Zone IA option is intended for the same purpose as the S3 IA, but is more suitable for data that does not require the same high availability as with S3 Standard and S3 IA. Since it is delivered within one zone with 99.99% durability in the AZ, the destruction of an availability zone will cause the data to be lost. Due to the data being tied to one AZ, the availability is also reduced to 99.5% for a given year. But the benefit of the One Zone IA is that it can deliver a 20% saving over using S3 IA replicated across multiple zones. This is a really good option when we have data that can be easily reproduced or is already replicated to multiple regions, and a loss of an AZ within one region will not affect the complete loss of data as it can be recreated or re-replicated.

S3 Reduced Redundancy Storage (RRS)

Similarly to the S3 One-Zone IA, the S3 RRS is designed for data that does not require the availability and durability that is delivered by S3 standard. RRS only replicates data within two availability zones, thus still making it 99.99% available and 99.99% durable, and giving it the ability to withstand the destruction of an availability zone. This still makes RRS about 400 times as reliable as a typical enterprise-grade disk. However, because it only has two replicas, it has less ability to recover from errors and thus less durability. But still, with RRS high performance, low latency, and all the other characteristics of S3 are available, while being delivered at a lower price than S3 Standard. RRS is, like One-Zone IA, intended for data that is easily reproducible from other sources.

Amazon Glacier

Amazon Glacier is the lowest cost-per-GB storage system, designed for the explicit purpose of long-term storage and archiving. The data has the same durability characteristics as S3, supports data encryption in transit, and automatically encrypts all data at rest with the 256-bit **Advanced Encryption Standard** (**AES**-256). Glacier ties in to the life cycle policies provided by S3, thus giving us the ability to archive data that is no longer needed to be accessed frequently from S3 or infrequently from S3-IA. With our previous example, the data would reside in S3 while it's less than 30 days old, then be migrated to S3-IA up until it is 90 days old, and then we can set it to be automatically sent to Glacier and stored as long as our compliance requirements need us to store that data for.

Once archived, if data needs to be accessed from Glacier there are several ways to request the data from Glacier. The standard request to Glacier will deliver the data within 3-5 hours, but if the data is needed as soon as possible, we can issue an expedited request, which can deliver the same data within 1-5 minutes. There is however limit per size of the request of 250 MB. The data retrieval rates for these two options differ as the expedited request is three times more expensive than a standard request per GB of data. We also have the ability to issue a bulk request; this is the lower cost option, usually costing 25% of a standard request per GB, and is intended for retrieving very large amounts of data. Bulk requests usually take 5-12 hours to deliver the data.

S3 bucket restrictions and limitations

Even though the S3 service provides unlimited storage space, there are certain service limits put on the service. Here are the most important limitations imposed on the S3 service:

- By default, there is a limit of 100 buckets per account, but that limit can be increased by submitting a request to AWS.
- The bucket names need to be unique across all of AWS; this is because all buckets are served via a unique global DNS name in the following format:

      http://{your-bucket-name}.s3.amazonaws.com

- Once a bucket is created, the region in which it is served cannot be changed.
- Buckets are not stackable; if you need to define a directory-like structure for your files, you can create a folder within a bucket to use object prefixes to organize the objects.
- A single `PUT` request can upload up to 5 GB of data, but multipart uploads can be used to store larger objects.
- A single object within a bucket cannot be bigger than 5 TB.

S3 performance recommendations

The S3 service is a highly scalable environment but there are some guidelines that need to be followed to achieve maximum performance from the S3 backend. Your data in S3 is distributed according to the *key* or *key name*, which is the name the object identified by in the bucket. The key name determines the partition the data is sotred on within S3. The key can be just the filename, or it can have a prefix. As objects in S3 are grouped and stored in the backend according to their keys, we can expect to achieve at least 3,500 `PUT/POST/DELETE` and 5,500 `GET` requests per second per prefix in a bucket. So, if we want to achieve more performance from S3, we need to address multiple partitions at the same time, by distributing the keys across the partitions. In this way we are able to get unlimited performance from S3.

So, let's imagine we have a service that stores images from photographers; they take the raw images and drop them into an S3 bucket. They take hundreds or thousands of photos per day and the images all have the following format: `IMG_yyyymmdd_hhmmss.jpg`. Here are a few examples:

```
Sam copies the following images:
IMG_20181110_151628.jpeg
IMG_20181110_151745.jpeg
```

```
IMG_20181110_151823.jpeg

Peter copies the following images:
IMG_20181110_180506.jpeg
IMG_20181110_180904.jpeg
IMG_20181110_190712.jpeg
```

All of these images will be stored very close by, as their keys are very similar, and all of the photographers will be sharing the 3,500 `PUT` requests that can be issued to one prefix. To give each photographer the maximum performance, you would want to distribute these image names by adding prefixes to the key. You can add a prefix that will group the keys together by creating a folder in the S3 management console and designating each photographer a separate directory, which will distribute the images across multiple keys. This also helps protect images with the same name by two photographers from being overwritten or versioned. It also increases security as we can give access to each photographer based solely on the key prefix.

So, now *Sam* would be working on the prefix `sam/` and *Peter* on `peter/`, and the uploaded images would be seen as follows:

```
sam/IMG_20181110_151628.jpeg
sam/IMG_20181110_151745.jpeg
sam/IMG_20181110_151823.jpeg
peter/IMG_20181110_180506.jpeg
peter/20181110_180904.jpeg
peter/20181110_190712.jpeg
```

By adding a prefix, we have doubled the performance of the environment. But, now we want a parallel processing environment to access the photographs from a distributed set of EC2 spot instances, and we want each instance to get maximum performance over these images. What we would want to do in this case is add a random prefix to the existing image prefix to distribute the files even further.

Let's say that once a day, we pick up the images and process them. Before processing, we can simply copy the images from the upload bucket where they are prefixed by username and move them to a processing bucket where the images are given a random prefix. After each image is copied, the original can be deleted from the upload bucket to save on space.

In this example, we will put an eight-character random prefix to the images. Once copied to the processing bucket, the image list will look like this:

```
2kf39s5f/sam/IMG_20181110_151628.jpeg
1ks9kdv8/sam/IMG_20181110_151745.jpeg
o9ues833/sam/IMG_20181110_151823.jpeg
kc8shj3d/peter/IMG_20181110_180506.jpeg
n8sk83ld/peter/20181110_180904.jpeg
u379di3r/peter/20181110_190712.jpeg
```

We have now even further distributed the images across the key prefixes, while also increasing the GET request capacity available for the processing of the images.

Whenever you are uploading large files to the S3 environment, you might see that you are not utilizing the full bandwidth of your uplink to S3. This can happen when you have hit the bandwidth limit for a single upload. To mitigate this issue, enable multipart uploads for your large files and send several parts at once. S3 will be able to handle much more traffic if you send a single file in multiple parts. Any file over 100MB should be considered as a good candidate for a multipart upload. You can have up to 10,000 parts in a multipart file, meaning you can easily distribute the traffic to S3 with up to 10,000 concurrent PUT requests. The PUT limits per key prefix per second do apply when using multipart uploads, so make sure you distribute the file wisely.

Amazon S3 and Glacier use cases

Due to the versatility of the S3 storage solution, it has many different potential use cases. We will try to capture a snapshot of possible use cases by outlining some of the common uses that S3 is perfect for. In this section, we will be looking at the following use cases:

- Serverless hosting
- Web-scale content delivery
- Data lakes for big data and machine learning
- Extending the capabilities of enterprise applications
- Backup and disaster recovery
- Archiving

Serverless hosting

S3 can be used as a frontend to our serverless environment. As we mentioned at the beginning of this chapter, and as we will demonstrate in our example later on, we can host a static website straight from S3 by providing an index document and uploading all our static website files. These files can also contain client-side scripts to extend their capabilities, and we can also give our end users the ability to upload data to S3. Any upload to an S3 bucket can be easily made to trigger a function that will process any information held in the uploaded file. The uploaded file can, for instance, deliver responses from a web form or it could be an image, video, or other file being uploaded that needs to be processed. Whatever the content, S3 is our starting point in building a web-scale serverless environment. The serverless function (or multiple functions) hosted on Lambda (which we will cover in a later chapter) can then take the place of our server-side processing features and perform any processing that would usually be processed within a web server: they can reply to the user, record data in databases, or perform powerful transformations on data and interact with other AWS services in the backend.

Web-scale content delivery

The highly scalable and highly available capabilities of S3 can be used to deliver content to millions or even billions of users from all around the world, without you having to worry about scaling your data delivery capacity and the bottlenecks common in traditional content delivery systems. Think of a traditional web server and the limitations it presents when we have a service that serves a lot of files. For example, let's say we are serving a marketplace where users upload images of items that they are selling to our system. Even with with a few thousand users selling a few items and each item having 5-10 images, this means the server will be storing tens of thousands of images in the backend. Any modern operating system can handle this scale.

Soon, our application becomes popular and suddenly our user base grows to all over the world, and we suddenly have hundreds of thousands or even millions of users. Our file base will now grow to tens or possibly hundreds of millions of files. Here is where the traditional operating system breaks down. We would require a very high performance backend to even enumerate the files in the file allocation table, let alone to be able to deliver this number of files with low latency to the end users. Also, this amount of files can mean that we will be storing tens or hundreds of TB of static data within a block device that is usually expensive to run.

Scaling this system and distributing it across multiple regions to reach its audience with the lowest latency would also mean having to replicate this huge amount of data across multiple servers, and that would be very inefficient.

We can simply redesign our application to allow end users to upload the images to an S3 bucket that can be used as a delivery mechanism, and our servers serving the website can be kept small, highly efficient, and easy to replicate across the world. We can even utilize the CloudFront environment (discussed in the next chapter) to cache frequently delivered S3 images and allow for lower latency and better performance for the end users.

Data lakes for big data and machine learning

Storing data at scale is made easy in S3 with its unlimited capacity. It can serve any big data and machine learning workloads with the ability to store data on a temporary or permanent basis.

For example, an insurance company needs to give its agents the ability to estimate the risk involved with a certain insurance contract, based upon the historical data of similar contracts. All the data can be easily pooled into an S3 bucket and the agent can call up visualization tools, like for instance Amazon QuickSight, select the data residing in S3, and deliver powerful ways of visualizing and getting a better understanding of the risk of a certain contract they are dealing with. This can help the insurance company be more responsive and more competitive in the way they provide their services to clients, and can be architected as a very low cost solution compared to traditional enterprise-grade onsite storage systems.

Another example is running training for a machine learning system. Let's say we are designing a neural network that needs to identify an image of a person or an object. That would be its only task, but the images it needs to recognize can be color photographs, black and white sketches, and even stylized images such as artwork. We would need to feed a lot of training data for the **machine learning** (**ML**) system to be able to start recognizing, so we can feed that training data to an S3 bucket, use it to train the ML system, and then we can easily delete that data as it is no longer needed with a simple CLI or API command, or a few clicks in the management console, so we can stop paying for the space consumed.

Extending the capabilities of enterprise applications

In the era of digitalization, enterprise applications have been known to struggle to serve content from traditional file-based storage backends that run on local disk filesystems. With the number of files increasing exponentially, it can become cumbersome and difficult to manage the sheer volume of content on a local disk system within a server.

Let's come back to our insurance company example. Now, before they can create a data lake of the historical contracts and risks involved, they need to capture that data somehow. As they want to capture as much historical data as possible, the company decides to scan and run **optical character recognition** (**OCR**) on all of their paper archives and unify that data into a new application. But the company's almost 100 years of records are going to consume massive amounts of data, as the images need to be scanned in at a high quality for the OCR process, and for the later archiving and replacement of the paper archive with a digital one.

The company already has an enterprise application that they have been using for a few years, where all contracts are now digital, indexed, and searchable. Now, they wish to add the OCR data and corresponding images to the new enterprise application. Adding the OCR data to their application proves to be simple, while adding hundreds of millions of files to the existing filesystem is determined to be too much for the on-premises application backend.

The images can be instead copied into S3 and the application can be extended by providing a link to the S3 image of the file when this file is required for review. This offloads the on-premises application from having to serve static content from an expensive enterprise-grade backend that was designed to run dynamic workflows such as the database that stores the index and content of the contracts.

Backup and disaster recovery

One of the common scenarios for using S3 is to utilize its cheap storage as a great way to perform backup and disaster recovery. For backups, S3 is perfect as it can hold snapshots and images for our EC2 instances, and also backups made by other providers for our on-site workloads and servers. There are plenty of open source scripts and commercial tools that allow us to use S3 as a backup and disaster recovery backend, and also utilize the built-in life cycle policies to push older data into long-term storage.

One of the typical simple backup scenarios for on-premises workloads is to create a process onsite that can deliver copies of data that can be restored to a newly deployed operating system. Let's take an example of a Linux server running an application with a MySQL backend. In this scenario, we need to ensure we have the following features backed up and delivered to the S3 storage:

- The application installer and configuration
- Any application-specific files
- A copy of the MySQL database and logs

Let's assume that the only dynamic content for this application is within the MySQL database. We need to then copy the data from which the database can be restored on a certain period to S3; let's say our **Recovery Point Objective (RPO)** is 24 hours and our **Recovery Time Objective (RTO)** is 4 hours. We need to copy the database in a timely manner that will help us achieve the RPO, perhaps every 12 hours so we have two backups to restore from, or even every 6 hours which would be a good option. Let's assume we will deliver incremental backups to S3 so we don't consume too much bandwidth daily, with a full backup every weekend. Also, every time upgrade the application, its configuration, or any application-specific files, we need to refresh these within the S3 backup.

To meet the RTO, we need to be able to deploy within 4 hours, meaning we have enough time to spin up a new server instance from EC2 (a few minutes), install the application, and restore its configuration (perhaps 30 minutes), and then copy the database from S3 to our instance. There is a lot of bandwidth between S3 and EC2; if the database is huge, we can attach and Elastic Network Adaptor to our EC2 instance and deliver 25 GBps of throughput from S3 to EC2, thus being able to restore up to 10 TB per hour.

Archiving

Any data from any of these examples stored in S3 can easily also be archived by implementing a life cycle policy and moving the data from S3 storage into Glacier. Being the cheapest solution and delivering secure data storage, Glacier is ideal for any archiving solution that needs to be compliant with the strictest of standards. We are also able to address the Glacier service as a **Virtual Tape Library (VTL)** through an AWS Storage Gateway, which can help us migrate any existing tape-based backup and archiving solutions to the cloud. This way, Glacier can become an inexpensive replacement to complicated, expensive tape storage systems, on top of which it delivers even higher durability of 99.999999999%, which no tape archiving system is able to deliver as tape fully degrades to a non-readable condition within 10-30 years, depending on the type of tape storage and the conditions of the storage environment.

Working with S3

In this example, we will show you several features of S3 and Glacier. We will perform the following tasks:

1. Create and S3 bucket
2. Host a static website within the bucket
3. Enable versioning and version the content

4. Enable life cycling for Glacier
5. Delete the bucket and it's content

Creating a bucket

1. To create an S3 bucket, we simply search for the S3 service in the management console and then click the **Create bucket** button in the Amazon S3 Dashboard:

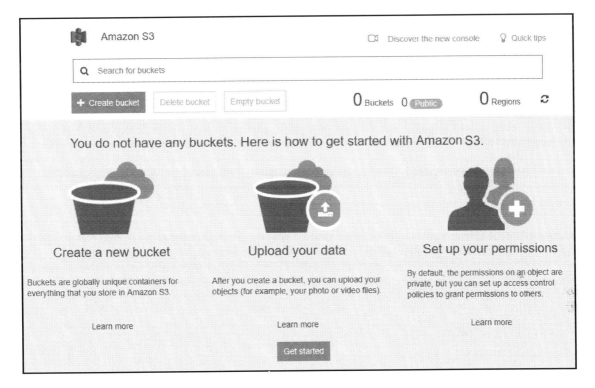

2. In the **Create bucket** dialog, we need to give the bucket a name. The name needs to be unique across all of AWS, as all of the buckets are automatically available via a unique DNS address in the following format:

```
http://{your-bucket-name}.s3.amazonaws.com
```

Usually, companies tend to find a good bucket naming schema, perhaps reversing the name of your domain like com-example-my-bucket-name or similar. The buckets also cannot contain any uppercase characters and must begin with a letter or number. Unique names between 3 and 63 characters are supported.

3. In our example, we will create a bucket with a random number, dash, and the name `mynewbucket`, specifically `685684-mynewbucket`. This bucket will be accessible via the following DNS name:

   `http://685684-mynewbucket.s3.amazonaws.com`

4. We also need to select a region where we want to store the bucket. In our example, we are using `use-west-2`, the Oregon region:

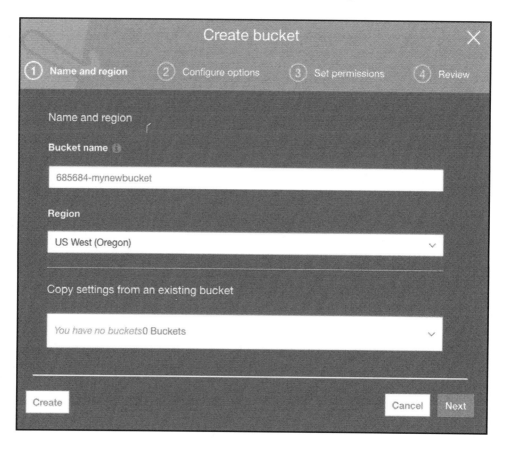

5. In the next step, we have the ability to configure versioning, which will enable us to maintain different versions of the same file name in the bucket. Think of this as a way to prevent content from accidentally being modified or deleted. Be careful to make sure to enable expiry of versioned objects as the full amount of space consumed by each version counts against your S3 usage. This is especially important when delivering temporary files and logs to S3.

6. In this step, we can also set up a log group and add tags to the bucket that help us identify the resource and maintain the inventory:

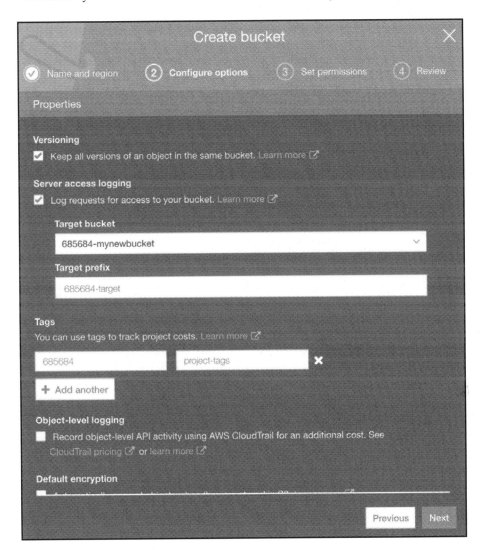

7. Scrolling down, in *Step 7* we can set the object-level logging, which allows us to use CloudTrail to determine and log each and every operation against each object. We can also deliver object-action metrics to CloudWatch. Both of these features carry extra costs. Objects can also be encrypted on the server side automatically at no additional cost. This should be enabled when compliance, governance, and other requirements need us to do so:

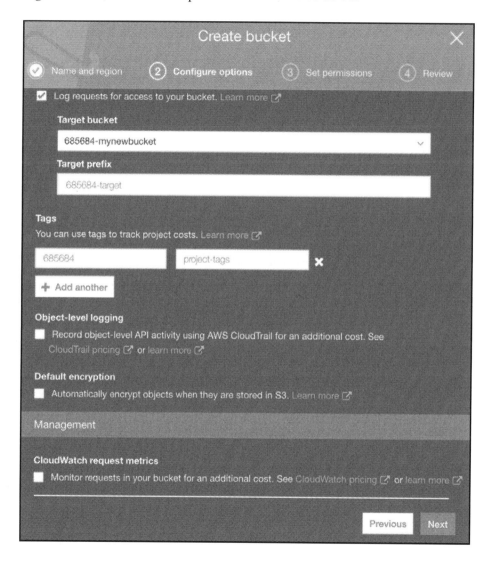

8. In the next step, we can publicly access system permissions. For our purposes, we will be making the bucket publicly accessible so we need to un-check the setting to disable blocking new public policies. We can also uncheck the blocking of public ACLs if we want to control the public access through ACLs. The bucket needs to be public so we can deliver the static web page from this bucket in the next part of this exercise:

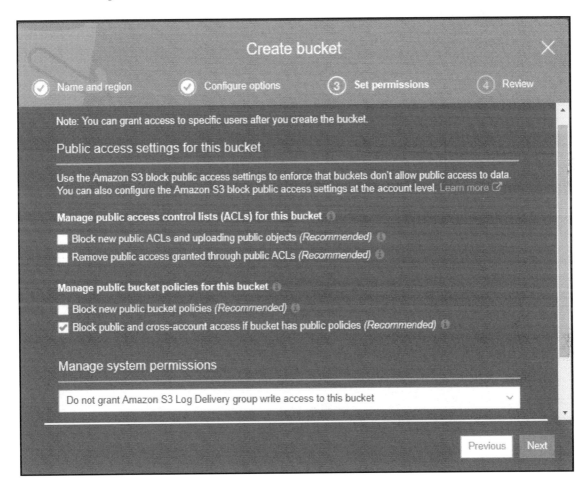

9. In the **Review** tab, we get a summary of all the features created, and we finish the task by clicking **Create bucket**:

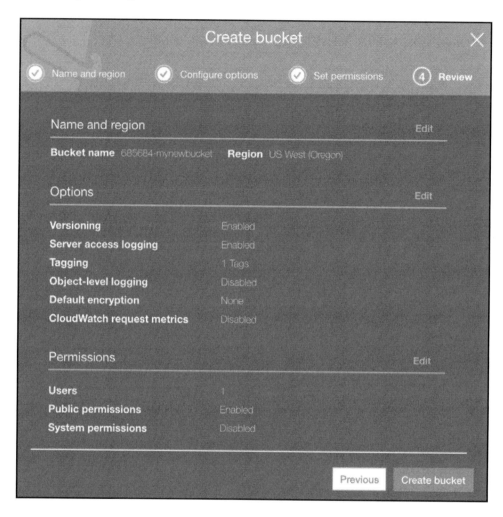

10. Once the bucket is created we will apply the following policy to make it public. Please replace the `685684-mynewbucket` with your bucket name:

```
{
"Version": "2012-10-17",
"Statement": [
{
"Sid": "PublicReadGetObject",
"Effect": "Allow",
```

```
"Principal": "*",
"Action": "s3:GetObject",
"Resource": "arn:aws:s3:::685684-mynewbucket/*"
        }
    ]
}
```

11. Click on the bucket, select **Permissions** and then Bucket policy. Paste the previous code into the bucket policy and then click **Save**. Your bucket will be made public this way:

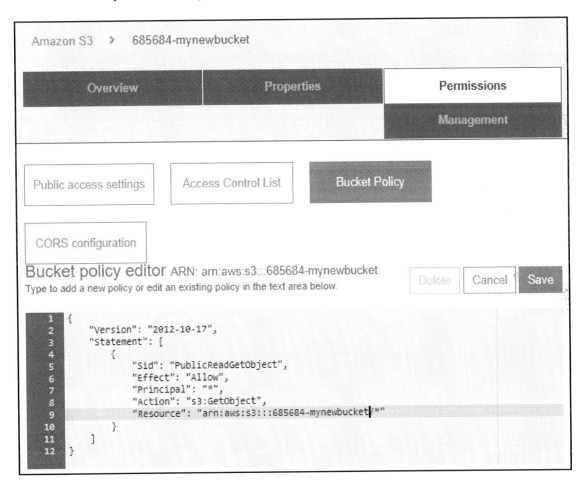

12. Once the bucket is created, we can see it in the list of our buckets within the S3 management console:

Setting up a static website

In this section, we will create a static website that is going to be hosted within our newly created bucket:

1. We need to first create a small `index` file, which will deliver some content we can view in our environment. For example, you can create a file named `index.html` and paste the following code that we are using in our example:

```html
<html>
<p>Everyone loves AWS!</p>
<p><a href="https://markocloud.com"><img
src="https://markocloud.com/wp-content/uploads/2016/02/markocloud-1
80.gif" alt="" width="180" height="155" /></a></p>
 </html>
```

2. We now need to save this file and upload it to the S3 bucket. Click on the bucket name on the previous screen and then select the **Upload** button:

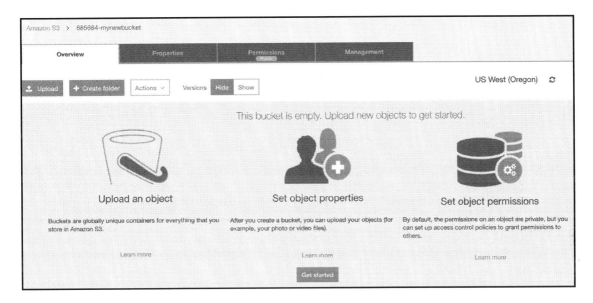

3. Add the `index.html` file to the **Upload** dialogue and skip through the permissions in *Step 3*, as we will maintain the same permissions as the bucket:

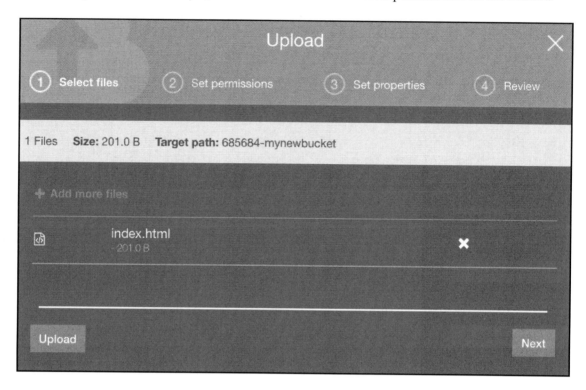

The `index.html` file should now be seen in the newly created bucket:

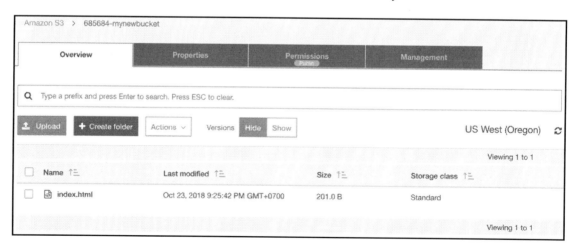

4. By clicking the file, we can see the properties of the uploaded file and the link at the bottom of the page. From this dialog, we can also modify the properties and permissions of the file:

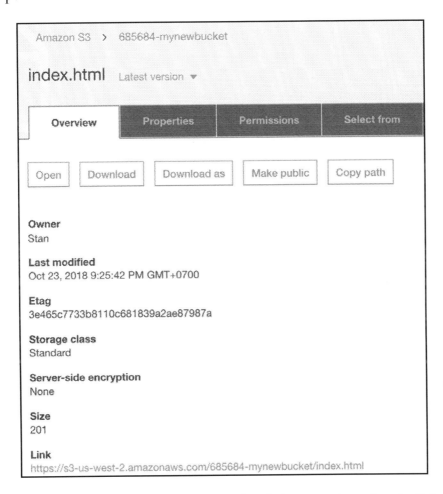

5. You can click on the link provided in this dialogue and see that the link opens the `index.html` file directly. Since this file is an `index` file, you can also browse the bucket DNS name and get the same result:

```
http://685684-mynewbucket.s3.amazonaws.com
```

Let's look at the following screenshot for the output:

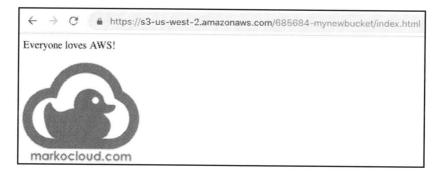

Versioning bucket content

We enabled versioning when we created the bucket. Now, let's say we want to upload a new image to the bucket and replace the image path in the index.html with this new image:

> 1. Select any image you like and upload it to the bucket:

2. Once you have uploaded the image, copy the image link from the properties of the newly uploaded file:

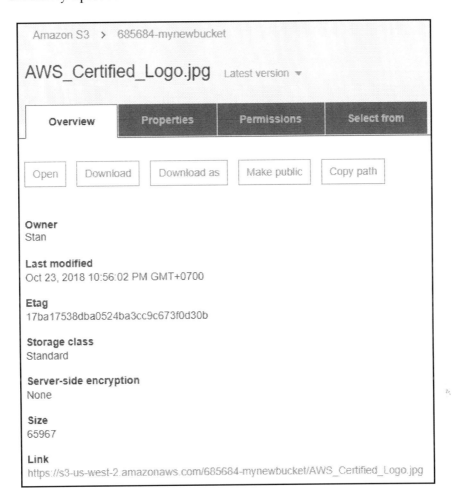

3. Now, open the `index.html` file and edit the code to replace `https://yourimagelinkgoeshere` with your image link:

```
<html>
<p>Everyone loves AWS!</p>
<p><a href="https://markocloud.com"><img
src="https://yourimagelinkgoeshere" alt="" width="180" height="155"
/></a></p>
 </html>
```

4. Now, save and upload `index.html` to the S3 bucket. You will now see that there are two versions of the `index.html` file in the bucket:

5. When you browse to the address, you should see the latest `index.html` with your new image served from the S3 service. As you can see, this is a good and easy way to maintain your content versions and easily restore any previous version with little management overhead:

Life cycling data to Glacier

Now that we have created some content in the bucket, we can also enable old content to be archived to Glacier automatically by enabling a life cycle policy on the bucket. To do so, we need to click on the bucket, select the **Management** tab, and click on **Add lifecycle rule**:

1. In *Step 1*, we need to create a rule name:

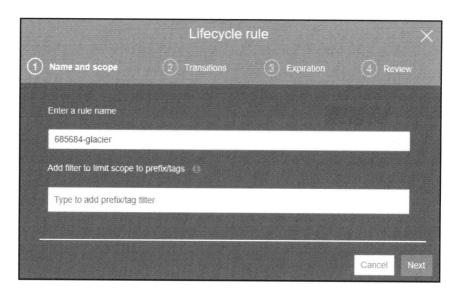

2. In *Step 2*, we configure the transitions. We can select either current or previous versions to be transitioned to Glacier or S3 Infrequent Access, and we can select the number of days after creation for the transition to be triggered. Here, we can create complex policies that match the guidelines set out in our compliance and governance policies:

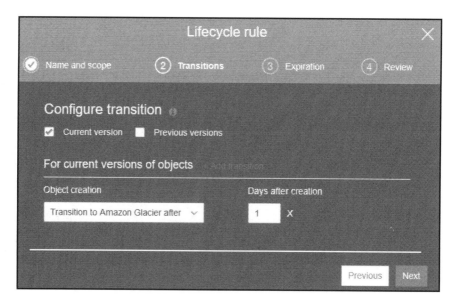

3. In the **Expiration** step, we can also configure when the objects expire. Object expiration automatically triggers the deletion of the objects within the life cycle rule. This helps automatically clean up data that is not required to be kept for compliance:

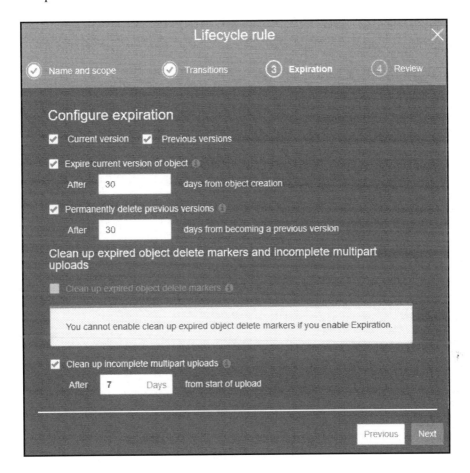

4. In the **Review** step, we can simply click **Save**. This will enable our life cycle rule on the bucket:

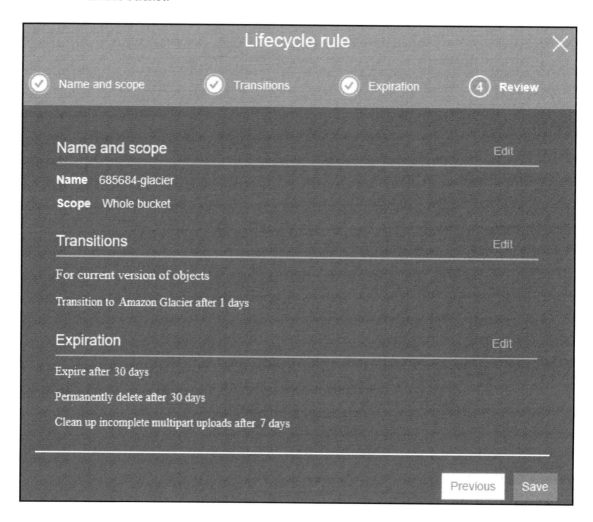

5. We can view the life cycle rules in the **Management** tab of the bucket properties:

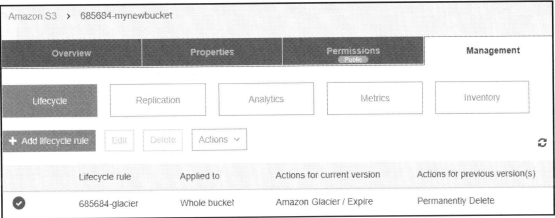

Deleting S3 buckets

Once buckets aren't required anymore, they can simply be deleted. Bucket deletion will permanently delete all the objects stored in the bucket, so make sure you consider what you are doing before proceeding:

1. To delete the bucket, simply select the bucket in the browser and select **Delete bucket**:

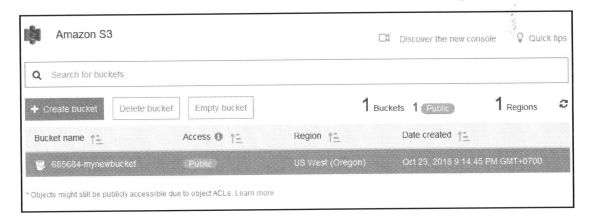

2. The **Delete bucket** dialog will make you write the bucket name to confirm bucket deletion and prevent any accidental delete actions, as this process is irrecoverable. Once you have typed in the name, you can click on **Delete bucket** and click on **Confirm**:

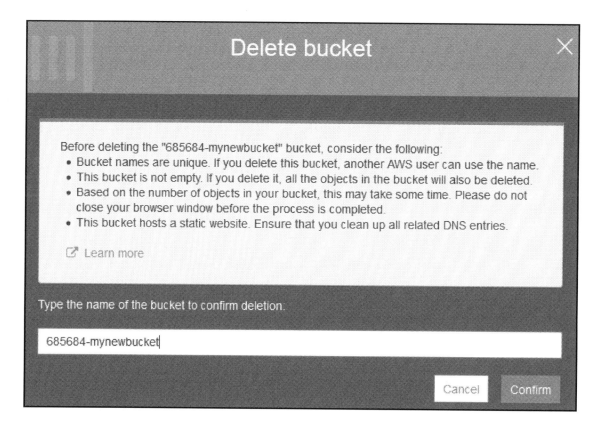

Before deleting the "685684-mynewbucket" bucket, consider the following:

- Bucket names are unique. If you delete this bucket, another AWS user can use the name.
- This bucket is not empty. If you delete it, all the objects in the bucket will also be deleted.
- Based on the number of objects in your bucket, this may take some time. Please do not close your browser window before the process is completed.
- This bucket hosts a static website. Ensure that you clean up all related DNS entries.

Learn more

Type the name of the bucket to confirm deletion:

685684-mynewbucket

Cancel   Confirm

3. Your S3 console should now have no buckets listed:

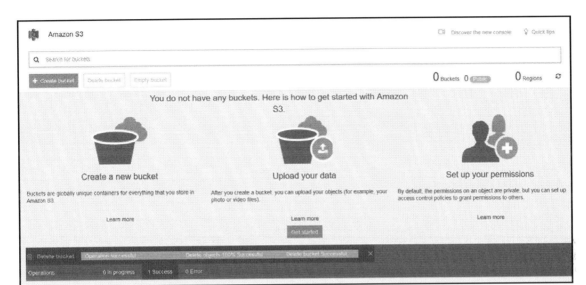

Summary

In this chapter, we learned about the S3 and Glacier environments, and the way data can be stored and served without requiring any servers to support the process. We discovered different versions of S3 that can deliver different availability (99.5% or 99.99%) and durability (99.99% or 99.999999999%) for our files. We also looked at different use cases for S3 and learned how to use S3 to serve a static website, implement versioning, implement a life cycle policy that can automatically archive data to Glacier, and delete an S3 bucket. In the next chapter, we will look into understanding content distribution with CloudFront.

Questions

1. What kind of data is S3 well suited for?
2. What kind of data is Glacier designed for?
3. What is the data durability of S3, Glacier, and S3-IA?
4. What is the maximum expected number of GET requests from an S3 key prefix?
5. Are there any cheaper options aside from S3 and S3 IA?

6. What do we need to upload to a bucket to serve a static website?
7. When we enable versioning on an S3 bucket, how many versions will be maintained?
8. In which example would it be useful to temporarily use S3 for huge amounts of data?

Further reading

- **S3 documentation**: https://docs.aws.amazon.com/s3/index.html
- **Glacier documentation**: https://docs.aws.amazon.com/glacier/index.html#lang/en_us
- **S3 object keys and metadata**: https://docs.aws.amazon.com/AmazonS3/latest/dev/UsingMetadata.html#object-keys
- **Object lifecycle management**: https://docs.aws.amazon.com/AmazonS3/latest/dev/object-lifecycle-mgmt.html
- **Virtual Hosting in S3**: https://docs.aws.amazon.com/AmazonS3/latest/dev/VirtualHosting.html
- **S3 Object Versions**: https://docs.aws.amazon.com/AmazonS3/latest/user-guide/view-object-versions.html
- **S3 FAQs**: https://aws.amazon.com/s3/faqs/
- **Glacier FAQs**: https://aws.amazon.com/glacier/faqs/
- **AWS Cloud VTL**: https://aws.amazon.com/storagegateway/vtl/
- **Network Bandwith for EC2 to S3**: https://aws.amazon.com/blogs/aws/the-floodgates-are-open-increased-network-bandwidth-for-ec2-instances/
- **S3 Storage Classes**: https://aws.amazon.com/s3/storage-classes/
- **S3 RRS**: https://aws.amazon.com/s3/reduced-redundancy/

8
Understanding Content Distribution with CloudFront

As we have seen so far, the majority of services that can be used to deliver web content in AWS are regionally bound. Since we have regions available in multiple geographies, we are always able to replicate our environment so that the content is delivered from the regions that are close to our users. But this approach might not be the most cost-effective, as replication between regions can be expensive. On top of that, users in geographies where no regions are situated close by will still see high latencies and slow delivery of content. We can improve this situation dramatically by delivering our content through the CloudFront content delivery network.

We will cover the following topics in this chapter:

- Overview of CloudFront
- Edge Locations
- Content delivery methods
- Cache behavior
- Working with CloudFront

Technical requirements

Basic knowledge of common web protocols, caching, and content delivery are required to benefit from reading this chapter.

Overview of CloudFront

CloudFront is a highly scalable, low-latency content delivery network that can help us efficiently deliver content such as static and dynamic website data, videos, images, and any application components that are allowed to be cached. CloudFront can dramatically lower the latency and cut down the delivery time for content from AWS data centers to the end users. CloudFront operates out of (at the time of writing) 150 Edge Locations worldwide, so any content delivered into CloudFront can be distributed to a global audience at the lowest latency possible.

Features of CloudFront

CloudFront has the ability to cache various types of data that can be presented via HTTP or HTTPS. To configure a CloudFront distribution, we need to specify an origin and its features. An origin can be an S3 bucket or an arbitrary DNS-resolvable HTTP/HTTPS server that can be hosted within AWS or anywhere on the internet. The **content delivery network (CDN)** is designed to deliver the distributions with the lowest possible latency. We also have some ability to control how the cache is retained and expired within CloudFront, allowing us to get the best out of the CDN.

CloudFront is fully addressable via its API and excels at programmability and the features that are offered as a service to extend its capability. We can control the behavior of the caching environment, define how to forward requests to the origin, choose what kind of compression to use, modify responses coming directly out of CloudFront, and detect the client type within the cache. CloudFront also has the ability to integrate with Lambda@Edge so developers can introduce cone execution patterns as close to the end users as possible. This can improve the performance and user experience in applications on various types of devices and operating systems.

Any data transfer between the AWS services and CloudFront is free, meaning we can cut down costs for delivering content from S3 as we are not subject to outgoing transfer pricing when using CloudFront. This also means CloudFront can be a cost-effective way to deliver content to our users, as we have the ability to implement it on an arbitrary basis and pay only while using it. Amazon also offers the ability to set up a committed private contract for CloudFront so that clients can take advantage of the service at a reduced price when they know their traffic patterns and are looking for a long-term solution.

Security

CloudFront is designed to be inherently resilient to DDoS attacks and can serve as an additional barrier of defense from attacks on the infrastructure that serves your web content. CloudFront also has a built-in capability that lets you simplify the process of encrypting your data in transit with SSL/TLS. Along with **AWS Certificate Manager (ACM)**, CloudFront gives us the capability of creating a free SSL certificate for our domain and attaching it to the CloudFront distribution. This free certificate can also be automatically renewed and re-applied, so we never have to worry about our SSL certificates expiring again.

CloudFront also offers the ability to restrict content to our data. There are several ways that access can be controlled with CloudFront:

- Restrict access to your application content with signed URLs or cookies
- Restrict access to content based on geolocation
- Restrict access to S3 buckets using **Origin Access Identity (OAI)**

Edge Locations

Edge Locations are located in data centers separate from the region and availability zone locations. Their location is designed to be closer to the users so they are situated nearer to large urban locations that might not be close to any physical location of an AWS region. In some geographies, such as South Africa at the time of writing, the Edge Locations are positioned where no region exists so that the experience delivered to the end users can be close to what it would be if a region was located there. Services running in Edge Locations at the time of writing are as follows:

- CloudFront
- Route 53 (discussed in Chapter 11, *Working with Relational Database Services*)
- Lambda@Edge (discussed in Chapter 17, *Overview of AWS Lambda*)

Regional Edge Cache

In 2016, AWS also introduced Regional Edge Caches. These sit between regions and the Edge Locations and have the ability to cache even more information than the Edge Locations themselves. For example, when a user is connecting to a CloudFront service sitting in an Edge Location and the requested data has expired in the cache, the content can be looked up in the Regional Edge Cache and delivered much more quickly than if it was requested from the origin server. This means that the request will only be served from the origin in case the data is not present in either the Edge Location or the Regional Edge Cache. This functionality is automatically enabled for all the services that run in the Edge Locations listed previously.

Content delivery methods

As well as serving your static content, CloudFront supports the delivery of dynamic content to the users by giving us the ability to configure the session HTTP/HTTPS termination at the CloudFront location. This feature allows us to secure and accelerate any application running either WebSockets or API calls. CloudFront can proxy the following HTTP methods to the origin servers or to the API Gateway:

- GET: A read operation against a HTTP server. Used for caching static content. GET retrieves a document.
- HEAD: Like GET it also reads, but HEAD retrieves just the header of the document without retrieving the body.
- POST: A write operation against a HTTP server that is commonly used to send textual information. CloudFront can proxy the POST request and deliver the content to the target more quickly through the AWS backbone.
- PUT: Like POST it also writes, but encloses a file or data blob that is to be stored on the server.
- OPTIONS: A general request to the server inquiring about the communication options available.

- DELETE: A write request to delete a certain resource on the HTTP server.
- PATCH: A write request designed as an extension to PUT that enables the requestor to modify an existing file or data blob on an HTTP server. Instead of re-uploading the whole file with PUT, we can use PATCH to upload only a certain section of bytes within the file itself.

Cache behavior

In CloudFront, we have the ability to control the behavior of the distribution we create in several different ways. We can decide what kinds of HTTP request methods we allow to be forwarded to our distribution. We can select three types of requests to be forwarded:

- **GET and HEAD**: Used for static content caching, such as media and static websites.
- **GET, HEAD, and OPTIONS**: Used for static content on servers that have several communication options enabled.
- **GET, HEAD, OPTIONS, PUT, PATCH, POST, and DELETE**: Used for caching and terminating dynamic HTTP sessions at the CloudFront Edge Location. This allows us to speed up the write requests to our backend API or WebSockets environment.

We can also control the **time-to-live** (TTL) of our cache by controlling the CloudFront distribution options. This allows us to automatically expire content and give the environment the ability to regularly refresh the content being served from the cache. We should set the TTL values appropriately, according to the way our content is life cycled. CloudFront distributions support the following options for setting TTL:

- **Min TTL**: Required when forwarding all headers. The value determines the minimum time our objects will be served from CloudFront caches. After the Min TTL expires, CloudFront will connect to the origin and check if the object has been updated. Min TTL will override any shorter TTLs defined for objects in the origin server.
- **Default TTL**: An optional value that can define the cache TTL if no specific TTL is defined in the origin. Must be longer than Min TTL if defined.

- **Max TTL**: Also optional and will define the longest possible period that objects can stay in the cache. This value, contrary to **Default TTL**, is only used with requests where the origin is specifying the cache data in the headers and is designed to override any cache control entries from the origin that are set too long.

Other cache control features allow control of the following:

- Traffic compression and encryption with the Compress and **FieldLevelEncryptionId** options
- Lambda function execution with the **LambdaFunctionAssociations** option
- Handling of strings, cookies, and patterns with the **ForwardedValues**, **PathPattern**, and **TargetOriginId** options
- Private and streaming content with the **TrustedSigners** and **SmoothStreaming** options
- How we treat HTTP and HTTPS requests with the **ViewerProtocolPolicy** option

Working with CloudFront

In this part, we will build on our previous exercise where we created a static website hosted on S3. If you are following along with this example, you are free to select any other custom origin as the source of the distribution to try the features out on your live data.

Creating a CloudFront distribution

We start by opening our AWS management console and navigating to the CloudFront section. Once there, we click on the **Create Distribution** button to begin the process:

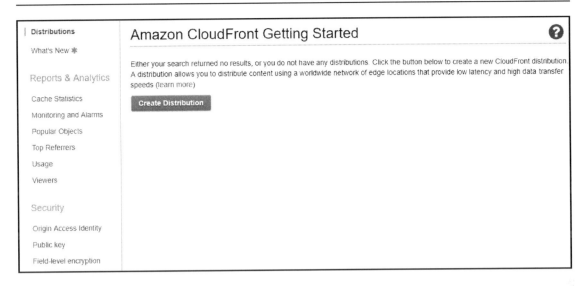

1. In *Step 1*, we will be able to select either a **Web** or **RTMP** distribution. In our example of caching the static website, we will select the **Web** distribution, but an **RTMP** one can be selected when delivering content using the Adobe Flash Media RTMP protocol. Click on the **Get Started** button below the **Web** distribution:

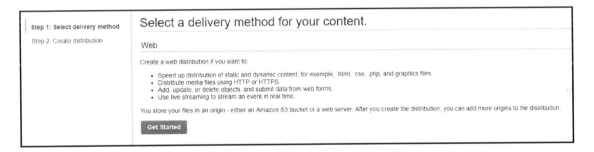

2. In *Step 2*, we will configure our Origin. For domain name, we need to specify our S3 bucket that is serving the static website. Instructions on how to set up the S3 static website can be found in Chapter 7, *Understanding Simple Storage Service and Glacier*, under the *Working with S3* section.

3. In the **Default Cache Behavior** section, we will select the **Viewer Protocol Policy** as **HTTP and HTTPS** and **Allowed HTTP Methods** as **GET, HEAD**. If you would like to read up on the HTTP methods themselves, please read the HTTP method definitions in the *Further reading* section of this chapter. We will not be modifying the headers, so under **Object Caching** we need to leave **Use Origin Cache Headers** selected:

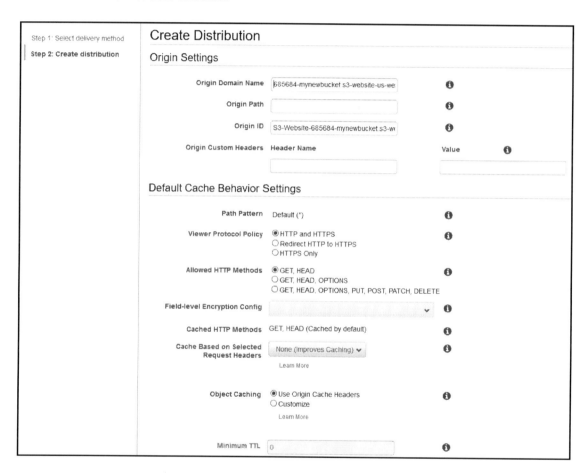

4. Once the distribution is created, you can see it in the CloudFront management console. The status will initially be **In-Progress** and should turn to **Enabled** as soon as all the distribution propagates across the CDN. Please record the Domain name as this will be the DNS name that we will be using to test the performance of the newly created distribution:

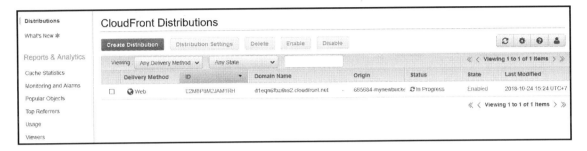

5. To test whether the performance of the static website has actually improved now that we have enabled the CloudFront distribution, we can browse to the CDN Performance Checker Tool
   at `https://www.cdnplanet.com/tools/cdnperfcheck/`.

6. We will initially enter our origin DNS name directly to get a baseline to which we can compare our CDN:

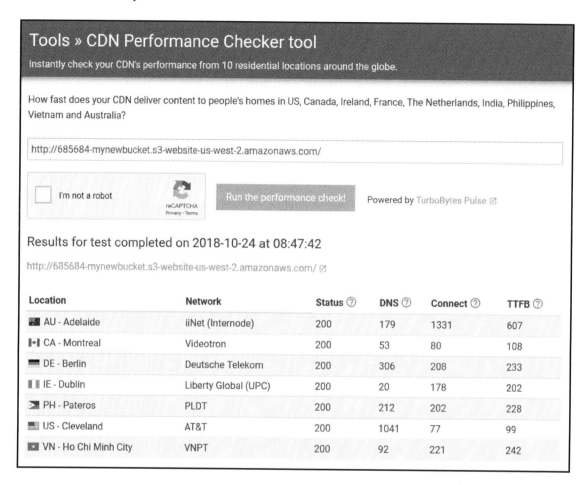

7. Once we have the metrics from our origin, let's enter the CloudFront distribution DNS name and test the performance of the website using the CDN. Make sure you run the performance checker at least twice as the CDN might not be populated on the first try and the content will be delivered from the origin instead. We should see the correct result on the second or subsequent tries:

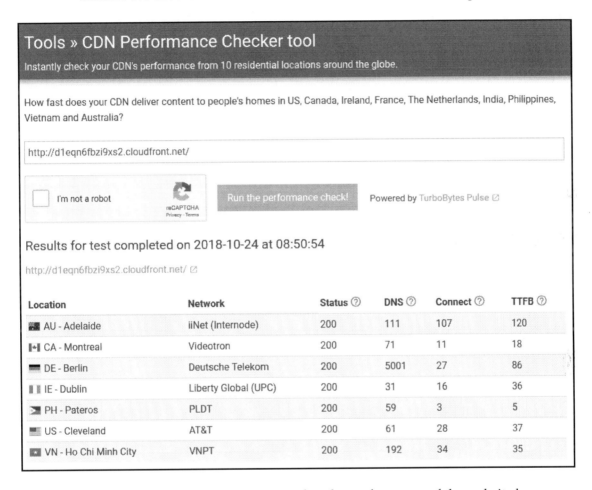

8. Comparing the metrics, we can see that the performance of the website has improved dramatically.

Deleting a CloudFront distribution

When the time comes to decommission the application, or the CDN is no longer required, we can simply delete the CloudFront distribution:

1. Before deleting, any enabled distribution needs to be disabled. Select the distribution you wish to delete and then click the **Disable** button:

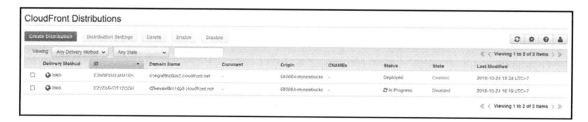

2. A confirmation window will pop up to disable the distribution, so please click on **Yes, Disable**:

3. Once you have initiated the disable process, please wait until the status changes to **Deployed**, which can take some time depending on the amount of content in the distribution. Once the status is reported as **Deployed**, we can again select the distribution and then click on the **Delete** button:

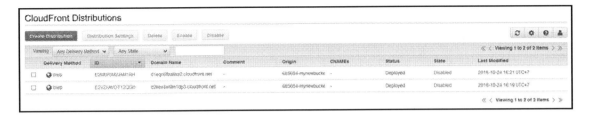

4. Another confirmation window will pop up and if we are sure we would like to delete the distribution, we can click **Yes, Delete**. This is the final step and will delete our CloudFront distribution:

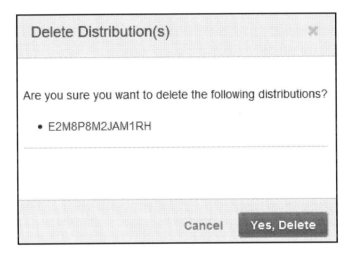

Summary

CloudFront is a CDN that can help improve the performance of our applications by delivering the content from AWS Edge Locations. Our content source, called an origin in CloudFront, can be either an S3 bucket or a DNS-resolvable hostname running within the AWS network or outside it. CloudFront can be highly customized and tied in with other AWS services to deliver content with lower latency and higher security, and at a lower cost. We have also taken a look at how simple it is to create a CloudFront distribution and how to measure the performance difference between our servers and the content being delivered through the CDN. In the next chapter, we will look into various storage options in AWS.

Questions

1. What is CloudFront?
2. What kind of content can be cached by CloudFront?
3. In CloudFront, what is the name given to a source server?
4. How do we enable DDoS protection on CloudFront?
5. What feature would you use to restrict access to S3 buckets?
6. What are the two types of distributions supported on CloudFront?
7. What do we need to do to be able to delete a CloudFront distribution?

Further reading

- **Key Features of CloudFront**: https://aws.amazon.com/cloudfront/features/?nc=snloc=2
- **CloudFront Pricing**: https://aws.amazon.com/cloudfront/pricing/?nc=snloc=3
- **Lambda@Edge**: https://aws.amazon.com/lambda/edge/
- **Restricting Access to Amazon S3 Content by Using an Origin Access Identity**: https://docs.aws.amazon.com/AmazonCloudFront/latest/DeveloperGuide/private-content-restricting-access-to-s3.html
- **HTTP method definitions**: https://www.w3.org/Protocols/rfc2616/rfc2616-sec9.html
- **CloudFront Cache Behavior**: https://docs.aws.amazon.com/cloudfront/latest/APIReference/API_CacheBehavior.html

AWS Storage Options 9

In our previous chapters on EC2 and S3, we have already discussed in detail how to store and deliver block-level and object-level data from AWS. While those two options can cover most of the scenarios for serving data, there are some cases where these storage options need to be extended with additional functionality. To achieve this, AWS has a wide ranging storage option portfolio that can enable customers to deliver, serve, back up, and access their data to and from AWS.

The following topics will be covered in this chapter:

- Overview of storage options on AWS
- Introduction to **Elastic File System (EFS)**
- Introduction to Storage Gateway
- Introduction to Snowball
- Introduction to Snowmobile

Technical requirements

The reader should be familiar with modern application storage requirements, and have a basic understanding of storage area networks and protocols, storage network data transfer characteristics and limitations, as well as common data migration and backup strategies employed in traditional on-premises data centers and the cloud.

Overview of storage options on AWS

Different types of data will require different services. AWS has solutions for all types of data with features that enable us to store classic block-level data, static web content, files, and solutions that emulate tape-based storage and help us efficiently transfer huge petabyte and exabyte datasets between our on-premises environment and AWS regions. The solutions available in AWS are the following:

- Amazon EBS and Instance Store (discussed in `Chapter 5`, *Managing Servers on AWS with Elastic Compute Cloud*)
- Amazon S3 and Glacier (discussed in `Chapter 7`, *Understanding Simple Storage Service and Glacier*)
- Amazon **Elastic File System** (**EFS**)
- Amazon Storage Gateway
- Amazon Snowball and Snowmobile

Introduction to Elastic File System (EFS)

Amazon EFS delivers a managed, high performance, highly available, and highly scalable network filesystem solution that we can use in the cloud. It is designed for applications and users that require the use of a common data storage area that can be accessed via a standard **Network File System v4** (**NFSv4**) protocol and is able to deliver NFS datastores of unlimited sizes.

While the EFS service has been designed to match the characteristics and durability and availability of S3, there is no upfront fee for using it and we only pay for the storage consumed. As of this writing, it does not have an officially published SLA to determine the exact percentage of availability, but since it is designed with replication across multiple availability zones within a region, it is highly available. Also, the backend is designed to maintain multiple copies of data, meaning it is highly durable.

The reads and writes are done through block-level access, which enables us to open files residing in a shared location without the need for downloading and reuploading, like S3 does. This enables us to run applications that require shared block storage backends. For example, a cluster of servers that needs to exchange some frequently changing file-based information or share a virtual disk device due to the cluster design requirements can use a file or virtual disk mounted directly from the NFS backed served by the EFS service.

Performance

The EFS backend is designed for high performance and can deliver in excess of 7,000 file operations per second per filesystem. However, this performance cannot be maintained for long periods of time, as each EFS filesystem that we create will be throttled according to the burst credits that it has. Due to the spiky nature of network filesystem patterns, the system environment was designed similarly to T-type burstable instances. A baseline performance pattern has been determined and clients are allowed to burst over the baseline with very high rates of file operations, but they use up burst credits when they do so. Once the performance is within the baseline, the filesystem earns burst credits that can be used when needed. The allotment of the burst credits is determined by the size of the filesystem.

Security and resilience of EFS

EFS also offers advanced features that help us manage the security and resilience of our data. We can enable EFS encryption, which can encrypt our filesystems with the standard AES256 encryption available within AWS. We can also integrate it with the KMS service if we would like to use custom encryption keys. EFS file sync also offers us the ability to synchronize our filesystems across multiple EFS locations in multiple regions or deliver synchronization of our NFS environments on-premises. We are also able to incrementally backup our EFS datastores with the EFS-to-EFS backup solution. To find out more about this solution, take a look at the link provided in the *Further reading* section of this chapter.

Introduction to Storage Gateway

AWS Storage Gateway is a software appliance that allows us to seamlessly connect our on-premises environment with AWS cloud-based storage backends. The Storage Gateway appliance can be run as a virtual machine in our on-premises data center and is able to deliver file-based storage, data volumes, and a virtual tape library device backed by Amazon S3 and Glacier backends.

The following configuration options are available with AWS Storage Gateway:

- **File Gateway**: A network filesystem service that allows you to access files on S3 via standard NFSv3, NFSv4.1, SMB 2, and SMB 3 protocols. The File Gateway is able to cache read and write requests on the locally deployed VM and deliver low latency responses to clients accessing the file server. In the backend, data is always stored on S3 so we can perform the typical S3 functions discussed in `Chapter 7`, *Understanding Simple Storage Service and Glacier*, such as server-side encryption, life cycling, and replicating the S3 bucket to another region for higher resiliency.
- **Volume Gateway**: A service that allows us to mount block-level volumes via the standard iSCSI protocol from the Storage Gateway device. The volumes created on the Storage Gateway are always backed by an S3 datastore; thus, we get the benefits of both worlds: block-level access and high durability and availability. The Storage Gateway appliance can cache the local volume in two different ways:
    - **Locally Cached Volumes**: Data is served from S3 and only caches frequently read data and buffers writes on the local Storage Gateway, thus enabling low latency and high performance to be achieved inside our on-premises environment.
    - **Locally Stored Volumes**: All data is served from the local volume and regular snapshots are taken of the local volume. The snapshots are asynchronously backed up to S3, thus giving us the ability to restore the data in case of a local Storage Gateway volume failure or data corruption.
- **Tape Gateway**: A service that presents a virtual tape library that can be used with our traditional on-premises backup solutions. The data is always delivered straight into Glacier, giving us the benefit of very low cost storage and very high durability of our archiving solution. The Tape Gateway can be used to replace existing tape libraries without the need for re-architecting the backup solution.

Introduction to Snowball

Although a Storage Gateway can be a great solution for delivering data from our on-premises data center into AWS, it is still dependent on the bandwidth of the internet connection. Sometimes, the datasets can be very large and for those datasets it can take a very long time, be very expensive, and be very inefficient to transfer across the internet.

For example, let's take a look how long it takes to transfer a certain large dataset across the internet. For example, let's consider a very common dataset of 50 TB of data. If we employ a dedicated 1 Gbps connection to transfer that dataset, it will take us about 125 hours to transfer all the data across that link to the target destination. This calculation is taken in ideal conditions and 100% link utilization. So, we can easily say that on a 1 Gbps uplink, which is a common corporate internet uplink these days, we are able to transfer that dataset in roughly 6 days. How about when that dataset is even larger, say 100 TB? That would take about 12 days. What about 1 PB? That would bring us closer to 4 months!

AWS Snowball was designed to enable us to quickly and efficiently transfer large datasets in exactly these kinds of scenarios. The Snowball device is a self-contained shipping unit that is able to deliver either 42 or 72 TB of data from on-premises locations into AWS. With much larger datasets, we can use multiple Snowball devices in parallel to quickly and efficiently transfer data at Petabyte scale to AWS. The device itself hosts an S3 compatible endpoint that you can plug into your network via a 10 GbE copper, SPF, or SPF+ connector located on the device. The service can then be addressed on the local network and the full transfer speed of the link can be utilized to copy data onto the device. With the 10 Gbe connection, we can fill up the 42 TB snowball with data in about 10 hours, while the 72 TB model will take about 18 hours to fill up with data completely. This means that a 1 PB dataset can be transferred to 22 smaller devices in about 10 hours and to 15 larger ones in about 18 hours when transferring the whole capacity in parallel.

Once completed, we simply power off the unit and call our local carrier. The unit has an E-ink label with the shipping instructions so we don't need to worry about anything else. Once the snowball arrives at the designated data center, the data is transferred to an S3 bucket in our account. We then have the option to perform any kind of action available on S3, such as life cycling and presenting the data via HTTP/HTTPS.

Security

There is no need to worry about the data while it is in transit, as the device itself is packed in a tamper-proof case and all the data that is being transferred is automatically encrypted via the AES256 encryption protocol. You have the ability to provide custom encryption keys via the KMS service when compliance requires you to control all aspects for encryption.

Snowball Edge

Snowball Edge combines the Snowball data migration device with the power of running EC2 instances and Lambda functions straight out of the device itself. This is perfect for any company that is developing or migrating a solution to AWS and would like to work out how the live data will be delivered by the AWS services. Snowball Edge devices are rack mountable so customers are able to temporarily build an AWS-like data center on-premises and work out the intricacies of migrating an environment or designing an application by using the live data from their on-premises environment. To learn more about *Snowball Edge*, take a look at the link provided in the *Further reading* section of this chapter.

Introduction to Snowmobile

When terabyte-scale devices won't do and we need to move Petabyte and Zetabyte scale data to the cloud, then the only option is the Snowmobile. The Snowmobile is a standard 45 ft shipping container delivered on a truck that has the capacity to retrieve and move huge amounts of data very efficiently. Each Snowmobile has 100 PB of capacity and has enough transfer capacity to fill up the disks in about 2 weeks of non-stop transferring. To achieve that transfer capacity, up to 1,000 Gbs of throughput is required, which would also need to be available on the data center side if we want to use all the capacity the Snowmobile has to offer. When we have more capacity available in our data center, multiple Snowmobiles can be used to deliver an even larger dataset or to increase the speed of the transfer of the data. Once a Snowmobile completes the data transfer, it will drive back to the designated data center where the data can be delivered straight into either S3 or Glacier.

Security

Of course, transferring such huge datasets can be a security challenge. The shipping container itself is tamper and weather proof, while all the equipment is climate controlled during use and transit, and has redundant disks where the data is stored. The data is also encrypted with AES256, while the shipping container and truck are also GPS tracked. We are also given the option to employ a security detail escort vehicle while the data is in transit if required.

Summary

There are multiple options for storing data in AWS and those depend on the type of data we need to store. For data that is not shared and requires block-level high performance access, we are always able to use EBS volumes. If we need to share that data, S3 is a great option due to its high availability and durability, backed by an SLA. Since S3 doesn't support block-level access, we can use EFS, which strives to provide an NFS compatible environment that is designed with the same HA and durability as S3. When data needs to be shared between our on-premises and AWS environments, an AWS Storage Gateway can be utilized to emulate a network filesystem, an iSCSI volume device, or a virtual tape library that we can connect to our existing backup infrastructure. There are some cases where the network connectivity does not allow us to efficiently transfer large datasets across the internet, and in such cases AWS has the Snowball and Snowmobile options, which can be used to physically transport data from our on-premises data center to AWS. In the next chapter, we will be working with Route 53 Domain Name System.

Questions

1. What are the three types of data that can be stored in AWS?
2. What kinds of protocols are supported by the EFS service?
3. What kind of SLA does the EFR service have?
4. What are the modes of operation available on the AWS Storage Gateway?
5. What two options for volumes does the AWS Storage Gateway support?
6. What options support transferring data from on-premises directly to Glacier?
7. Which AWS feature would you use to transfer 1 PB of data if you had unlimited time?

Further reading

- **AWS Storage Options Whitepaper**: https://aws.amazon.com/whitepapers/storage-options-aws-cloud/
- **AWS EFS**: https://aws.amazon.com/efs/
- **EFS to EFS backup**: https://aws.amazon.com/answers/infrastructure-management/efs-backup/
- **AWS Storage Gateway**: https://docs.aws.amazon.com/storagegateway/latest/userguide/WhatIsStorageGateway.html
- **AWS Snowball**: https://aws.amazon.com/snowball/
- **AWS Snowball Edge**: https://aws.amazon.com/snowball-edge/
- **File Transfer Calculator**: https://techinternets.com/copy_calc
- **AWS Snowmobile**: https://aws.amazon.com/snowmobile/

10
Working with the Route 53 Domain Name System

On the modern internet, one types in a name of a website and almost instantly the content is presented via the browser. This feature of the internet is often taken for granted both by regular users and by IT professionals, since it is considered a given. In the background, the **Domain Name System** (**DNS**) makes sure this feature is available and has simplified the way we access the internet since the 1980s. But the traditional DNS system has its own drawbacks and limitations, which is why AWS set out to modernize the way we deploy, manage, and deliver DNS services by building the Route 53 system.

The following topics will be covered in this chapter:

- Introduction to Route 53
- Route 53 supported DNS resource record types
- Registering a domain and creating a zone
- Routing policies
- Health checking
- Best practices

Technical requirements

A basic understanding of internet addressing, the Domain Name System, and name resolution is required to get a comprehensive grasp of the subject at hand.

Introduction to Route 53

We probably wouldn't have the internet as we know it now if it wasn't for the work of Paul Mockapetris in the 1980s. In the early days of distributed networks, scalability started becoming an issue as there were hundreds of servers connected with hundreds of IP addresses that would need to have been used to access the content served on these servers. Back in the day, one would use a directory of websites to IP addresses and punch in an IP to access the content. Paul Mockapetris's contribution to ARPANET essentially created the automated resolution of names to IP addresses today known as the **Domain Name System**, or **DNS** for short.

Traditional DNS system design features

Traditional DNS systems maintain a mapping of **Internet Protocol** (**IP**) addresses to **fully qualified domain names** (**FQDN**) in files called zone files, and those are usually text or binary format files that are maintained on one or more servers. Usually, the way the DNS operates is that we have one server that hosts the master DNS zone and one or more read-only replicas that host the slave DNS zone. The master is where we make the changes and the changes then propagate to the slaves through zone replication. This does provide high availability but if the master zone is disabled because of a failure, the DNS itself might become read-only so any updates to the DNS will need to wait for the master to recover.

One feature of the traditional DNS server types is that they are designed to update zones manually on the master server, and those that do have programmable access provide that access essentially on top of a traditional manually modified system. Another fairly common feature of the traditional DNS architecture is that the DNS servers themselves are not connected to the records they host; the servers will deliver a mapping between a name and an IP address, and all features beyond that operation are not included. For instance, if a request is made for a website that is currently not operational, the DNS will respond with the address but has no way of delivering any information on whether there is anything responding on the IP address provided.

In modern applications, however, we strive to deliver the highest availability possible within our application, and we also want to automate the provisioning tasks and deliver the website from multiple backends in case of hardware or other failures affecting our availability.

AWS identified that an application will be only as highly available as the sum of the components providing the features of the application, and one crucial feature is the DNS. Without the ability to resolve names to IP addresses, our application is essentially non-functional. And if the DNS service has an SLA of 99.9%, then we can theoretically never guarantee the delivery of any higher level of availability. To overcome the limitations of traditional DNS architectures, the engineers and architects at AWS decided to develop the Amazon Route 53 service.

Amazon Route 53 features

The Amazon Route 53 service is essentially a *smart* DNS service, sometimes even hailed as *the next generation of DNS*. The Route 53 service is the only service that has a 100% SLA for service delivery and is designed to withstand massive, multi-regional service and data failures and still deliver the DNS services at the same performance and quality. The service is so reliable that the only event that will cause Route 53 to stop working would be an extinction-level meteor impact on planet Earth; that is, until AWS establishes its first Mars region of course.

Amazon Route 53 is not just a classic resolver; it delivers the ability to mange the traffic flow to our application by understanding the origin and the destination of the DNS queries. Essentially, it is designed to interact with the backend and identify the servers that are capable of serving specific content, and only then delivering the correct resolution parameters to the client. Also, Route 53 is API addressable, so we can easily automate the provisioning of our infrastructure and build the DNS assignments into the code of our application. Route 53 helps us deliver our application with the correct content to the correct user and mitigate any disruptions in availability at the DNS level with the following features:

- Built-in DNS health checks and DNS failover allow us to automatically exclude IP addresses of servers that are non-operational from the DNS response
- Latency-based, weighted round-robin routing and Geo DNS allow us to target specific audiences based on proximity and geolocation so that we can deliver the right service to the right user in the fastest manner
- Integration with CloudFront, S3, and ELB allow us to easily configure and maintain the websites served through these services on Route 53

Route 53 supported DNS resource record types

Amazon Route 53 is designed to support the most common DNS record types. While a huge subset of record types exists, the AWS team has designed the service to be as inclusive as possible and to provide the record types that are most commonly used with internet-based applications and websites. The following resource types are supported on Route 53 at the time of writing:

- A and AAAA records are designed to resolve IPv4 (A) and IPv6 (AAAA) server names to IP addresses and allow browsers and applications to access our content via FQDN names
- CAA records are designed to allow us to specify which **Certificate Authority (CA)** servers are allowed to issue certificates for our domain and thus increase the security of our websites
- **CNAME** or **Common Name** records allow us to resolve complex DNS names to simpler or more general DNS names; for instance, the name `www.example.com` can have a CNAME record that points to the public S3 bucket DNS name
- **MX** or **Mail Exchanger** records are used to determine the mail server(s) that receive email for a particular domain
- **NAPTR** or **Name Authority Pointer** is used by the **Dynamic Delegation Discovery System** (**DDDS**) to dynamically determine application or service endpoints; for example, NAPTR can be used to convert telephone numbers to SIP endpoints
- **NS** or **Name Server** records are used to determine which DNS server is authoritative to serve responses to DNS queries for the domain
- **PTR** or **Pointer** records allow us to look up DNS records in reverse by specifying an IP address and then determining the FQDN
- **SOA** or **Start of Authority** records are mandatory records for each domain that determine the authoritative DNS servers and keep a timestamp and version record of the domain zone
- **SPF** or **Sender Policy Framework** records allow email systems to determine whether the email sender is authorized to send messages on behalf of the domain
- **SRV** or **Service** records are designed to help us deliver information about the ports the host serves its services on
- **TXT** or **Text** records are designed to allow us to share arbitrary strings of text within the DNS service and thus extend the functionality or security of our domain and the services running on the servers belonging to our domain

Registering a domain and creating a zone

Amazon Web Services have made it very easy for us to register a new domain from the AWS Management console. The first time we navigate to the Route 53 management console, we will see a short introduction to the Route 53 service:

1. We can select the feature we would like to get started with; in this demo, we will select **Get started now** under **Domain registration**:

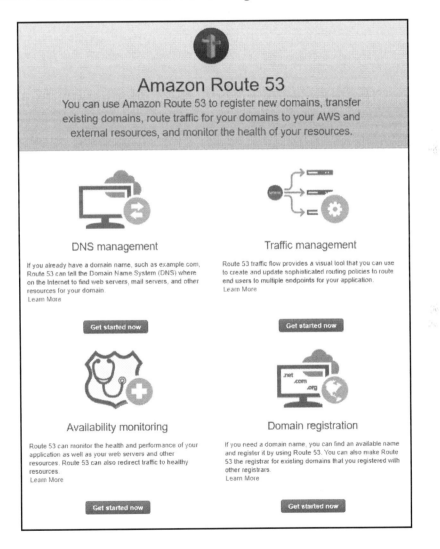

2. Once we are in the domain registration console, we have the option to register a new domain or transfer an existing domain registered at a different provider. We will take a look at the process of registering a domain by clicking on the **Register Domain** button:

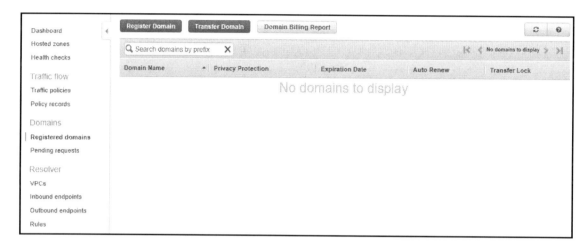

3. In the **Choose a domain name** dialog, we can simply write the domain name that we wish to register and then click on **Check**, which will enable us to search for the existence of the domain.

4. If the domain already exists, AWS will also give us suggestions on other domain names similar to ours that might be available. Once you are ready to select your domain, just click on **Add to cart** and then click on **Continue**:

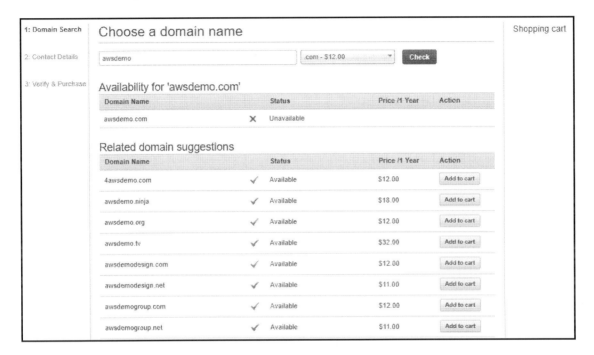

5. In the next step, we simply fill out the registration contact information and then proceed to **Verify & Purchase** to verify the details and complete the purchase:

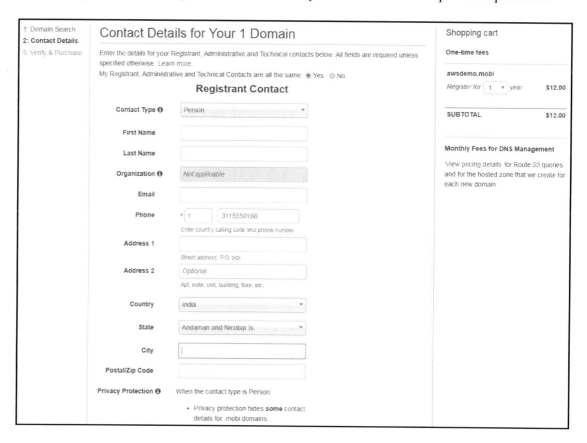

6. Once we have our domain, or when we would like to move the DNS functionality to AWS, we can create a hosted zone. In the Route 53 management console, just select **Hosted zones** from the menu and then click on **Create Hosted Zone**:

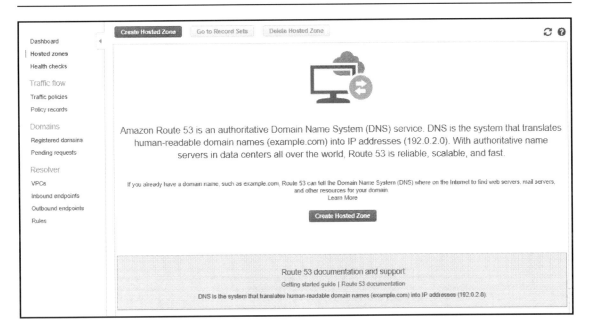

7. In the zone creation dialog, enter the domain name of the zone you would like to create and select whether it is a public-hosted zone or a private zone available from your VPC only.

8. With private zones, you also have the ability to host internal domains that can be used within your application. Once you have entered the name, simply click on **Create**:

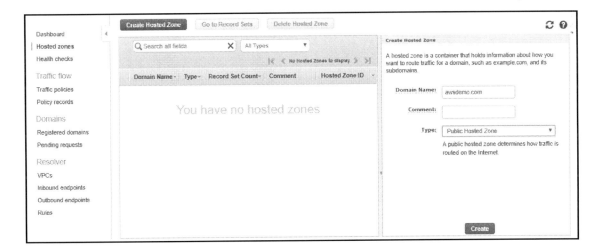

9. After creating the hosted zone, you can start editing it. As you will see, the SOA is automatically created and the NS names will appear in the SOA also.

10. You would use these NS names with your registrar if you have not registered your domain with AWS. To create a record set in the zone, click on **Create Record Set:**

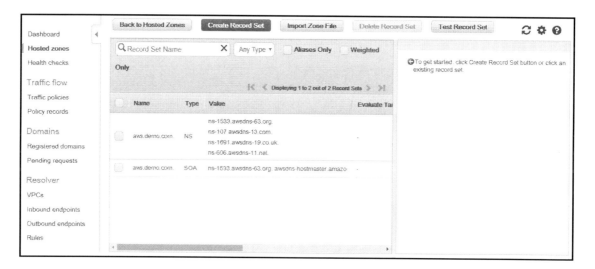

11. In the record set dialog, you can select your record name and type, and then assign a value to the record. In our example, we are creating a record with the name test, the type is **A**, and the value is 1.2.3.4; as you can see, we have previously created a record with this name and it is also visible in the records next to the SOA and NS. You can also select a TTL for the record if you need a TTL that is different from the default, and a routing policy:

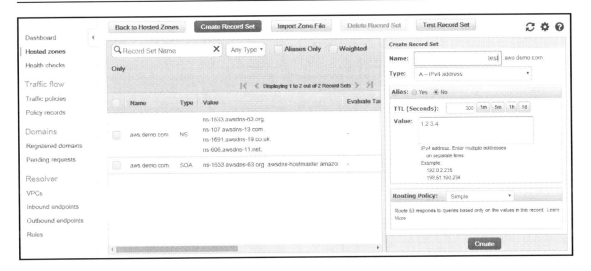

We have now registered a new domain and created a DNS zone for this domain. We can now add any number of records into this domain and AWS will serve them through the servers listed in the NS records.

Routing policies

The internet now has a global audience, and we need to design our applications to reach our global audience and deliver the content in the fastest way possible with the least disruption possible. We also want to deliver custom content to users in different geographical areas, based on the language, compliance with regulations and laws, and other principles that determine how we present our content to our users. Routing of DNS requests with routing policies allows us to control the traffic flow and delivery of our content to our users. We have several different options available when creating records, and, for each record, we can choose the following:

- Simple routing
- Latency-based routing
- Weighted routing
- Fail-over routing
- Geolocation routing
- Multi-value response

Simple routing

This is the default way the DNS response operates if you do not select an alternate routing option. It returns one resource IP or DNS name for one FQDN address. So, when looking up `www.example.com`, it will return the IP address if the record is **A**, or the DNS name if the record is **CNAME**.

Latency-based routing

Latency-based routing (**LBR**) helps us deliver content from the AWS endpoints that reside in different regions and locations, and determines which AWS endpoint to serve the content from based on the network proximity of the user to AWS. That enables us to deliver the content in the fastest possible manner and increase the performance of our applications. LBS is very useful when we are looking to distribute the same content across a wide geographical area or globally, and we would like to present the content in the quickest possible manner to the users.

Weighted routing

Weighted routing allows us to deliver the content from several AWS endpoints and determine how much traffic or *weight* we want to put on each entry in the DNS record. This record type allows us to design environments that handle different traffic with different backends:

- Solutions with asymmetrical multi-regional deployments that can be used as a primary/failover location for our production application
- Blue-green deployment migration by increasing the weight of the new deployment
- Testing our applications with canary and A/B environments

Failover routing

Like weighted routing, failover routing allows us to deliver content from several AWS endpoints but with an active/passive approach, where one endpoint is active and taking all the traffic, and a secondary endpoint is the passive one that is designed to take the traffic of the active one if that one fails. This approach is useful when we have an application that synchronizes the content only from the active to the passive endpoint asymmetrically.

Geolocation routing

Geolocation routing allows us to determine the location of our users by geolocating the source IP addresses the requests for the DNS are coming from, and then delivering the endpoint that is designed to serve the specific region. With geolocation routing, we can design applications that are able to deliver custom content based on the country or region our users are coming from, in the appropriate language, and with the appropriate compliance with local laws and regulations. For instance, if we have an application that is designed to deliver content to users from the US and EU, we can have the US content served from the US regions and the EU content from the EU regions, and then use geolocation routing to forward requests from the appropriate geographical area to the appropriate servers. This enables us to easily comply with the local laws and also maintain all the user data within the data governance-required geographical area.

Multi-value response

With multi-value answers, we can design a DNS response that will deliver a list of possible servers that the client can choose from. This is very beneficial for applications that require enumeration of all the possible servers that can serve the content, such as direct peer-to-peer-based applications for services such as video streaming.

Health checking

Route 53 also supports health checks that allow us to determine the healthy and unhealthy AWS endpoints. It supports simple TCP port checks and more advanced HTTP and HTTPS health checks where it looks for either a 200 or 300 response with an additionally optional string matching functionality that can check your website for a specific string of text to determine if the site content is actually being served.

The health check can also determine the health based on the response time, a response threshold where we can define a number of required successful responses from the endpoint before determining it is healthy, and the CloudWatch alarm metrics collected for the AWS endpoint itself.

Health checks are performed from the global Route 53 endpoints and the service determines an endpoint healthy if more than 18% of the Route 53 endpoints report the service as healthy. This number was chosen in consideration of the number of regions and an understanding that the internet routing might make a health check fail from some regions at certain times.

Best practices

As you can see by now, Route 53 is quite a powerful service, but even with the most powerful service, we have the responsibility to make sure our DNS records are designed in the best possible way so they are secure and correct. Here are some best practices to follow when designing domains with Route 53:

- Enable domain auto renew to ensure your domain is automatically renewed
- Enable privacy protection for domains that require the contact information to be kept private and secure
- Do not enter private records into public zones
- Monitor Route 53 configuration changes to detect any rogue entries or actions
- Enable domain transfer lock, which can prevent your domain from being hijacked

Summary

The Route 53 service is the next generation DNS service, which is a fully managed, highly available, and high performance DNS solution and is the only AWS service with a 100% SLA. Route 53 allows us to manage DNS names in a programmable manner and deliver features that can enable a high level of traffic shaping, depending on the location latency and design of our application. We have also discussed the supported DNS resource records and health checks available in Route 53. In the next chapter, we will be working with relational databases.

Questions

1. What is the purpose of the DNS service?
2. What areas of the DNS does the Route 53 service improve upon?
3. Your application is synchronizing a database from the primary to secondary site and presents the content through an EC2 instance locally. What type of DNS routing policy would be appropriate for this setup?
4. You need to make sure your content adheres to the GDPR for all users from the EU. What kind of routing policy would be applicable in this case?

5. You are designing a health check for a custom application that sends custom traffic via SSL on port 443 to the server. What would be the appropriate health check in this case?

6. Your application needs to be protected from web page hijacks and you want to eliminate any hijacked servers from responding to your clients. How can Route 53 help?

7. A peer-to-peer streaming service needs to deliver a list of servers that serve the video stream to the clients. Which routing policy would deliver this kind of response?

Further reading

- **Route 53 features**: https://aws.amazon.com/route53/features/
- Route 53 record types: https://docs.aws.amazon.com/Route53/latest/DeveloperGuide/ResourceRecordTypes.html
- **List of DNS record types**: https://en.wikipedia.org/wiki/List_of_DNS_record_types
- **Choosing a routing policy**: https://docs.aws.amazon.com/Route53/latest/DeveloperGuide/routing-policy.html
- **Route 53 health checks**: https://docs.aws.amazon.com/Route53/latest/DeveloperGuide/dns-failover.html

11
Working with Relational Database Services

Data is king, and it does not matter what kind of application you are designing: every application will at one point in processing the data need to store that data in a persistent and reliable way. We have already looked at several different ways of storing data in AWS for several different data types, from objects to block data to files, and we have learned how to use EC2 to provide an operating system where we can install applications such as a database server. But what if we don't have the resources to manage our own database server? Or we just want a simple way to consume a database from the cloud? One way this can be done is by using a managed database service such as the Amazon **Relational Database Service** (**RDS**).

The following topics will be covered in this chapter:

- Introduction to RDS
- RDS engine types
- Best practices for deploying RDS instances
- Changing RDS instance types
- Read replicas
- Sharding data over RDS instances
- Creating and restoring snapshots

Technical requirements

An understanding of operating and managing relational databases and the **Atomicity, Consistency, Isolation, and Durability (ACID)** database types is required to follow along with this chapter.

Introduction to RDS

Whenever you are planning to consume cloud computing resources, there is always a balance that needs to be achieved between the requirement of maintaining control of the environment and instantiation, and having the ability to focus on the task at hand. This is true for the need to use a relational database. In AWS you have a choice: you can either deploy your own EC2 instance with a database engine on it to maintain control of the configuration and the underlying operating system, or you can choose to use an RDS instance that can provide the same functionality and deliver a database service with minimal management overhead.

The decision to use RDS will be driven by the business driver of cloud adoption. Sometimes the business driver behind the use of cloud services is simplifying the management; in this case it is always easier to use the RDS service instead of managing your own server. In other cases, the business driver is increased flexibility and automation; again, RDS comes out on top as the flexibility of being able to deploy new RDS instances straight out of the SDK and managing the RDS infrastructure straight out of the code can be a big benefit.

Features of RDS

RDS is a managed service that is able to provide a highly scalable and high-performance relational database backend to your applications. All RDS instances are backed by SSD disks and the latest-generation instance types. It is easily scalable both in size and performance and it has built-in features that allow you to create highly available synchronous and asynchronous replicas to be used as fail-over or read replicas. The environment also offers very high data durability by enabling automated and manual snapshots of the database instances to be taken to provide a backup of your data. All snapshots are stored to S3 and are inherently as durable as the S3 service. RDS seamlessly integrates with the AWS monitoring and auditing tools to provide a complete overview of performance and the state of your database environment.

RDS engine types

RDS supports the creation and management of different relational database backends. As business needs change and applications evolve, different database backends will be required to run the applications. RDS offers the following database engine types to support as much compatibility as possible with your current and future applications:

- RDS for MySQL, MariaDB, and PostgreSQL
- Amazon Aurora
- RDS for Oracle
- RDS for SQL Server

RDS for MySQL, MariaDB, and PostgreSQL

Amazon RDS supports MySQL, MariaDB, and PostgreSQL, three of the most popular open source relational databases that have become the industry standard for deploying enterprise applications on open source databases. All of the engines support the ability to deliver Multi-AZ, highly available, master-slave synchronous copies of databases in one region and the capability to deploy multiple read replicas in the same region or across other regions. The RDS service supports the following versions of the open source databases:

- Drop-in compatible engines for MySQL Community Edition versions 5.5, 5.6, 5.7, and 8.0
- Drop-in compatible engines for MariaDB Server versions 10.0, 10.1, 10.2, and 10.3
- Any version of PostgreSQL with version 9.3.5 and later supporting Multi-AZ and read replicas

To protect data at rest, the databases support instance volume encryption and have the ability to use SSL to protect data in transit.

Amazon Aurora

Amazon Aurora is an AWS-optimized relational database engine that supports running either MySQL or PostgreSQL databases. The service is drop-in compatible with MySQL 5.6 and later, and provides a migration tool that is able to assess and migrate a PostgreSQL database into the Aurora environment.

Amazon Aurora enables very simple management of the database while delivering high availability and high performance. The design behind an Aurora cluster differs slightly from the way the open source databases are delivered. With the open source databases, the Master database can have a synchronous slave replica within another availability zone, and then on top of those, we can deliver asynchronous read replicas that can be used to offload the read requests to the database.

An Aurora cluster is designed to always have one master instance, the so-called primary instance, and then multiple replica instances. Both the primary and the replicas have access to the same synchronously replicated backend storage volume. The instances themselves are stateless and are designed to only provide the database service and respond to database queries. The primary instance allows write access to the cluster volume while the replicas allow only for reads. To deliver high availability, the storage and the replicas are distributed across two or more availability zones. If the primary instance becomes unreliable or unavailable, Amazon Aurora will instantly promote one of the replicas to the primary role and deliver instant fail-over of all write traffic to that instance.

In essence, the design of Amazon Aurora enables us to have all nodes in the cluster take some work from the clients and, by having synchronous read replicas within one region, there is no lag in data being delivered out of the database which can be caused by asynchronous replication. The cluster can scale quite a bit since it supports delivering up to 15 replicas in addition to the primary instance, and also allows us to create global database clusters that can have an additional 16 replica instances deployed in other regions.

One feature of Amazon Aurora that is highly anticipated by some is the ability to provide multi-master clusters within our environment. At the time of writing, a preview program for the feature is available and you can sign up for the preview by following the link provided in the *Further reading* section of this chapter.

Oracle and Microsoft SQL on RDS

RDS also supports Oracle (version 11g and newer) and Microsoft SQL (2008 and newer), two industry standard licensed relational database products that are commonly used in enterprise applications. The ability to consume these database types from the cloud gives us the flexibility of choosing the RDS option when migrating to the cloud for these two database types.

To protect data at rest and in transit, **Transparent Data Encryption** (**TDE**) is supported on both of these instances. With TDE, the encryption is delivered in a transparent manner that does not require any management or configuration overhead on the client side. Both of these database types require a license and are able to be consumed as a service or as a bring-your-own-license model. For more details on licensing, please follow the links on Oracle on RDS and MS SQL on RDS in the *Further reading* section of this chapter.

Deploying an RDS database

Let's perform the following steps to deploy an RDS instance:

1. To deploy an RDS instance, we navigate to the **Amazon RDS** console and click on **Create database**:

2. We need to select an engine to deploy. The recommended option for **Amazon Aurora** will be selected but you can select any of the other engines. In this example, we will choose a **MySQL** instance and then click **Next**:

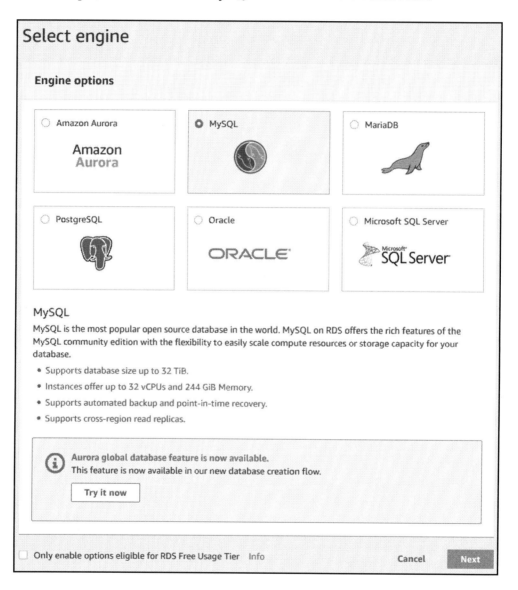

[246]

3. When choosing a **MySQL** instance, Amazon Aurora will be recommended for production as the engine is superior to the MySQL engine in all respects. We will choose the **Dev/Test - MySQL** option for our purposes:

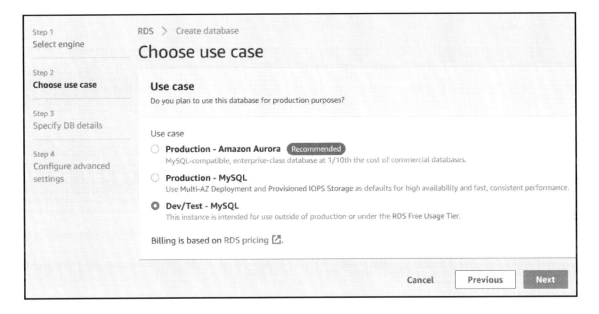

4. In *Step 3*, we need to specify the setup for the database. We can choose the license model and DB engine version, and the instance class, which determines the size of the instance serving our database (in our example, we are selecting `db.t2.small`). We also have the chance to select the option to create a Multi-AZ deployment to make the database highly available:

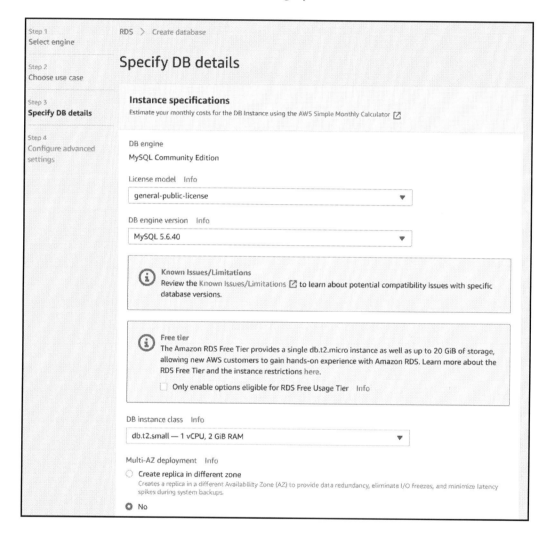

5. Next, we select the storage type and size, and enter the name for the database instance, and the username and password for the database administrator. After we have completed *Step 3*, we click **Next**:

6. In the advanced settings, under **Network & Security**, we can select the VPC in which we want to deploy, whether we want the instance to be public, and the availability zone in which to deploy, as well as the security group that will allow access to the database server from our instances:

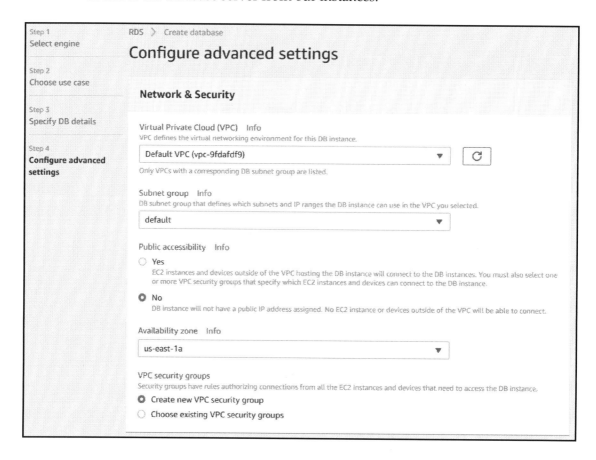

7. The **Database Options** section will let us create a default database, set the port, select the database parameters and options that allow us to tune our RDS databases, and enable or disable database user authentication via IAM:

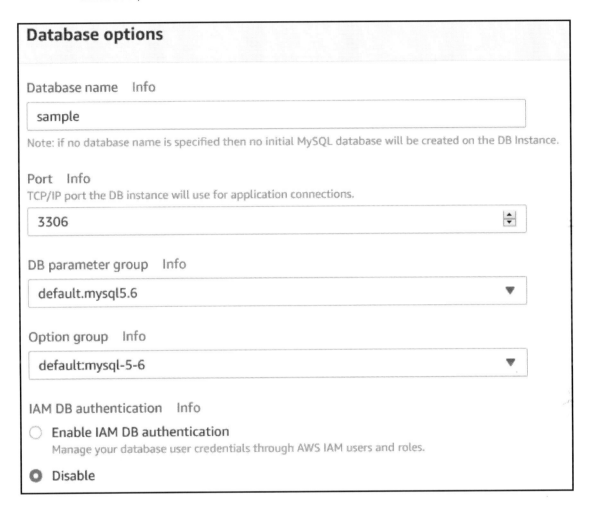

8. In the next section, we can also enable encryption, configure automatic backups, enable detailed monitoring, and enable the publishing of logs to CloudWatch:

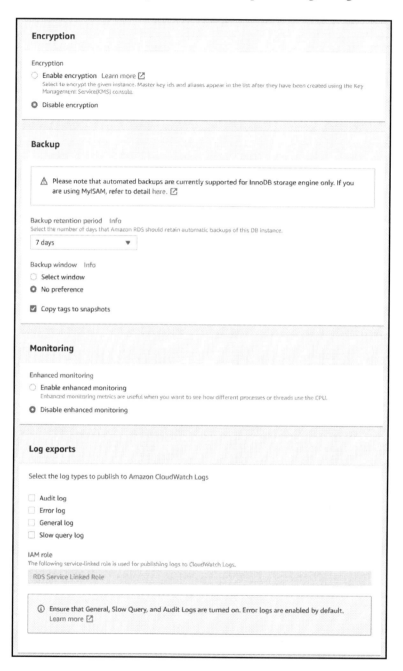

9. Under **Maintenance**, we can select whether we want to allow minor upgrades to the DB engine and select a maintenance window if required. For production databases, deletion protection is also available. After completing this part, we click on **Create database**:

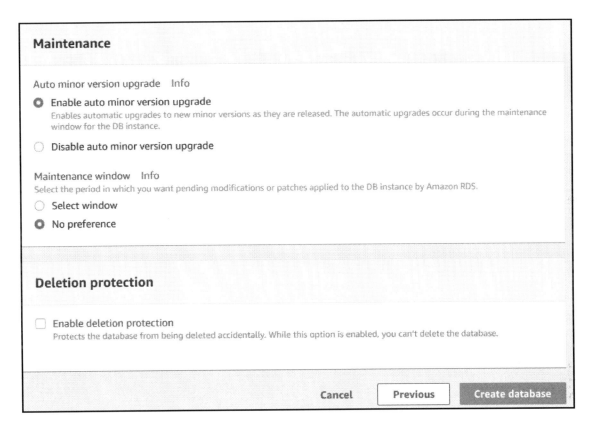

10. We will get a notification once a database is created. On this page, we can click on **View DB instance details**:

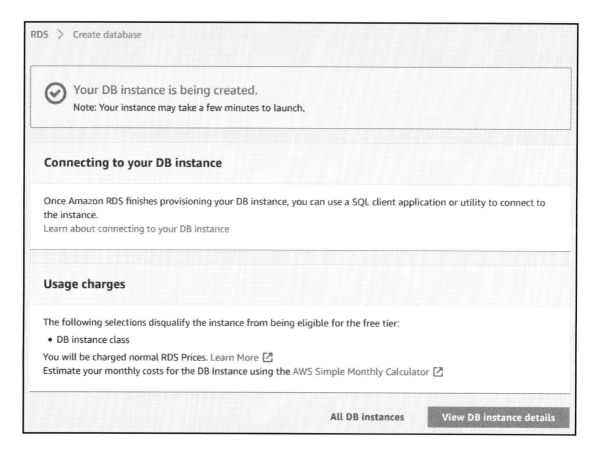

11. In the instance details, we can see the performance metrics for our database:

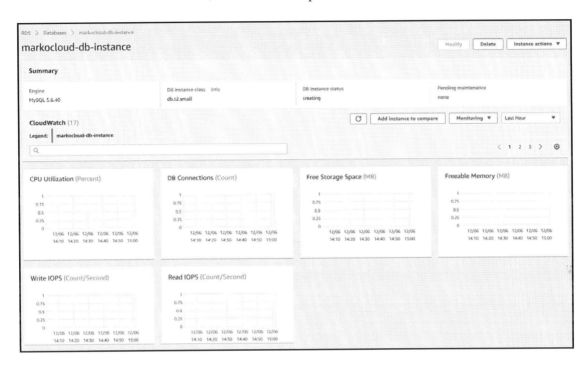

12. To connect to the database, find the endpoint DNS name and port that the database is available on:

As you can see, it takes much less effort to create a database instance than it would if we were deploying it on an EC2 instance. Two more benefits are that it is very easy to configure and deploy a database through the same process, and that we are provided with a DNS name that we can easily connect to and use in our application.

Best practices for deploying RDS instances

When deploying RDS instances in our VPC, we need to consider the following requirements of the database service:

- Security requirements, to prevent unauthorized or unnecessary access
- High availability requirements
- Performance requirements

RDS security

Within a VPC, RDS instances will need to be deployed with a security group that only allows communication from the correct source. For example, when using EC2 instances to communicate with RDS instances, always specify only the security group of the instances themselves. This will allow for you to dynamically replace application instances in the EC2, for example, when working with autoscaling EC2 clusters. The best practice for database instances is that they should also always be deployed into private subnets, as there is generally no requirement for a database backend to have any public access from the internet. When designing security groups, always make sure to open only the port the database service responds on, as no other access to the RDS instances should be allowed. In the case of NACL creation, don't forget to create both the incoming and outgoing rules for your RDS instance subnets. When troubleshooting connectivity to the RDS instances, you should be using the VPC flow logs for the subnet that the instances reside in to identify the cause of connectivity issues.

Multi-AZ RDS

For high availability, Multi-AZ deployments are recommended. All engine types support the ability to distribute data across two (or, in the case of Aurora, more) availability zones. This feature enables our database to survive any failures in one particular availability zone. The Multi-AZ feature allows us to access the database via a DNS name that automatically fails over to the secondary instance in case the primary fails. It also allows for ease of management as backend management functions do not affect the availability of the database.

Performance best practices

To achieve the best performance from our instances, always consider the data access pattern, the throughput required to the database, and the memory requirement for your database servers; this will allow you to select the appropriate instance type. Once in production, the instance should be monitored for I/O and latency, and of course, disk and memory usage. We can monitor our instances using CloudWatch, and we can also set up alarms on CloudWatch to determine when our instance health or resource usage is spiking and an action would need to be taken to resolve the issue. There are four ways to increase the performance of our clusters:

- Change the instance type to increase the performance of the instance
- Add read replicas to distribute the read load over more instances
- Shard the data to multiple instances
- Add caching to offload the read operations to the cache (discussed in `Chapter 12`, *Introduction to ElastiCache*)

Changing RDS instance types

The simplest way to get more performance from our database is to increase the instance size of our RDS instance; this can be done with very little effort in RDS as we are able to initiate an instance resize from the management console, CLI, or SDK. Once initiated, the instance is shut down and the instance type is changed; this is essentially done in the same way as with EC2 instances. For a single instance RDS, this means that the service will see a disruption as the instance needs to be shut down. In a Multi-AZ deployment, the secondary instance will be resized first, then the traffic will be redirected to the secondary while the master instance is resized.

With an Aurora cluster, the instance replicas are replaced with larger ones and one of the larger instances is promoted to primary, while the smaller instances are shut down. With highly available options, the instance type resize happens transparently in the background:

1. To change the instance type, select the instance that you have created and click on **Modify**:

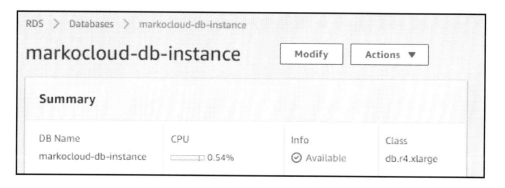

2. Next, select the new instance type and proceed to the next step:

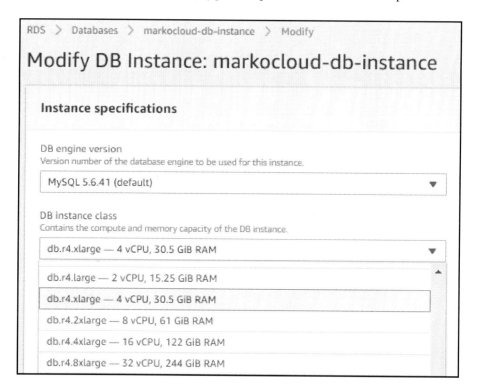

3. In the next step, you will see a summary of changes that will show how the database will be modified. You need to select **Apply during the next scheduled maintenance window** or **Apply immediately** if you would like to resize it right away, then click on **Modify DB instance**:

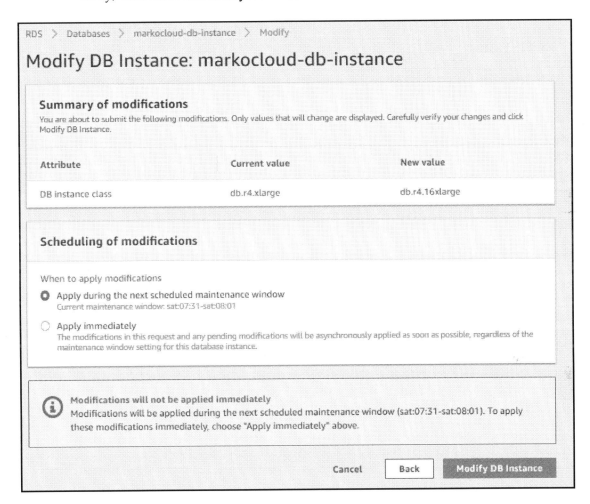

As you can see, it is very easy to change the instance size from the management console.

Read replicas

The second way to get more performance out of our cluster is to introduce read replicas. With typical relational databases, the read-to-write ratios are usually in favor of reads by a factor of a few. Typical access patterns could be as high as 80% read and 20% write, or even as high as 90-10 or more. By introducing read replicas, we allow the application to distribute the reads to the read replicas and relieve the master or primary instance of the reads.

With the MySQL, MariaDB, and PostgreSQL engines, the read replicas can be created within the same region or another region and are done with the engine's native asynchronous replication capabilities. This means that the data in the read replicas might see a bit of a lag and serve stale data, so we need to handle this in the application we are deploying. This can be useful for **business intelligence** (**BI**) or analytics platforms that need to perform end-of-day analysis on our data and project that into reports. If your application cannot handle stale data, then introducing caching (discussed in `Chapter 12`, *Introduction to ElastiCache*) will be the appropriate option with these database types.

With Amazon Aurora, the read replicas are essentially built into the cluster and retrieve data from the shared backend volume, meaning there is no replication at the instance level required and the data delivered from the read replicas is never stale.

 Oracle and Microsoft SQL RDS instances do not support read replicas.

1. To add read replicas, navigate back to the databases section in the RDS management console and select **Actions** and then **Create read replica**:

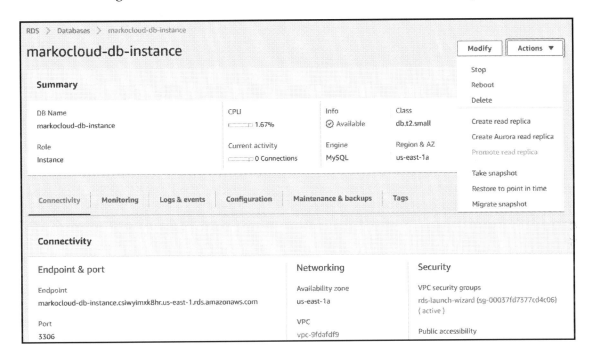

2. In the read replica dialog, we can select the destination region and availability zone, and we can also configure whether we would like to make the read replica publicly available:

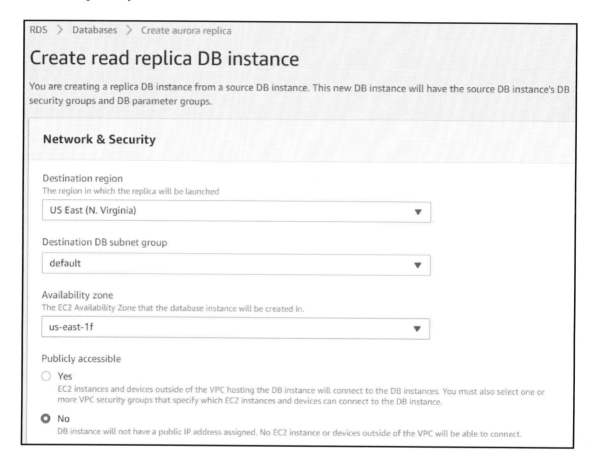

3. We can also encrypt the database, select an instance size for the replica, configure Multi-AZ, the database settings, monitoring, logging, and the maintenance window, just like we did when we created the initial database. After we are satisfied with our selections, we can click **Create read replica**:

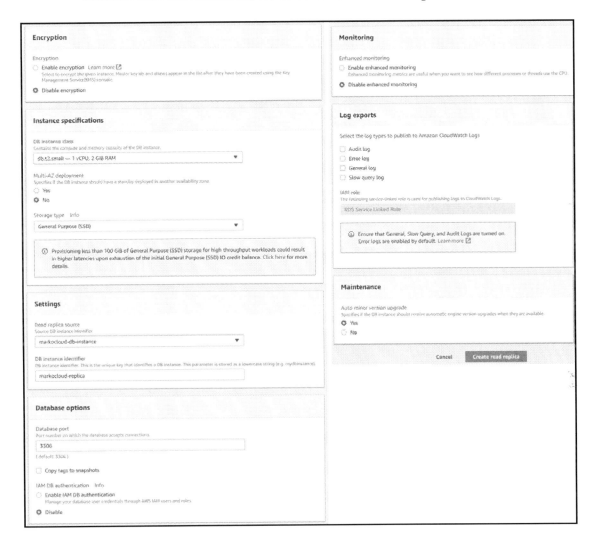

4. When replica creation starts, we will see another instance in our list of databases in the RDS management console:

Sharding data over RDS instances

Another consideration for your data in RDS instances is sharding. When the data access pattern allows it and the distribution of the data is relatively uniform across the database, sharding can be a way of storing data that can almost linearly increase the write performance of our databases. With sharding, we can distribute the data to several RDS backend clusters; for example, if we have a phone directory and we are storing names from A-Z, these names are more or less evenly distributed. We can introduce sharding and distribute the names from A-M in the first shard on one cluster and the names from N-Z to the second shard residing on the second cluster.

Sharding is a good way of increasing the performance of our database clusters when the data is evenly distributed, but it does have some inherent drawbacks, such as the complexity of performing data projections, table joins, and other complex SQL transactions for which we usually employ ACID-compliant relational databases. For example, a BI report might need to source and compare data from several databases and compile the appropriate relationships on the BI server instead of in the database, if the BI server even supports this kind of approach.

Creating and restoring snapshots

The RDS service supports creating database snapshots (sometimes also called database backups), which are point-in-time copies of a complete volume where the database resides. The snapshots are created incrementally, meaning that only the blocks of the volume that have changed since the last snapshot are saved to the next snapshot. This essentially means that the same characteristics apply to RDS snapshots as EC2 snapshots, with one exception: when creating an RDS snapshot, the instance I/O will be frozen due to the fact that the RDS snapshots need to be consistent and can be used as ACID-compliant backups of your database. This will mean that, when using a single instance, the instance will become unavailable for anywhere from a few seconds to a few minutes while the snapshot is being taken, depending on the size of the data in the snapshot being taken:

1. To take a manual snapshot, select the database, click on **Actions**, and then select the **Take snapshot** option:

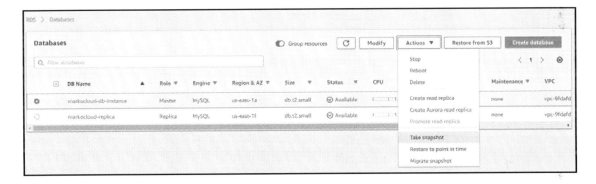

2. In the snapshot, we will need to define a snapshot identifier, then click on **Take snapshot**:

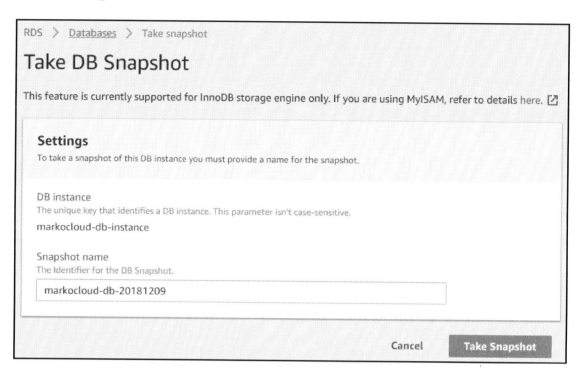

3. When the snapshot commences, we will be able to see the process in the **Snapshots** section of the RDS management console:

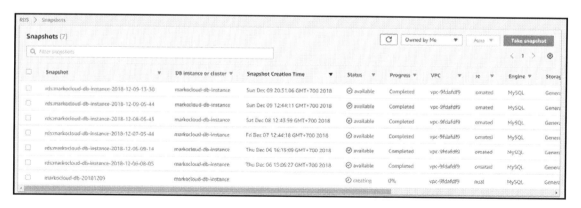

We now have snapshots from which we can restore the data to a new RDS instance.

Multi-AZ snapshots

Taking a snapshot in a Multi-AZ deployment will not affect the availability of the database. With a Multi-AZ deployment, the snapshot is taken from the secondary instance while the master is still available to take queries and writes. We should consider that, when many writes are happening on the master instance during snapshot creation, those need to be replicated after the snapshot completes to the secondary, thus we might see a spike in latency in our CloudWatch monitoring due to the fact that the secondary instance is being replicated after the snapshot completes.

In Amazon Aurora, snapshots are even more transparent. Aurora instances are stateless, so a snapshot of the backend cluster storage is taken during an RDS snapshot operation. Aurora snapshots are thus referred to as cluster database snapshots.

Automated backups

The RDS service allows for the creation of automated backups that are taken once daily during a predefined or user-defined backup window. Automated backups can be retained backups for up to 35 days, allowing us to comply with most typical enterprise policy requirements out of the box. On top of automated backups, we can always take manual snapshots if longer retention is required for a certain snapshot, that is, a monthly backup or an end-of-year backup is required.

The automated backup can be configured during the initial setup of the database in the section displayed here:

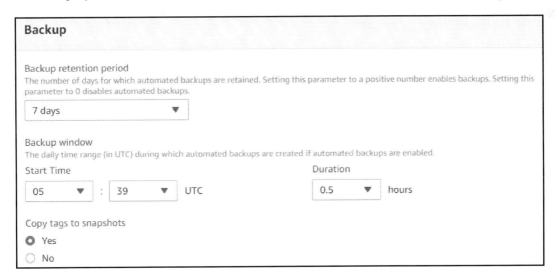

We can also view the backup configuration in the **Maintenance & Backup** section:

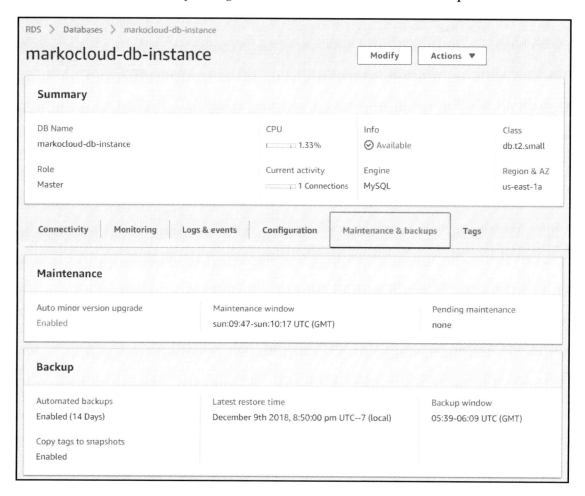

Restoring RDS instances from a snapshot

If restoring one of the database backups is required, a database restore can be completed from an RDS snapshot. We need to consider that an RDS snapshot cannot be restored over an existing database instance or cluster; only a new database instance, or database cluster in the case of Aurora, with the same or newly selected characteristics can be used to restore the database in question.

Summary

We have now covered the RDS service, which gives us the ability to deliver fully managed relational databases from the cloud. We have learned about the different database engine types that are available in the RDS environment and the different features these database engines support. We have also learned how to deploy, manage, scale, and back up the RDS databases, how to make the database service highly available and secure, and how to scale the RDS clusters in several ways to increase cluster performance. In the next chapter, we will be introducing ourselves to ElastiCache.

Questions

1. Name the engines supported by RDS.
2. How do read replicas differ from Multi-AZ deployments with the MySQL, MariaDB, and PostgreSQL engines?
3. What are the two instance types in Amazon Aurora?
4. How long will an Amazon Aurora cluster be unavailable during snapshots?
5. What are the steps to restore a DB snapshot to an existing Aurora cluster?
6. You are implementing a BI system that will issue end of day reports. You currently run a Multi-AZ cluster. What is the easiest way to support your BI requirements?
7. You are developing an application with a MariaDB backend. The architecture defines two public subnets, one for the EC2 instances and one for the RDS instances. The RDS security group allows traffic from the EC2 instance subnet to the RDS subnet. How can you increase the security of your RDS cluster?

Further reading

- **RDS for MySQL**: https://docs.aws.amazon.com/AmazonRDS/latest/UserGuide/CHAP_MySQL.html
- **RDS for MariaDB**: https://docs.aws.amazon.com/AmazonRDS/latest/UserGuide/CHAP_MariaDB.html
- **RDS for PostgreSQL**: https://docs.aws.amazon.com/AmazonRDS/latest/UserGuide/CHAP_PostgreSQL.html
- **Amazon Aurora**: https://docs.aws.amazon.com/AmazonRDS/latest/AuroraUserGuide/CHAP_AuroraOverview.html
- **Aurora Multi-master Preview**: https://aws.amazon.com/about-aws/whats-new/2017/11/sign-up-for-the-preview-of-amazon-aurora-multi-master
- **Oracle on RDS**: https://docs.aws.amazon.com/AmazonRDS/latest/UserGuide/CHAP_Oracle.html
- **MS SQL on RDS**: https://docs.aws.amazon.com/AmazonRDS/latest/UserGuide/CHAP_SQLServer.html
- **Creating RDS Snapshots**: https://docs.aws.amazon.com/AmazonRDS/latest/UserGuide/USER_CreateSnapshot.html
- **Restoring RDS Snapshots**: https://docs.aws.amazon.com/AmazonRDS/latest/UserGuide/USER_RestoreFromSnapshot.html
- **RDS Automated Backups**: https://docs.aws.amazon.com/AmazonRDS/latest/UserGuide/USER_WorkingWithAutomatedBackups.html

12
Introduction to ElastiCache

One of the ways to deliver content much more quickly is to offload our infrastructure and deliver common responses from a middle, cached data layer that can provide much better responsiveness and higher performance for our application. When we talk about accelerating applications, we have several options on AWS and one of them is a dedicated, managed caching service called ElastiCache.

The following topics will be covered in this chapter:

- What is ElastiCache?
- Engine types
- Caching strategies
- Best practices

Technical requirements

A high-level understanding of common data access patterns in modern application designs is a prerequisite to understanding the way caching improves application performance.

What is ElastiCache?

ElastiCache is a managed service that helps simplify the delivery and consumption of caching services in the AWS cloud. Caching is a very important tool in the arsenal of any cloud architect since the way modern applications operate can always be improved. When delivering applications from the cloud, it is imperative to deliver operational excellence, which means we should always be striving to consume only the amount of resources that is required to deliver our application services at the level defined by the **Service Level Agreement (SLA)**.

In short, we want to deliver the maximum amount of performance for the minimum amount of cost. One way to optimize the performance of your application is to relieve the backend from constantly having to deliver the same result from the same request.

Think of a game on your device; thousands, possibly millions, of users are going to be requesting dynamic information such as who has the top score. Now, if we have thousands (or millions) of instances of the same request being sent to the backend database, that might become very expensive. Why not store the response in some kind of cache and deliver the response to all of those users without having to involve the database server at all? And if the leader changes and the scoreboard only shows the new leader and score in a few seconds or minutes, it will not affect the game at all.

Engine types

ElastiCache was designed to deliver exactly that kind of functionality to a broad range of applications. No matter whether your application requires just a simple place to store simple values that it retrieves from the database or whether it requires a scalable, highly available cluster that offers high-performance complex data types, ElastiCache can deliver the right solution for the right purpose. This is why we are able to choose from two different engine types in ElastiCache: Memcached and Redis.

Memcached

When a high-performance distributed in-memory caching system is required, Memcached is the answer. Commonly used in web applications to deliver fast performance for storing simple datasets and relieving the database of commonly returned responses, Memcached works as a distributed cluster so the data being stored on the nodes is redundant and can be delivered to multiple nodes or multiple threads within our application at the same time.

One use case for Memcached is storing user sessions. Say we have an application that handles sessions within the application. Now, that works fine on one server as the application is receiving all the traffic and handling it on its own. Now, scaling this application is going to be difficult since, if we slice it up into a cluster, each node is going to only be aware of its own sessions. Once a node dies and the load balancer redirects the user sessions to another node, all the user session information will be lost.

So instead of having stateful nodes, we should be introducing an external data store to handle sessions. One way to do this is to set up a Memcached cluster and direct all our nodes to write the sessions to Memcached instead. It is multi threaded so all the nodes can read and write at the same time, and it uses a simple connection and data model so very little needs to be done to redesign our applications to use Memcached.

Another really good scenario is when we require a high-performance cluster to store common responses from our database. Like in the example when we were calling the database thousands, possibly millions, of times to get the leader, we can set up a small Memcached cluster and store those responses from the first node that reads the database. All the consequent reads can be directed to the cache and thus our database load decreases dramatically.

Redis

When simple models supported by Memcached just won't do, we can use Redis. Redis is an in-memory data repository that can be used not only as a caching environment but also as a persistent database. It also has the ability to deliver message brokering with a publisher/subscriber model, allowing us to deliver services that do much more than just simple caching. While Memcached supports just simple values to be stored in the data structure, Redis is capable of storing advanced datasets such as strings, hashes, lists, sets, bitmaps, geospatial indexes, and so on, and supports performing complex transactions on the data with the Lua scripting language. It also supports the ability to create a cluster with one read/write node and up to five replicas. This means that, when there are a lot of concurrent writes from multiple nodes or multi-threaded applications, Redis might not be the correct choice, but it can still perform spectacularly well under heavy read load from multiple targets at once. Redis can also be deployed as a Multi-AZ cluster, making sure the data is replicated synchronously across availability zones for applications that require highly available caching, in-memory databases, or very fast messaging solutions.

Creating an ElastiCache service

1. To build an ElastiCache cluster, navigate tor the **ElastiCache Dashboard** in the management console and click on the **Get Started Now** button:

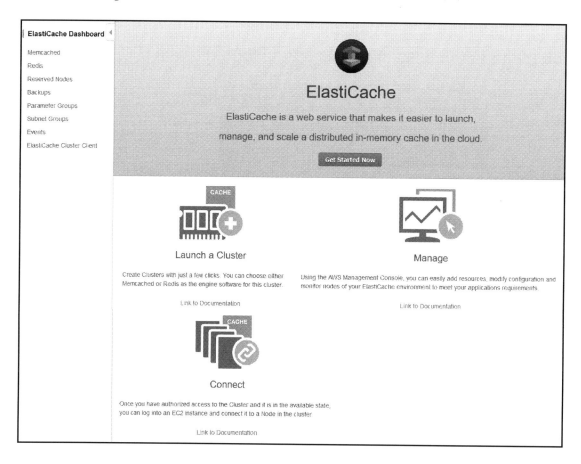

2. When creating the cluster, we need to select the engine and the settings applicable to each engine. We will take a look at the **Redis** cluster in this example. Once you have selected the Engine type and configured settings such as the engine version, the port on which to communicate, the parameter group for caching, and the node type, we can simply click **Create**. In this example, we are creating a `cache.t2.small` instance size:

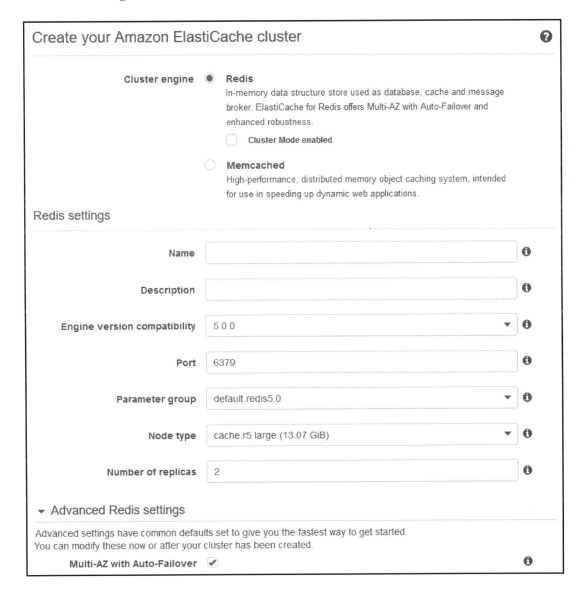

3. With Redis, we are also able to create a Multi-AZ cluster that will allow us to build a highly available cache environment. With Multi-AZ, we need to select the networking information such as the VPC and the subnets the cache nodes need to reside in:

4. We are also able to determine how to store the cache on the nodes in shards:

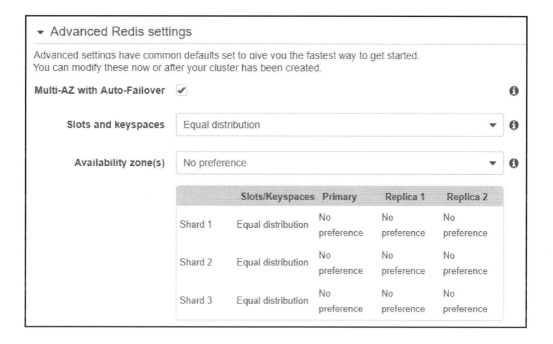

5. Lastly, we can configure the automatic backup features, define the backup window, and select the security policies to apply to the cluster:

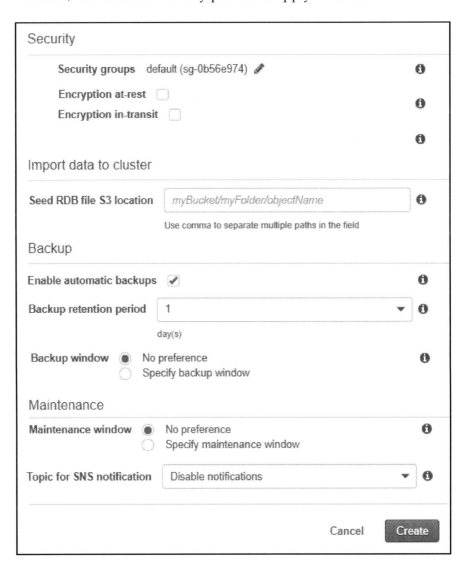

6. Once the cluster is created, we will be able to see it in the dashboard. The initial state will always be **creating**:

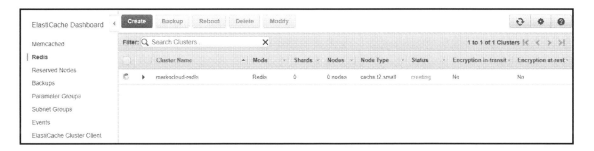

7. Once the cluster becomes available, we can click on it to get more details about the cluster we configured:

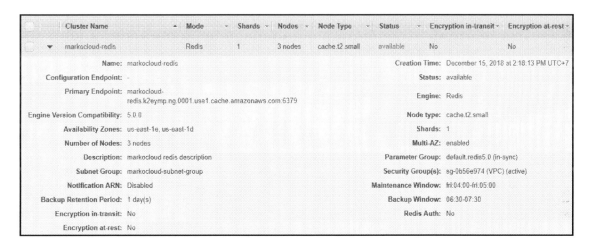

As you can see, with a few simple clicks it is easy to create and enable even a complex caching mechanism such as Redis. There is very little management required. This makes sure that we can focus on our application and the things that are important. For instance, we can make sure our environment is performing at its best, instead of focusing on maintaining and running Redis clusters, updating them, and making sure they are patched.

Caching strategies

When performing caching, there are several ways to control the behavior of our cache system depending on our requirements. These are called caching strategies, and we can put different caching strategies to work when we have different data requirements.

So, let's see how caching can be implemented to offload a database. Any time we are implementing a caching solution, we treat the cache as a separate data store that can hold some or all of the data being used in our application. The first read request will thus always be directed towards the cache, and the cache will either respond with a piece of data that it has – a so called **cache hit** - or it will not have the data and that would be a **cache miss**. When the data is not in the cache, there are several more steps that need to be undertaken. First, we need to direct the read at the database and request the database to provide us with the piece of data, or to perform a complex transaction that will create that piece of data. Once we have the response, we can write to the cache and update the contents so that if another node from our cluster or another user requests that same piece of data, it can be delivered straight from the cache. The following diagram shows how this model functions:

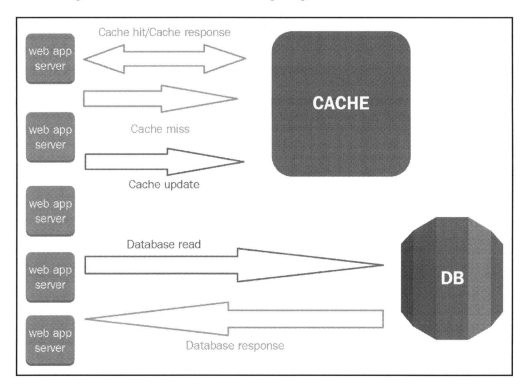

As mentioned before, there are essentially two ways to control the contents of an ElastiCache cluster:

- Write-through data loading
- Lazy data loading

Write-through

The write-through model assumes we are starting with an empty database and we are performing writes to the database, after which reads will start very shortly. We write each piece of data to the caching cluster and to the database, thus every read will potentially result in a cache hit and the read performance will be dramatically increased. This model is perfect for offloading databases with very simple queries, since performing complex transaction requests will still generate responses that cannot be cached through just a write process. Also, since we are caching all writes, this can be very heavy on the caching system and can cause a lot of cache churn and a lot of data that is never read to be written into the cache.

Lazy loading

Instead of writing everything into the cache, we can perform lazy loading, which is essentially caching all the responses from the database to the cache. Our application, starting from scratch, will always have a cache miss, but as soon as reads to the database are performed from the server, they are cached for other nodes to be able to get that same result. This approach might mean a high cache miss rate in the beginning, but we are able to store results from complex queries and the cache consumption is not as high as with the write-through approach. It is a bit heavier in the beginning but it makes up for it in the long run, especially if we need to cache frequent very heavy transaction responses from the database. To make sure the responses do not become stale, we can implement custom TTL values that help us expire the data in the cache after a certain time, and thus the lazy loading will start over for all the cached responses that expire, making sure we are getting fresh data into our application.

Best practices

When delivering ElastiCache clusters, the best practices will always depend on the type of data that needs to be stored. The best approach to choosing and scaling your caching solution is to ask yourself the following questions:

- What type of data am I storing?
- What is the volume, frequency, and concurrency of data coming in/out of the cache?
- Do I need support for transactions on the cache?
- Do I need high availability and high resilience of the caching cluster?

When choosing your cache, the first question will be the most important. The data type will determine which of the two services you can use: is it just values that I want to store, or is it complex datasets? We also need to ask ourselves what the data update volume is: do we need very high parallel performance, or is the application single-threaded? Is there any requirement to support transactions on the caching cluster, and should it be highly available and resilient? These questions are going to determine which caching engine to use and what best practices to apply against it. Is it simple datasets and simple values that we need to store? Then, go with Memcached. Is the application multi-homed or multi threaded? Memcached. No need for transactions and no need to deliver cross-availability zone clusters? Again, Memcached.

In pretty much all other cases, Redis should be considered as it can deliver high availability and read replicas, and supports complex datasets and the other features mentioned before. However, being quite a beast of a service, Redis has some specifics we need to look out for. Specifically, any commands requiring administrative privileges will not be available on an ElastiCache Redis cluster.

Being an in-memory database, Redis is tricky to manage when we need to persist the data on it. We can take snapshots of our Redis database state at any time, but of course that will consume additional memory so we need to make sure we have an instance that has enough memory for the active dataset of which the snapshot is being taken, and any data coming into the cluster while the snapshot is taking place. We also assign reserved memory to the Redis cluster and this is used for non-data operations such as replications and failover; we will need to scale our reserved memory accordingly. Configuring too little memory will potentially cause failover and replication to fail. When you run out of memory in a Redis cluster, you can always resize the environment quite easily:

1. We can simply log in to the management console, select our existing Redis cluster, and select a new size for the instances that are running Redis. In the console, select the cluster and click **Modify**:

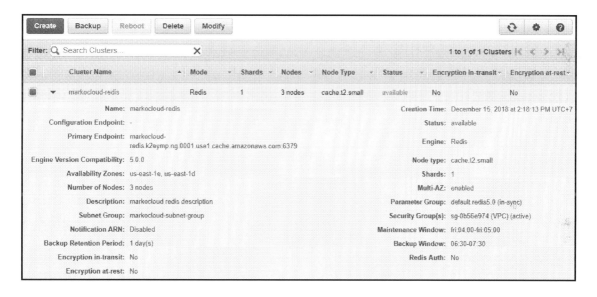

2. In the **Modify Cluster** dialog, simply select the new size; here, we have chosen to increase our **cache.t2.small** to any available larger size. Next, click **Modify**:

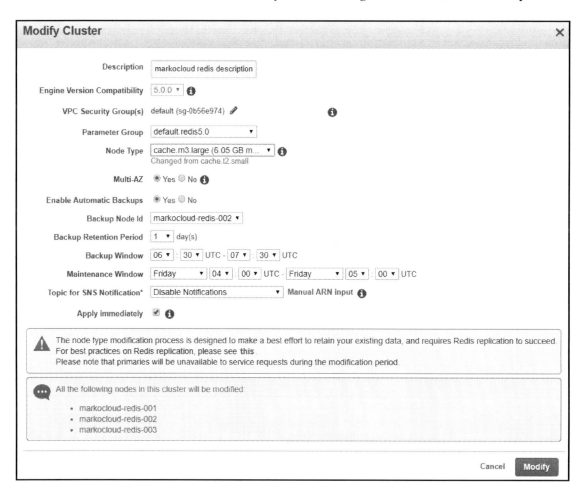

3. After you have completed the process, the cluster will be in the **modifying** state until the instances are replaced with bigger ones. When you have read replicas in your cluster, this operation will be performed without downtime:

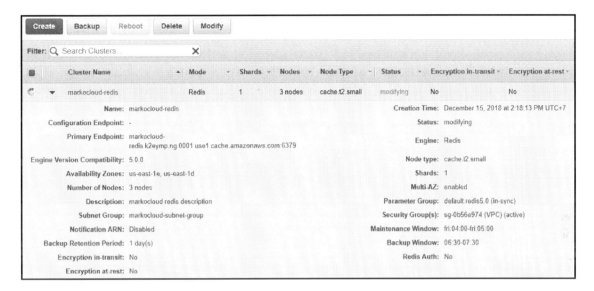

We should also be considering the caching strategy to use and the TTLs to deliver by determining whether we are storing the data as is or we need to retrieve responses via complex queries from the database. We will also need to determine the TTL for the data and decide on the caching strategy to best suit our needs.

Summary

We have taken a look at the two caching technologies, Redis and Memcached that AWS provides in its ElastiCache service. We have also looked at the different ways these two technologies can be used to deliver an efficient caching store that can be used to offload database burdens, store session and other simple data type information, and also deliver an in-memory database that supports complex queries and data types. We have looked at the caching strategies that allow us to control our data in the cache and got an overview that will help us to choose the right solution for our data and what we need to be careful of when using caching. In the next chapter, we will look into Amazon DynamoDB which is a fully managed NoSQL database service that provides fast and predictable performance with seamless scalability.

Questions

1. Name a few reasons for implementing caching in our applications.
2. What engines does ElastiCache support?
3. What is the difference between the ElastiCache engines when it comes to data?
4. An application is storing HTTP sessions in the local memory. How can we improve the availability of this application?
5. You need to store your data in a write-through manner to keep as much data as possible cached. One part of your application needs to perform complex transactions using the SQL query language on the cache. Which engine would you choose for this setup?
6. You have a multi threaded application using Redis. An administrator recommends adding three more Redis read/write nodes to the cluster. How will this improve the performance of the application?
7. During the workday, your application is using Memcached to store transaction responses using lazy loading. Every night, your BI system needs to replay a lot of these transactions for the end-of-day analysis. Your managers are complaining about getting data that is several days old whenever the BI system runs. How would you fix this problem?

Further reading

- **ElastiCache for Redis**: https://docs.aws.amazon.com/AmazonElastiCache/latest/red-ug/WhatIs.html
- **ElastiCache for Memcached**: https://docs.aws.amazon.com/AmazonElastiCache/latest/mem-ug/WhatIs.html
- **Caching Strategies and Best Practices**: https://docs.aws.amazon.com/AmazonElastiCache/latest/red-ug/BestPractices.html

13
Amazon DynamoDB - A NoSQL Database Service

Modern applications need to store and process many different types of data. From files to streams, to relational data, to simple values; each type of data has an appropriate backend store that can be used in AWS. Amazon DynamoDB is a NoSQL database service that can be a great fit for an application requiring a backend that can store many NoSQL-compatible data types with reliable performance at scale.

The following topics will be covered in this chapter:

- Introduction to DynamoDB
- ACID versus BASE
- Relational versus non-relational DB
- How DynamoDB works
- DynamoDB core concepts
- Read consistency
- Creating a DynamoDB table
- DynamoDB provisioned throughput
- DynamoDB partitions and distribution
- Accessing DynamoDB
- User authentication and access control
- DynamoDB service ceiling

Technical requirements

To follow along with this chapter, a basic understanding of application data types and the HTTP protocol is required. An additional understanding of NoSQL databases can be beneficial to the learning process. Please refer to the GitHub link for this chapter: `https://github.com/PacktPublishing/AWS-Certified-SysOps-Administrator-Associate-Guide/tree/master/Chapter13`.

Introduction to DynamoDB

DynamoDB is a *NoSQL* or *Not only SQL* database solution designed for web-scale applications and delivered as a managed service from the AWS cloud. It allows us to create a NoSQL database with a few clicks or one CLI command. DynamoDB is designed for storing datasets of unlimited sizes at predictable performance rates at any scale. DynamoDB uses standard HTTP methods for storing and retrieving data. These capabilities are augmented with the use of JMESPath query language so that we can perform a lot of server-side functionality when crawling through our data.

ACID versus BASE

How we write, read, and use our data is the determining factor that will define which database type to use. There are generally two types of requirements for data storage in databases that require two very different approaches to storing data, and these are governed by two acronyms: **Atomicity, Consistency, Isolation, and Durability (ACID)** and **Basically Available, Soft state, Eventual consistency (BASE)**. Like the two liquids with opposing pH factors, ACID and BASE are two completely different approaches to storing data that are incompatible with each other.

ACID compliant data

ACID compliant data is required to have these abilities:

- To be accessed at the lowest level of the dataset (Atomicity)
- For the same data to be returned from all nodes at all times (Consistency)
- To isolate concurrent transactions from each other (Isolation)
- Once the data is stored, it is stored permanently and can be recovered even in the case of system failures (Durability)

Relational databases are usually designed to be ACID compliant and enable the same data to be stored in the database by only one writer at a time. Relational databases introduce a locking mechanism to prevent data from being written at the same time by multiple writers (Isolation), and that feature means that we can keep a lock on newly written data until it is replicated across the cluster (Consistency). This locking also enables us to only change atomic parts of each piece of data by locking a table, index, or part of an index and writing changes to it (Atomicity). The data in relational databases is stored durably and there are special provisions usually put in place that enable us to make sure the data that is stored will be recoverable and restorable in case of failures (transaction logs, snapshots, backups, and so on).

BASE-compliant data

BASE-compliant data essentially throws those concepts out the window and starts with a clean slate. It relies on the findings of the CAP Theorem, also known as Brewer's Theorem, which states that there are three stem requirements that modern, highly distributed, scalable applications will strive to deliver: Consistency, Availability, and Partition Tolerance. The crux of the research is that only two of those can ever be delivered simultaneously if we want the system to operate in real time.

For example, if we want the system to be fully consistent at all times, this can only be done by sacrificing availability or partition tolerance. A single-partition system is fully consistent and available at all times but there is no tolerance of failure. A multi-partition system can be designed to be consistent, but to achieve consistency all partitions need to be synchronized at the same time, meaning the system will be unavailable during the consistency window. We can make this system partition-tolerant and available, but it will never be fully consistent due to this same fact.

So, BASE-compliant databases were introduced as a way to acknowledge what the CAP theorem tells us about distributed systems. If you want to scale your relational ACID database beyond a certain number of nodes, you will have to sacrifice one of the features of the CAP theorem and then your database will not be ACID compliant anymore. That is why most modern NoSQL solutions opt for unlimited scalability across multiple nodes, which delivers partition tolerance and high inherent availability over consistency.

In NoSQL databases, we talk about eventual consistency as a way to describe what is happening in the backend: data is written to one node and then replicated over to others. While the data is being replicated, the system is available and will still serve either old or new data, making the data inconsistent during a replication window. This is an underlying reality of distributed systems that cannot be overcome, and we essentially need to embrace it in our application design and run with it.

Relational versus non-relational DB

So, besides ACID and BASE compliance, what is the real difference between relational and non-relational databases? Essentially, we have the ability to provide roughly the same features from both of these database types: storing data, both can do that; support for transactions and scripting, yup, we can do that on both as well. It's just that the database types are better at doing one specific thing. Relational databases are better at scripting, complex transactions, table joins, and so on, whereas non-relational databases are better at storing huge datasets of simple values that we need to retrieve at very high performance rates; some non-relational databases support scripting and transactions, but they are much less efficient at it.

The biggest difference is probably in the datasets themselves. Relational databases are designed to store data according to a schema; imagine a table with columns and rows. Each column has a purpose and each row is treated as a separate entry with atomic pieces of data that can be addressed separately. With non-relational databases, an entry could be any kind of piece of data: a document, a value for a key, a map, a graph, a stream, and so on. Non-relational databases typically do not have a schema and can store variable sizes and types of entries in the same table.

Now, let's compare the data for a real-world example; relational database entries will look like this:

Index	Name	Surname	Position	Active
1001	Johan	Dohe	Engineer	Y
1002	Ben	Dopher	Administrator	Y

We can see that each entry has its own index and each entry has specific values for each field.

In a NoSQL database, the data might be stored in a JSON format like so:

```
{
  "Index":"1001",
  "Name":"Johan",
  "Surname":"Dohe"
  "Position":"Engineer"
  "Active":"Y"
}
```

Essentially, instead of formatting the table, we create a document repository, and when we upload the document, the service might present those values as entries in a table to achieve the same purpose.

How about when we need to change the data and add more information to the user? Let's say we want to give the group information only for all the administrators in our database. With a relational database, we would need to extend the schema to accommodate new entries for each index, whereas with the NoSQL database, there is no schema. We can simply add information to our user by adding more key-value pairs like so:

```
{
  "Index":"1001",
  "Name":"Ben",
  "Surname":"Dopher"
  "Position":"Administrator"
  "Active":"Y"
  "Group Membership": [
  {
  "Sales":"Administator",
  },
  {
  "Tech":"Member",
  }]
  }
```

This adds more attributes to the entry on the fly without having to extend the schema of the database, a clever feature of NoSQL databases that can make quite a difference.

DynamoDB core concepts

In DynamoDB, the core concepts for storing data are the following:

- Tables, into which we store items
- Items, which are composed of attributes
- Attributes, which represent the data being stored in DynamoDB

DynamoDB is a distributed database running on a large number of servers, so the data needs to be stored in some kind of order. The way we determine the storage backend is with the primary key. The primary key is the attribute of an item we select for providing an even distribution of data across the cluster. There are also secondary indexes available in DynamoDB, so we can perform data ordering on attributes other than the primary key. To track changes to DynamoDB, the database service allows us to enable DynamoDB streams that help us track changes being made in the tables.

Tables

A table is a collection of items. When creating a DynamoDB table, we will always need to specify a name that is unique in the region; however, we can have multiple tables with the same name in different regions. We will also need to assign a primary and optional sort key for the data being stored into the table. Furthermore, we are able to adjust additional properties such as any secondary indexes, the capacity units, and optionally the autoscaling of capacity units, which we will discuss later in this chapter. We can also encrypt the tables upon creation and decide whether we want to use the default encryption or a custom key that we can create and manage in the **Key Management Service** (**KMS**). Once a table is created, we can start creating items.

Items

Items are collections of attributes that are written to and read from a DynamoDB table. The maximum size of a DynamoDB item is 400 KB, which includes all the attribute names and values. We can issue standard HTTP PUT/GET/UPDATE/DELETE requests to perform **Create, Read, Update, and Delete** (**CRUD**) operations. We are able to address each item individually by specifying the primary key and a sort key if one exists. We are also able to perform batch read and batch write operations against a table. Batch read operations are able to retrieve up to 100 items of up to 16 MB in size, whereas batch write operations can create up to 25 items at a time.

Attributes

The attributes within an item in DynamoDB are represented as key-value pairs. Each value can have a single entry or can consist of a list of entries, a map, or a set of other key-value pairs. The values support nesting of other values within an attribute up to 32 levels deep, as long as the item does not exceed the 400 KB maximum size; this means we can store complete documents within an attribute.

Naming rules and data types

All DynamoDB tables and attributes need to have a UTF-8-encoded name, and there are some rules to how we can name them:

- Table and index names can have 3 to 255 characters which can include both upper case and lowercase letters, numbers, underscores, dashes, and dots.

- Attribute names can have 1 to 255 characters.
- When using expressions, there are certain reserved words that cannot be used as attribute names. Please refer to the *Expression Attributes and Reserved Words* links in the *Further reading* section of this chapter in case you need to use reserved words as attribute names.

Within attributes, the DynamoDB service supports the following data types:

- **Scalar Types**: A number, string, binary, Boolean, and null
- **Document Types**: A complex structure with nested attributes, such as a list or a map
- **Set Types**: Multiple scalar values represented as string set, number set, and binary set

Here are some examples of these data types that would be stored as an attribute written in JSON format and their representation in a DynamoDB table.

Scalar type key-value pairs

For each attribute name such as `username` the value is one single string such as `thownsr` in our example:

```
{
 "username" : thownsr,
 "lastname" : "Thowns",
 "firstname" : "Rick",
}
```

These would be represented in a DynamoDB table as follows:

username	last_name	first_name
thownsr	Thowns	Rick

Document type – a map attribute

Here, for each attribute name there are several values represented as a mapping of nested attributes to nested values:

```
{
"date_of_bith" :
 [
 "year" : 1979,
```

```
"month" : 09,
"day" : 25
]
}
```

This would be represented in a DynamoDB table as follows:

username	last_name	first_name	date_of_birth
thownsr	Thowns	Rick	year: 1979 month: 09 day: 25

Set type – a set of strings

Here, for each attribute name there are several values represented as a comma-separated set of string attribute values:

```
{
  "group_membership" :
  ["Users", "Admins", "Engineers" ]
}
```

This would be represented in a DynamoDB table as follows:

username	last_name	first_name	date_of_birth	group_membership
thownsr	Thowns	Rick	year: 1979 month: 09 day: 25	Users, Admins, Engineers

Primary and sort key

When we create a table, we are required to select one of the attributes from our dataset as the primary key. As we have already discussed, the primary key is used to distribute the data across the cluster and to identify the item when performing CRUD operations. The primary key should be selected so that the data is easily identifiable and distributed evenly across the keys. We should always use a many-to-less relationship when choosing our primary key to ensure that the distribution of data will be as even as possible.

For example, in our DynamoDB table with our users, it would be wise to choose the **username** as the primary key as it is unique and it would ensure that each set of attributes for each username is evenly distributed across the cluster. Finding a user's other attributes is done by specifying the primary key, in this case the username, since DynamoDB keeps a data index that contains the primary key and its storage location.

But sometimes it is not efficient to sort the data with the key that will give us the best distribution, and for these kinds of situations we can add an optional sort key to our data. So, for example, we can use the `last_name` attribute as the sort key in our table, ensuring that the index is created with both the `username` and `last_name` attributes, meaning we are able to retrieve the attributes for each item by simply specifying the last name.

Secondary indexes

If we need to project even more attributes into an index, we have the ability to create secondary indexes. There are two types of secondary indexes available in DynamoDB:

- **Local secondary index (LSI)**: A local secondary index gives us the ability to project another sort key into the index and allows for additional data access patterns to be created for our items. A local secondary index supports both strong and consistent reads across the key data and is created locally at the key partition, meaning each key will have a local index created for it. A local secondary index consumes the read and write capacity units of our table. For example, let's say we are tracking our user logins with timestamps in a DynamoDB table. Each time one of our users logs in, they create an entry with their username and a timestamp. We can select the timestamp as the local secondary index, and this way we can filter the login dates according to a time frame that we specify in our query. With a local secondary index, we always need to specify the key in our query as the index is local to the key.

- **Global secondary index (GSI)**: With global secondary indexes, we can achieve an even more advanced design of secondary indexes, as the primary key and the sort key of a global secondary index are going to be separate from the partition key and the sort key defined in the table. A global secondary index thus allows us the ability to create a completely different set of attributes with which we can access our data. For example, we can project the timestamp in the global secondary index, and by searching on a particular time range with our query, we will now be able to retrieve not just one user's login times but the times of all users in our table. The global secondary index also has its own read and write capacity units assigned to it, but is only able to retrieve eventually consistent reads from the table.

DynamoDB streams

Another way to track changes in a DynamoDB table is to enable streams. A stream is able to output all changes being made in the DynamoDB table to an interface where other services are listening for changes.

For example, when our users log in, we want to have a system that tracks the login time and performs some kind of advanced security check on top of each login event. As soon as the user logs in to the environment, a login entry will be created in the DynamoDB table. That record can be instantly output into the stream and a security service can listen on the backend to the stream and perform the necessary security check for each entry.

The streams can output information about each item that is being changed and we can configure the delivery of just the partition key, the old data in the table, the newly written data in the table, or both the new and the old data simultaneously. DynamoDB streams can also be utilized to trigger lambda functions, to provide real-time analytics, or output the changes of a DynamoDB table to another DynamoDB table or any other compatible AWS service.

Read consistency

Due to the reality of the CAP Theorem, discussed in the *ACID versus BASE* section of this chapter, DynamoDB chooses availability and partition tolerance over consistency. The consistency of DynamoDB is still remarkable, as any changes to an item will be replicated to the backend within a second of the write occurring. But a second can be a fairly long time when we possibly have thousands or even tens of thousands of concurrent reads happening every second against our DynamoDB table.

This fact essentially means that a piece of data that we have just written might be inconsistently delivered to thousands of clients during the time it takes to replicate the new data across the cluster. We try to mitigate this fact by providing the ability to perform both eventually consistent and strongly consistent reads from our DynamoDB table. We are able to select either read type for each and every query we perform on a DynamoDB table.

Eventually consistent reads

Eventually consistent reads are essential reads that are performed against one node of our cluster. When an item is updated, an eventually consistent read will return either an old piece of data or a new piece of data. If our operation is not time-sensitive, then eventually consistent reads are a great approach.

For example, if we have a game scoreboard that we record in DynamoDB and we have millions of users playing the game and viewing the scoreboard, it would be very inefficient to make sure the new scores are up to date at the exact time as they probably change quite a lot. Also, when a user sets a new high score, it is not important if the other users see this change exactly at the time it happens or a few seconds after the score was recorded.

Strongly consistent reads

When we have time-sensitive queries where we require the data to be correct at the exact time the change goes into effect, we can strongly use consistent reads. Essentially, when performing strongly consistent reads, we need to read the data from two sources. This means that we can achieve double the capacity when using essentially consistent reads versus strongly consistent reads. This drawback, however, is a requirement if we want the correct data to be returned.

For example, let's say we have three cluster members: `server01`, `server02`, and `server03`. When updating an item value from *OLD* to *NEW*, our write will be received by `server02` and the write will be committed to local disk. In that moment, before the replication happens to `server01` and `server03`, all reads from the other two members will still return *OLD* as the correct value. If we perform an eventually consistent read, we might get *OLD* from `server01` and `server03` and *NEW* from `server02`. A strongly consistent read at this moment performs two reads and might return the following:

- `server01` and `server02`: OLD and NEW
- `servero2` and `server03`: NEW and OLD
- `server01` and `server03`: OLD and OLD

In the case of `server01` and `server03`, the value will be considered strongly consistent due to Byzantine redundancy. The term Byzantine redundancy comes from the court of Byzantium, where there would be three judges giving verdicts; thus, if one says *guilty* and the other two *not guilty*, the majority vote would stand. In the same case, the majority vote of two equal values would determine that the OLD value is correct.

In the case of both of the other situations, where there are two different responses, the service would have to perform an additional read from `server03` or `server01`. Since the replication starts immediately after the item is stored, the responses of the servers in question might have changed in the time it took to re-read the data from the backend, so in this case the third write would either return the value as NEW if the replication has been completed, or OLD if the replication to that node has not been completed yet.

So, for time sensitive operations, it is crucial to understand the data structure of a distributed system like DynamoDB and how consistency is delivered and determined. Strongly consistent means that we are confident that the majority of the servers are responding with this value. The new data is thus not considered consistent until it has been replicated to a majority of servers, which can affect the way a time-sensitive operation is performed.

Creating a DynamoDB table

1. To create a DynamoDB table, we can simply open up the DynamoDB Dashboard and select **Create table**:

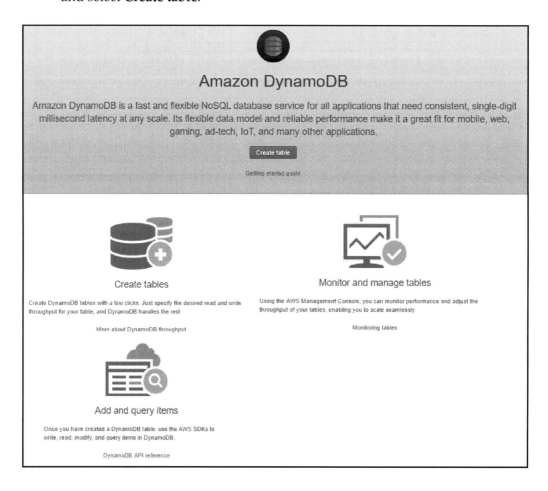

2. In the **Create DynamoDB** table dialog, we will need to assign a name and a primary key. Optionally, we can select **Add sort key** and add a sort key to our table if our data model requires it:

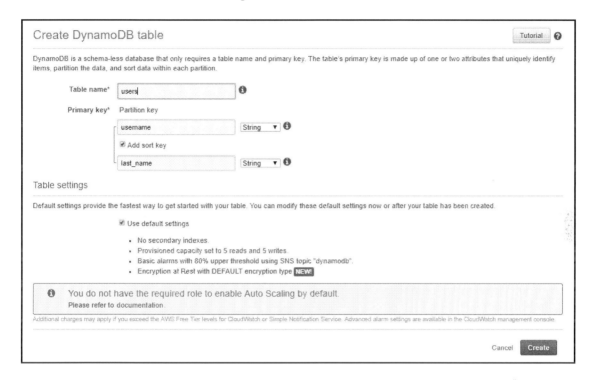

3. We also have the ability to deselect **Use default settings**; this will give us the ability to customize the table while we are provisioning it. Customizing the table gives us the ability to select read/write capacity mode and create secondary indexes. To create a secondary index, click on **+Add index**:

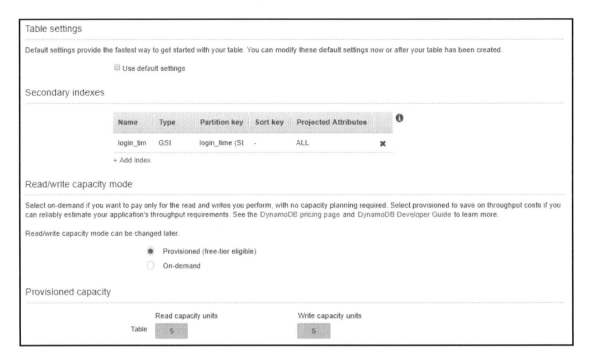

4. In the **Add index** dialog, we need to select the primary key. Using the same key would create a local secondary index, while adding a new primary key will add a global secondary index. We can also add a sort key to the table and we will of course have to name it. We can also select the attributes we would like to project into the index:

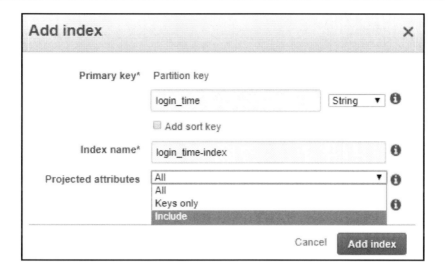

5. Further down, we can customize the provisioned capacity if we selected provisioned capacity mode and add the read and write capacity units. We can also configure capacity autoscaling, which we will discuss in the *DynamoDB provisioned* throughput section of this chapter:

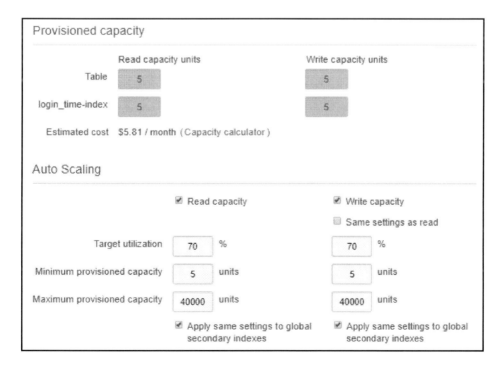

6. We are also able to select a role for Auto Scaling or use the **DynamoDB AutoScaling Linked Role**. Right at the bottom of the dialog, we are able to select the encryption and decide whether we want to use the default encryption key or use our own CMK from the KMS service. After we have completed the customization, we can click **Create** to create the table:

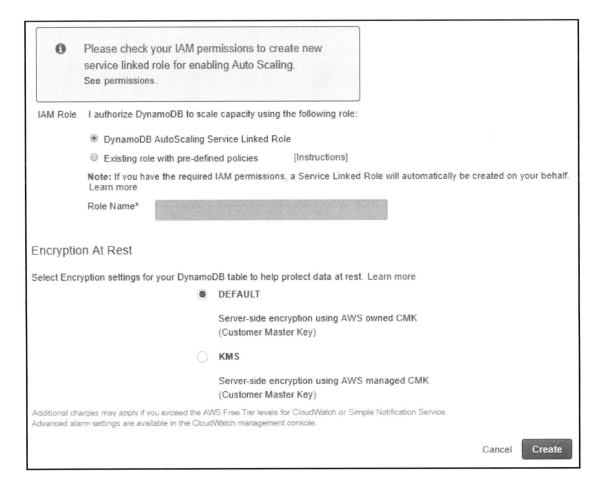

7. Once the table is provisioned, we can manage it from the DynamoDB management console and address it via the CLI and SDK:

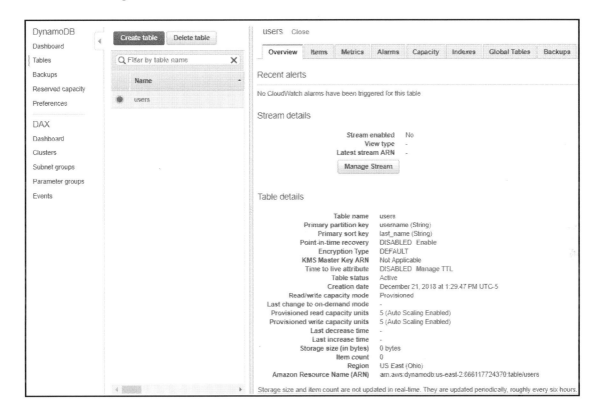

DynamoDB provisioned throughput

There are two ways of assigning the capacity units to our DynamoDB service: provisioned capacity units mode on-demand capacity mode. The default way of operating is with provisioned capacity units. This mode of operation requires us to specify the capacity units that we are going to be consuming from DynamoDB. Essentially, we reserve the capacity on the backend and ensure that the backend always works with the assigned set of capacity units.

The provisioned capacity mode of operation is useful when we have predictable application performance or when we have a certain SLA or budget that we do not wish to exceed. Provisioned capacity mode is also eligible for the free tier, meaning it is the right approach for any proof-of-concept or small-scale application.

If our traffic pattern is unknown or unpredictable, we can still use provisioned mode with auto-scaling, where we set the minimum and maximum provisioned capacity and the target utilization. The capacity units will increase above the target utilization to allow spikes in traffic and decrease if we are well below the target utilization, helping us to save money on the provisioned capacity.

Determining required read/write capacity units

When using provisioned capacity mode, we will need to determine the capacity units for our database table, based on the characteristics of the **read capacity units (RCUs)** and **write capacity units (WCUs)**:

- A RCU is defined as one strongly consistent read or two eventually consistent reads of 4 KB in size.
- A WCU is defined as one write request of 1 KB in size.

For example, if we know our application is sending in data at a rate of 1 MB per second in writes of exactly 1 KB in size, then we need to assign 1,024 capacity units to the application. The writes are rounded up to the 1 KB unit size, so if your 1 MB per second rate is composed of 500-byte writes, then you will consume 1 WCU for each 500-byte write. This means you will require approximately 2,000 WCUs to achieve the same 1 MBps throughput to the table. If your writes are up to 2 KB in size, then each write will consume two WCUs, meaning a 500-byte and 2 KB write will both require about 2,000 WCUs at 1 MB per second, while a 4 KB write will consume 4,000 WCUs.

Reads are also rounded up to 4 KB when they are smaller, meaning our 500-byte, 1 KB, 2 KB, and 4 KB items would each consume 1 RCU regardless of their size. Reads of more than 4 KB would of course consume two or more RCUs.

This pattern means that we need to design our item sizes correctly to make the best use of the DynamoDB tables. As mentioned before, the item sizes can be up to 400 KB in size; such an item would consume 400 WCUs when written, 100 RCUs when read with strong consistency, and 50 RCUs when read with eventual consistency, as eventually consistent reads can perform up to two 4 KB reads per RCU.

On-demand capacity mode

The second approach to unknown or unpredictable patterns is on-demand mode, where we do not control the capacity but instead rely on AWS to scale the service on demand to meet the traffic volume automatically. This can scale to thousands and even tens or hundreds of thousands of reads and writes per second completely seamlessly. Essentially, we point our application toward a DynamoDB table and then the service determines the sustained performance of our application and allows us to peak at double the sustained rate.

For example, if your application is writing at a sustained rate of 10,000 capacity units, the service will allow the handling of up to 20,000 capacity units of peak traffic. Once our application's sustained rate increases or decreases, the peak rate will be automatically adjusted up or down accordingly.

DynamoDB partitions and distribution

We already mentioned that DynamoDB is a distributed cluster that stores our data in a redundant and distributed manner. The data is stored in partitions, which are distributed and replicated across availability zones for fault tolerance, high availability, and redundancy. The partitions are fully managed by AWS, but we can determine the pattern of distribution of our data across partitions with the partition key.

DynamoDB will, in principle, always assign enough partitions to your table to handle the provisioned capacity for your tables. But it is on us to make sure the performance is always up to the capacity defined, since the data is stored in the partitions using the partition key. If our partition keys have a bad distribution, then we could create a so-called *hot partition* where a lot of items with the same partition key are stored.

For example, when our partition key is username and the sort key is login_time, we could get a lot of entries for one particular username and all those will be sitting on the same backend partition. This does not become a problem until we try to perform operations that will consume more than 3,000 RCUs or 1,000 WCUs on that particular partition, as this is the limit of the per-key performance that DynamoDB can muster.

The way DynamoDB determines the partition is by running a hash operation against the partition key values when we write them. This means that a good distribution of our partition keys is crucial to the performance of our tables. When there is no other option but to use the same partition key, we can always add a calculated suffix to the data instead of using the same entry for the partition key for each time the user logs in:

username	login_time
thownsr	2018-09-11-18:30:07
thownsr	2018-09-13-12:18:46
thownsr	2018-09-15-19:21:13

We can use a calculated suffix derived from the data of the login and make sure our application understands that `username.wxyz` is the same as `username` without the suffix, like so:

username	login_time
thownsr.2106	2018-09-11-18:30:07
thownsr.2116	*2018-09-13-12:18:46*
thownsr.2095	2018-09-15-19:21:13

In this example, we get three different partition keys for the same username by calculating all the numbers in the date like so:

$$2018+09+13+12+18+46 = 2116$$

This makes the suffix in this example `.2116` and the partition key `thownsr.2116`.

This approach gives us a whole new range of partition keys that will have a whole new range of hashes, thereby avoiding having a hot partition without having to change the data model.

Accessing DynamoDB

We can access the DynamoDB table through the AWS management console directly by clicking on the items tab in the table selection and reading and writing items there directly. This is, however, inefficient, as no modern application would have us enter values manually into an interface that is grammatically accessible.

The most powerful feature of DynamoDB is of course its REST API where we can send standard HTTP `PUT`/`GET`/`UPDATE`/`DELETE` requests. With this programmatic approach, we can send commands to the DynamoDB table through the AWS CLI. It is very well integrated with all the SDKs, and, of course, we can always perform API calls straight to the DynamoDB API.

Accessing DynamoDB through the CLI

When accessing the DynamoDB service via the CLI, we can use the AWS CLI integrated shorthand or direct JSON commands and JMESpath scripting. In the next example, we will be creating the same DynamoDB table as before: users, with primary key (also known as the **HASH** key) username and lastname as the sort key (also known as the **RANGE** key). Once we have our AWS CLI set up, we simply send the `aws dynamodb create-table` command with the following attributes:

- `--table name`: Defines the name of the table
- `--attribute-definitions`: Defines the attributes
- `AttributeName`: The name of our attribute (not the value!)
- `AttributeType`: The type of value (S = string, N = number, B = binary)
- `--key-schema`: Defines the primary and sort key to use
- `KeyType`: HASH defines the primary key, RANGE defines the sort key
- `--provisione-throughput`: Defines the RCUs and WCU

So, now, let's put all of this together:

```
aws dynamodb create-table \
--table-name users \
--attribute-definitions \
AttributeName=username,AttributeType=S \
AttributeName=last_name,AttributeType=S \
--key-schema AttributeName=username,KeyType=HASH
AttributeName=lastn_name,KeyType=RANGE \
--provisioned-throughput ReadCapacityUnits=100,WriteCapacityUnits=400
```

Now that we have the table, we can address the table and write items with the `aws dynamodb put-item` command:

- `--table-name`: Specifies the table we want to write into
- `--item`: Defines the item in key-value pairs
- `"keyname": {"data type":"value"}`: Defines the key we are writing to, the data type (S/N/B), and the value of the data being written

So, let's put this all together:

```
aws dynamodb put-item \
--table-name users \
--item '{ \
"username": {"S": "thownsr"}, \
"last_name": {"S": "Thowns"}, \
"first_name": {"S": "Rick"} }'
```

If we want to know how many capacity units our write has consumed, we can add the `--return-consumed-capacity TOTAL` switch at the end of our command to determine the TOTAL number of capacity units the command consumed in the API response.

To read the whole item from the DynamoDB table, we can issue the `aws dynamodb get-item` command, where we need to specify the `--table-name` for naming our table and `--key`, which is the primary and optionally the sort key for the item. To retrieve the data from the DynamoDB table for our user with the primary key `username:thownsr` and sort key `lastn_name:Thowns`, we would issue the following command:

```
aws dynamodb get-item \
--table-name users \
--key '{ \
"username": {"S": "thownsr"}, \
"last_name": {"S": "Thowns"},
```

The response from the query would be the following:

```
HTTP/1.1 200 OK
 x-amzn-RequestId: <RequestId>
 x-amz-crc32: <Checksum>
 Content-Type: application/x-amz-json-1.0
 Content-Length: <PayloadSizeBytes>
 Date: <Date>
 {
"Item": {
        "username": { "S": ["thownsr"] },
       "last_name": { "S": ["Thowns"] },
```

```
        "first_name": { "S": ["Rick"] },
    }
}
```

For each command, we can source the information from a file by specifying `file://input-file.json` as the value for each shorthand command. This gives us the ability to easily import large datasets from JSON-formatted files into DynamoDB. As you can see, the DynamoDB service can be easily controlled through the CLI and this gives us a lot of power when performing queries.

Table scans and queries

But what if we find ourselves in a situation where we are unable to determine the correct key to use to retrieve the data? Then, we can use a table scan. A scan operation is simply an operation that will essentially read all the items from the table, starting with the first item and then continuing with the next until it has read through all the items in the table. With a table scan, we can retrieve all the attributes stored in all the items, or we can perform filtering on the data with a filtering expression to match only the data you are looking for.

Scanning and then filtering, however, is inefficient. We always get charged for the whole scan, even if the data returned is highly filtered. This is why we should always try to perform the operation as a query. For a query, we will need to supply the primary key and an operator to be run against the sort key. For example, if we are only retrieving a certain date range from the sort key for our user logging in, we can construct a query with the date range, and the data-retrieval process will find the appropriate items on the server and return them in the response.

Pagination and limits

To further optimize reads against the DynamoDB tables, we have the ability to paginate the results; essentially, it's returning results in pages of up to 1 MB in size. The results of a scan or query operation are thus returned in pages, and if the result we are looking for is on the page, we can stop the query or scan operation once the required value has been retrieved.

We also have the ability to limit the number of results from scan or query operations. Let's say we want to pick the first 100 items from the table to perform a test on our data. We can put a limit on the number of returned results and thus get only the first 100 items.

Conditional and atomic writes

There is some transactional support available in DynamoDB, and those transactions can be executed against data in the table with conditional queries and atomic writes.

For example, let's say we want to force users to change their password when it is 90 days old or older. Before the user is logged in, we can perform a query against the table where we specify `last_password_change_date` as the attribute and the value calculated as follows:

```
current_date - last_password_change_date => 90 days
```

We then set the write condition to change `force_password_change` to `true` and force them to change their password if the condition matches.

User authentication and access control

DynamoDB integrates with IAM to control access to both the service and the data in the tables. There will be two types of access for DynamoDB granted to our IAM users:

- **Administrative access**: IAM users or roles with permissions to create and modify DynamoDB tables
- **Data access**: IAM users or roles with specific permissions to read, write, update, or delete items in one specific table

When designing your application, you can therefore give the code the ability to provision its own tables; this is very useful when your application works in cycles.

For example, an application that records sessions could be trusted to automatically create a new sessions table at the start of the day, and remove the old sessions table from the previous day. This would keep the DynamoDB table lean and clean as there would never be any session data more than 24 hours old in the table.

The same approach can be used for a sales application that records sales metrics each month. The application could be trusted to create a new table every month with the production capacity units, but maintain the old tables for analytics. Every month it would reduce the previous monthly table's capacity units to whatever would be required for analytics to run.

On the other hand, some applications need only strict access to certain data in a particular DynamoDB table. For example, we can create a role and attach it to a federated identity for a mobile application that uses DynamoDB as a backend catalog. We could very well lock down the application to only that one particular table by adding a deny rule on anything other than the table, to prevent any leaks of data through a potential misconfiguration of the application or AWS security.

To achieve this, we could implement a policy that looks like this:

```
{
  "Version": "2012-10-17",
  "Statement":[{
  "Effect":"Allow",
  "Action":["dynamodb:*","s3:*"],
  "Resource":["arn:aws:dynamodb:us-east-1:111222333444:table/catalogue"]
  },
  {
  "Effect":"Deny",
  "Action":["dynamodb:*","s3:*"],
  "NotResource":["arn:aws:dynamodb:us-east- 1:111222333444:table/catalogue"]
  },
  ]
  }
```

The `Allow` effect specifies a specific DynamoDB table and the `Deny` effect specifies anything that is NOT the specific DynamoDB table. This means that, even if any misconfiguration, breach, or fault in the application happens, access to any other table in DynamoDB is explicitly denied and takes precedence over any other allow.

When applying permissions to a DynamoDB table, we should of course always remember the best practice of least privilege when defining permissions, and the practice of using a role for our applications and users.

DynamoDB service ceiling

Like other services in AWS, DynamoDB has some default soft limits set on the service to prevent us from consuming the backend resources unintentionally. If required, the service soft limits can be extended by contacting AWS. The soft limits in DynamoDB are set as follows:

- Depending on the region, each DynamoDB table will be limited either to 10,000/40,000 read and 10,000/40,000 write capacity units per table and double that for all tables in the account in provisioned mode. There is no soft limit on the cumulative RCU/WCU capacity for all on-demand capacity mode tables.
- Up to 256 tables of unlimited size per region per account.
- A maximum of 20 global secondary indexes per table.

There are also some limitations in the service itself due to the service design, and these are as follows:

- One RCU = one strongly consistent read of up to 4 KB or two eventually consistent reads of up to 4 KB
- One WCU = one write of up to 1 KB in size
- Transactional requests require 2 RCUs and 1 WCU to update the item
- A maximum of five local secondary indexes
- Partition key values are limited to between 1 and 2048 bytes in length
- Sort key values are limited to between 1 and 1024 bytes in length
- Strings and binary values are limited to 400 KB in size
- Number values can have up to 38 digits of precision
- Nested attributes in values can be up to 32 levels deep
- Only two processes can read from a DynamoDB stream shard at the same time

There are some additional limitations for queries, transactions, and APIs, and, as we have mentioned before, DynamoDB has some reserved words that cannot be used as attribute names. For a complete list of these, please see the links in the *Further reading* section of this chapter.

Summary

We have learned that the DynamoDB service is a very powerful NoSQL solution that supports writing and reading data at very consistent performance rates. We have learned about the differences between NoSQL and SQL databases, and the data that is suitable for each database type. We have also discussed the data structure and learned about how to manage DynamoDB, as well as how to access the data within the DynamoDB service. One very nice feature of the service is the ability to address it via HTTP, with standard PUT, GET, UPDATE, and DELETE methods. In addition, we can use JSON and JMESpath scripting to support some transactions, atomicity, and some other features usually reserved for SQL databases. In the next chapter, we will look into one of the message brokering services offered in AWS such as Simple Queue Service (SQS).

Questions

1. True or false: DynamoDB is a fully managed highly available NoSQL service that is addressable via a standard SQL interface.
2. What is the difference between ACID and BASE data as far as consistency is concerned?
3. You have an application that requires storing session data for a complex web application that performs BI on a very large backend dataset. Which database type is suitable for storing sessions for this application?
4. Which HTTP methods map to CRUD (create, read, update, and delete)?
5. Describe the relationships between tables, items, and attributes in DynamoDB.
6. What is the maximum item size in DynamoDB?
7. What are the two ways of determining capacity units in DynamoDB?
8. You have an application that collects metrics from industrial sensors at a rate of 50 MB per second. Each entry is 1.5 KB in size and the performance is consistent. You set up a DynamoDB table with on-demand provisioning in the US West (Oregon) region to ingest all the writes. You run a test and find that not all the values are being stored. You look at the sensor logs and see a lot of `ProvisionedThroughputExceededException` errors in the logs. What could be the problem?

9. You need to gather metrics from an online test from thousands of students. The current database is MySQL and the proposal is to move to DynamoDB. How would you choose the partition and sort key according to the following requirements:
    1. Retrieve the score per user by entering the username
    2. Rank by the date the test was taken (a user can take the test multiple times)
    3. Rank and sort users according to their scores

Further reading

- **Working with DynamoDB**: https://docs.aws.amazon.com/amazondynamodb/latest/developerguide/WorkingWithDynamo.html
- **DynamoDB Backups**: https://docs.aws.amazon.com/amazondynamodb/latest/developerguide/BackupRestore.html
- **Secondary Indexes**: https://docs.aws.amazon.com/amazondynamodb/latest/developerguide/bp-indexes-general.html
- **Naming Rules and Data Types**: https://docs.aws.amazon.com/amazondynamodb/latest/developerguide/HowItWorks.NamingRulesDataTypes.html
- **Reserved Words**: https://docs.aws.amazon.com/amazondynamodb/latest/developerguide/ReservedWords.html
- **Expression Attributes**: https://docs.aws.amazon.com/amazondynamodb/latest/developerguide/Expressions.ExpressionAttributeNames.html
- **Managing throughput**: https://docs.aws.amazon.com/amazondynamodb/latest/developerguide/ProvisionedThroughput.html
- **Table scans**: https://docs.aws.amazon.com/amazondynamodb/latest/developerguide/SQLtoNoSQL.ReadData.Scan.html
- **Table queries**: https://docs.aws.amazon.com/amazondynamodb/latest/developerguide/Query.html
- **Limits in DynamoDB**: https://docs.aws.amazon.com/amazondynamodb/latest/developerguide/Limits.html

14
Working with Simple Queue Service

We have now looked at services that provide the capability to store and process data. With modern application designs, the storage and processing are distributed among several layers of servers or services, and these need an effective way to communicate information among themselves. One way to perform this is to hardcode the network names and addresses of all the servers into each server. While this is doable on a small scale, keeping track of hundreds or thousands of servers and dynamically determining their addresses can be quite difficult. The other way to exchange messages among services and servers is by using a message brokering service. One of the message brokering services offered in AWS is **Simple Queue Service (SQS)**.

The following topics will be covered in this chapter:

- Introduction to queuing
- How a queue works
- Managing queues
- Working with messages
- Queue limits
- Queue security

Technical requirements

A basic understanding of modern application architectures, distributed systems, and messaging services is required to understand this chapter fully. Please refer to the GitHub link for this chapter: `https://github.com/PacktPublishing/AWS-Certified-SysOps-Administrator-Associate-Guide/tree/master/Chapter14`.

Introduction to queuing

When operating distributed clusters of servers, we need to figure out a good approach to meet the need to communicate with the servers and the services they offer. Imagine a cluster of hundreds, thousands, or even tens of thousands of servers running on an environment such the spot service, across several regions and availability zones. Now, imagine having to determine the following at any given time:

- The network address or DNS name of each server
- The current load on the server
- Which server is available to take a request and process it

This would be a daunting task with a stable environment, let alone a spot environment where the servers can pop in and out of existence on the EC2 compute layer.

So, instead of trying to figure out which server I should send my request to, we can simply let the servers themselves decide when there are enough resources to process a request. In this kind of setup, we need to post the request on a message broker layer where the message can be queued up for processing and stored until the worker comes along, reads the message, and processes it.

In essence, this type of message queue service decouples the relationship of the producer of the request and the worker that consumes and processes the request. Before implementing a message queue service, we would have needed to keep track of all the servers and account for their load before we would be able to select the most appropriate server to process our request. After introducing the message queue service, the only configuration on both layers is the endpoint address of the message queue service and the protocol it operates on.

How a queue works

The Simple Queue Service is a service that delivers a highly available message queue service and operates on a standard HTTP access model. It has the potential to deliver unlimited message capacity for any application size and is delivered as a pay-per-request service, so your costs of running the queue service automatically scale with the size of your application.

A queue is essentially used as a message repository that stores the message on a distributed cluster of servers. Once the message is stored, it can be made visible for consumers to read or made invisible, which means stored but not ready to be read. When messages are produced, they are stored on the cluster with a randomized distribution, as shown in this diagram:

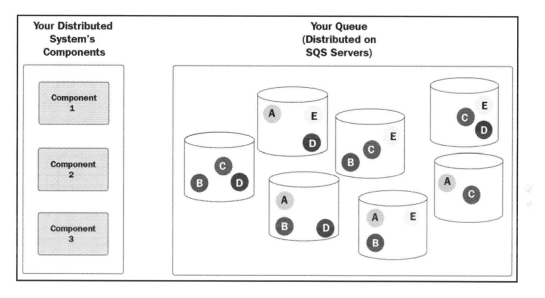

Here, we see the messages **A**, **B**, **C**, **D**, and **E** which were produced in that sequence being randomly distributed across a set of hosts in the cluster. Not all messages are present on all hosts, but all messages will be present on multiple hosts for high availability and durability.

Messages that are being consumed will be read from the cluster by polling the cluster. We can implement short polling, which is the default for the SQS, where we call up the service, sample a few nodes from the cluster, and retrieve a message. For example, a short polling request would sample just a small subset of hosts and each would serve one message, thus the reader would retrieve the messages B, A, and D from the example diagram before closing the connection to the server.

If we want to read the maximum possible amount of messages, then we can introduce long polling to our message read requests. This gives us the ability to poll for up to 20 seconds and sample all the servers in the cluster. With long polling, we can batch read up to 10 messages at a time. In our example, the servers would serve perhaps B, A, D, E, and lastly C as the messages from the queue.

Long polling can also help reduce the number of requests being sent to the queue when queues are empty. We need to remember that we pay for every request against the queue service, even if the response is empty. So when queue responses are empty, we should always try to perform the next read with exponential back-off so that we aren't reading an empty queue at a constant rate. For example, if the response is empty, we retry in 2 seconds instead of 1, and after the second one is empty, we can retry in 4 seconds, then 8, then 16, and so on.

Standard queues versus FIFO queues

There are two queue types that can be configured with the SQS: standard and FIFO queues. The standard queue type does not compensate for the randomness of the message distribution across the backend. This means that, when reading messages from the cluster, the messages will try to be delivered with a *best effort* concept for the message order.

But there are some applications where the message order is important, and in these situations we have the ability to preserve message order as follows:

- Implementing our own message numbering
- Creating producer timestamps
- Configuring FIFO queues

With FIFO queues, the message order is strictly preserved and the messages are sent out to producers in the strict order that they were received. FIFO queues, however, need to compensate for the randomness of the backend distribution, and this means that the FIFO queue service is throttled to up to 300 transactions per second, whereas the standard queues have an unlimited rate at which they can operate. FIFO queues also deliver the message only once, and we need to maintain a processing state separate from our queues, whereas the standard queues introduce a mechanism to deliver the message at least once.

Visibility timeout

When reading a message from a standard SQS queue, the reader is able to read the message and, once read, the message becomes invisible. This visibility timeout enables the message to automatically become visible if the first consumer that has read the message does not delete the message before the visibility timeout expires.

For example, let's say we have a task that takes up to 30 seconds to process on our consumer application. We set the visibility timeout to 45 seconds to make sure we have enough time to process the message and delete it with our consumer application. The consumers are distributed across a cluster of EC2 instances. Instance number 10 picks up message A and starts processing it. The visibility timeout kicks in and, if the instance successfully processes it within the time frame, it will delete the message while invisible as the task is completed. But if the instance fails during processing, then the task has not been completed, and after 45 seconds the visibility timeout will make the message visible again, and another instance can come along, pick that message up, and process the task at hand:

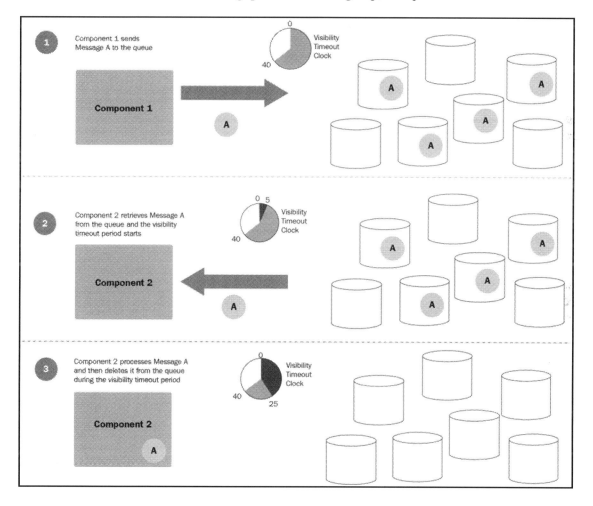

The message in the queue must be deleted after it has been successfully processed, as the visibility timeout will make the message visible again if the message is not deleted. This is why we say that the standard queues have an at least once delivery implemented.

This functionality is not enabled on FIFO queues; once the message is received with a FIFO queue, the message is automatically deleted from the queue and the service does not keep a copy. With FIFO queues, we need to handle backend failures and message histories with a different approach as, once a consumer fails, the message will not be retrievable from the queue.

Dead letter queues

But what if the error causing a failure to process a message is not in the consumer application but in the message content? Then, the first consumer processing the message will keep processing it until the visibility timeout expires, and then the second one will start processing, and so on. What can we do in this case?

The SQS supports implementing dead letter queues when using standard SQS queues. The dead letter queues are designed to prevent a message with corrupt content being processed into infinity, and allows us to develop the application to detect such messages, dequeue them from the main queue, and queue them up into the dead letter queue. This queue is then used by developers and administrators who can take a look at the message and determine the cause of the processing failure.

Use cases for queues

There are numerous reasons why one would introduce a queue in an application design. Everything from making sure the application components are decoupled to using the queue as a buffering interface, to making sure we can send requests that would otherwise be consuming other services and providing a batch distribution endpoint. To give you a better idea of how one can use a queue, we are going to discuss a few examples.

Example 1 – decoupling

As we have already mentioned, queues can be used to decouple groups of servers. As a message broker, the SQS is perfectly designed to maintain any number of messages between any number of producers and consumers, and can operate at any rate of performance.

Example 2 – buffering

The SQS is also a really good option for request buffering. Let's say we have a consumer application that can consume and process up to 10,000 messages per second, but the rate of these messages coming in from producers is very variable; anywhere between 1,000 and 100,000 messages per second are being produced. The queue service can queue up the spiky requests and the consumer application can easily process the messages from the queue at a constant rate.

Example 3 – request offloading

The SQS can be used to offload requests from another service onto the queue. For example an application with several services stores its state in a relational database. If one of the services changes state, then all the others would need to check the database for changes. This would mean the services would constantly scan the database and look for changes. Instead of doing this, the service that changes state can inform one or multiple services of the changes via the message queue. The message can contain the exact index that has changed in the database, and the receiver now only needs to look at that index in the database to determine how the state has changed.

Example 4 – batch operations

When performing batch operations, traditionally, the service is sent as a list of operations to one target and they are executed sequentially by that one system. This can mean that operations can take a long time to complete. If we are able to execute any of the batch operations in parallel, then we can slice up any batch operation and send each command to be executed as a separate message in the message queue. A number of backend systems can then be spun up and thereby can execute these operations in parallel, thus improving performance and completing the batch job in an exponentially shorter time.

Managing queues

Now, let's take a look at the administrative operations available from the SQS. In this section, we will be doing some management through the management console, but since the power of SQS is best shown with a programmatic approach, we will be demonstrating some examples with the AWS CLI.

Creating and listing queues

Let's first create a queue by executing the following steps:

1. In the management console, we can simply navigate to the SQS dashboard and, when presented with the initial screen, choose **Get Started Now**:

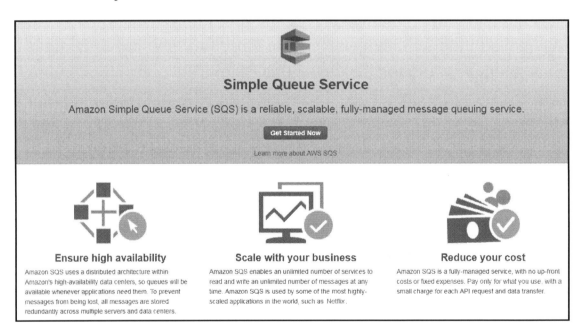

2. This will immediately be followed by the **Create New Queue** dialog, where we can enter a queue name and then click **Quick-Create Queue** or click **Configure Queue**:

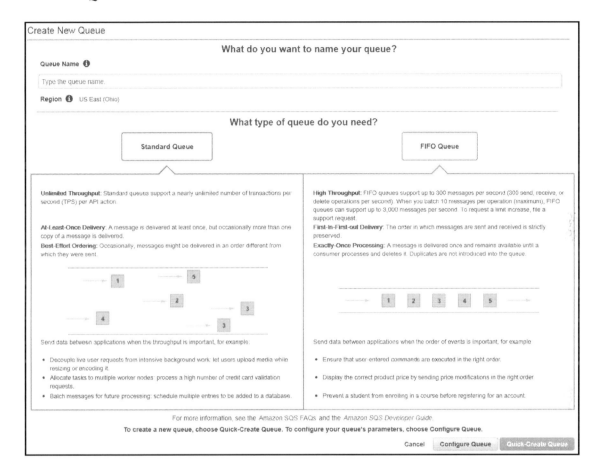

3. By clicking **Configure Queue**, we are able to configure features such as the visibility timeout; how long we want to retain the messages in the queue, the maximum message size; the delivery delay, which makes the message invisible for a certain period before enabling it to be read; and short or long polling by defining the receive message wait time of up to 20 seconds. We can also configure a dead letter queue and server-side encryption here:

You can change these default parameters.

Queue Attributes

Default Visibility Timeout ⓘ	30	seconds ▼	Value must be between 0 seconds and 12 hours.
Message Retention Period ⓘ	4	days ▼	Value must be between 1 minute and 14 days.
Maximum Message Size ⓘ	256	KB	Value must be between 1 and 256 KB.
Delivery Delay ⓘ	0	seconds ▼	Value must be between 0 seconds and 15 minutes.
Receive Message Wait Time ⓘ	0	seconds	Value must be between 0 and 20 seconds.

Dead Letter Queue Settings

Use Redrive Policy ⓘ	☐	
Dead Letter Queue ⓘ		Value must be an existing queue name.
Maximum Receives ⓘ		Value must be between 1 and 1000.

Server-Side Encryption (SSE) Settings

Use SSE ⓘ	☐	
AWS KMS Customer Master Key (CMK) ⓘ	▼	
Data Key Reuse Period ⓘ		▼	This value must be between 1 minute and 24 hours.

Cancel   Create Queue

4. After the queue is created, the management console will show the queue and its properties:

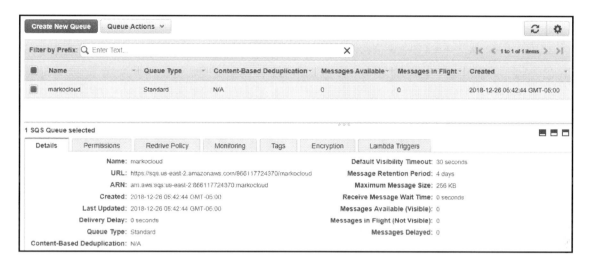

5. Creating a queue can be done via the CLI with the use of the `aws sqs create-queue` command. The only required attribute for this command would be `--queue-name`, while all the optional advanced options can be used to configure the same properties as the **Configure Options** operation. Please see the CLI reference in the *Further reading* section of this chapter for all the possible options for the `create-queue` operation.

6. To list the queues in the AWS CLI, we can run the `aws sqs list-queues` command, which should give us a response that outputs the **QueueUrls** key with the value representing the full HTTPS path to the queue that we can address directly:

```
{
  "QueueUrls": [
  "https://us-east-2.queue.amazonaws.com/866117724370/markocloud"
  ]
}
```

Adding user permissions to a queue

Let's perform the following steps:

1. To add permissions to the queue, we can simply open the **Permissions** tab and click on **Add a Permission**:

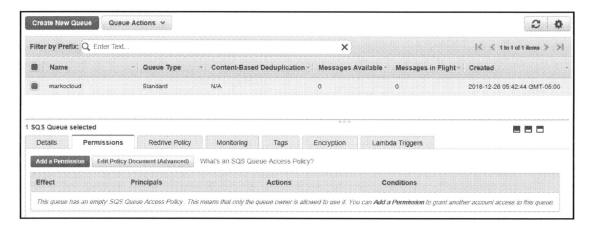

2. In the **Add a Permission to markocloud** dialog, where `markocloud` is the `queue-name`, we can simply select the effect, who to give the permission to, and which AWS account, or we can share it anonymously along with what actions are allowed. We click the **Add Permission** button to apply it's features:

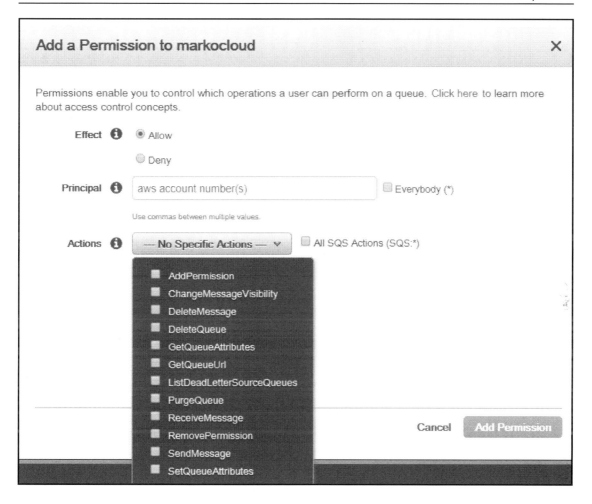

3. Once applied, the permission is visible in the **Permissions** tab in our SQS management console:

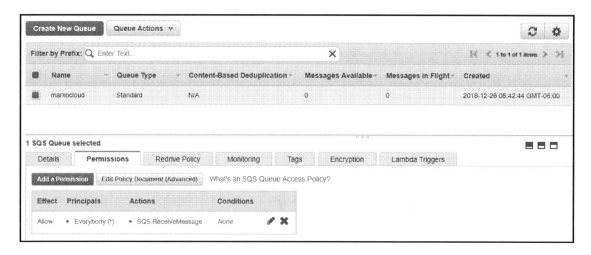

In this example, we have enabled everyone (anonymous sharing) to receive a message from this message queue. All we would require for them to achieve this would be the queue DNS name, which can be retrieved with the `list-queue` operation or seen in the **Details** tab of the queue.

Deleting a queue

To delete a queue, we can simply go the management console and select **Queue Actions** and then **Delete Queue**. This operation deletes a queue and all the message held within the queue:

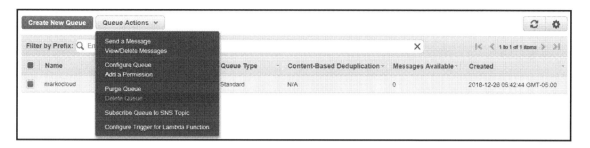

Working with messages

Sending, receiving, and deleting messages from the message queue can partially be done via the management console, but the most power can be achieved programmatically by using the AWS CLI or the SDKs. We will take a look at some examples in the management console and some in the AWS CLI.

Sending a message in a queue

Please perform the following steps:

1. To send a message to the queue, we can simply choose **Queue Actions** in the management console and then select **Send a Message**. The same result can be achieved with the `aws sqs send-message` command, but for simplicity we will demonstrate only the management console in this example:

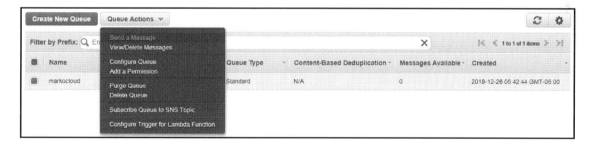

2. In the **Send a Message to markocloud** dialog, where `markocloud` is the queue-name, we can simply write our message and send it. The message might contain actual commands to be run or other information relevant to our application that can be encoded in JSON:

3. Once the message is sent, we will get a response with a Message ID and an MD5 hash of the message body. This helps us maintain a record and the consistency of the messages being sent to the service:

4. We can also see that one message is now visible in the **Messages Available** column of our queue:

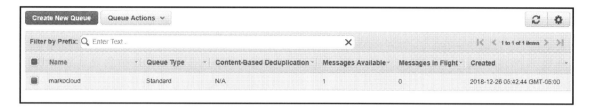

Receiving and deleting a message

To receive a message, we will use the command line with the `aws sqs receive-message` command; we will need to specify the `--queue-url` attribute to point our command at the queue.

In our example, the command to run would be this:

```
aws sqs receive-message
--queue-url "https://us-east-2.queue.amazonaws.com/866117724370/markocloud"
```

And the response would be as follows:

```
{
 "Messages": [
 {
 "Body": "This is a test message\n", "ReceiptHandle":
"AQEBE9Pi+P5RP9FoZxgQ8xtDVT4qetd060GmD6LVr3s3iltZpAixsujI/2xEE4FqD/Mrxa4H98
hSxT6Gcn215L0jtJRlrtVK9kl/xpjwjQqoTsEh5i9B9WWDly/QQPj6RpeL7BvfytoQ7I25DqlTH
wZQMEhGgD29vJ5FzYFi8WSc7+mVozTwSOsqXM0PeoCOMnlP8UaBFniRCIVvk9HbNFE198zC+F1b
DL682NfRJA7SBgRMyjaVxSauQ9hkh/5UZJE1SHiYaJtEKKbYXzfosaAeHq3BNEZGQk2KV33IAnJ
Jx1H2w7g6tODAeRF7yhVOuWAsVXfm1eSFQ46DCH9o7kAAsxEYXYO19o0uNyjMwadHA0U0CD/4in
oehQAtugF2AlNEzoyTaYVLCz+ZKRVbe9wSMw==",
 "MD5OfBody": "2309502dc5493f110869b570d9028942",
 "MessageId": "2e50bc36-90d6-4ef9-82d2-5769462394f0"
 }
 ]
}
```

The structure of the response is as follows:

- `"Body"`: Represents the message content
- `"ReceiptHandle"`: Is the unique identifier for the message that was received
- `"MD5OfBody"`: The MD5 sum of the body of the message, used for delivery consistency
- `"MessageId"`: The identifier of the message in the queue

After we have finished processing the message, we can delete the message by specifying the `aws sqs delete-message` command with the `--queue-url` and `--receipt-handle` options, which are required to identify the message queue and message we are deleting. In our example, this command would look like this:

```
aws sqs delete-message \
 --queue-url
"https://us-east-2.queue.amazonaws.com/866117724370/markocloud" \
 --receipt-handle
"AQEBE9Pi+P5RP9FoZxgQ8xtDVT4qetd060GmD6LVr3s3iltZpAixsujI/2xEE4FqD/Mrxa4H98
hSxT6Gcn215L0jtJRlrtVK9kl/xpjwjQqoTsEh5i9B9WWDly/QQPj6RpeL7BvfytoQ7I25DqlTH
wZQMEhGgD29vJ5FzYFi8WSc7+mVozTwSOsqXM0PeoCOMn1P8UaBFniRCIVvk9HbNFE198zC+F1b
DL682NfRJA7SBgRMyjaVxSauQ9hkh/5UZJE1SHiYaJtEKKbYXzfosaAeHq3BNEZGQk2KV33IAnJ
Jx1H2w7g6tODAeRF7yhVOuWAsVXfm1eSFQ46DCH9o7kAAsxEYXYO19o0uNyjMwadHA0U0CD/4in
oehQAtugF2AlNEzoyTaYVLCz+ZKRVbe9wSMw=="
```

The CLI command would now remove the message from the queue, and there are now no messages in the message queue.

Purging a queue

Sometimes, the messages in the message queue cannot be processed or have become stale, and we do not want to use the processing power in AWS to process them as they are irrelevant. If we need to clean up a queue, we can perform a queue purge. This will delete all the messages in the message queue and can be achieved in the management console by selecting **Queue Actions** | **Purge Queue**, as shown in the following screenshot, or by running the `aws sqs purge-queue` command from the CLI:

Queue limits

When working with SQS queues, the service is designed to have some limitations as far as the size and duration of operations are concerned. The following limits apply to the SQS:

- The queue names need to be unique within a region and can have up to 80 characters
- The queues should have no more than 50 tags associated with them
- The maximum message size is 256 KB (including all metadata)
- A maximum of 10 metadata attributes are supported per message
- The message delivery timeout can be between 0 and 15 seconds
- The message retention period can be between 60 seconds and 14 days (default is 4 days)
- The visibility timeout can be set between 0 seconds and 12 hours (default is 30 seconds)
- The FIFO queues support up to 300 transactions per second (3000 messages in batches)
- Batches of up to 10 messages can be read or written to the queue

Other limitations apply to policies and more fine-grained details of the message queues. For a full list, please refer to the SQS Limits link in the *Further reading* section of this chapter.

Queue security

There are several ways to protect the data in the SQS:

- Encryption
- Access control
- VPC endpoints

The data is protected in transit with encryption, as the service always uses the HTTPS protocol when responding to requests. We also have the ability to enable server-side encryption for data at rest. We have the ability to select the default server-side encryption with an AWS SQS managed key, or we can use our own key via the KMS service with a **customer managed key (CMK)**.

We can assign permissions to our own account users and roles to perform operations against the SQS service. Proper controls need to be put in place, and least privilege permissions need to be applied when using IAM to control access. For public access, we are also able to add permissions to a particular queue to other accounts and anonymous users. Remember that, when sharing queues, it is the owner of the queue who pays for all requests against a queue.

If the queues need to be kept within the private network, we can attach a VPC endpoint to a queue and thus allow for private communication that never passes over the internet within a region.

Summary

We have now taken a look at how messaging can be used to decouple our application, to create a workload buffer, or to offload requests from other services. We took a look at the details of the SQS and saw how we can manage queues, create and read messages, and delete them, and we learned about the visibility timeout. We also learned about the performance of the two types of queues and the limitations of the SQS itself. We also discussed security via encryption, access control, and VPC endpoints. In the next chapter, we will be introducing ourselves to SNS to distribute one message to multiple consumers at the same time.

Questions

1. What are the two types of queues supported by SQS?
2. What is the performance limitation of the FIFO queue?
3. What protocol does SQS use to deliver messages?
4. What is the visibility timeout?
5. When reading a message, what metadata is delivered alongside the body?
6. Which piece of metadata is needed to delete the message?
7. You have built an application that sends and processes exactly 10 messages per second. Your application has been working fine for days, but now you discover that there are over 100 messages in the queue and the number is growing. What might be the problem?
8. You have purged the queue and would like to recover the purged messages. How can you achieve this?

Further reading

- **SQS documentation**: https://docs.aws.amazon.com/sqs/index.html
- **SQS architecture**: https://docs.aws.amazon.com/AWSSimpleQueueService/latest/SQSDeveloperGuide/sqs-basic-architecture.html
- **SQS CLI reference**: https://docs.aws.amazon.com/cli/latest/reference/sqs/
- **SQS Limits**: https://docs.aws.amazon.com/AWSSimpleQueueService/latest/SQSDeveloperGuide/sqs-limits.html
- **SQS Security**: https://docs.aws.amazon.com/AWSSimpleQueueService/latest/SQSDeveloperGuide/sqs-security.html

15
Handling Messaging with Simple Notification Service

As we have already seen, message brokering is an important part of modern applications. In the case of SQS, we had a producer-consumer model, but in some cases we need to distribute one message to multiple consumers at the same time. For many-to-one use cases, we introduce **Simple Notification Service** (**SNS**).

The following topics will be covered in this chapter:

- Introduction to SNS
- SNS use cases
- Working with topics
- Managing SNS access

Technical requirements

As with the SQS chapter, a basic understanding of modern application architectures, distributed systems, and messaging services is required to understand the content.

Introduction to SNS

The SNS provides us with a very effective mechanism that allows us to send messages from one publisher to multiple subscribers. In contrast to the SQS, where the relationship is one-to-one and the messages had to be pulled by the consumers from the queue, the SNS pushes the messages to the subscribers immediately upon the posting of the message in the service. There is also no persistence in the SNS queue and, once sent, the message cannot be recalled.

The SNS service is a fully managed, highly available service that allows us to send messages via the following supported protocols to clients:

- **HTTP** and **HTTPS**: Uses standard HTTP POST commands to deliver messages
- **EMAIL** and **EMAIL-JSON**: Uses SMTP to send (JSON-formatted) emails
- **SMS**: Uses SMS text messaging to send data to mobile phones
- **Application**: Sends JSON-encoded messages to an endpoint ARN for mobile devices
- **SQS**: Integrates with the SQS service
- **Lambda**: Sends JSON-encoded messages to Lambdas

SNS use cases

In this section, we are going to take a look at how we can make use of the SNS service to implement advanced message delivery scenarios.

SNS fan-out

An application design will sometimes require us to take one message and deliver it to multiple different groups of systems for processing. The SNS service is able to take one message and deliver it to multiple SQS targets. This allows us to extend the functionality of the SQS service from a standard one-to-one approach to a service that can provide a one-to-many delivery. In this example, one message is sent to three different backends and each can perform the task in a different way.

For example, whenever a new image is posted to our website, we need to format it into several standard sizes: a thumbnail, a mobile size, and a standard web-optimized size. We can send the message of the image's upload to the SNS topic, which in turn pushes the message into the three different SQS queues where the respective workers are listening and will perform the task of creating the thumbnail and the web-optimized and the mobile-optimized images in parallel:

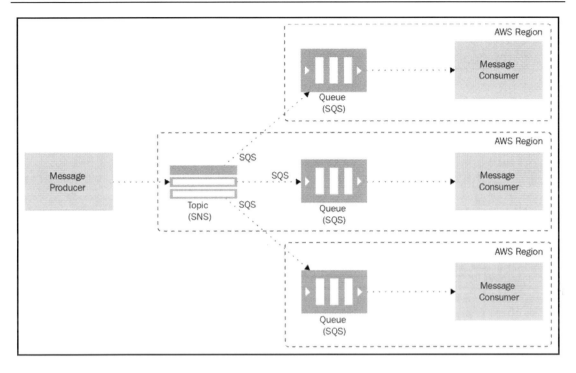

We can also use the fan-out approach to notify completely different services of an event that happened, for example, if we have an application where an event or message needs to be processed in several ways by several completely different components. In this example, the message being sent to the SNS service is processed in three different ways:

- The SQS queue takes the message for the workers to process the content.
- The Lambda function reads the metadata from the message.
- The HTTP endpoint records the message in an archive.

The following setup of an SNS topic, where an HTTP endpoint, a Lambda, and an SQS service are subscribed, will allow us to process the message, record its metadata, and archive it in parallel:

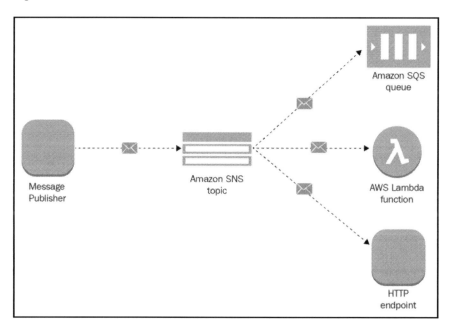

Application and system alerts

Pretty much all the AWS services can post messages to an SNS topic, and CloudWatch is no exception. With CloudWatch, we can collect metrics from our operating system, as well as from our applications. On top of the metrics, we also have the ability to create alarms. When creating an alarm, we would need to define a threshold for a certain metric and the duration of the threshold breach.

For example, when monitoring our EC2 instances in our environment, we can set a threshold for the CPU usage of 80% and a duration of 10 minutes. When an EC2 instance's CPU usage goes above 80% for more than 10 minutes, a CloudWatch alarm will trigger. That trigger can send a message to an SNS topic, which can in turn notify a certain email address or perform other actions, such as triggering a Lambda function and so on. It is also fairly easy to design the alarm notifications, as we can customize which topic each alarm will post messages to, so we can divide the tasks among teams responsible for their own region or account, or aggregate all our accounts and regions into one email:

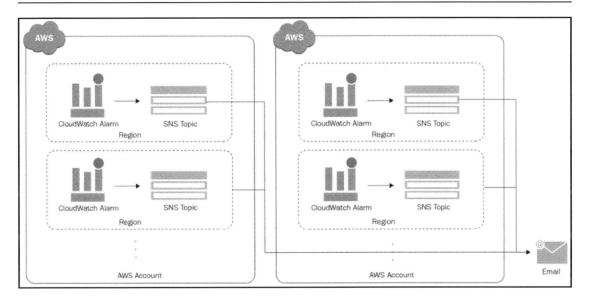

Push email and text messaging

Since the SNS service delivers the notifications immediately, it is a great system to use when events in our application require a user to be notified via an email or a text message. For example, let's assume we have an e-commerce website that takes orders. Once an order is taken, there are usually quite a lot of actions that need to be performed before the order is finalized. An example scenario would be composed of the following steps:

1. The user puts the product(s) in the cart.
2. The user clicks on **Proceed** to checkout.
3. The user enters payment details, address, shipping method, and so on.
4. The system creates a draft order.
5. The draft order is sent for payment processing.
6. Once confirmation is received, the system notifies the user and sends an email with the order details or payment issue.
7. The system continues processing the order by sending the following:
    - The order details to the fulfillment department
    - The shipping details to the shipping department
    - The financial details of the order to accounting
    - Updates the user's account with the order status

8. Any time a change of order is detected, the system will update the user's account with the order status.
9. Once the shipping and delivery date is determined, notify the user of the shipment's arrival via email or SMS.
10. Once the shipment is received, the order will be closed.

As you can see, there are several locations where an immediate notification via either email or SMS would be very useful in this case. Some actions require sequential processing (shipment after payment, for instance), while others can be executed in parallel (for instance, actions in *Steps 6* and *7*).

Since the proposed e-commerce solution already speaks HTTP, it can easily make use of the SNS service whenever it needs to notify a user. Notifications can be sent when the order is received and potentially when the order status changes. This can increase the quality of service for the e-commerce website, as the clients can easily select what kinds of notifications they wish to receive, and the site can keep them updated about their order in real time.

Mobile push notifications

As with email and text notifications, mobile push messages to iOS and Android devices are also supported with SNS. This is a really neat feature that can be used to do the following:

- Communicate messages about updates, changes, and new features for your mobile applications
- Communicate information about services offered in a certain geographical area
- Target a certain audience that will likely respond positively to the notification

One example would be a mobile application offering information about pop-up restaurants and street vendor locations to users. Due to the fact that street vendors cannot always sell their food at the same spot, the application would track the vendor locations. The vendor locations would be shown to users when they open the application.

Chapter 15

An added feature of the application could allow the user to select their favorite food trucks. The application could match the user locations to the vendor locations, and then notify the users of their favorite food truck location when the vendor is in roughly the same area. The user could also request to be notified of all the vendors in their area at lunchtime, which would let them choose their lunch much more easily than searching all the vendors or phoning to find their locations.

Working with topics

Now, let's take a look at how easy it is to work with SNS and how we can perform complete management of SNS tasks from the SNS management console. The real power of SNS of course lies in the programmable access and the ability to automate the creation of topics and distribution of messages, but, to demonstrate the way SNS operates, the management console will suffice.

Creating a topic

Let's perform the following steps:

1. To create a topic, navigate to the SNS management console and select the **Create topic** action:

2. In the **Create new topic** dialog, we can select the **Topic name** and the **Display name** that we will be using for this topic. Note that the **Display name** is only required when sending SMS messages and is limited to 10 characters, whereas the **Topic name** is the name that will be used as the identifier for this topic and needs to be unique within a region:

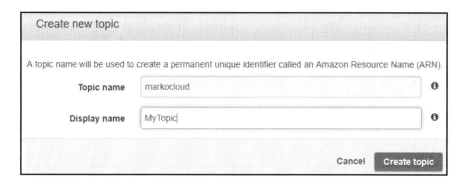

3. Once a topic is created, we can select it and view the details, including the topic ARN, which can be used by other AWS services to publish messages, the region, the display name, and, most importantly, the subscriptions. The topics are of course created without subscribers, and if we would like to subscribe to the topic, we can click the **Create subscription** button:

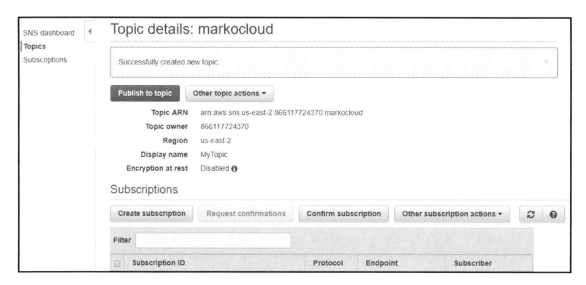

Subscribing to a topic

Let's perform the following steps:

1. In the **Create subscription** dialog, we need to select the protocol (**Email**, **SMS**, **HTTP**, and so on) and the endpoint that represents the user's email address, phone number, HTTP endpoint, and so on:

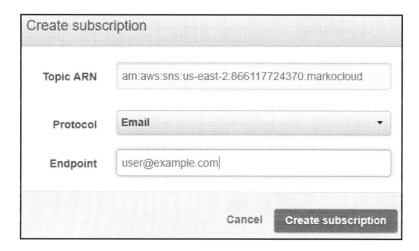

2. Once a subscription is created, it will be visible in the **Subscriptions** section of the topic details. Note that, when subscribing an end user via protocols such as email, the user will receive a subscription confirmation and will be in the **PendingConfirmation** state until they confirm the subscription:

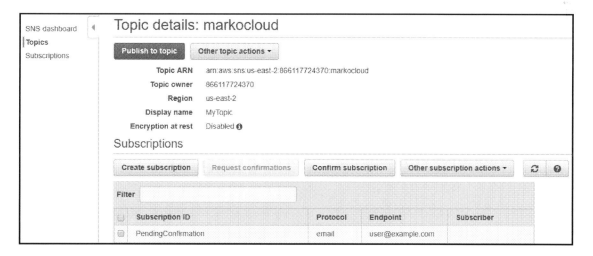

Publishing to a topic

Once we have our topic set up, we can click the **Publish to topic** button in the topic details and start creating a message. We can add a subject and the message body straight into the web interface. We also have the ability to select the message to be **Raw** (without formatting) or **JSON**-formatted:

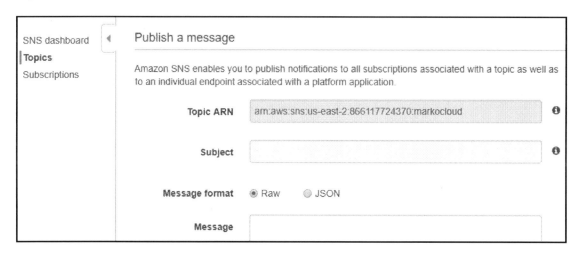

Below the message body section, we also have the JSON message generator, which can help us create a message in the appropriate JSON format for each protocol:

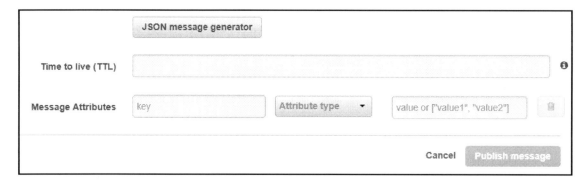

With the JSON message generator, we can simply enter the message into the body and then select the targets that will receive the messages from the topic:

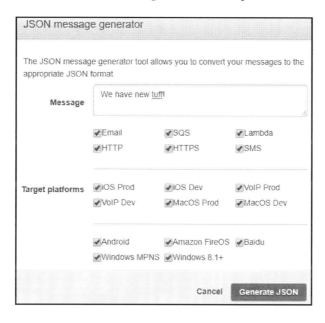

When the JSON format is generated, the window is populated with the appropriate metadata for each type of communication protocol and the format automatically changes to JSON:

We can now simply click **Publish Message** at the bottom of the dialog and the message will be push-delivered to the subscribers. As you can see, it is very simple to create a topic and a subscription, and post messages straight from the management console.

Deleting a topic

To delete a topic, simply select a topic from the **Topics** section of the SNS management console and select **Actions**, then **Delete Topics**. Exercise caution when deleting the topics, as it is easy to select multiple topics from the list and delete them with this one move. You can always recreate the topic, but you will also need to recreate the subscriptions:

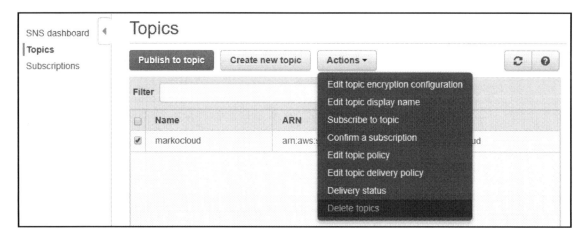

Managing SNS access

Any topic created by an IAM user is automatically owned by that IAM user, and the default policy only allows the owner to publish and subscribe to the topic itself. This is of course very limiting, and in reality we would require the ability to assign fine-grained permissions to different security principals, or even anonymous publishers, to create messages in the SNS topic we have created.

Access control

With most services, control of the resource is governed directly through IAM. As we have learned, some services have resource policies and, with SNS, the resource policy will be the place where we will control access on a per-topic basis. While we have the ability in IAM to control access to the SNS service, once a user, role, or group is allowed access, the IAM policy applies globally to all topics. On top of that, for each topic separately, we have the ability to allow access to either an IAM security principal or an anonymous user (everyone). For each topic, we have the ability to edit the default Access Policy and thus control access to the topic.

Access policy concepts

An access policy allows us the ability to control who can post a message to a topic and who can subscribe to a topic. It is based on a similar approach to the S3 resource policy and allows us the ability to maintain fine-grained control over access to the SNS topic:

1. To edit the policy, simply select the SNS topic and select **Edit topic policy** from the **Actions** menu:

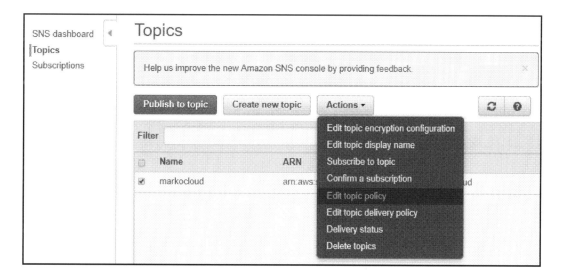

2. There are two views, **Basic** and **Advanced**; in the **Basic view**, we can select who we would like to allow to publish to the topic, but are limited to either the topic owner, everyone, or specific AWS IAM users. The same goes for the subscriptions; only a limited set of options is available for subscriptions:

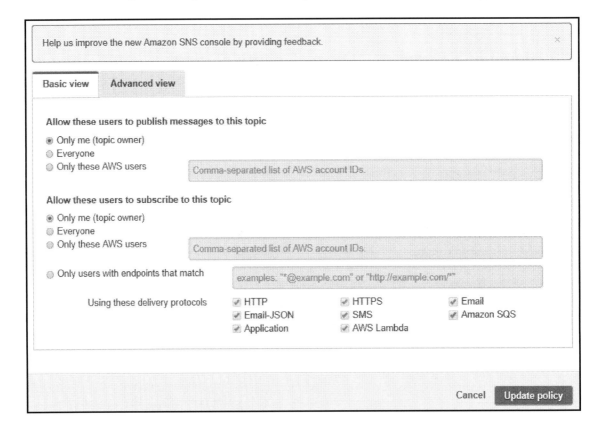

3. With the **Advanced view**, we have the ability to edit the policy in JSON using the SNS Access Policy Language:

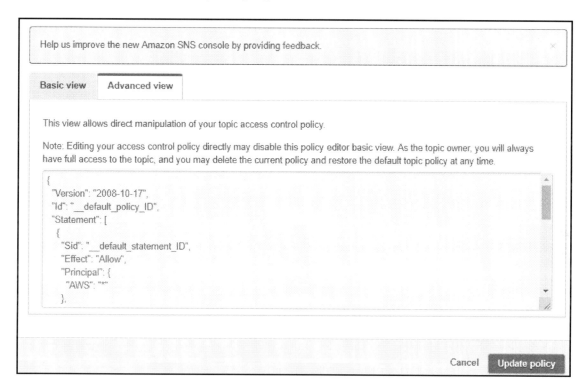

4. Once we are done editing the policy to our satisfaction, we simply click **Update policy** and the access policy is updated.

 If you would like to learn more about the SNS Access Policy Language, please take a look at the link in the *Further reading* section of this chapter.

Access request evaluation logic

When evaluating access to the topic, a combination of all policies is going to be considered for each individual accessing the topic. If a user, group, or role does not have permission to access SNS, the service will implicitly deny all access. But once access to SNS is allowed, a combination of the IAM SNS policy and the topic's own access policy will be applied. Be careful when setting explicit denies in either the IAM policy or the access policy, as any explicit denies will of course override any explicit allows, thereby potentially causing valid actions to be unavailable.

Summary

We have seen how we can use SNS as a powerful tool for message distribution in our AWS environment. The service is essentially very easy to use and there are numerous use cases that could utilize SNS. It is especially valuable when we require a serverless component that can react to an event or an incoming message and distribute that message to multiple entities, either for processing or as a notification service. In the next chapter, we will get started with Simple Workflow Service.

Questions

1. Is JSON supported as an SNS transfer method?
2. Name the special SNS topic property that needs to be configured when sending SMS.
3. In what way does SNS enhance SQS with fan-out?
4. Which protocols would make sense for your Android application to use to deliver notifications to your users?
5. You are sending CloudWatch alarms to a global topic to alert your response team of issues. Your managers now need you to identify the number of issues in each region and bill that separately to each department that is responsible for the region. How could you easily implement this?
6. You've created an email subscription, but you are not receiving emails from the topic. What would you check first?
7. A service outside of AWS requires the ability to send a message to an SNS topic. How can we protect the topic from anyone sending to it?

Further reading

- **SNS Documentation**: https://docs.aws.amazon.com/sns/index.html#lang/en_us
- **SNS Subscribtions**: https://docs.aws.amazon.com/sns/latest/api/API_Subscribe.html
- **SNS CLI Reference**: https://docs.aws.amazon.com/cli/latest/reference/sns/index.html
- **SNS Service Limits**: https://docs.aws.amazon.com/general/latest/gr/aws_service_limits.html
- **SNS Access Policy Language**: https://docs.aws.amazon.com/sns/latest/dg/AccessPolicyLanguage_KeyConcepts.html

16
Getting Started with Simple Workflow Service

One way of maintaining the state of our application is to continuously exchange messages between all services that need to be informed of state changes. But when working with technologies that allow us to design applications that are serverless, we might find it difficult to coordinate the message relaying between all of the components. Also, manual tasks in our business process might be difficult to implement through messaging alone. We need a tool to enable the simple coordination of automated and manual activities that map to our business process, and the **Simple Workflow Service** (**SWF**) provides just that capability.

The following topics will be covered in this chapter:

- Introduction to SWF
- Components of SWF
- Managing access with IAM

Technical requirements

A general understanding of modern distributed application design and the concept of maintaining state in distributed applications is required to fully comprehend this chapter.

Introduction to SWF

The SWF is a fully managed solution in AWS that allows us to track the state of our applications and coordinate the tasks and activities within our environment that map to the needs of our business processes. Tracking the state in distributed applications that require coordination between multiple instances of a component, or multiple different components, can be challenging. The SWF gives us the ability to reliably track the state and coordinate tasks among multiple units of data transformation and processing.

The SWF integrates with fully managed services and allows us to automate the provisioning of the service that will perform the task as soon as it is generated. This makes the service highly flexible, as we never need to run any idle components to be able to perform our tasks, and also highly scalable, as the service can spin up its own infrastructure and scale to the size required to meet the number or scale of the tasks at hand.

The SWF enables us to logically separate the processing plane from the control plane as all control, state-tracking, and coordination operations are performed in the SWF service, and the processing and data transformation are performed by other AWS service components that the SWF orchestrates.

For example, in the previous chapter we defined a 10-step order process in an e-commerce website that had multiple tasks and activities that needed to be completed sequentially or in parallel. The state of the order needs to be tracked somewhere and we have found that we can use a database and a message queue to notify components of state changes. To simplify the need to program all of these state notifications into our application, the whole orchestration scenario can be built in SWF.

Components of the SWF

The SWF is designed to be simple to use and design straight out of the management console. The service itself has some basic concepts that we need to understand before we can start designing our workflows. We are going to take a look at the following concepts:

- Workflows
- Workflow execution history
- Activities and tasks
- Actors
- Domains

- Object identifiers
- Task lists
- The workflow life cycle and execution closure
- Polling for tasks
- Endpoints

Workflows

The workflow represents our business process in the SWF. The workflow contains activities and tasks that need to be completed. It will include all of the orchestration logic that connects the activities together, which defines what kind of actions need to be performed in what sequence, or under which circumstances, and in what order.

For example, we will create a workflow for our ten-step order-processing example from the previous chapter, and each of the ten steps will be represented as a task in the workflow. Each task in the ten steps of the workflow will then either invoke another task or, if it is the last task invoke the completion of the workflow; or send out a failure or timeout notification if the task is not able to complete successfully.

The invocation of other tasks or the decision to mark the process as failed or timed out is carried out by the decider. Each workflow contains deciders that have the ability to perform task scheduling and pass data to the tasks. They also make sure to track events within the workflow while it is in progress. The deciders also close the workflow when completed or upon failure.

Workflow execution history

Each change to the state of a task being performed is recorded as an event within the workflow execution history. The events record different aspects of the state changes of each task, which include the successful completion of the task or an error or timeout within the task execution scenario. The workflow execution history is a stateful and authoritative recording of the progress of the workflow execution.

When processing our ten-step order, each step, once complete, will register an event that will record whether the order has been received and processed, the user notified, and so on. The workflow can then also be used as a record of action in the order-fulfillment environment.

Activities and tasks

There are two types of tasks that will be contained within a workflow: the activity task, which contains information about the actions that need to be completed, and the decision task, which will invoke the decider to perform the next action from the previous activity task, according to the output of the activity task.

When defining an activity task in the workflow, we will need to specify the activity type, the name and version, the domain it belongs to, the task list, the task start schedule, and task timeouts. This will specifically identify the task at hand and allow us to control the behavior of the task.

For example, in our ten-step order, we will define each of the ten steps as a separate task that will have a different definition of the task and a different timeout. An email notification task will be a fully automated task that will invoke the SNS and send a message to the topic to notify the user. This task will probably be defined with a timeout of five minutes, whereas the order-fulfillment task might well be a manual task since the package needs to be prepared and sent off to shipping manually, and will have a longer timeout of, for example, 24 hours.

The work in this example will be processed by the activity task and the logic by the decision task.

Actors

Any task or activity will always be performed by an actor. An actor, sometimes be referred to as an activity worker, can be any kind of entity that can perform the task at hand. Actors can be represented as software components or a person that needs to complete a manual process to perform the task. When performing a task manually, the activity worker software can be used to receive the task details and perform the action that completes the task.

In the ten-step example, any task, such as the email or SMS notifications, payment processing, and account updates, will be performed by the software actors, whereas tasks such as order fulfillment, shipping, and so on will be performed by a person.

Domains

Domains are used to logically group and separate workflows. We can have multiple workflows run in a domain, and these workflows have the ability to interact. We also have the ability to have multiple domains within our AWS account, and any workflows in separate domains will be completely isolated from each other.

Object identifiers

Each workflow and each object in a workflow will have unique object identifiers attached to it. Here is a list of object identifiers that are attached to each SWF concept:

- A workflow or an activity within the workflow is identified by its domain, name, and version.
- A task is identified by a unique task token automatically generated by SWF.
- A workflow execution is identified by the domain, workflow ID, and run ID.

Task lists

A task list provides the ability to store information about what processing actions need to be performed for the task to be completed. We can think of the task list as a queue within each activity that delivers a list of actions to be processed by the workers. The task list is dynamically populated by the SWF service according to the input parameters.

For example, in our ten-step order the client might buy one or several items within the order process, and the SWF service will then populate the task list with one or several tasks for each of the activities defined in the workflow.

The workflow life cycle and execution closure

Once we run a workflow execution, it is considered open, and the actions are coordinated between activity tasks, which perform the work, and decider tasks, which perform the logical operations. Once the life cycle has completed all the tasks, the workflow execution will be closed. We could also manually cancel the workflow execution, then the closure will be recorded as cancelled. In the case of a failure or a timeout of a task or activity, the workflow execution will be closed as failed, or timed out. Workflow execution closure is always handled by a decider.

Polling for tasks

All task components of a workflow will always poll the SWF service using long polling. If an action is available for a particular activity or decision task, the service will immediately respond. When there are no tasks, the long polling request will allow the service to wait for a message about an action for up to 60 seconds. After 60 seconds, the service will respond with an empty request and close the connection. If an empty response is received by the task worker, then the worker will need to poll for the task again.

When developing a worker, the developers might implement an exponential back-off algorithm for polling, which will delay the polling attempts for longer and longer if an empty response is received. Make sure you understand that there is a possibility of a very long delay between polls due to exponential back-off when diagnosing the SWF. If the developer implements the delay by doubling it every time, the delay might quickly get very long.

For example, every time an empty response is received, the application waits for an amount equal to the poll length before polling again. Once a second empty response in a row is received, it will double the wait time before polling again. In this example, the poll length is one minute, so the back-off algorithm will make the application wait for another minute before polling again. If another empty response is received, then the application will double the wait time to two minutes before polling again. If a third empty response is received, then the wait time will double to 4 minutes and then 8, 16, 32 , and so on. As you can see, this kind of approach works well when polls are short but with long poll times, it might get very long very quickly.

Endpoints

The SWF endpoints are different for each region, and a list of the current SWF endpoints can be found in the link in the *Further reading* section of this chapter. Since the service endpoints are regionally bound, the domains, workflows, and components executing workflow tasks must also exist within the same region, as per the requirement that they all communicate with the same endpoint. This means that any SWF components, such as domains, workflows, and tasks, created in one region will not be available in the other region. If we have an application that is distributed across multiple regions, we will need to create multiple workflows, each responsible for a certain regional part of the application if the architecture of the application requires us to do so.

Managing access with IAM

The SWF service allows us to control access to the SWF resources directly via IAM. Each actor in the workflow is required to use a secret key and access key to sign each and every request to the SWF service endpoint. The best practice will be to design our actors with roles that have the correct permission to access a certain workflow, and they can be issued temporary credentials to access and poll the SWF service. This means we do not need to expose our secret key and access key when designing our application. We can, however, maintain access with our secret key and access key when performing manual tasks or designing and troubleshooting the workflow itself.

There are two types of permissions that can be applied to each IAM security principal to control access to SWF:

- **Resource permissions**: Allow us to define the resources that a user, group, or role is able to use within a domain
- **API permissions**: Allow us to define which API actions the user is allowed to perform against the SWF API

A coordination of these two permissions will allow us to create fine-grained control over the SWF resources and adhere to the least privilege principle. For example, we can allow a certain security principal the following:

- Full control over all resources in all domains or in a certain domain
- Read-only permissions over all domains or all resources in a certain domain
- Read-only permissions over a certain workflow within a certain domain
- A combination of full control and read-only access to specific resources in specific domains

Summary

We have taken a look at the SWF service and how the SWF service can be used to create and manage a serverless application's processing logic and maintain the state. With SWF, the workflow can easily be designed in the management console. We have taken a look at the components of SWF and have discussed how to control access to the resources created within the SWF service. In the next chapter, we will look into the most powerful component of the AWS cloud: the AWS Lambda service.

Questions

1. The SWF can be used to separate which two parts of an application?
2. Fill in the blank: Within a workflow, a _____ task is used to close the workflow execution.
3. True or false: An actor is a person that need to perform an action.
4. True or false: A task list is populated with activities manually when creating an activity task.
5. How do the workers poll the service in SWF?
6. True or false: We can use the global endpoint for SWF or we can create regional endpoints to save on cross-region traffic?
7. A secret key and access key will need to be assigned to each actor within the SWF. What will be the best practice for key distribution within the SWF?

Further reading

- **SWF Documentation**: https://docs.aws.amazon.com/amazonswf/latest/developerguide/swf-dg-intro-to-swf.html
- **SWF Service Endpoints**: https://docs.aws.amazon.com/general/latest/gr/rande.html#swf_region
- **SWF IAM Access Control**: https://docs.aws.amazon.com/amazonswf/latest/developerguide/swf-dev-iam.html

Overview of AWS Lambda
17

In the preceding chapters, we demonstrated the ability to use different serverless environments to store files and database content, provide content distribution and caching, implement messaging, and coordinate tasks within the AWS cloud. To process information, the AWS environment offers another serverless environment that can be run on demand and with the greatest of ease. This is probably the most powerful component of the AWS cloud: the AWS Lambda service.

The following topics will be covered in this chapter:

- Introduction to AWS Lambda
- Supported languages
- Creating a Lambda function
- Supported AWS services
- Business cases

Technical requirements

To get the most benefit out of this chapter, a basic understanding of the way an application processes a piece of code in a modern operating system is required. Basic familiarity with different programming languages, their structure, and their features is a benefit.

Introduction to AWS Lambda

The AWS Lambda service is a fully managed, highly available and highly scalable, processing environment that allows us to process code written in multiple different programming languages without the need to run and configure any infrastructure.

When working with Lambda, the service will orchestrate the creation of the resources required to run our code. Everything from the allocation of resources, building the operating environment, the code interpreter, and the programming language runtimes will be made available by Lambda. All we need to do is bring our code and any dependencies to run it.

Packaging a function

To run our code, we need to package it in a ZIP or WAR file and then either upload it to S3 and reference the location or author the code directly within the Lambda service upon function creation. Within the package, we would include the following:

- The code to run
- Optionally any dependencies, libraries (even native ones), and any executable files that your code will be calling

The optional components are stored in Lambda layers. Each layer represent a simple way to logically separate parts of the package. This way we can maintain, secure, distribute, and update each layer separately. The code package you provide is called a function.

Functions, runtimes, sources, and resources

A function in Lambda always processes some kind of input data, be it an event or any other type of trigger that can invoke the Lambda function from an event source. An event source can be another AWS service, or from any other compatible source inside or outside AWS. When configuring a Lambda function, we always need to define a runtime, as this will ensure that the appropriate programming language support is available in the Lambda execution environment.

Once the event source invokes a function, the execution starts and a Lambda function that is running will push out metrics and optionally any kind of application log output to a log stream. Log streams are stored in CloudWatch and give us the ability to analyze the performance and learn the characteristics of our Lambda functions so we can optimize them and achieve peak performance.

Once the function completes its task, the output is either returned to the requester or stored in so-called downstream resources. Downstream resources can be any type of environment that Lambda can write to, such as an S3 bucket for outputting files, DynamoDB to output key-value pairs, another Lambda function to perform additional processing, and so on.

The Lambda invocation architecture is displayed in the following diagram:

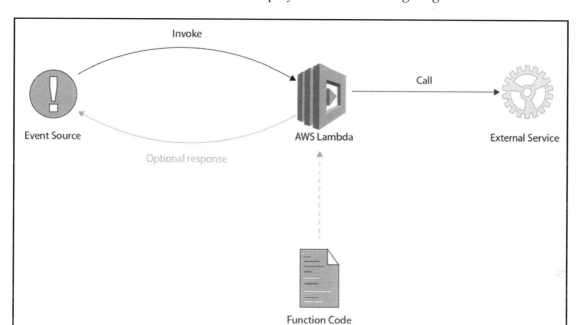

Supported languages

The Lambda service operates an Amazon Linux operating system to provide the resources necessary to execute the code. Usually, this is a stable version of Amazon Linux with a kernel that is destined for long-term support. At the time of writing, the Linux kernel in the Lambda environment is 4.14, which is quite a modern kernel so we can expect a large number of runtimes to be supported. To look up the latest version, please take a look at the link under **Lambda Current OS Version** in the *Further reading* section of this chapter.

The programming languages currently supported natively within the Lambda environment are Java, Go, PowerShell, Node.js, C#, Python, and Ruby, but Lambda also provides a runtime API that allows us the ability to use any other programming language to run our functions.

When a Lambda function is executed, an execution environment will be created, and this execution environment has the ability to provide support for any of the following:

- A single version of a single programming language
- Multiple versions of a single programming language
- Multiple programming languages

When a Lambda function that has previously been executed is run again, the service will try to reuse the existing execution environment. This can speed up provisioning for a Lambda function dramatically. Due to the ability to support multiple versions and languages, we have the ability to easily integrate newer versions of code into existing Lambda execution environments, and also the ability to swap out the programming language.

When invoking the same function from multiple sources at the same time, multiple execution environments will be provisioned. This is important as each execution environment will create its own log stream in the CloudWatch logs, so we will need to be mindful of that fact when troubleshooting a Lambda function that has potentially run in parallel.

Creating a Lambda function

We can easily create a new Lambda function from the management console by navigating to the AWS Lambda section and execute the following steps:

1. Click on **Create function** to begin the process:

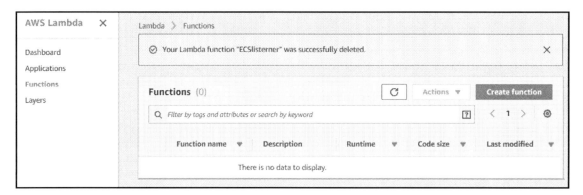

2. The **Create function** dialog will give us the option to select the following:

   - **Author from scratch**: Write our own function that will be completely custom
   - **Blueprints**: Use a template that AWS has provided for us to help with authoring the function
   - **AWS Serverless Application Repository**: A repository for predefined Lambda functions

3. We will select the **Author from scratch** option, to write our own function in this scenario:

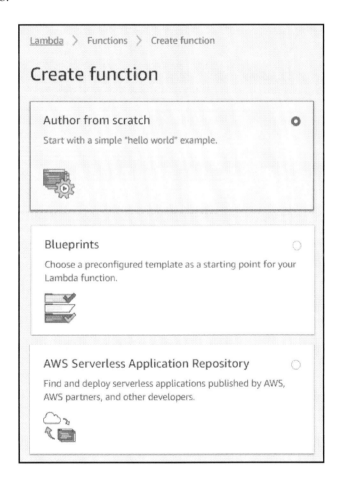

4. In the **Author from scratch** section, we need to name our function, select a runtime, and create or select an existing role if we have one, so that the Lambda function will have the necessary permissions to execute the code:

5. After the function is created, a window with the function configuration details appears. Here, we have the ability to use the **Designer** tool. This is an invaluable resource for building Lambda functions, as it can help us complete common tasks by giving us the ability to quickly integrate our Lambda function with triggers that will invoke a function and downstream resources that will receive its output:

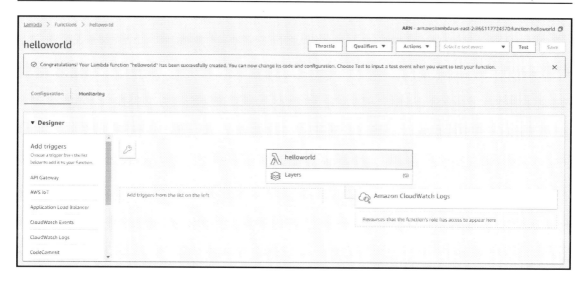

6. Further down, we can scroll to the **Function code** section. Here, we can author our code straight from the browser and save it into our function package. In our example, we will be using a simple Node.js function that replies with Hello, World! when invoked:

```
exports.handler = function(event, context) {
context.succeed('Hello, World!');
};
```

7. After changing the function, we will need to hit the **Save** button in the top-right to save the function configuration. We can also use the IDE provided in Lambda to easily create new files and add other components needed to run our code:

8. Further down, we can set **Environment variables** that can be used directly by our function code. We can also add additional key-value tags that will only be seen from the AWS management environment:

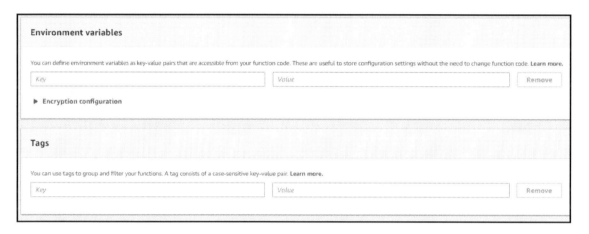

Environment variables

You can define environment variables as key-value pairs that are accessible from your function code. These are useful to store configuration settings without the need to change function code. **Learn more.**

| Key | Value | Remove |

▶ **Encryption configuration**

Tags

You can use tags to group and filter your functions. A tag consists of a case-sensitive key-value pair. **Learn more.**

| Key | Value | Remove |

9. Going further, we get to the **Execution role** section, where we can modify the execution role to change the permissions for our function code. We can also set the size of our function in the **Basic settings** section. Here, we can set the memory we want to use for our function. The amount of memory defines the amount of CPU to be added to the function; these scale together, as does the price of each function execution. We also have the ability to set the timeout. Initially, the timeout was limited to 300 seconds, but it has been extended to 900 seconds since November, 2018.

 Note that the Lambda change to a 15-minute timeout might not yet be reflected in the exam, and the old five-minute value may be the correct answer!

Please refer to the following screenshot:

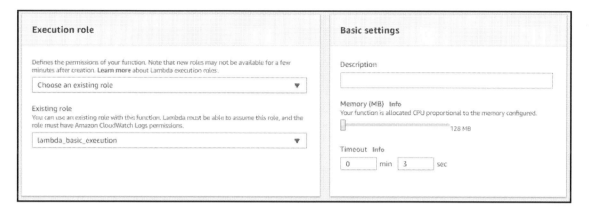

10. At the bottom of the page, we can configure the network. We can either run the Lambda with the default (recommended) network environment, or we can tie the Lambda into a VPC. We would usually only do so if some kind of compliance or governance reason existed.

11. We can also configure the Dead Letter Queue in the **Debugging and error handling** section. Here, we can specify how to handle executions that fail. We can specify how many retries we want to have and, if the function fails on all retries, to forward the diagnostic output to a Dead Letter Queue.

12. By default, each region in each account has the ability to execute 1000 concurrent Lambda executions. In the **Concurrency** section, we have the ability to either use the default concurrency or reserve a certain amount of concurrent executions for our function. We would preferably do that for mission-critical Lambda functions. This is a soft limit, and if you require the ability to execute more than 1,000 concurrent Lambda functions in a region, you can contact AWS support to raise your account limit.

13. Lastly, in the **Auditing and compliance** section, we have the ability to tie in the Lambda function with CloudTrail, which can record each and every API call to the Lambda function, thereby giving us a complete auditing trail of all actions and invocations of the Lambda function:

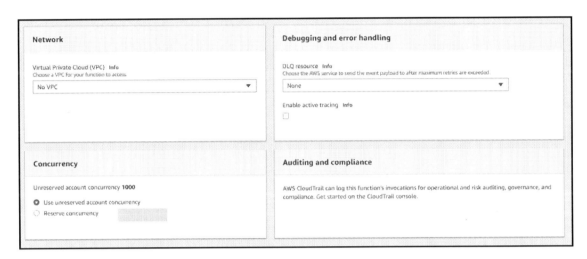

14. Now that we have reached the end of the configuration section, we can scroll up and click on the monitoring section. Here, we have a quick overview of the execution statistics and performance of our Lambda function. For detailed information, we would still be using the CloudWatch interface, which we will look at in the next chapter:

Our function is now ready for invocation, and now we can configure the appropriate triggers that will invoke the service and execute the function.

Supported AWS services

Lambda supports triggers from almost any AWS service, including, but not limited to, the following:

- Amazon S3
- Amazon Kinesis
- Amazon SNS, SQS, and SES
- Amazon Cognito
- AWS CloudFormation and AWS Config
- Amazon CloudWatch Logs and Events (supports scheduled events)
- Amazon API Gateway (including custom invocations through HTTP links)
- AWS CodeCommit, CodeBuild, IoT Button, Alexa, Lex, CloudFront, and so on

There are two types of invocations supported for the Lambda service:

- **Push**: An event in an AWS service or a custom event can invoke the lambda function
- **Pull**: The Lambda service polls an AWS services stream or queue and retrieves tasks

An example of a push-based Lambda invocation would be an image-processing app. The users would upload files to an S3 bucket, and the event of the S3 file being uploaded can trigger a Lambda function. That Lambda function can then pick up an image, extract the metadata from the image, and output the information (such as size, type of image, date, and S3 location) to a DynamoDB table. In this case, we need to also provide the appropriate invocation permissions to the S3 bucket to be able to invoke the Lambda, and of course provide Lambda with the appropriate role with permissions to write to DynamoDB.

An example of a pull-based Lambda invocation would be the second part of the same image processing app. Once the first Lambda function records the metadata in the DynamoDB table, a second Lambda function that listens to the DynamoDB stream will pick up the changes and create a static website file in S3 with the information from the DynamoDB table, so that the image will be served on the static website. In the pull scenario, we need to allow the lambda to read the DynamoDB stream by providing permission in the Lambda execution role.

Business cases

When it comes to using Lambda, the use cases are literally unlimited. Anywhere there is a need to process some kind of information or process/transform/extract some kind of data, we can simply write a Lambda function to perform the task. The main business driver behind Lambda functions is that we never pay for any idling infrastructure and are able to match the cost of processing to the demand for services.

Lambda is also extremely cost-effective. When we start using Lambda, we get an indefinite free tier. The first million requests and 400,000 GB-seconds fall under the free tier; that is a lot of processing time that we essentially get for free. At the time of writing, the cost per request beyond the free tier is $0.0000002 and the cost per GB-second is $0.00001667. Putting that into perspective, if our website has 1 million visitors per day:

- Each visitor would represent one lambda invocation.
- Each response would take 100 ms to process the query from the user.
- Our lambda function would have 128 MB of memory assigned to it.
- The total cost for this application would be **under $10 per month**.

Web applications, microservices, and backends

A Lambda service can essentially be only invoked from within AWS. But, we have an option to use another AWS service as a frontend to our Lambda service. For example, we can use the API gateway or an S3 bucket to provide our trigger for our Lambda function.

A typical web application will have some kind of input that will be collected from the user and then processed by the backend in the web server. But what can we do when we host our website on a static content service such as S3? There is no server-side processing in S3, so how do we implement this functionality? We can use a Lambda function (or multiple Lambdas) to provide the same functionality a feature-rich dynamic website would. Two typical approaches for triggering a Lambda from a static website would be as follows:

- Using client-side scripts, we can generate and upload documents with the content entered by the user to a *trigger* S3 bucket. Each document that is uploaded invokes a Lambda function that reads the information and records it into a downstream resource.
- Using a link in the static website to an API gateway, which invokes the lambda function and forwards the request to be processed by Lambda.

The API gateway approach can also be used to front Lambdas that can act as microservices. Each Lambda function can represent a microservice that runs only upon invocation from the API gateway. The API Gateway can also be used to invoke different Lambda functions, according to different input methods or different data paths being accessed in the incoming request.

Asynchronous data processing

Lambda supports both synchronous and asynchronous invocations. The asynchronous response model lends itself well to asynchronous data-processing requests. We can issue as many requests in parallel as our soft limit for concurrent Lambda executions allows us to do (by default, up to 1,000 per region).

A good example would be an image-processing application. We mentioned such an application in `Chapter 15`, *Handling Messaging with Simple Notification Service* when we talked about an image-resizing tool that would take an input from an S3 bucket and resize it to a web format, a mobile format, and a thumbnail. The processing itself can be done with a Lambda function (or three Lambda functions, one for each format), which can easily be invoked by the act of the image being uploaded to S3. As soon as the image is uploaded to the source bucket, the Lambdas pick up the original image, transform the image to the desired sizes, and then store the output to one or several S3 buckets so that the image can be displayed on the website.

Live support and chatbots

One way automation is coming into our everyday lives is with user support. Almost every service provider website nowadays has a support chat popup that tries to help us find the right solution. Usually the *person* chatting with us awkwardly offers help with a standardized sentence, and then when we respond with our question, we will usually be redirected to some general responses in the Q/A or the provider's knowledge base. But in some cases, these chat systems have been designed to be quite intelligent in the way they respond to questions; in some cases, it is getting hard to distinguish between a person with poor grammar skills and a chat bot.

The Lambda service is perfect for implementing chat bot logic as the service is highly scalable and can meet the needs of hundreds of thousands of users concurrently out of the box. Using Lambda as a chatbot backend is also very economical, as there are never any idle resources running when using Lambda.

Intelligent scaling and IT automation

Lambda can also be used in combination with monitoring platforms such as CloudWatch. We can create alarms and invoke Lambdas when our application usage reaches a certain threshold. The Lambda function can then perform additional analysis of the data being recorded from the application and determine the pattern of the traffic increase or decrease, and the best way to scale the application at hand. Lambdas can do more than just scale EC2 instances like the AutoScaling feature; Lambdas can scale databases instances, create read replicas, manage caching, and so on.

Essentially, scaling is only the beginning. We can use the Lambda service to continuously monitor streams or logs from our mission-critical applications and enhance the way we manage our applications. They can provide advanced warning of failures or errors in our application, and can perform remediation actions in our infrastructure. Everything will fail, all the time, but with intelligent IT automation with Lambdas, we can make it seem as through that failure never even happened.

Summary

In this chapter, we took a look at the Lambda service and how we can implement serverless processing in our application design. We took a look at some features of the Lambda service and saw an introduction to creating and configuring a Lambda function. We also discussed what other services can invoke a Lambda function and how it can be integrated to provide different kinds of processing, with either the push or pull mechanism. Finally, we took a look at some use cases that give a good overview of how we can use Lambda and what kinds of services it can help us deliver. In the next chapter, we will be monitoring resources with Amazon CloudWatch.

Questions

1. Which operating system does the Lambda service use to provide the execution environment?
2. Which programming languages are supported by Lambda?
3. What is a downstream resource in Lambda?
4. What does the Lambda Designer help us with?
5. True or false: The Lambda service has a public endpoint that defaults to the North Virginia region, but other regional endpoints can be created if required.

6. Your Lambda service requires read access to the S3 bucket named `images` and read-write access to the bucket named `thumbnails`; how would you configure permissions for the Lambda function?

7. An Amazon Kinesis Stream needs to invoke the lambda service; you are creating the invocation role for Kinesis but are unable to find where to apply this permission on the Kinesis stream. Why is this?

8. You have a requirement to invoke the Lambda function from a public website hosted at another provider. How can you achieve this?

Further reading

- **AWS Lambda Documentation**: https://docs.aws.amazon.com/lambda/latest/dg/welcome.html
- **Writing Lambda Functions**: https://docs.aws.amazon.com/lambda/latest/dg/lambda-introduction-function.html
- **Lambda Layers**: https://docs.aws.amazon.com/lambda/latest/dg/configuration-layers.html
- **Lambda Runtimes**: https://docs.aws.amazon.com/lambda/latest/dg/lambda-runtimes.html
- **Lambda Current OS Version**: https://docs.aws.amazon.com/lambda/latest/dg/current-supported-versions.html
- **Lambda Runtime API**: https://docs.aws.amazon.com/lambda/latest/dg/runtimes-api.html
- **AWS Serverless Application Repository**: https://docs.aws.amazon.com/serverlessrepo/latest/devguide/what-is-serverlessrepo.html
- **Supported AWS Services**: https://docs.aws.amazon.com/lambda/latest/dg/invoking-lambda-function.html
- **Lambda Pricing**: https://aws.amazon.com/lambda/pricing/

18
Monitoring Resources with Amazon CloudWatch

A crucial aspect of running any application is having the ability to look into its performance and operating characteristics. Implementing monitoring is a crucial step that helps us understand the application's behavior and operational performance patterns. Only when we understand how our application performs will we be able to improve the application and deliver a better service to the end users. I like to say to my clients: *Running an application without motioning is like flying an airplane with sunglasses on... at night.*

The following topics will be covered in this chapter:

- Introduction to Amazon CloudWatch
- How CloudWatch works
- Elements of CloudWatch
- Metrics and alarms
- CloudWatch dashboards
- Monitoring EC2
- Monitoring RDS
- Monitoring ElastiCache
- SQS monitoring and logging
- Monitoring SNS with CloudWatch
- Monitoring Elastic Beanstalk environments
- Billing alerts

Technical requirements

A basic understanding of performance monitoring and metrics analysis of modern computing systems is required to get the most out of this chapter. Please refer to the GitHub link for this chapter: `https://github.com/PacktPublishing/AWS-Certified-SysOps-Administrator-Associate-Guide/tree/master/Chapter18`.

Introduction to Amazon CloudWatch

Any application that consumes any kind of compute, storage, or network resources should be monitored. The term *monitoring* is commonly used in place of four separate features that allow us to get complete insight into the state of our applications:

- Resource usage metering
- System and application log collection
- Resource utilization graphing
- Alarming upon predefined trigger

We need to collect metrics and logs to be able to determine patterns of usage. The metrics, logs, and patterns will allow us to understand the resource consumption characteristics of an application, and once we have understood the way our application consumes resources, we can create alarms that are usually represented as certain thresholds, beyond which our application operates in an abnormal state.

Many monitoring systems are available as open source products or proprietary solutions. Some have the four previously mentioned characteristics, while others are very focused tools. Some monitoring systems also upgrade the four characteristics by providing us with mechanisms that can connect to resources and perform actions over these resources. While CloudWatch itself does not provide any actionable items, it can work together with other AWS services such as SNS, autoscaling, and Lambda to perform any kind of action that can be automated.

Amazon CloudWatch is a fully managed, fully integrated metering, log collection, graphing, and alarming utility for resources running in the AWS cloud and any on-premises resources connected to the AWS cloud.

How CloudWatch works

The CloudWatch service collects the metrics and the logs from any systems it monitors. Each and every AWS service that we create and use in our account automatically starts reporting its metrics to CloudWatch. If the default metrics are not sufficient to paint a complete image of the state of our application, we have the ability to create custom metrics and send any kind of relevant custom data to the service.

Any metrics, logs, or custom data that CloudWatch receives are stored into the CloudWatch repository, which is stored within the region that the services operate in. This means that any data stored in one region will never be replicated to any other region. Any on-premises or remote services where we enable log delivery to CloudWatch will also have to be configured with one of the CloudWatch regional endpoints which will, of course, mean that the data will be stored within that region.

To retrieve the metrics, logs, and statistics from the CloudWatch environment, we can use the CloudWatch management console, the AWS CLI, and the SDKs. We will of course have to select a region in any of those tools due to the previously mentioned regionally bound metric storage.

We also have the ability to perform actions upon certain conditions called alarms. A CloudWatch alarm can send a notification or inform other services that a certain metric has breached a threshold, and the recipient can then perform some kind of manual or automated action to remediate the situation.

The following diagram represents the CloudWatch architecture:

Elements of CloudWatch

When publishing metrics and logs to CloudWatch, each service or custom component is required to adhere to the CloudWatch data structure. In this section, we will be taking a look at the following components of the CloudWatch service:

- Namespaces
- Metrics
- Dimensions
- Statistics
- Percentiles
- Alarms

Namespaces

Each and every piece of data that is sent to CloudWatch has to have a namespace attribute assigned to it. There is no default, and each service will usually be using a namespace in the form of `AWS/servicename` that corresponds to the name of the service. This allows us to easily distinguish between groups of metrics, whether accessing them from the console, the CLI, or SDK.

When publishing custom metrics that have no AWS analog, we will also be required to specify a namespace. When creating metrics, we have complete freedom for choosing our namespaces as long as they do not exceed 256 alphanumeric characters (0–9, A–Z, and a–z). The following special characters are also allowed: period, hyphen, underscore, forward slash, hash, and colon.

Metrics

Metrics are one of the core concepts within the CloudWatch environment. A metric is a data point collected at a certain point in time that represents a numeric value of the resource consumption. For example, a metric can be expressed as the current utilization of the CPU or current write queue length of an EBS volume and so on. Metrics can be standard AWS resource metrics or custom metrics. Metrics can be collected in normal or detailed periods.

Normal and detailed metrics

By default, all metrics created by any AWS service are collected on a 5-minute intervals. These are the so-called *normal* metrics. But AWS has enabled us to allow detailed metrics within a high number of services; the detailed metrics available from the AWS services are available in 1-minute intervals. The detailed metrics enable us to perform actions upon alarms from triggers that are much closer together than with the normal metrics. For example, when performing an action on two consecutive triggers, we will need to wait 10 minutes before the action is performed, while with detailed monitoring we can do it in only 2 minutes. While normal metrics are free, enabling detailed monitoring will mean that we will incur an additional cost for collecting the metrics with a higher frequency.

But is 1 minute detailed enough? Modern applications running in containers or as serverless Lambda functions can be scaled in under a second, and data that is minutes old might be too old. This is why CloudWatch enables us to collect custom metrics from our environment for a period as short as 1 second. Collecting metrics as frequently as 1 second apart will allow us to react to any kind of change in our application in real time.

Data retention for metrics

As you can imagine, the amount of metrics that CloudWatch collects from all clients in AWS is absolutely mind-boggling. Anyone who has ever designed or maintained any motoring system and the database the system relies on will appreciate the skill of the AWS CloudWatch team. The fact that CloudWatch is able to collect and store millions (or perhaps billions?) of data points concurrently is quite a feat. All I can say is kudos to the CloudWatch team!

The sheer volume of data being collected means that it is literally impossible to store the data indefinitely, which is why AWS has defined a retention period for each of the previously mentioned metrics as follows:

- Any metrics with a collection interval of below 1 minute is available for 3 hours
- 1-minute metrics are available for 15 days
- 5-minute metrics are available for 63 days
- 1-hour metrics are available for 15 months

Once the retention period expires, the data is aggregated to the next level and retained accordingly. For example, 1-second metrics will be aggregated to 1-minute metrics after 3 hours. The 1-minute metrics will in turn be aggregated to 5-minute metrics after 15 days. All 5-minute metrics are aggregated to 1-hour metrics after 63 days, and all metrics are discarded once they are more than 15 months old.

Dimensions

Each metric has to be identified somehow, and with CloudWatch this is done through dimensions. Dimensions are key-value pairs that identify metrics. For example, each EC2 instance will have a dimension of `instance-id` that will have a value of that instance's ID.

Each metric can have up to 10 dimensions assigned to it. By adding additional dimensions we have the ability to present the data according to those additional dimensions. For example, when our application is composed of hundreds of instances that belong to different development environment such as production, test, and staging, it might be difficult to understand which parts of the application are consuming how many resources. We can project additional dimensions on the metrics from our environment to group and isolate different parts of an application in our data analysis, graphing, and reporting procedures.

Statistics

Statistics are represented as metrics that have been aggregated over a period of time. Statistics help us discover performance and operational characteristics of our application such as service ceilings, averages, and percentages. The following statistics are available in CloudWatch:

- **Minimum**: The lowest value within a certain period
- **Maximum**: The highest value within a certain period
- **Sum**: The sum of all values within a certain period
- **Average**: An average of all values within a certain period
- **SampleCount**: The number of values within a certain period
- **pNN.NN**: The value of the percentile (for example up-time percentage) up to 2 decimal points

Percentile

The percentile represents the relative position of a specific metric compared to other metrics within the dataset. For example, the 50th percentile means that half of the values in the dataset are lower, while half are higher. The 90th percentile would mean that 90% of the data has a lower value. Percentiles are typically used when performing a statistical analysis to determine any outliers or anomalies in the datasets that we are working on. At the time of writing, percentiles are available with metrics from the following AWS services:

- Amazon EC2
- Amazon RDS
- Amazon Kinesis
- The application and classic load balancer
- The API Gateway

CloudWatch Logs

On top of metrics, CloudWatch also has the ability to accept logs from our operating system or our application. The CloudWatch Logs component stores the logs into the same data store as the metrics but maintains the logs indefinitely. We can also set the retention period or we can create a procedure for shipping logs to the S3 service for long-term retention and life-cycling into archive. We are able to deliver logs to CloudWatch Logs via the CloudWatch agent that can be installed on any EC2 instance or on-premises server with a compatible operating system.

Alarms

CloudWatch alarms give us the ability to create actions upon any kind of metric, log or event. Before creating alarms, we will always need to determine the reason for the alarm. There are numerous reasons why we would require an action to be performed on a metric and we will look at some examples, namely the following:

- Notifications
- Autoscaling
- Auto-recovery
- Event-based computing

The simplest goal for alarms is notifications. We can create an alarm that will notify us of a certain metric being above a certain threshold for a certain period of time. For example, we need to be aware of any RDS instance where the available space is below 10%. We can simply create an alarm that will send an email via an SNS topic to our incident response department to deal with the issue and increase the size of the volume or handle it in another appropriate manner.

We can also use the alarms to enable autoscaling for our applications. As discussed in the EC2 chapter, we can use CloudWatch to scale our EC2 clusters if the CPU metrics are above a certain percentage for a certain amount of time. For example, if the aggregate CPU usage of the cluster is above 80% for 5 minutes, the CloudWatch alarm can notify the autoscaling service and a scaling action that will increase the number of instances in the cluster will be performed.

The same approach can be used for auto-recovery. For example, we have an application where our developers have identified an issue that causes the instance to continue processing requests even after the session has been closed. Instances affected by this issue will start exhibiting a continuous increase in the CPU utilization, which does not affect the application until it hits 100% and cannot take on any new requests. The developers are working on a bug fix that should be due out in a few days, but in the meantime we need to make sure we implement a temporary solution that will reboot any affected instances before they hit 90% CPU utilization. We can simply create an alarm, for which we set an EC2 action to reboot the instance when the CPU reaches the desired threshold. This is a simple solution that will allow our application to survive until the bug fix is in place.

CloudWatch alarms can also be used as triggers for event-based computing. Literally any metric and any threshold can be used to trigger some kind of function or other process that will perform some kind of intelligent action. For example, when monitoring our RDS volumes, instead of only notifying the incident response team, we can also subscribe a Lambda function to the same SNS topic, and that Lambda function can have the appropriate permissions to modify our RDS instances. In this case, we could enable the Lambda function to automatically increase the size of the RDS volume and completely automate the response scenario in this example.

Creating a CloudWatch alarm

To create a CloudWatch alarm, we can simply navigate to the CloudWatch management console and select alarms from the menu:

1. We click the blue **Create Alarm** button to open the **Create new alarm** dialog:

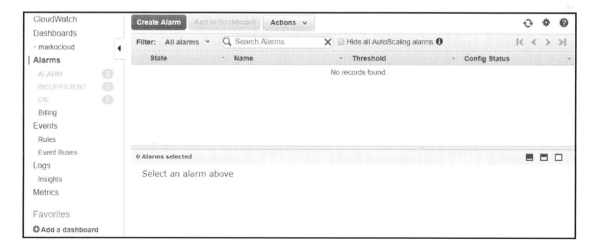

2. In the **Create new alarm** dialogue, we need to first select a metric by clicking on the **Select metric** button:

3. This will open another dialogue where we can select the metrics. We have the ability to select metrics from different categories and drill down to the exact metric that we would like to set a threshold on. In this example, we selected **EC2** and the **Per-Instance Metrics** where we selected the **CPUUtilization** metric to use in our alarm. We also have the ability to rename the metric by clicking on the little pencil icon in the upper-left corner of the dialogue.

Once we are satisfied with our selection, we click on the **Select metric** button:

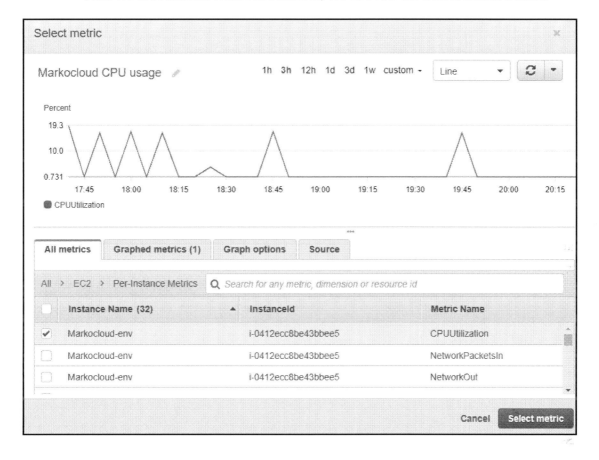

4. Going back to the **Create new alarm** dialogue, we will now see the metric and a preview of the graph. We will need to scroll further down to configure the alarm:

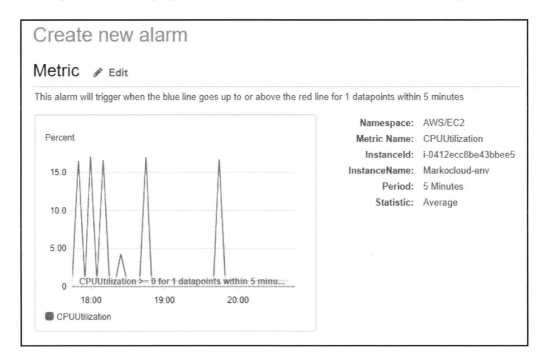

5. Scrolling further down, we need to name the alarm and optionally give it a description. In the **Alarm** details, we also need to configure the threshold and the duration of the threshold breach before the alarm is triggered. As we can see in the example, we have selected that the alarm will be triggered when the CPU utilization is above 80% for two out of five sequential data points:

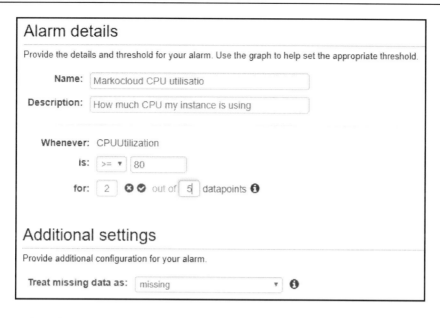

6. Further down, we will create an action. In the example, the action is just a notification that will be sent out to a notification SNS topic that has previously been created within our account. We are also able to add additional actions including autoscaling actions that can increase or decrease the number of instances in our autoscaling group and EC2 actions that can perform a recover, stop, terminate, or reboot action on our EC2 instance:

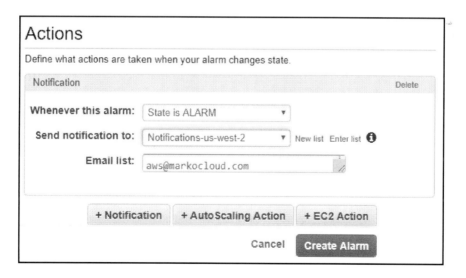

7. Once the alarm is created, the service will display the alarm in the management console:

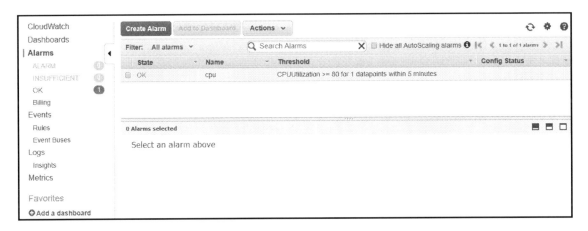

In this example, we configured an alarm that will notify us of an abnormal EC2 instance condition via an email that is sent out via the SNS service. This is a very useful alarm that can be implemented not only on single instances but on fleets of instances running in our EC2 environment.

CloudWatch dashboards

Whenever we provision any kind of resource, we will automatically get an overview of the metrics of that resource available from the CloudWatch **Overview** section, as can be seen in the following screenshot:

By clicking the **Overview** section, we have the ability to select each service individually and take a look at a nice graphical representation of the metrics for each service:

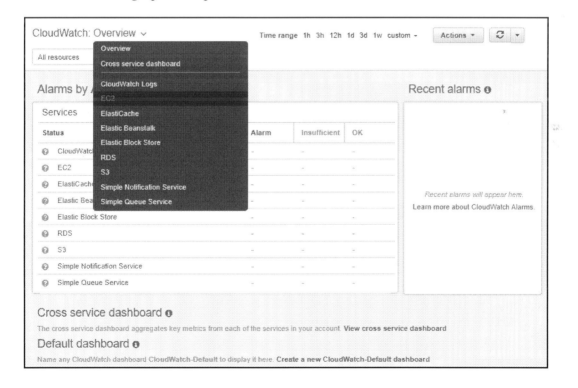

When the **Overview** section does not provide the metrics that we want to quickly glance at, we have the ability to create dashboards where we can customize the way the metrics are displayed. We can select metrics from one service or metrics from different services in one dashboard and thus create a simple way to view the metrics that are relevant to the health of our application.

Creating a CloudWatch dashboard

1. To create a new dashboard, simply select **Dashboards** from the menu in the CloudWatch management console and then click on the **Create dashboard** button:

2. In the **Create new dashboard** dialogue, we simply name the dashboard and click **Create dashboard**:

3. Once the dashboard is created, a pop-up window allowing us to add widgets to the dashboard is presented. Here, we have the ability to choose line and stacked graphs, current metrics, and more complex query results to be displayed. We also have the ability to create a text window with markdown formatting where we can include direct links to services, documentation, wikis, and so on:

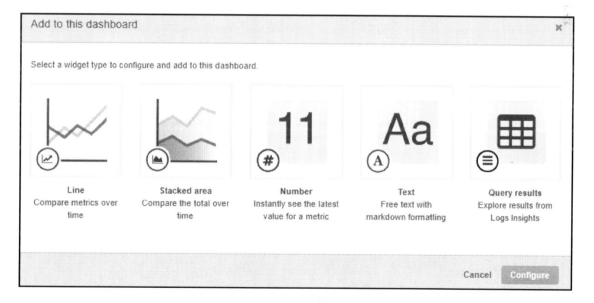

4. In our example, we will first select a line graph and fill it up with relevant metrics about our application. The categories presented here are the same as when creating the alarm and we are able to drill down upon or search identifiers, service types, and tags:

5. Once we have selected our metrics, a preview graph is presented and we simply need to click on **Create widget**:

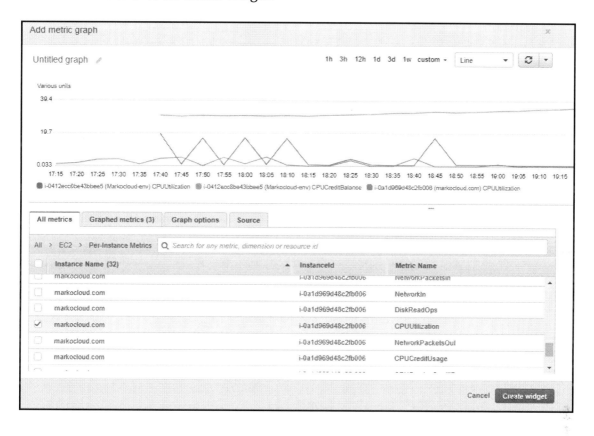

6. Once the widget is added, we need to also click on **Save dashboard** to keep the widget in the dashboard. We can also resize and reposition the widget to our liking before clicking **Save**:

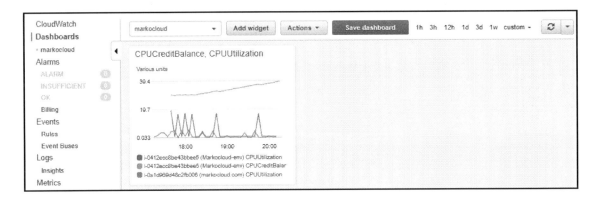

7. By clicking on **Add widget**, we can add additional widgets that will display additional information on our dashboard and the end result could look something like this:

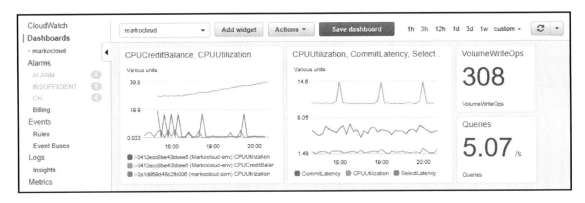

Dashboards are an easy way to create an environment where only relevant metrics are presented to the user that creates the dashboard. We would normally use only the metrics that can help us quickly gauge the health and state of our application in a dashboard to make the best use of this feature. We can create multiple dashboards and completely customize them in a way that fits our requirements.

Monitoring EC2

When working with our virtual machine instances in EC2, we are provided with standard metrics that can help us determine the performance and state of our instance. For each instance, we are able to enable detailed metrics if required and install a CloudWatch agent that can provide us with custom metrics and the ability to export system and application logs into the CloudWatch Logs component.

By default, the CloudWatch metrics being collected for EC2 instances are any metrics related to CPU, disk, and network utilization as well as the status check that determines the instance health. Most new users to EC2 are astonished to find that no information about memory usage is provided within the CloudWatch metrics. There is a simple reason for that: AWS has no access to the operating system and thus has no way of correctly determining the amount of memory the instance is consuming. It is true that these metrics could be retrieved from the hypervisor and delivered to CloudWatch, but since the hypervisor has no way of knowing how the memory is actually being consumed within the operating system, this metric would be useless in a lot of cases.

Take, for example, a database server. The database will try to grab as much available memory as possible to utilize as much of the memory for caching and other performance enhancements as possible. The hypervisor would suddenly determine that the instance is consuming 99% of its memory.

Because of this fact, AWS leaves it up to the customer to determine if the memory utilization metric is important, and when it is important it can be delivered to the CloudWatch service as a custom metric with the CloudWatch agent straight from the operating system. Alongside the metric, we can also include logs that provide diagnostic information or a better interpretation of memory usage. In any case, it is a best practice to select an instance that will have the exact right amount of memory assigned to it, so a high memory utilization is nothing but a sign of success, as far as the SysOps team is concerned.

As soon as we start an EC2 instance in any availability zone within a region, the CloudWatch management console will provide us with an overview section for the EC2 service:

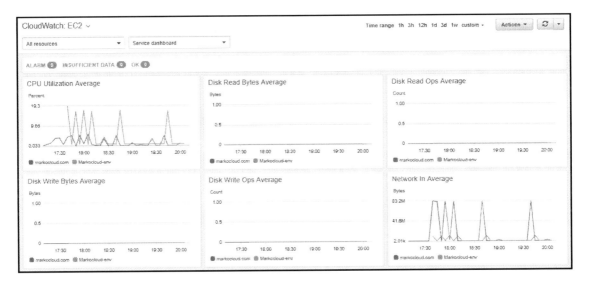

The overview will show aggregated performance metrics across all of our instances so the graphs in this section can become quite oversaturated, so perhaps a better approach would be to use a custom dashboard for sets of EC2 instances that belong to each application, as represented in the following screenshot:

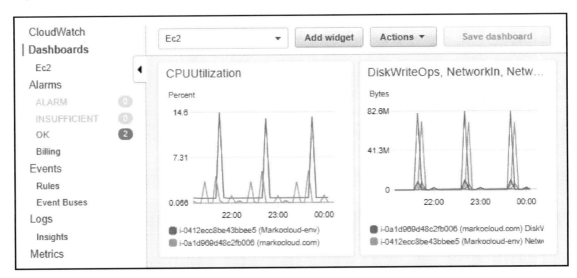

EC2 status troubleshooting

With EC2, we also have the ability to perform basic troubleshooting and recovery by monitoring the status check metric of our instance. As soon as the status check is undetermined or failed, we can trigger an alarm that will auto-recover or reboot our instance so that it is restarted on another host and the status check is resolved. This is a really good feature to implement on any mission-critical instances or instances that cannot be clustered due to licensing or other limitations:

1. To enable the status check alarm, we simply need to navigate to the EC2 management console and select our instance. Then we select the **Status Check** tab from the instance properties and click on **Create Status Check Alarm**:

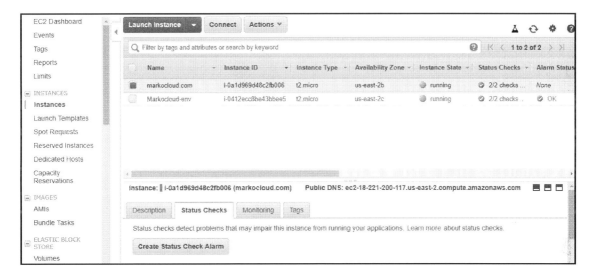

2. In the **Create Alarm** dialogue, we can select whether to send a notification or take an action on the instance (or both). We also have the ability to control under what condition to trigger the alarm. When finished, we simply click **Create Alarm**:

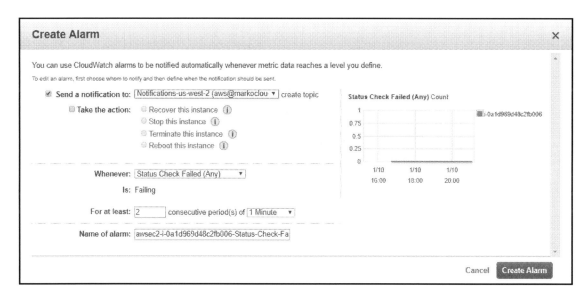

3. A pop-up window appears that informs us of the alarm's creation, and a link that will lead us directly to the alarm is presented. We can either click the link or click **Close** if we are done:

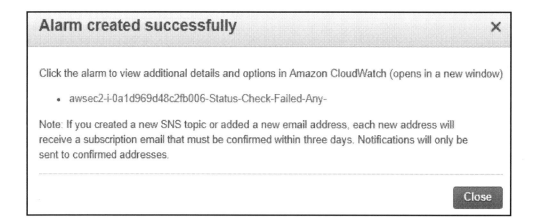

4. Clicking on the link provided in the previous dialogue will display the alarm in the **Alarms** section of the CloudWatch management console:

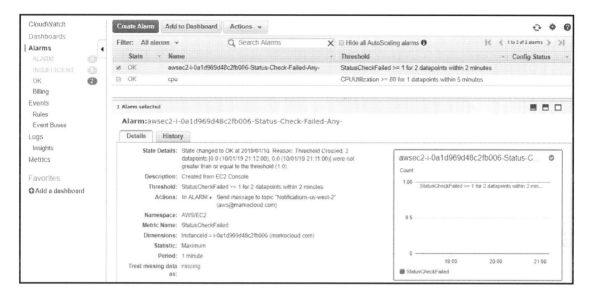

We have now created an alarm that will perform an action if our instance fails a status check.

EC2 custom metrics

As we have mentioned, there are many scenarios where publishing custom metrics is required. Either it is because we require operating system metrics that are not provided by default or because we are looking to post metrics from our own application to the CloudWatch service. We have the ability to use the CloudWatch agent, the AWS CLI, and the CloudWatch enhanced monitoring scripts that are downloadable.

Reporting custom metrics using the AWS CLI

We can use the AWS command line to report metrics to the CloudWatch environment. First, we need to make sure the account that we are using has permissions to post to CloudWatch. When automating, it is always preferable to attach the permissions to the EC2 instance role than to hard-code the credentials into the EC2 instance.

To report metrics, we can use the `aws cloudwatch put-metric-data` command within the instance that is able to read the metrics being written to CloudWatch. The required operators are as follows:

- `--metric-name`: The name of the metric
- `--namespace`: The namespace the metric will be recorded to
- `--value`: The current value that was collected from the system
- `--timestamp`: The time and date when the value was collected

Putting it all together would look something like this:

```
aws cloudwatch put-metric-data --metric-name WebsiteVisitors --namespace
markocloud --value 37 --timestamp 2019-01-09T20:02:17.344Z
```

As you can see, it is fairly easy to script the delivery of custom metrics via the AWS CLI itself. In a real-world scenario, the value and timestamp would be represented as variables sourced from a certain application and the operating system itself, of course.

Reporting memory utilization using the CloudWatch enhanced monitoring scripts

The CloudWatch team has made it easy for us to report metrics with the use of the CloudWatch enhanced monitoring scripts. The script we are going to use in this example will allow us to report memory metrics from the operating system to the CloudWatch environment. The setup is quite straightforward and easy to do with minimal Linux command-line knowledge.

Before we start, we need to make sure we install the prerequisites. On an Amazon Linux instance, all we need to install are a few `perl` packages as the script is written in `perl` and requires these to run:

```
sudo yum install -y perl-Switch perl-DateTime perl-Sys-Syslog perl-LWP-
Protocol-https perl-Digest-SHA.x86_64
```

Next, we need to retrieve and install the monitoring scripts from the repository:

```
curl
https://aws-cloudwatch.s3.amazonaws.com/downloads/CloudWatchMonitoringScrip
ts-1.2.2.zip -O && \
 unzip CloudWatchMonitoringScripts-1.2.2.zip && \
 rm CloudWatchMonitoringScripts-1.2.2.zip
```

Once unzipped, a new directory called `aws-scripts-mon` is created. We will need to enter the `aws-scripts-mon` directory by running `cd aws-scripts-mon` and test the monitoring script:

```
./mon-put-instance-data.pl --mem-util --verify --verbose
```

This will test if we have all the prerequisites and permissions required to write to CloudWatch. No data will be written during this test, and the response of the `test` command should look something like this:

```
[ec2-user@ip-10-0-0-127 aws-scripts-mon]$ ./mon-put-instance-data.pl --mem-util
--verify --verbose
MemoryUtilization: 12.9875018822466 (Percent)
Using AWS credentials file <./awscreds.conf>
Endpoint: https://monitoring.us-east-2.amazonaws.com
Payload: {"MetricData":[{"Timestamp":1547167690,"Dimensions":[{"Value":"i-0a1d96
9d48c2fb006","Name":"InstanceId"}],"Value":12.9875018822466,"Unit":"Percent","Me
tricName":"MemoryUtilization"}],"Namespace":"System/Linux","__type":"com.amazona
ws.cloudwatch.v2010_08_01#PutMetricDataInput"}

Verification completed successfully. No actual metrics sent to CloudWatch.
```

If the test has completed successfully, then we can now try to publish our memory metrics to CloudWatch:

```
./mon-put-instance-data.pl --mem-used-incl-cache-buff --mem-util --mem-used
--mem-avail
```

The response of the publishing command should look something like the following screenshot:

```
[ec2-user@ip-10-0-0-127 aws-scripts-mon]$ ./mon-put-instance-data.pl --mem-used-
incl-cache-buff --mem-util --mem-used --mem-avail

Successfully reported metrics to CloudWatch. Reference Id: a2ff3003-153a-11e9-b3
e5-ef42ef31d503
```

Once happy with the setup, we can create a cron job that sends the custom metrics to the CloudWatch environment based on your preferences. The following example sends metrics every 5 minutes:

```
*/5 * * * * ~/aws-scripts-mon/mon-put-instance-data.pl --mem-used-incl-
cache-buff --mem-util --disk-space-util --disk-path=/ --from-cron
```

Monitoring EBS

Like the EC2 instances, monitoring block volumes is critical to understanding the operating pattern of our application. Critical information about the performance of our disk, the latencies, I/O operations, and response times can be obtained through the CloudWatch service. We can overview the EBS metrics in the CloudWatch overview section by selecting **Elastic Block Store**, as shown in the following screenshot:

It is recommended to create a dashboard and appropriate widgets that represent a complete overview of the volumes being used by your applications. Remember that there are sometimes multiple volumes attached to one instance and the EBS metrics are bound to get even more complicated when looking at them in the overview section.

A dashboard for EBS volumes might look something like this example:

Monitoring ELB

When working with load balancers, we have a nice overview in the CloudWatch management console that already provides us with a nice set of metrics that we would typically be tracking with ELB. Possibly the most important part of monitoring ELB services is the ability to understand the load our application is under at any given time and the way it is responding to the load. A crucial metric to follow would be the number of requests and the latency of the response. We will be striving to maintain a low latency under a high load at all times, since the application user experience is directly tied to these two factors. When latencies rise upon an increase in the number of connections, our application is probably not scaled appropriately.

In the ELB metrics, we can also find the backend connection errors. We will either be looking at the combined number of backend errors, as we can see on the right-hand side of the following screenshot, or we can create a dashboard and collect 400 and 500 error metrics separately:

Monitoring RDS

Looking further into backend performance, we would also need to understand the performance of our databases. Relational databases are not as easy to scale horizontally. Scaling a database usually entails the following:

- **Vertical scaling**: Resizing the instance type to get more memory, CPU, and network performance
- **Adding a read replica (or replicas)**: Distributing the read operations on the read replicas and offloading our master database
- Increasing the size of the volume when space is low

To detect the need to scale or optimize the performance of our database, we can use CloudWatch. The RDS overview in the CloudWatch management console gives us a good, quick look at the operation of our databases, but, as with the EC2 service, it can get crowded when running a lot of RDS services.

The default overview, however, does give us a good insight into the operational statistics, as can be seen in the following screenshot:

But, of course, the way we use RDS is going to be very application-specific, and if we want to get the most out of the CloudWatch service, we will create a dashboard that will give us an overview of the metrics that matter. For example, a dashboard with the number of queries, the relevant database latencies, and throughput can easily be created by selecting the correct metrics. A custom RDS dashboard might look something like the following screenshot:

A big benefit of the CloudWatch service is that it also collects the logs from our RDS database. We can simply select **Logs** from the CloudWatch management console, followed by **Log** groups, and then the group name that starts with `/aws/rds/`.... In the following screenshot, we can see the error log that is being collected for the `markocloud` database cluster:

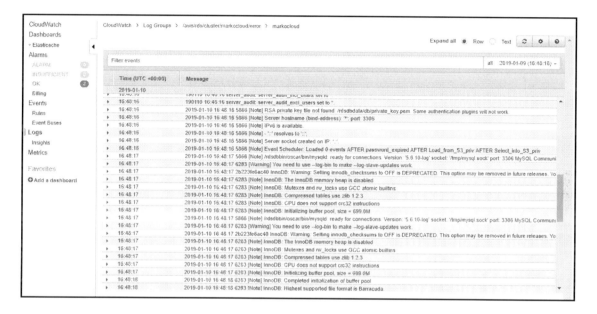

Monitoring ElastiCache

Like the database metrics, we also need to understand the metrics in our ElastiCache clusters. In the CloudWatch **Overview** section, we can select the ElastiCache service where we can get a great overview of the commonly monitored metrics in ElastiCache clusters. We can see the CPU utilization for our hosts, the memory consumption, and network statistics:

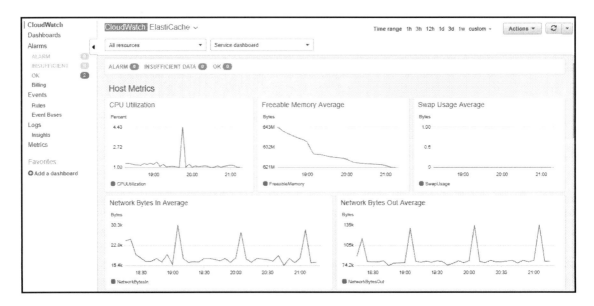

But, due to the fact that every application uses cache in a slightly different manner, the ability to create custom dashboards is crucial for ElastiCache clusters. Providing a dashboard with the right metrics that will give us the ability to quickly assess the health of the ElastiCache cluster is crucial. An example dashboard for ElastiCache would look something like the following screenshot:

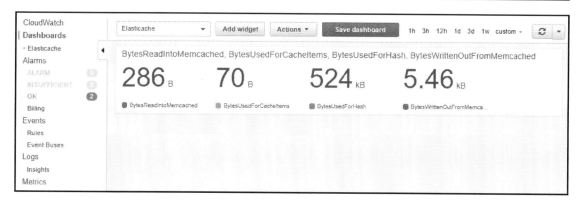

SQS monitoring and logging

As part of monitoring our backend components, we will need to gain an insight into the messaging statistics. The SQS is designed to provide essentially unlimited performance for our messaging needs, so the metrics being collected from the SQS will not have any information about the performance of the service. However, there will be crucial information about the delivery of messages that can help us gain insight into the messaging component of our application.

The CloudWatch overview console for the SQS provides us with a common set of statistics that we need to track, as can be seen in the following screenshot:

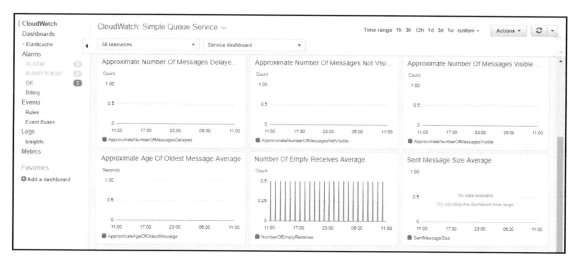

There are several important metrics that will tell us if our application is performing correctly. For example, a continuously growing number of messages in our queue could indicate that the workers are unable to process the messages in time. This could be because of messages that are broken and cannot be successfully processed. These should be moved to a dead letter queue.

We should also be mindful of the number of empty responses, as the service charges will apply even to GET requests that receive an empty response. When we have a lot of empty responses, we should implement an exponential back-off strategy to reduce the amount of GET operations against the SQS and thus reduce our costs of retrieving messages from the queue.

Monitoring SNS with CloudWatch

To fully understand our messaging infrastructure, we should also be looking at the SNS service. The CloudWatch overview console gives us a good glimpse into the operation of our SNS service. With the SNS, we will also be getting information about our messages rather than performance, but there are two crucial metrics to monitor when operating an SNS topic:

- Number of Notifications Delivered
- Number of Notifications Failed

These two metrics will help us get an overview of whether the topics are actually working and if the messages being published are being delivered or failed. In any scenario, there are bound to be failed messages, and we need to maintain a low number of failed messages versus a high number of delivered ones. Both of these metrics can be fed into a query result to create an alarm when the percentage of failed messages goes above a certain threshold. An overview console example is displayed in the following screenshot:

Monitoring Elastic Beanstalk environments

We will discuss Elastic Beanstalk in more detail in the next chapter, but essentially our Elastic Beanstalk environments are self-contained applications that provide all the services required to run our code. The environments themselves are created in a transparent manner and should be monitored according to the features that are created within the environment.

For example, an Elastic Beanstalk application could be composed of EC2 instances, an ELB, a RDS database, an SQS queue, and so on. All of these components need to be monitored in the same way as if we created those services ourselves. We do have an additional set of metrics that we can follow in the CloudWatch overview section when selecting Elastic Beanstalk. Here, we can see the environment health status and the HTTP response codes ordered by class (200, 300, 400, and 500 errors) that our application is responding to requests with.

An example of an Elastic Beanstalk CloudWatch overview is provided in the following screenshot:

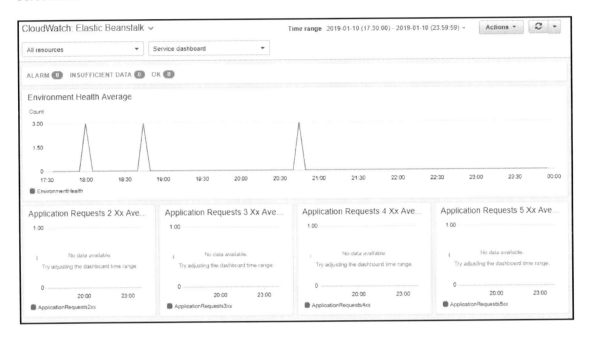

B10030_18_36

Billing alerts

CloudWatch also has the ability to provide us with billing alerts when the monthly usage of our resources hits or exceeds a certain threshold. Billing alerts can easily be configured in the management console. CloudWatch displays all billing data and alarms in the US East (N. Virginia) region, so the first thing we need to do is to select our region as **N. Virginia** or **us-east-1**. To create a billing alarm, proceed to the **Billing** section under **Alarms** in the CloudWatch management console:

1. In the **Billing Alarms** section, we will be reminded to enable the option to **Receive Billing Alarms** in the **Account Billing** console of our AWS account. We can click the link in the page that will redirect us to the billing dashboard:

2. In the **Account Billing** console, we will need to select **Preferences** in the left-hand navigation pane, and then check the checkbox next to **Receive Billing Alerts**. After we click **Save preferences**, we can browse back to CloudWatch:

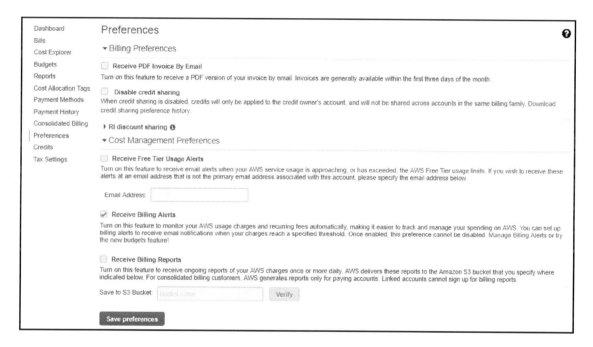

3. In the CloudWatch console **Billing alarms** section, we can now create an alarm by clicking on the **Create Alarm** button:

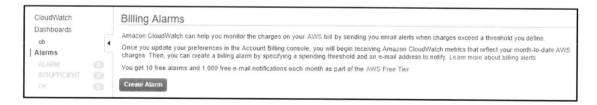

4. To create a new alarm, we can simply enter an amount at which to alert and an email address to send the notification to. This will send a notification when the cumulative consumption within our account exceeds the set amount. We can either click **Create alarm** or create a more detailed alarm by clicking the **Edit** button next to **Metric**:

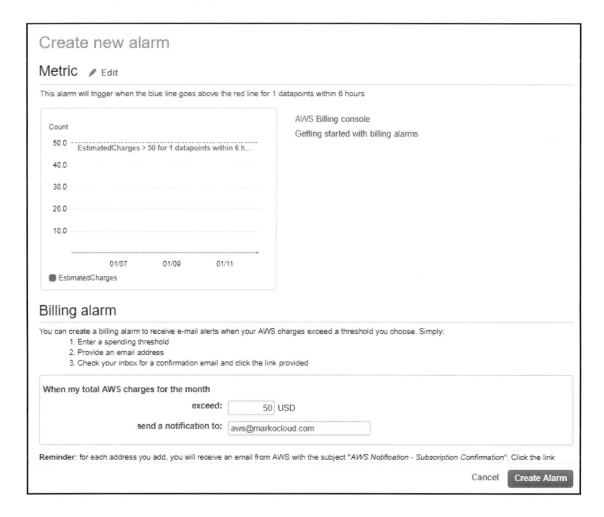

5. To create a more detailed alert, we have the ability to edit the metrics upon which the alerts will be sent out. For example, we can select the metrics by service and receive an alert when a service passes a consumption threshold or we can select a linked account:

6. The procedure of digging deeper into the detailed metrics is exactly the same as with the creation of the performance metric alarms. We can select the exact service or the exact account we want to create a billing alert for. Once we have decided on a metric, simply click on **Select metric**:

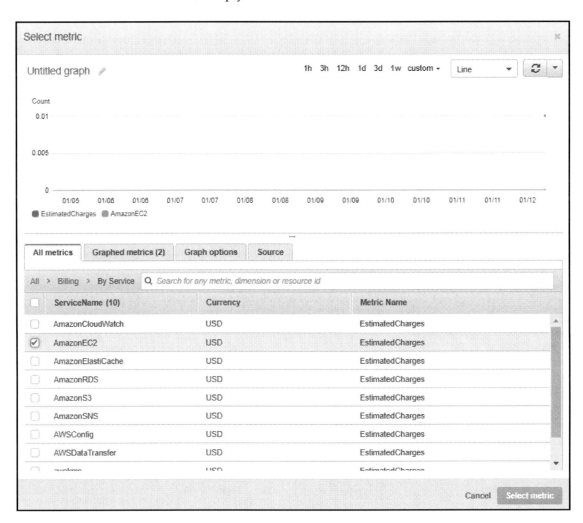

7. After we have completed configuring the alarm and created it, we will be presented with a pop-up dialogue that will instruct us to confirm the subscription to the alarm. An email will be sent to the emails we subscribed to the topic and we need to click the link in the email to subscribe. Once we have confirmed the email address, we will be able to click **View Alarm**:

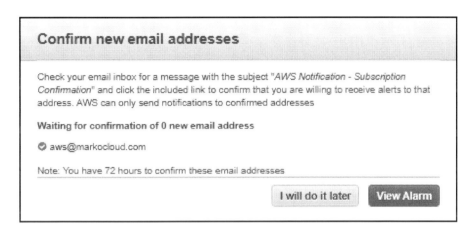

8. When the alarm is created, it will have a status of INSUFFICIENT_DATA:

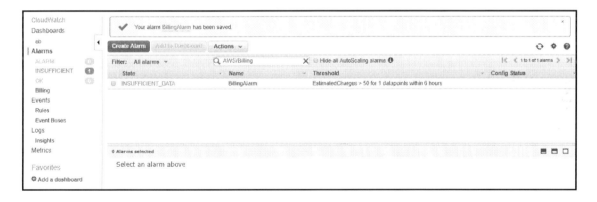

9. The alarm state should shortly change to **OK**. We can now select the alarm and view or modify its details:

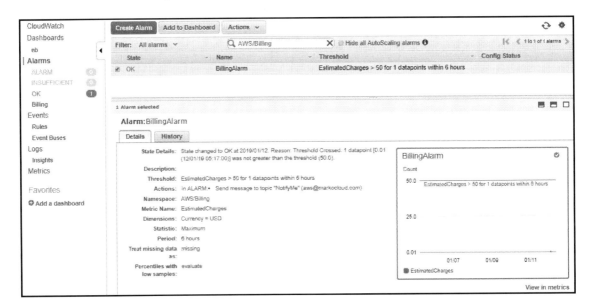

In this example, we have created a billing alarm that will notify us of any usage that will consume $50 or more in our account. This is a valuable feature that will help us control the service cost and enable us to stay within the SLA of the application we are running in AWS.

Summary

CloudWatch is an invaluable tool that helps us understand the performance and health of the environment created in our AWS account. We have the ability to track and monitor our application with standard metrics, that are collected every 5 minutes at no cost. We also have the ability to enable detailed metrics for AWS services that can be reported every minute or store custom metrics that can be reported with intervals under 1 minute, down to as little as 1 second apart. As well as metrics, CloudWatch also has the ability to store and display logs. Furthermore, we can create alerts upon certain thresholds being breached and perform notifications or inform other AWS services of an event. We have also taken a look at the way we can monitor different common AWS services with CloudWatch. In the next chapter, we will understand how we can reduce the management overhead using Elastic Beanstalk.

Questions

1. True or false: A CloudWatch namespace must be preceded with AWS.
2. True or false: Metrics come in two types: Normal and Detailed.
3. True or false: Metrics are aggregated to the next tier after their retention period expires.
4. A new compliance requirement has been introduced in your company that dictates that all EC2 system slogs need to be redirected to a central data store where they can be accessed and then stored durably in an archive. How could you achieve this?
5. Your application is divided into three functional environments: Test, Staging, and Production, each composed of EC2 autoscaling clusters, RDS databases, and ElastiCache cluster. A requirement to maintain alerts of CPU usage on all instances only on the Production environment is set out by a governance policy. How can you implement your CloudWatch Alarms to achieve this in the most efficient manner?
6. What would a number in a CloudWatch Dashboard represent?
7. You are asked by your developers to create an alarm when 10% of the SNS messages to a particular topic are not delivered. How could this be done?
8. You are running an e-commerce application that starts performing slowly when the number of concurrent connections to your frontend is above 100,000. This kind of volume is unusual and only happens during seasonal sales (3–4 times per year). During the last sale, you analyzed the metrics and discovered that your ELB and your EC2 instances are responding correctly and the latency issue is being caused by the RDS backend being hit by a high number of requests. Due to the fact that you need to keep costs as low as possible, increasing the size of your instance permanently isn't an option. You know the thresholds at which the application starts to perform slowly. Come up with a solution that will temporarily increase the performance of the database during these few events

Further reading

- **CloudWatch Docs**: https://docs.aws.amazon.com/AmazonCloudWatch/latest/monitoring/WhatIsCloudWatch.html
- **CloudWatch Regional Endpoints**: https://docs.aws.amazon.com/general/latest/gr/rande.html#cw_region
- **EC2 Custom Metrics**: https://docs.aws.amazon.com/AmazonCloudWatch/latest/monitoring/publishingMetrics.html
- **CloudWatch Agent**: https://docs.aws.amazon.com/AmazonCloudWatch/latest/monitoring/install-CloudWatch-Agent-on-first-instance.html
- **CloudWatch Enhanced Monitoring Scripts**: https://docs.aws.amazon.com/AWSEC2/latest/UserGuide/mon-scripts.html
- **CloudWatch Alarms**: https://docs.aws.amazon.com/AmazonCloudWatch/latest/monitoring/AlarmThatSendsEmail.html

19
Understanding Elastic Beanstalk

As we saw in previous chapters, AWS provides us with many different products that can provide services for our computing needs. All of the different options that are available help us to use AWS according to our business driver for cloud adoption. When the demand for ease of use and reduction in management overhead is identified, then we should look toward Elastic Beanstalk.

The following topics will be covered in this chapter:

- Introduction to Elastic Beanstalk
- Supported platforms
- Supported AWS services
- Deploying an application with Elastic Beanstalk
- Managing Elastic Beanstalk environments
- Updating Elastic Beanstalk environments

Technical requirements

A basic understanding of Elastic Beanstalk applications and their operating environments is necessary to understand this chapter. Readers with any level of understanding of programming languages that are used in Elastic Beanstalk applications, as well as the maintenance and upgrading of the application, should benefit from this chapter.

Introduction to Elastic Beanstalk

Running modern Elastic Beanstalk applications can be quite a daunting task. To be able to run the Elastic Beanstalk application code, the operations team will usually be required to maintain a set of inter-dependent resources consisting of the following:

- A host with an operating system
- A programming language interpreter
- An application server with prerequisites such as frameworks, runtimes, libraries, and modules
- An HTTP service to present the Elastic Beanstalk application
- External components such as load balancers, databases, message queues, and so on

A whole lot of resources can be spent operating, maintaining, updating, patching, and making sure that the service is reliable, resilient, and highly available. Sometimes, it feels like it would be wonderful to have a service that could do all of this for us. Well, we have one—the AWS Elastic Beanstalk.

When our business requirements dictate that we need to reduce the management overhead in our development cycle, then Elastic Beanstalk is the perfect solution. With Elastic Beanstalk, the complete set of underlying resources is managed by AWS and we simply provide the code and a definition for the running environment. Being able to put 100% of our focus on the code frees our developers and SysOps engineers from having to design, deliver, operate, and maintain the infrastructure and lets us cut down on management overhead by a sizeable factor.

Elastic Beanstalk basics

There are three components that are defined within the Elastic Beanstalk service:

- Application
- Environment
- Configuration

An application is a logical grouping for multiple environments that belong to an application. Each environment will be running a specific platform. An overview of an application will display, showing different environments in the management console, like so:

When creating an environment, we'll need to specify a tier that will define the services that are provided by the environment. There are two tiers to choose from:

- **Elastic Beanstalk tier**: An application frontend that serves the Elastic Beanstalk page
- **Worker tier**: An application backend that performs tasks

The Elastic Beanstalk tier will usually be fronted by a load balancer, unless we're building a single instance in a non-highly available setup. The worker tier is fronted by an SQS queue where the requests for the worker tier are posted.

We can have multiple application versions within each application. An application version will be defined by the developers and will reflect the version of the code. Once deployed, we can select different versions for an environment and perform upgrades and rollbacks of an environment from within the Elastic Beanstalk's management. Application versions can be viewed in the management console, as demonstrated in the following screenshot:

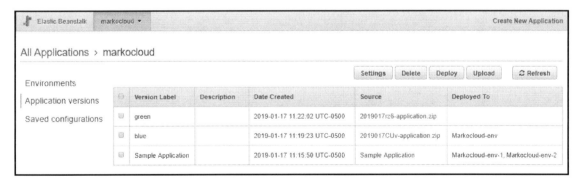

Each environment will also have a configuration. This configuration will contain all of the necessary information for the Elastic Beanstalk service to build, deploy, and even customize the environment before it's ready to serve the code. When customizing an Elastic Beanstalk configuration, it is wise to save the environment configuration as it can be used to deploy new environments or as a backup in case we break our current configuration. We can take a look at the saved configurations in the management console, as demonstrated in the following screenshot:

Supported platforms

When deploying an application with Elastic Beanstalk, we simply provide a package containing our code in one of the supported platform formats to the Elastic Beanstalk service. We can then use the management console, the AWS CLI, the Elastic Beanstalk CLI, or the SDK to configure the application we are running. We'll, of course, have to name the application and select the platform on which to run the code. The supported platforms at the time of writing are as follows:

- **Packer Builder**: An open source tool that can help us create and manage AMIs in AWS
- **Docker**: An open source container engine that supports single and multi-container deployments
- **Go**: Supports the Go programming language 1.11 version 2.9.4
- **Java SE and Java on Tomcat**: Supports Java SE 7 and 8 and Java 6, 7, and 8 on Tomcat Elastic Beanstalk server
- **.NET on Windows Server with IIS**: Supports a variety of the .NET Framework and Core versions running on Windows server 2008-2016 and IIS Elastic Beanstalk server version 7.5, 8, 8.5, and 10
- **Node.js**: Supports the Node.js language versions 4, 5, 6, 7, 8, and 10

- **PHP**: Supports the PHP language versions 5.4 to 7.2
- **Python**: Supports the Python language versions 2.6 to 3.6
- **Ruby**: Supports the Ruby language versions 1.9 to 2.6

We are also able to customize the environment from the management console when deploying the application environment or by providing customization straight in the package with the `.ebextensions` file. Within the customization, we can specify other AWS services and features, such as packages to install and commands to run on startup.

Supported AWS services

In Elastic Beanstalk, there's support for automatically configuring and running other AWS services. The following AWS services can be used or controlled when configuring an Elastic Beanstalk environment directly from the environment deployment:

- AWS X-Ray daemon
- Log and metric collection with CloudWatch
- Log delivery to S3
- Elastic Load Balancers
- RDS databases
- SQS Queues

By default, each environment we create can be configured to have the AWS X-Ray daemon installed to help with distributed tracing when using X-Ray. We also have the ability to deliver logs either to S3 or to CloudWatch, and we can configure the enhanced CloudWatch metric collection. With Elastic Beanstalk tier environments, we are able to configure and customize a load balancer to receive the requests for our application, whereas, with a worker tier, we can configure the SQS for requests. We are also able to add an RDS database to the environment and configure the details on the fly from the deployment. However, adding a RDS database is not the best practice as the environment owns the database and deleting the environment would also delete the database.

If we require additional services and would like to configure them and attach them to the Elastic Beanstalk application, we certainly have the option to do so. We can either use the `.ebextensions` file to configure the AWS CLI commands that will configure the services or we can simply build the service configuration into the code and execute the commands from the SDK. With Elastic Beanstalk, the only limitation is that the environment is configured via code deployment so even minor changes to the environment will need to be delivered via an application version update.

Deploying an application with Elastic Beanstalk

An Elastic Beanstalk environment is designed to be very easy to deploy. In this section, we will demonstrate the features of how to create and manage an Elastic Beanstalk environment in the management console. Take a look at the following steps:

1. We need to open the Elastic Beanstalk management console so that we can create an application and environment. Initially, if we have no Elastic Beanstalk deployments, we will see an introductory screen with a short description of Elastic Beanstalk. We can click the **Get started** button to initiate the creation of an environment:

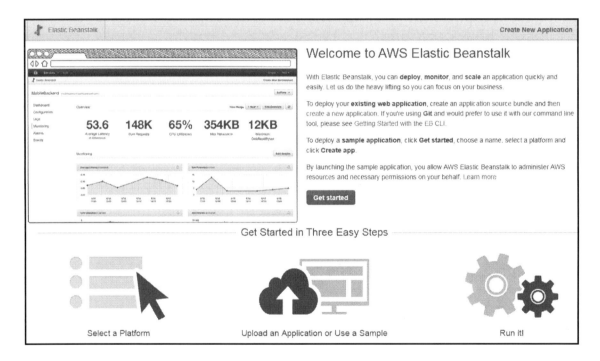

2. The **Get started** button automatically starts a Elastic Beanstalk app creation dialogue. The Elastic Beanstalk console assumes that we need to have an Elastic Beanstalk tier application before we can add any kind of worker tier. The next time we create an environment, a choice between the worker and Elastic Beanstalk tier will show but, for now, we will create the *Elastic Beanstalk* app. We need to specify an application name that will be used to group different application versions and environments, and we will need to choose a platform. In the following example, the choice of platforms is displayed:

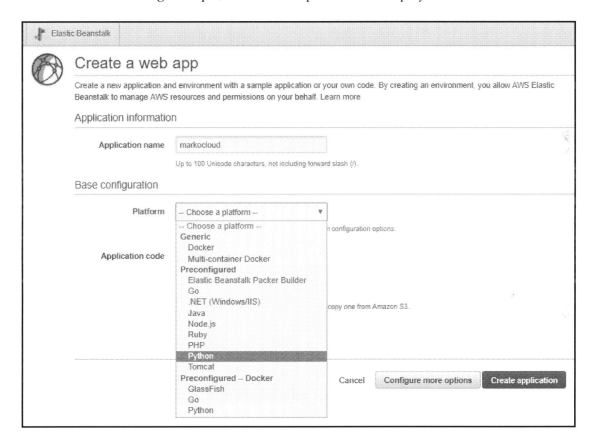

3. After we have chosen a platform, we need to either select a sample application that will show a sample Elastic Beanstalk page written in the programming language of our choice or upload our code. To upload custom code, select the **Upload your code** selector and then click on **Upload**:

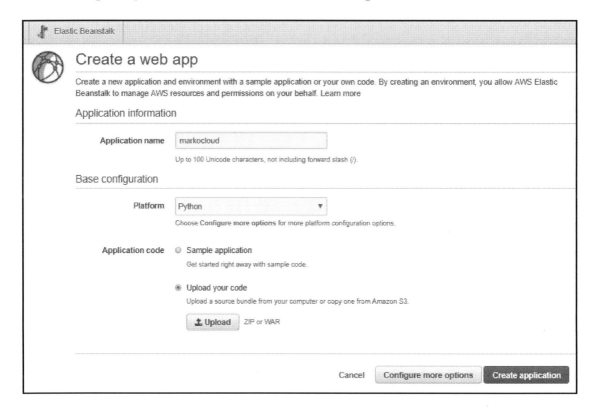

4. In the **Upload your code** dialog, we can select a local file from our computer or a file that has been posted in an S3 bucket. Using S3 here is a good idea as we can use the built-in versioning on S3 to deliver the latest or other previous versions directly by specifying the appropriate S3 path. We can think of the S3 option as a poor man's code repository. After we are happy with our selection, we also need to give the code a version label. This should reflect the application code version that you are deploying and will be visible in the application versions menu:

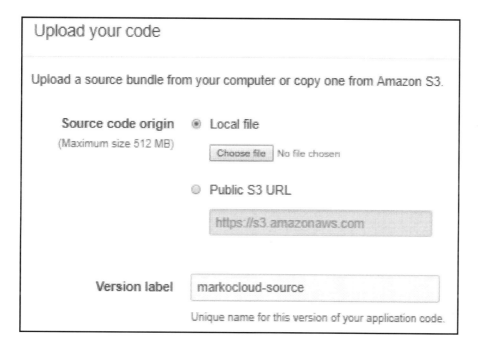

5. At this point, we can click the **Create Application** button to begin the application creation or we can select **Configure more options** to open the option configuration dialogue that's shown in the following screenshot. As you can see, there are multiple options that can be configured in the configuration dialogue. We can choose to modify and configure any aspect of the environment. When we choose to configure more options, the following dialogue will open. Here, we can control the aspects of the operating system that help manage our software such as configuring and running the AWS X-Ray agent and redirecting logs. We can also modify instances, select the number of instances in a highly available deployment group, configure the load balancer, and manage security. More importantly, we also have the ability to control the way software updates will be preformed when updating the application:

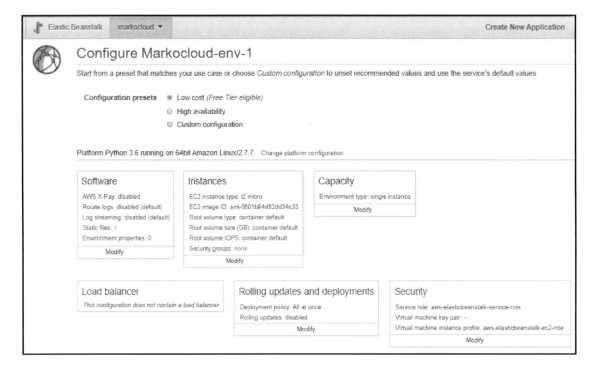

6. Selecting instances in the previous dialogue will allow us to modify the tape of an instance and the AMI ID to deploy from, as well as configure the root volume and EC2 security groups. When we have finished the selections, we can click on **Save** to return to the previous window:

7. Clicking on the **Security** section will open up the security configuration of the application. Here, we can modify the service role ID that's required and select an instance profile, as well as add an EC2 key-pair for the instances that are created through Elastic Beanstalk. We will click **Save** to return to the previous window:

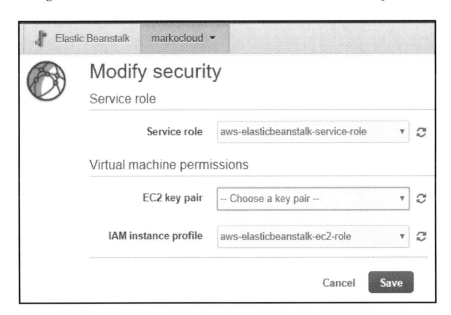

8. By scrolling further down in the configuration dialog, we will see configuration options for monitoring, where we can select either detailed and standard monitoring. If we select detailed monitoring, we have the ability to select which metrics to deliver in a detailed manner. We can also control the managed updates that are delivered by AWS to patch and update our operating system and receive notifications about our environment. We can also control the network layout and place the application in a certain VPC. We also have the ability to create and add a database layer by using RDS. We can choose the engine the application will use and the type of instance to run, as well as whether we want to make the database highly available.

Finally, we can add tags to our environment so that it is easier to manage:

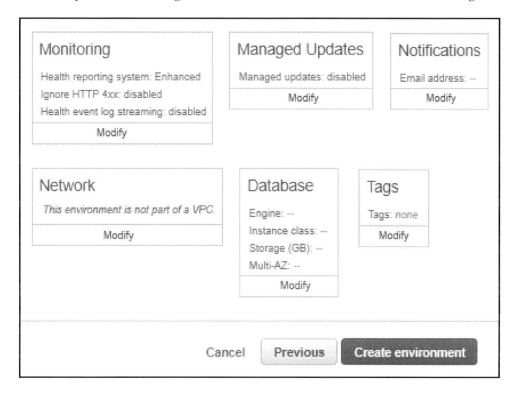

9. After we are happy with our selections, we can click the **Create environment** button and the creation will begin. A window displaying the creation process and output will be presented, as shown in the following screenshot:

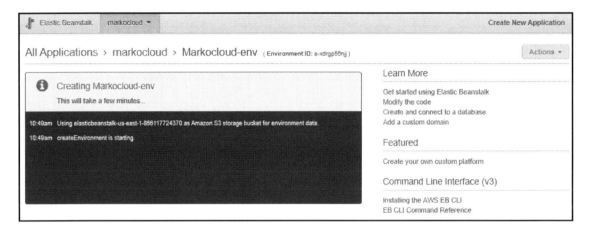

10. Once the application has been created, we will be able to click on the environment URL that's displayed next to the environment name:

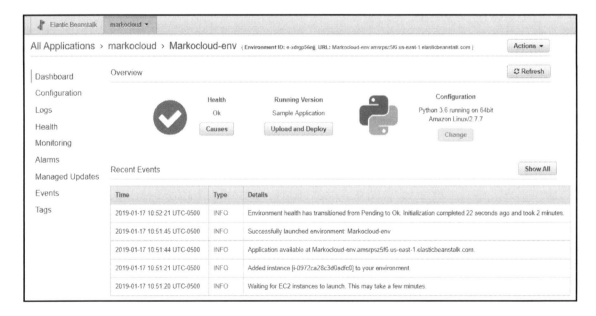

11. Clicking on the environment URL opens up the Elastic Beanstalk site in a browser window, as demonstrated in the following screenshot:

As you can see, managing an Elastic Beanstalk environment is very easy and gives us a lot of options when we want to configure the environment straight out of the box. In this example, we were able to deploy a fully operational application in just a few minutes.

Managing Elastic Beanstalk environments

Once we have deployed an Elastic Beanstalk environment, we will of course have to operate and manage that environment. The Elastic Beanstalk environment is designed for developers in fast-paced DevOps teams who are conforming to Agile development strategies. This allows them to quickly iterate among the version of their application and deliver new functionality and fixes of their application with high velocity. We also have built-in recovery options. When updates don't perform as well as expected, we have the ability to easily roll the application version back to the previous version with several supported update strategies.

Managing application versions

A deployed environment in Elastic Beanstalk will always be deployed with a certain application version. We are able to manage application versions straight out of the management environment by providing different packages or different S3 paths to the packages that exist in our environment. When deploying an environment in an application that has existing application versions, the deployment dialogue changes and the application code will get an **Existing version** selection available. Here, we can select any existing versions to deploy to the environment, as shown in the following screenshot:

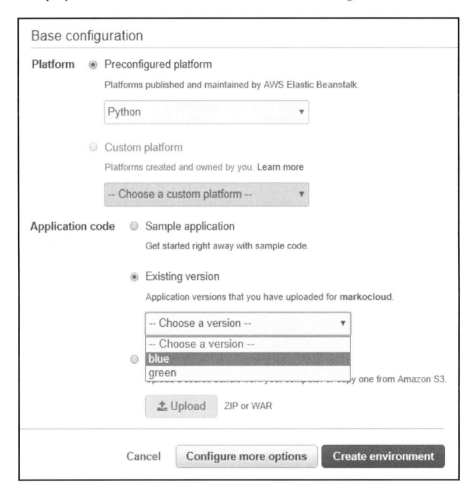

Being able to maintain several versions of the code in these environments is crucial as development usually has several stages that the code passes through. For example, we can easily maintain a development environment as well as a test, staging, and production environment, all running independently with different versions of code, as demonstrated in the following screenshot:

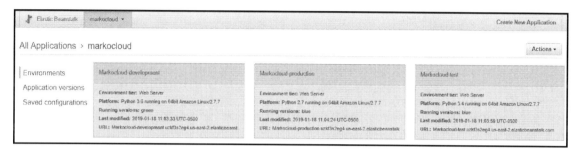

Configuring application version life cycle settings

Elastic Beanstalk allows us to store up to 100 versions of an application. This might seem like a lot, but with today's fast-paced development that perhaps deploys and tests multiple versions of an application every day, this limit can be reached fairly quickly. This limit is set on a per-application basis, so each application's life cycle policy needs to be managed separately. Follow these steps to get started:

1. To enable application life cycling, we can simply navigate to our **Application versions** section and click the **Settings** button:

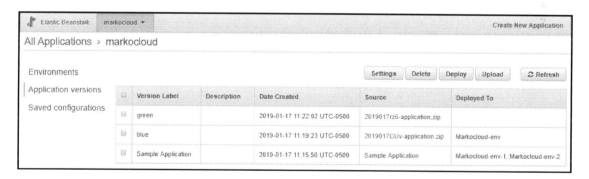

2. In the **Application version lifecycle** settings dialogue, we can enable the policy and then select whether we want to limit the application version to a certain number of versions or a certain age in days. Limiting to a number of versions is appropriate for an application with a fast development cycle, whereas the age limit is useful when we have an SLA that defines the age we are required to maintain. After creating the policy, we click on the **Save** button to enable the life cycle policy on the application versions:

Creating a source bundle

Application versions are always created as packaged bundles. These are required to be either ZIP or WAR files of up to 512 MB in size. The application is required to be stored in the root of the file, but it can have as many subdirectories as needed. The package can also contain additional customization that's defined in the `.ebextensions` file and additional packages, libraries, and other bundles that are referenced by `.ebextensions`. When deploying a worker environment, we are required to include a `cron.yaml` file where we define and configure the cron jobs that will initiate the worker process in the application.

Updating Elastic Beanstalk environments

Once we have deployed the packages and have created multiple versions of our application, we will eventually need to update an existing application. For example, when we have completed the development of the application, we need to update the test environment to the same version and then, of course, the same will be done for staging and production. Several upgrade options are supported in Elastic Beanstalk, and some of them are as follows:

- All at once
- Rolling updates
- Immutable updates
- Blue/green deployment

All at once

The simplest way to perform updates is by taking all instances running the current version out of service and updating them with new instances. This is the cheapest way as the size of your environment doesn't increase during this type of update and it is efficient when unpredictable behavior can occur while running multiple versions of the application in the same autoscaling group. The drawback of all at once is that the application will be unavailable while the update is being performed.

Rolling updates

To avoid any kind of downtime of our environment, we can perform a rolling update. A rolling update replaces instances in a particular order. By default, we can choose to either replace one instance at a time or replace half at a time, but we can also customize the replacement order if required. The rolling update will replace the instances with newer instances in the same autoscaling group so that, at a certain point, there will be different versions (the old and the new) running and accepting calls from clients, which might cause issues in certain applications.

Immutable updates

To avoid issues with application version mismatches in the same autoscaling group, we can use immutable updates. Immutable updates are performed by adding an additional temporary autoscaling group in the background of the Elastic Beanstalk environment that's connected to the same load balancer. The immutable update creates a new instance and waits for all of its health checks to pass, then loads a subset of traffic alongside the original group to the new instance. It then proceeds to create the same number of instances that exist in the current autoscaling group and waits for the health checks to pass. Once all of the new instances are healthy, the immutable update process moves the instances into the existing autoscaling group and deletes the old instances and the temporary autoscaling group that was created during the update.

Blue/green deployment

A blue/green deployment strategy takes the dynamic infrastructure advantage of cloud computing and uses it as a basis for updating applications. Instead of running new instances in the existing environment, a new environment is created. The existing environment is now designated as **blue** and the new one is designated as **green**. Usually, a switchover of the DNS will be preformed to redirect the traffic from the blue application to the green application. This can be done gradually with a weighted round robin approach or instantly by switching the DNS over fully. Elastic Beanstalk allows us to switch the DNS over from one environment to the other within the management console or via the CLI:

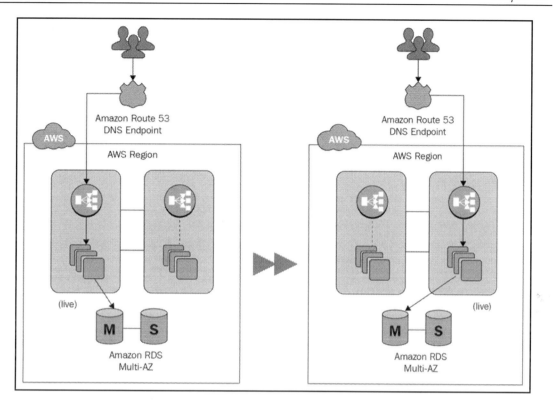

Summary

Elastic Beanstalk is a great solution when the cloud adoption driver is the reduction of management overhead. It's also very useful when a small development team needs to focus 100% on the code and not worry about managing the infrastructure. In this chapter, have taken a look at how to create and manage Elastic Beanstalk applications and environments and the different strategies that exist for updating. In the next chapter, we will be studying automation with the CloudFormation Service.

Questions

1. True or false: Elastic Beanstalk requires us to maintain and manage our code and takes care of each and every aspect of the infrastructure.

2. True or false: An Elastic Beanstalk environment creates a transparent environment that we can see in our EC2, ELB, RDS, and other consoles.
3. True or false: Elastic Beanstalk environments are one-click deployments that can't be customized.
4. What is the type and maximum size of the source bundle that can be created for use with Elastic Beanstalk?
5. What is the maximum number of versions supported in each application?
6. A SLA requires you to maintain the application versions for 30 days and then discard them. What feature of Elastic Beanstalk can help you adhere to the SLA?
7. You have deployed an Elastic Beanstalk application. Now, you need to modify the instance type of the running application. How would you go about doing this?
8. Your application needs to be updated as inexpensively as possible. Which update option is the best for this approach?
9. You have been tasked with an application update. You need to make sure that the uptime of the application is maintained as close to 100% as possible, even during the update process, regardless of cost. Which update option would you choose and why?

Further reading

- **Elastic Beanstalk Documentation**: https://docs.aws.amazon.com/elasticbeanstalk/latest/dg/Welcome.html
- **Elastic Beanstalk Supported Platforms**: https://docs.aws.amazon.com/elasticbeanstalk/latest/platforms/platforms-supported.html
- **The .Elastic Beanstalkeextensions File**: https://docs.aws.amazon.com/elasticbeanstalk/latest/dg/ebextensions.html
- **Life Cycling**: https://docs.aws.amazon.com/elasticbeanstalk/latest/dg/applications-lifecycle.html
- **Creating Elastic Beanstalk Bundles**: https://docs.aws.amazon.com/elasticbeanstalk/latest/dg/applications-sourcebundle.html
- **Elastic Beanstalk Updates**: https://docs.aws.amazon.com/elasticbeanstalk/latest/dg/environments-updating.html
- **Blue/Green Updates with Elastic Beanstalk**: https://docs.aws.amazon.com/elasticbeanstalk/latest/dg/using-features.CNAMESwap.html

20
Automation with the CloudFormation Service

Now that we have taken a look at Elastic Beanstalk, we have seen that we can instruct AWS to create complete environments in an automated manner. But what if Elastic Beanstalk is not enough? What can we do when we need to create a custom application in AWS that's delivered in an automated manner? In these kinds of situations, we can use CloudFormation—a cloud orchestration tool that can create resources from a specification document.

The following topics will be covered in this chapter:

- Introduction to CloudFormation
- CloudFormation basic elements
- How CloudFormation works
- Creating an EC2 instance using template (code example)

Technical requirements

An understanding of cloud orchestration and automation is required to get the most out of this topic. Additionally, familiarity with the JSON or YAML documentation notation is a useful resource. Please refer to the GitHub link for this chapter: `https://github.com/PacktPublishing/AWS-Certified-SysOps-Administrator-Associate-Guide/tree/master/Chapter20`.

Introduction to CloudFormation

CloudFormation is an AWS service that helps us to define resources in a specification document and deploy them. We create a document in a unified manner and then feed that definition document to the CloudFormation service through the management console, the CLI, SDK, or directly through the CloudFormation API. The CloudFormation service will, in turn, deploy all of the resources that we have specified and configure them accordingly. In case of any failures upon deployment, the CloudFormation service will also automatically be able to roll back the resources it created so that we never have half-functional CloudFormation deployments in our AWS account.

The power that CloudFormation gives us is the ability to create complete environments in a repeatable and automated fashion. By removing manual activities from deployments, we make the application inherently more reliable and allow for advanced deployment scenarios where not only humans but other automation systems and the code itself call up the CloudFormation service, provide a specification document, and create resources that are required. This enables us to treat our infrastructure as code, which means doing the following:

- We define the infrastructure in a document.
- We maintain that document in a repository.
- We version the document whenever changes occur.
- We deploy the infrastructure with the same tools that we deploy our code with.

Infrastructure as code is a prerequisite to being able to create a fully automated development, testing, and deployment scenario while at the same time empowering our developers, operations engineers, and administrators by relieving them of the mundane, task-based manual deployments that have a lot of unreliability built into them. The goal of infrastructure as code is to let the computers do the mundane, repeatable tasks that computers are good at while humans do the complex tasks such as writing code, designing, optimizing, estimating, and thinking outside of the box.

CloudFormation basic elements

In CloudFormation, there are some basic elements that we need to understand before we can proceed with deployments. We always write templates from which we deploy stacks. Once a stack is deployed, we can create a change set and compare this change set against a deployed stack before eventually applying the changes.

Templates

As we have already mentioned, we will be providing a specification document called a Template to the service. A template can be created in a text editor and written either in JSON or YAML. We can also use the AWS CloudFormation Designer or any other **What You See Is What You Get** (**WYSIWYG**) design tool that's compatible with AWS CloudFormation. In the template, we define each resource and how that resource should be configured. Within a template, we will find the following sections:

- **AWS Template Format Version**: The AWS Template Format Version is an optional component of the template and will denote the CloudFormation template version that the template conforms to.
- **Description**: The description can include any arbitrary string of text that will help us to understand what the template does and what services are deployed. The description must always follow the template format version section, otherwise it is optional.
- **Metadata**: In the metadata section, we can optionally include any information that we would like to pass to the services and instances that are being deployed. This can be represented as tags or other information that needs to be passed on to the environment.
- **Parameters**: The parameters represent the values to be passed to the resources section. This is an optional part of the template that can be used whenever creating a resource and when we would like certain information to be provided at run time into the configuration of the resource. For example, an instance type can be specified as a parameter to an EC2 resource that's being created.
- **Mappings**: Mappings can optionally be created to apply the appropriate parameters to the appropriate environment or region. For example, we can create mappings for the AMI ID to use, depending on the region that the CloudFormation template is being deployed in.
- **Conditions**: Conditions can optionally determine whether a resource is created or not, depending on a certain value. For example, we can create a condition that creates a load balancer and an autoscaling group for the application, but only when the environment tags denote the deployment as production.
- **Transform**: The Transform section can optionally be used with AWS Serverless components such as AWS Lambda to define specifics and versions of the AWS Serverless Application Model to be used in the template.

- **Resources**: This is the only mandatory part of the template as it defines the actual resources that the CloudFormation service will be creating. Here, we specify all of our networks, routers, gateways, EC2 instances, databases, S3 buckets, and so on.
- **Outputs**: When required, we can use the Outputs section to return a certain piece of information upon deployment. For example, when creating a load balancer, we would like to know the address of the load balancer instead of having to look it up with a separate task. We can simply specify the URL of the load balancer to be outputted upon template creation.

Stacks

A stack is a set of resources that's created by a template. A stack can represent a complete application or a part of the resources that are deployed from a specific template. For example, we can use separate stacks to create separate layers of our application. These can be deployed by separate teams, and these teams are hence able to maintain the segregation of duties, even when working in the cloud.

In the real world, the network team would be in charge of creating the VPC, internet gateways, VPNs, and Direct Connect connections. The Security team would then take over and create the NACLs, and the Security Groups would provision the groups, users, and roles, and then define permissions. A shared resources team would deploy a stack with the queues, the SES and SNS services, and other shared resources. The database team would then be able to deploy the databases and tables, and lastly the application team would deploy the servers and connect them to the resources being deployed by the other teams.

Each stack in this scenario would only be controlled by the team that deployed it. For example, the server team would have no way of modifying the network stack as their stacks only create the servers and vice-versa.

We can also specify stacks as part of templates, hence sort of nesting stacks within stacks. Supplying nested stacks allows us to create dependencies on complete stacks. For example, we would not want to deploy an EC2 stack before the VPC stack completes as there would be no VPC to deploy into and server stack creation would fail.

Change sets

Once we have deployed a stack and the resources are running, there is a possibility that we will need to change those resources. Whether it is through optimization or through the normal application life cycle, the need for changing a stack is almost a given for any deployment. Change sets help us with delivering updates and changes to the stack that we have deployed in our AWS account.

With change sets, we create changes that we would like to perform on the environment we deployed. Once the changes have been created, we can run a comparison against our existing stack and get a detailed report of how these changes will impact the stack. There are three types of changes in any CloudFormation deployment:

- **Non-disruptive updates**: These operations don't have impact on running resources, for example, changing CloudWatch alarms within a template.
- **Disruptive updates**: These operations disrupt running resources for a certain period of time, for example, changing the instance type will require a reboot.
- **Replacement updates**: These operations terminate an existing resource and deploy a new resource with a new ID, for example, changing an RDS engine from MySQL to Aurora.

With change sets, we get a detailed description that can give us a deeper understanding of which kind of update is taking place and hence we can determine the broader impact of the change set's execution on our application. Once we are happy with these changes, we can execute the change set and the CloudFormation service will deploy the changes.

How does CloudFormation work?

Once we provide a template to the CloudFormation service, the service stores that template in an S3 bucket. It simultaneously reads the inputs in the template and processes them in parallel. We have to take this into consideration whenever we have resources that need to be created in sequence.

To create resources in sequence, we can implement the CloudFormation `DependsOn` attribute. The `DependsOn` attribute gives us the ability to wait for a certain resource to be created before another resource creation is started. For example, we can specify a `DependsOn` attribute that will wait for an RDS instance to be created and available before it starts an EC2 instance creation.

Stack creation

The template is analyzed for the correct syntax and, if the syntax is correct, the parameters are verified against the AWS account. If any of these are not correct, the CloudFormation service will throw an error before it begins the deployment of resources. If the syntax and parameter check passes, the service will initiate creation.

In the creation process, the CloudFormation service will call up other AWS services via their corresponding APIs and initiate the creation of resources. We can control the permissions that CloudFormation has over the environment with the different predefined and custom CloudFormation service roles. This way, we also have the ability to create a granular definition of which users, groups, and roles initiate CloudFormation and what resources they can create.

During stack creation, a status will be displayed in the management console or when listing the stack details via the CLI. For the sake of simplicity, we will discuss the following end states of a stack creation process:

- CREATE_IN_PROGRESS: The stack is being created. By default, a stack creation process does not have a timeout defined and will run indefinitely as it waits for the resources to be completed. It is always useful to define a timeout in the template itself, as providing the timeout gives ample time for the creation of all the resources in the stack. Note that a stack creation can run several minutes to several hours.
- CREATE_COMPLETE: A stack creation has completed successfully. When a stack creation has completed successfully, then a CREATE_COMPLETE will be displayed and all of the sources will be operational. We will be aiming for all of our stacks to end in a CREATE_COMPLETE status.
- CREATE_FAILED: A stack creation has failed. There's always the possibility of errors being introduced through the template (wrong name, ID, and so on) or errors in the backend services that can cause our stack creation to fail. Any error in any of the resources defined in our stack will cause the stack to fail and push a rollback action. The rollback action will either delete the resources that were newly created or roll back the resources to the previous versions (when an update of a stack with a change set fails).

Other intermediate states and states during updates and deletion not described in this chapter can be found by following the link for **CloudFormation Stack States** in the *Further reading* section of this chapter.

Stack deletion

Performing stack deletion is as simple as issuing a command to the CloudFormation service. A stack will be deleted only if there are no dependent resources using the resources that were created by the stack. For example, this occurs when we create a VPC and an EC2 instance with a separate stack and then we want to delete the VPC. The deletion will fail, while the EC2 instance still exists in the VPC that was created in the stack that we are trying to delete.

Creating an EC2 instance using a template (code example)

In the following example, we will create a simple stack containing one EC2 instance that will enable us to SSH into it with our chosen SSH key. We will first take a look at the template in segments and then assemble the template and look at the process of deploying the template in the management console.

Template analysis

The template has the typical structure that we would find in other CloudFormation templates and is written using JSON notation.

Version and description

The template starts with a version and description that tell us a bit about the template and which version of CloudFormation notation it conforms to:

```
{
  "AWSTemplateFormatVersion" : "2010-09-09",

  "Description" : "This template creates a t2 EC2 instance using the Amazon
Linux AMI in one of the US regions and allows SSH access.",
```

Parameters

The `Parameters` section defines the parameters we need to specify when deploying the template. In our scenario, the `"KeyName"` parameter defines that we need to select an existing key pair to log in to the instance:

```
"Parameters" : {
 "KeyName": {
   "Description" : "Name of an existing EC2 KeyPair to enable SSH access to
the instance",
   "Type": "AWS::EC2::KeyPair::KeyName",
   "ConstraintDescription" : "Must be an existing EC2 KeyPair."
 },
```

Next, the `"Instancetype"` parameter allows us to choose an instance type from a few available options. The `"AllowedValues"` parameter defines the instance types we can select:

```
"InstanceType" : {
 "Description" : "The EC2 instance type",
 "Type" : "String",
 "Default" : "t2.micro",
 "AllowedValues" : [ "t2.micro", "t2.small", "t2.medium", "t2.large"],
 "ConstraintDescription" : "Must be one of the t2 EC2 instance types."
 }
 },
```

Mappings

In the `Mapping` section, we define the mappings for our `T2type` architectures:

```
"Mappings" : {
 "T2type" : {
   "t2.micro" : { "Arch" : "HVM64" },
   "t2.small" : { "Arch" : "HVM64" },
   "t2.medium" : { "Arch" : "HVM64" },
   "t2.large" : { "Arch" : "HVM64" }
 },
```

The "RegionID" mapping helps the template determine the correct AMI ID to use when starting the EC2 instance. The AMI IDs are region-dependent, so this mapping has a separate AMI ID for every available region:

```
"RegionID" : {
    "us-east-1" : {"HVM64" : "ami-0ff8a91507f77f867", "HVMG2" :
"ami-0a584ac55a7631c0c"},
    "us-west-2" : {"HVM64" : "ami-a0cfeed8", "HVMG2" :
"ami-0e09505bc235aa82d"},
    "us-west-1" : {"HVM64" : "ami-0bdb828fd58c52235", "HVMG2" :
"ami-066ee5fd4a9ef77f1"},
    "us-east-2" : {"HVM64" : "ami-0b59bfac6be064b78", "HVMG2" :
"NOT_SUPPORTED"}
  }

},
```

Resources

In Resources, we will define our EC2 instance. The "Properties" section defines calling up the "InstanceType" and "KeyName" parameters that were defined in the beginning of the template, as well as the "SecurityGroup" resource to connect to; it picks up the security group ID to connect the instance to during stack creation. It also calls up the "ImageId" parameter that references the map of images, called "RegionID", to look up the correct AMI ID for the correct region:

```
"Resources" : {
  "EC2Instance" : {
    "Type" : "AWS::EC2::Instance",
    "Properties" : {
    "InstanceType" : { "Ref" : "InstanceType" },
    "SecurityGroups" : [ { "Ref" : "SecurityGroup" } ],
            "KeyName" : { "Ref" : "KeyName" },
    "ImageId" : { "Fn::FindInMap" : [ "RegionID", { "Ref" :  "AWS::Region"
},
  { "Fn::FindInMap" : [ "T2type", { "Ref" : "InstanceType" }, "Arch" ] } ] }
  }
  },
```

We are also defining a security group to be created for this instance so that we can connect to the SSH port. This resource defines the Ingress port and protocol via the `"SecurityGroupIngress"` parameter, and allows access by defining the `"CidrIp"` parameter from the IP address range `0.0.0.0/0` – meaning everywhere:

```
"SecurityGroup" : {
  "Type" : "AWS::EC2::SecurityGroup",
  "Properties" : {
    "GroupDescription" : "Enable SSH access via port 22",
    "SecurityGroupIngress" : [ {
      "IpProtocol" : "tcp",
      "FromPort" : "22",
      "ToPort" : "22",
      "CidrIp" : "0.0.0.0/0"
    } ]
  }
},
```

Outputs

The outputs of the template are the instance IDs, so we can find it easily in the EC2 management console and the Public IP address. This means that we can get the IP to connect to the instance straight out of CloudFormation's output:

```
"Outputs" : {
  "InstanceId" : {
    "Description" : "InstanceId of the newly created EC2 instance",
    "Value" : { "Ref" : "EC2Instance" }
  },
  "PublicIP" : {
    "Description" : "Public IP address of the newly created EC2  instance",
"Value" : { "Fn::GetAtt" : [ "EC2Instance", "PublicIp" ] }
  }
}
}
```

Template deployment

Now, let's look at how we can deploy the template through the console. Follow these steps to get started:

1. We need to navigate to the CloudFormation management console and click on the **Create new stack** button:

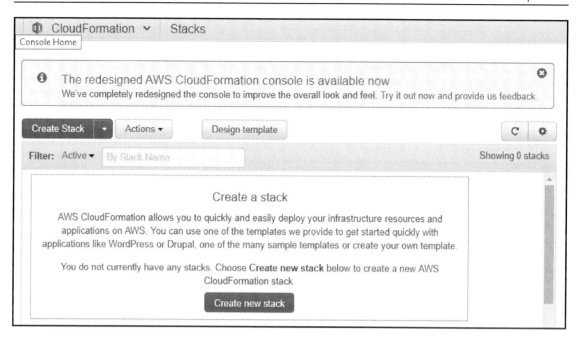

2. We need to upload a template to Amazon S3 and select the file from the samples provided by clicking **Choose file**, selecting the file, and then clicking **Next**:

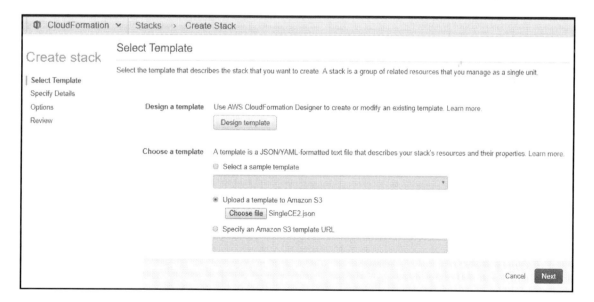

3. In the **Specify Details** section, we will be required to name the stack and specify the parameters that are defined in the template. We will need to select an instance type from the list and an EC2 key pair from any of our existing key pairs and then click **Next**:

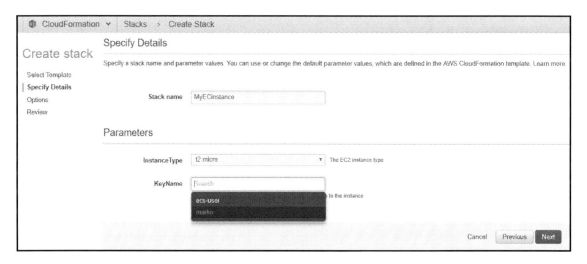

4. In the **Options** section, we have the ability to add tags to the stack. Adding tags is highly recommended so that we can easily identify the resources that have been created by the stack when browsing other management consoles. Optionally, we can also assign a role that CloudFormation will use to create these resources:

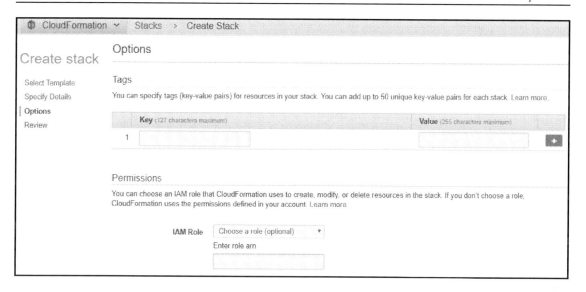

5. When running fully automated template deployments, rollback triggers are an important part of the configuration as they can automatically help us to determine whether the application has been deployed successfully or not. Additionally, we can also set advanced options for our stack like a stack policy that can help us to secure the stack. Once we are done with these settings, we can click **Next**:

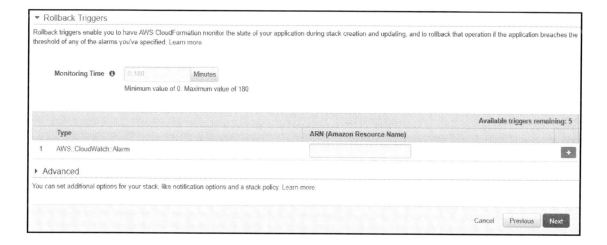

6. We are presented with a review window in which we can verify our selections and configurations of the CloudFormation stack. We are presented with the template URL and the details from the second step:

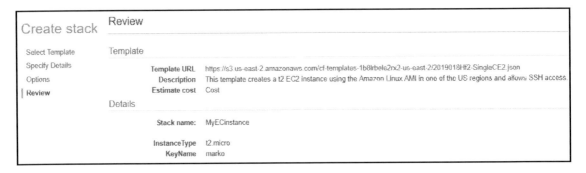

7. We are also met with options such as tags and rollback that we configured in the previous step. Once we are happy with these selections, we can click **Create** to initiate the creation of the stack:

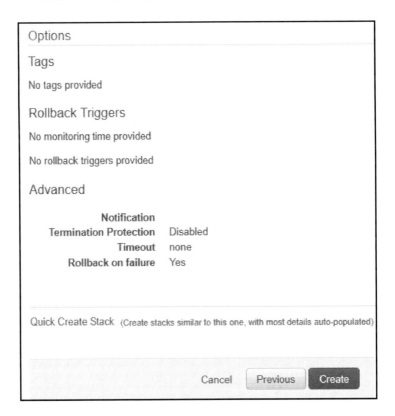

8. The stack will start to be created and will initially be seen with a status of **CREATE_IN_PROGRESS**:

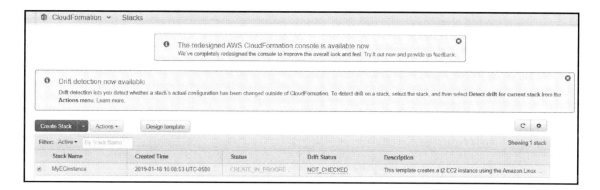

9. After stack creation completes, we will see the status change to **CREATE_COMPLETE**. We can click on the stack and then select the **Outputs** tab on the bottom. Here, we have the instance ID and the IP address to which we can now test our SSH connection to:

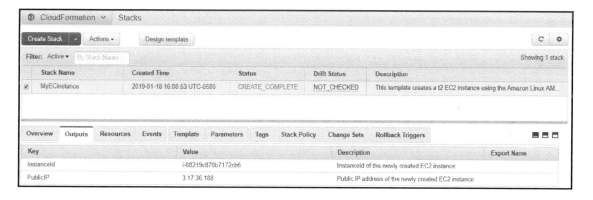

10. To connect to the IP, use your favorite SSH client with your ssh key. To verify that the instance's public IP address is really the one we want to connect to, you can run the following command, which looks up the public IP from an external service:

```
curl https://ipinfo.io/ip
```

Let's look at the following output:

Our stack was successfully deployed and our instance is running. We were able to connect to the instance because a security group allowing SSH was created by the template and the SSH key that we specified in the template creation process was added to this instance.

Summary

CloudFormation is the perfect tool when we need to automate our AWS environment. This service enables us to implement an infrastructure as code approach to our AWS deployments and deliver the applications that are running in AWS in a much more automated fashion. In this chapter, we took a look at the elements of CloudFormation and the way it works and we took a detailed look at a sample template and the procedure to deploy the template. The next chapter will help us understand how OpsWorks comes in handy when we do not have a complete control of our environment.

Questions

1. What is an environment deployed in CloudFormation called?
2. What notation formats are supported in CloudFormation templates?
3. When designing a CloudFormation, we need to restrict the users to just a few images that can be used with the template. Which section of the template can help us achieve this?

4. We would like to see the URL of the load balancer when stack creation completes. Which section of the template can help us achieve this?

5. We have deployed a stack with a VPC, Security Groups, EC2 instances, and an RDS instance in a Multi-AZ configuration. The stack keeps failing after it starts. What could be the reason for this failure?

6. You are tasked with designing a three-tiered application where each tier is designed and managed by a separate team. A network team is responsible for providing connectivity for the application. What design approach would you use in CloudFormation to separate the duties and responsibilities between the teams and how?

7. You have just joined a DevOps team where you are responsible for the infrastructure. You are shown some automated and manual processes that need to run to deliver the infrastructure for a new deployment. The automated processes are focused around the deployment of the application and the manual processes are AWS CLI commands that need to be run to provide the instances to install to. How could you improve this process?

Further reading

- **CloudFormation Documentation**: https://docs.aws.amazon.com/cloudformation/index.html#lang/en_us
- **CloudFormation Templates**: https://docs.aws.amazon.com/AWSCloudFormation/latest/UserGuide/template-guide.html
- **Cloudformation Designer**: https://console.aws.amazon.com/cloudformation/designer
- **CloudFormation Stacks**: https://docs.aws.amazon.com/AWSCloudFormation/latest/UserGuide/stacks.html
- **CloudFormation Samples**: https://docs.aws.amazon.com/AWSCloudFormation/latest/UserGuide/sample-templates-services-us-west-2.html
- **CloudFormation DependsOn Attribute**: https://docs.aws.amazon.com/AWSCloudFormation/latest/UserGuide/aws-attribute-dependson.html
- **CloudFormation Stack States**: https://docs.aws.amazon.com/AWSCloudFormation/latest/UserGuide/using-cfn-describing-stacks.html
- **CloudFormation Rollback Triggers**: https://docs.aws.amazon.com/AWSCloudFormation/latest/UserGuide/using-cfn-rollback-triggers.html

21
Cloud Orchestration with OpsWorks

Both Elastic Beanstalk and CloudFormation can orchestrate and automate the complete deployment of an application within AWS and deliver changes to existing applications through a redeployment. These two solutions are handy, but don't give us complete control of our environment. For example, neither of these solutions are effective when running legacy systems, where redeploying is not an option, or running hybrid environments both in AWS and on-premises. This is where OpsWorks comes in.

The following topics will be covered in this chapter:

- Introduction to OpsWorks
- How OpsWorks works
- Components of OpsWorks

Technical requirements

A basic understanding of enterprise orchestration and automation is required to get the most out of this topic. Additional familiarity with the operational aspects of the Chef and Puppet open source orchestration environments is beneficial.

Introduction to OpsWorks

When there's a requirement for orchestration and automation that goes beyond what Elastic Beanstalk or CloudFormation can offer, then AWS OpsWorks is the right solution to choose. OpsWorks is a highly available, highly scalable, fully managed configuration management service that delivers a cloud-based Puppet Enterprise or Chef Automate environment. OpsWorks takes care of the installation, scaling, and high availability of the solution while we maintain the same level of access as with a standalone installation of either Chef or Puppet.

With OpsWorks, we get complete control within our operating system. We can control any aspect of the configuration, including the following:

- Software, patch, and update installation
- Controlling system configurations and operating system settings
- Running scripts and applications
- Performing regular maintenance jobs
- Modifying files

Essentially, we are able to control any aspect of the operating system with changes ranging from a few characters in a file to a completely automated install and configuring tasks.

OpsWorks examples

Some typical examples that we should consider when using OpsWorks are as follows:

- Legacy applications where a redeployment is not an option
- Hybrid environments where we need unified control of both AWS and on-premise resources
- Compliance with a certain configuration
- Large clusters with a lot of small dynamic changes
- Updating and patching fleets of servers
- Migrating existing Chef or Puppet environments to a managed solution

Legacy applications

Migrating a legacy application to the cloud is just a part of the challenge. Making sure that the application is performing well and that the operating system is patched and secured is another part. With OpsWorks, we can install the appropriate agent on a server running a legacy application and include the legacy server in our automated maintenance, updating, and patching scenarios. OpsWorks can simplify the way we manage legacy applications and help to bring them into the 21st century.

Hybrid environments

With OpsWorks, we have the ability to control any operating system, regardless of where it is running. We can install the agents on both the AWS instances as well as on-premise virtual and physical servers. With OpsWorks, we gain a single point of management for both our cloud and on-premise servers and are able to ensure that the complete hybrid environment is managed in a unified manner.

Compliance

OpsWorks can be used as a compliance tool. We can use OpsWorks to continuously monitor and maintain the configuration of our servers. Whenever a server that does not have the correct configuration is detected, the server can be automatically brought back to the baseline. For example, when an administrator opens a port on a server manually that should not have been open, the OpsWorks solution can detect this change and apply the correct configuration on the server.

Clusters with small dynamic changes

When we are running clusters where a high number of dynamic changes are required, we would have a lot of difficulty achieving this by just using CloudFormation. With CloudFormation, we would need to redeploy the instances with even minor changes to the configuration, while the same can be achieved on a running instance with OpsWorks. For example, when deploying an application with a DevOps process with extremely high velocity, there is a possibility that we will be performing a deployment multiple times per day. When such a high frequency of deployments is required, OpsWorks can be a great solution as it can manage and update an existing environment without a requirement for redeploying.

Updating and patching

Updating and patching are one of the most important security aspects of modern operating systems and application platforms. Almost every major breach that has been announced in recent years has happened due to environments that were not patched or were patched too late to prevent the attack. Exploiting known vulnerabilities has been proven as the easiest and most effective way for an unauthorized actor to enter our environment. OpsWorks is a great solution for operational tasks that can help us to update and patch a variety of operating systems and all of the applications running on top of these operating systems.

Migration of Chef or Puppet

OpsWorks is the right choice when running an existing installation of Chef or Puppet configuration management, and the business driver for cloud adoption identifies the need to reduce management overhead. OpsWorks gives us the exact same level of access and control to a Chef or Puppet environment as a standalone installation would. The OpsWorks solution is fully managed, which means that we will never need to worry about making sure that the Chef or Puppet environment is running, making it highly available, scaling it, and keeping it patched and updated. All of this is taken care of by AWS. We do, however, have the option to fully customize and tune the Chef or Puppet solution within OpsWorks so that we can extract all of the power we require from our chosen configuration management tool.

How OpsWorks works

OpsWorks is a system that essentially takes care of installing and running a selected orchestration environment for us. Once we have selected our solution, we need to install and configure the correct agent or client on the operating system that will be managed by OpsWorks. We can introduce the client straight away to the AMI for any newly created EC2 instances that we deploy. We can also retrieve downloadable installer packages and install the agent or client of existing EC2 instances or on-premise virtual and physical servers. Once the operating system starts, the agent or client will be connected to the centralized configuration management environment and changes can be applied.

At the time of writing, two options exist when configuring an OpsWorks cluster:

- AWS OpsWorks for Chef Automate
- AWS OpsWorks for Puppet Enterprise

AWS OpsWorks for Chef Automate

OpsWorks for Chef Automate lets us install and run Chef Automate servers in our AWS account. The installation is completed in minutes and the system is fully usable and configurable from that point on. When running OpsWorks for Chef Automate, we will need to install chef-client on the servers and instances that we want to manage. Chef uses a push-based approach where the instances running chef-client register to the server, but no configuration is sent to the client until a recipe is applied to the group the instances belong to. Once we apply a configuration, the server pushes these changes to the clients.

AWS OpsWorks for Puppet Enterprise

OpsWorks for Puppet Enterprise lets us install and run Puppet Enterprise servers in our AWS account. Like with Chef, the installation is completed in minutes and the system is fully usable and configurable from that point on. When running OpsWorks for Puppet Enterprise, we will need to install `puppet-agent` on the servers and instances that we want to manage. Puppet uses a pull-based approach where the instances that are running `puppet-agent` register to the server and continuously poll the Puppet master server for any changes that need to be applied. These changes are stored in Puppet modules that we can write and store on the Puppet master. This is a really good approach when we need to make sure that a configuration is maintained because of compliance as the system has been designed so that the instances and servers initiate the checks and essentially manage themselves.

Components of OpsWorks

When running cloud environments, we usually group resources together in groups that represent an application or another logical grouping. As with CloudFormation, the resources that are logically bound to one another and will be managed as a single entity are grouped together in stacks. Each stack can have multiple layers representing the logical separation of a function within a stack. Within layers, we will find instances that represent computing resources that are managed by OpsWorks. Instances run apps, which are representations of applications, patches, and other software that we apply to the instances. We maintain the configuration of the server by using Cookbooks, Recipes, Manifests, and Modules. A complete architecture of the OpsWorks environment is represented in the following diagram:

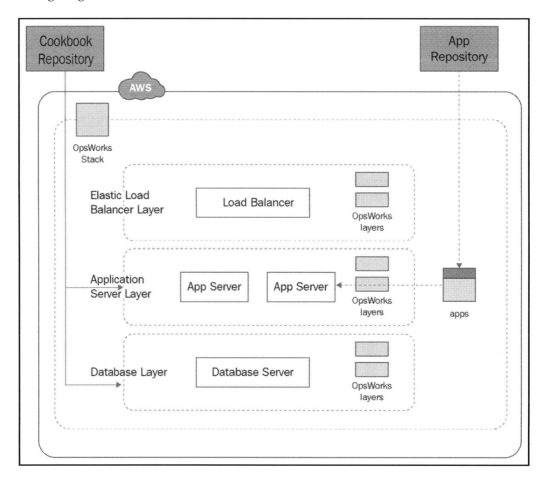

Stacks

A stack is a connected set of resources within an OpsWorks environment. We would create stacks to logically group together resources belonging to a certain application or another logical grouping. We would typically allow stacks to be provisioned and managed as a whole unit, but we can logically separate the functional parts of a stack into layers. A stack is required to have at least one layer.

An example of a stack that would manage a three-tier application would contain the following:

- A load balancer server recipe or manifest
- A web frontend server recipe or manifest
- A database server recipe or manifest

We would usually group the applications into stacks according to the purpose they serve, so we would typically find a development stack, a testing stack, and staging and production stacks being managed for one application within an OpsWorks environment.

We can also use stacks when performing blue/green deployments to update our application. Any existing stack can easily be cloned to a new stack, and a DNS switch-over can be performed to swap the environment URLs from the blue to the green environment, as represented in the following diagram:

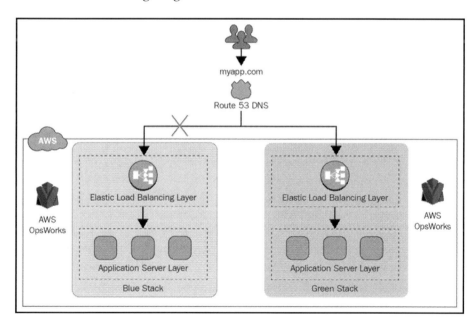

Layers

Layers represent a functional part of an application. For our three-tier application, the stack would have the following three layers:

- A load balancer layer
- A web frontend layer
- A database layer

Each layer is required to have an instance assigned to it, and each instance is required to be a part of one or multiple layers within OpsWorks. We can assign an instance to multiple layers to reduce the cost of the service we are running. For example, in a development stack, we might assign only one instance to all of the layers as the software development process would only require a functional environment, not a complete replica of the production setup.

Service layers

In AWS, there are, of course, managed services within the infrastructure. This is why service layers were introduced. Service layers differ slightly from OpsWorks layers in the sense that there are no instances with agents within a service layer, but rather other AWS services, including the following:

- Elastic load balancing layer
- Amazon RDS service layer
- ECS cluster layers
- Custom layers

All of these can be used to extend the functionality of the OpsWorks environment to include AWS resources as layered representations. A typical representation of a mix of service and OpsWorks layers in the management console would look similar to the representation that's displayed in the following diagram:

Instances

Instances represent our server computing resources. An instance can run any supported Linux or Windows operating system, must run a chef-client or `puppet-agent`, and can reside either in AWS or on-premise. Once an instance starts, the agent or client will register to the centralized management and poll for changes (in case of `puppet-agent`) or wait for changes to be pushed to it (in the case of chef-client). Instances must be a member of at least one OpsWorks layer to be able to be controlled by OpsWorks.

Apps

Any applications, patches, and updates that we would like to apply to our instances within a layer of a stack are represented as apps. An app needs to be delivered from a repository such as an S3 bucket or Git. Once we have published an app in the repository, it can be applied to a layer. Once an app has been assigned to a layer, each instance that becomes a member of a layer will have all of the layers apps automatically installed.

Each app is composed of the following sections:

- **Settings**: This represents the name of the app and its document structure.
- **Application Source**: This represents the sources for the installation of applications, such as repositories and bundles that need to be made accessible to the instances that are managed by OpsWorks.
- **Data Sources**: These represent databases that need to be attached to the application if required.

- **Environment Variables**: These represent application-specific variables that can be passed into the instance upon deployment of the application.
- **Domain and SSL Settings**: These represent domain and SSL certificates that are being configured on the instance.

Cookbooks, recipes, manifests, and modules

To control the configurations of our instances and on-premise servers within an OpsWorks environment, we will be using standard Chef Automate Cookbooks and Puppet Enterprise Manifests. Cookbooks contain recipes, whereas manifests contain modules. We can use both the official cookbooks from the Chef Supermarket and manifests from the puppet main manifest, or we can enable the use of custom cookbooks and manifests from any compatible versioned repository. Recipes and modules can be executed as follows:

- Automatically, during a stack's life cycle events
- Automatically on a schedule
- Manually

Life cycle events

Within each layer, the following life cycle events can be triggered:

- **Setup**: Once the instance starts and the agent or client reports to the server, the setup event runs the recopies or modules that configure the instance to the base specification of the layer.
- **Configure**: A configure event occurs whenever an instance is added or removed from a layer or whenever network interfaces or load balancers are connected to the layer.
- **Deploy**: Whenever a deployment of an application is initiated, the deployed life cycle event will pick up the recopies or modules that need to be executed on the instances. We can use deploy to update our software or patch our servers.
- **Undeploy**: We can use undeploy to remove an application or roll back changes that have been made by a deploy operation.
- **Shutdown**: The shutdown life cycle event is triggered upon shutdown of an instance. This gives the instance time to leave a cluster, record any data, or transfer any logs to an external source before it is terminated.

Timed and manual deployments

We can also run recipes or manifests on a schedule. We can always configure the server to apply certain configurations on a timely basis. This is a very good option if we have the need to maintain a configuration over time due to compliance requirements, laws, or regulations. We can prevent the configuration from straying from the baseline by continuously passing the recipe or manifest that handles the base configuration to the servers so that if any changes that are not compliant have been made, the system can easily be made compliant again.

If required, OpsWorks also gives us the ability to easily run a certain recipe or manifest manually from the management console, the CLI, or the SDK.

Summary

OpsWorks is a great solution when we require full control of our environments at all times. OpsWorks is fully compatible with Chef Automate cookbooks and recipes and Puppet Enterprise manifests and modules. The solution is fully managed, but also supports full customization as we are able to configure each and every aspect of the service to get the most out of the product. In this chapter, we have taken a look at the structure of the OpsWorks system and learned a bit about what each functional component of OpsWorks represents. The next chapter mainly deals with the tips and tricks we can use to prepare and pass the AWS Certified SysOps Administrator – Associate exam.

Questions

1. True or false: OpsWorks is a configuration management tool that supports Chef Automate and Puppet Enterprise and allows us to control our instances running in AWS.
2. True or false: OpsWorks supports both OpsWorks and Service layers to provide the capability to use both EC2 instances and other AWS services from the same stack.
3. When running OpsWorks, which component can we use to install applications to instances within a stack?
4. You have a multi-tier application. How would you separate the functional aspects of this application within OpsWorks?

5. Your development environment is deemed a success and you wish to create four similar environments (test, QA, staging, and production) based on the settings and characteristics of the development stack. What is the easiest way to do that in OpsWorks?

6. You have a requirement to maintain a configuration across time on a certain set of instances due to compliance reasons. How would you go about automating the compliance requirements with OpsWorks?

7. You are running an application with infrequent heavy changes being delivered to the instances that are running in AWS. You are currently using a manual process with an AWS CLI script and a JSON input file to create and deploy a new AMI and then deploy the new instances and terminate the old instances. There is a need to automate the deployment with a CI server that can generate the JSON input file automatically. What would be a good solution to implement in this scenario and why?

Further reading

- **OpsWorks Documentation**: https://docs.aws.amazon.com/opsworks/latest/userguide/welcome.html
- **OpsWorks fro Puppet**: https://docs.aws.amazon.com/opsworks/latest/userguide/welcome_opspup.html
- **OpsWorks for Chef**: https://docs.aws.amazon.com/opsworks/latest/userguide/welcome_opscm.html
- **OpsWorks Components**: https://docs.aws.amazon.com/opsworks/latest/userguide/welcome_classic.html
- **Chef Automate Open Source**: https://docs.chef.io/chef_automate.html
- **Puppet Open Source**: https://puppet.com/docs

Exam Tips and Tricks 22

This chapter is intended to provide a deeper understanding of what the AWS Certified SysOps Administrator – Associate exam is and how to prepare to pass the exam.

The following topics will be covered in this chapter:

- Introduction
- Monitoring metrics and managing cost
- High availability and scaling
- Analysis of your AWS environment
- Deployment and provisioning
- Data management
- Security
- Networking

Technical requirements

In this chapter, we'll be broadly discussing the complete scope of AWS technologies that we described in the previous chapters and what to look out for when taking the exam. To get the most benefit out of this chapter, it's recommended to read through and understand the topics from all of the previous chapters of this book.

Introduction

As you have seen from the content of this book and the exam blueprint, a broad range of knowledge is required to pass the AWS Certified SysOps Administrator – Associate exam. AWS recommends that anyone attempting to pass the exam have at least one year experience working with AWS. In my own opinion, that's a reasonable requirement, but due to the broad range of topics that we have covered, anyone working with AWS for one year might not even scratch the surface.

Due to different business drivers for cloud adoption, some SysOps engineers might be highly proficient in EC2, RDS, S3, load balancing, VPCs, and other network components, but due to the nature of the applications they maintain in AWS, they might have never even touched any of the serverless technologies. Quite the opposite might occur on the other side, where the business driver is getting rid of servers—anyone who is highly proficient in building and operating serverless solutions might struggle with EC2. I have even seen examples of hardcore OpsWorks/Chef engineers with several years of experience struggle with the SysOps topics just because they weren't familiar with all of the AWS offerings that are covered in the exam.

The reason why I'm stressing this is not to put you off or make you feel like the exam will be difficult. Rather, I would like to make everyone reading this book understand that it is highly likely that you will find that you have strengths and weaknesses when it comes to your knowledge of AWS, and that's due to the fact that not everyone is going to be equally exposed to these technologies.

However, the exam does take this into account somewhat. You shouldn't be expecting the questions to be very specific. The questions will be focused on revealing whether you have enough of a broad understanding of the technologies in AWS, whether you know what the best practices are and how to apply them to the configurations in AWS, and whether you are able to identify the technology based on its description or vice versa.

My recommendation to you is to identify the strengths, level of understanding, and weaknesses that you may have in your knowledge and understanding of the topics that were covered in this book. Once you have identified your level of knowledge and understanding for each topic, then make sure that you also have enough hands-on experience. Whether it is through daily tasks at work or by experimenting with a free-tier account, make sure that you are actually working with these solutions. There is no book, no exam guide, no sample question set—not one thing that can replace the experience and the time you spend actually working with the technologies covered in this book.

If I had to choose one piece of advice among everything, I would sum it up in three words: experiment, experiment, and experiment!

Monitoring metrics and managing cost

The exam covers different domains of knowledge and the first one focuses on testing your understanding of how to monitor your environment and manage costs in your environment. This section will look at your ability to understand the CloudWatch monitoring environment and what kinds of metrics and logs it can store and display in the management console. There are several crucial aspects to remember about CloudWatch:

- By default, there's no cost associated with the metrics unless you enable detailed monitoring.
- You can deliver any kind of custom metrics to CloudWatch with detailed monitoring down to one second.
- CloudWatch doesn't have access to the EC2 operating system, meaning that any metrics or logs that can't be collected by the hypervisor require the delivery of custom metrics or the use of the CloudWatch agent to stream logs.
- Remember, you can always deliver logs either to CloudWatch or store them in S3
- Tagging is very useful when monitoring as it can help analyze metrics from several different services in one visualization.

To test your understanding of how to understand and control costs in AWS, the exam will probe your general understanding of how billing works in AWS and what the cost structure of services in AWS is. You should be able to demonstrate a fairly high level of understanding of costs—for example, whether it is cheaper to store files on S3 or EBS. There are several crucial aspects to remember about cost management:

- Make sure you understand which services are charged on what kind of use. Some services have charges for provisioned resources, some for requests, some for the amount or time consumed, and so on.
- CloudWatch billing alarms can help with controlling costs and projecting usage amounts.
- Consolidated billing is the right approach when you need to centralize billing for several AWS accounts.
- Read the questions carefully and look for the crucial metric that would cause one service to be more expensive than the other—be it the number of requests, the size of the data, whether the data is being sent in out of AWS, are we crossing regions, and so on.

High availability and scaling

In the high availability and scaling section of the exam, you can expect questions that will test how well you understand the AWS architecture and how to make sure that the services are highly available and scalable within the scope of AWS. Make sure not to forget that some services are highly available and/or scalable by default, while some will take some architecting to achieve that. There are several crucial aspects about high availability and scaling that you should remember:

- Make sure you understand high availability across availability zones and regions.
- Understand what can impact the availability for an availability zone or a region.
- Make sure you know how to make a VPC and its components highly available.
- Understand the high availability and scaling of EC2 and RDS instances.
- Familiarize yourself with the SLA, that is, the availability and scaling of managed services in AWS.
- Explore the AWS disaster recovery scenarios.
- Understand how to use ELB, Autoscaling, CloudWatch, and Route 53 for high availability.

Analysis of your AWS environment

Once crucial aspect of every SysOps engineer's job is understanding the environment that they operate on. AWS wants you to be able to understand how your application behaves and be able to analyse and detect when your environment is operating out of bounds. You will be thoroughly tested on this topic and it should not be taken for granted. When preparing for the exam, crucial aspects to take a look at would be as follows:

- Make sure you know how to read metrics and understand what each metric is telling you about the state of your environment
- Make sure you understand the soft and hard limits that are put on AWS services
- Make sure you understand how to collect logs and diagnostic data when an issue is present
- Understand how to analyze trends in AWS

Deployment and provisioning

Another crucial part of the operation team's job is being able to deploy and provision resources in a timely and correct manner. In AWS, there are several technologies that can help you provision resources and deploy applications and that provide you with complete control of the infrastructure components. The exam will test your knowledge of deployment and provisioning practices and will try to determine whether you are able to identify the right solution to use for the right type of application. Sometimes, the driver for selecting a certain tool would also be what the enterprise is currently using or the need to reduce the management overhead, increase automation, or integrate with other environments. Crucial aspects to remember about deployment and provisioning would be as follows:

- Understand the differences between Elastic Beanstalk, CloudFormation, and OpsWorks
- Understand the basic practices that are used in cloud and on-premise orchestration
- Make sure you are able to select the right solution—the cheapest, easiest, or most compatible with the current setup

Data management

Managing data is also usually part of an operation team's responsibilities. Being able to identify the correct solution to store the data that will be the most efficient as far as costs and resource usage is concerned is a crucial part of this domain of the exam. On top of that, you need to learn about the backup strategies for each data type, the approaches to life cycling, and making sure that the data residing on a certain data store is compliant with regulations and laws. When preparing for this domain, keep the following points in mind:

- Understand the different data types and the data stores that are available in AWS for each data type
- Be able to differentiate between S3, S3-IA, S3-RRS, Glacier, instance store, EBS, and EFS
- When to upload and when to use Snowball/Snowmobile
- Use AWS built-in tools and external tools/scripts to backup and snapshot EC2 and RDS instances and other AWS services
- Understand compliance with availability, durability, regional compliance, and data sovereignty

Security

Security is possibly the most discussed topic as far as the cloud is concerned. Whether it is about securing your services on the network, making sure your applications are secure, encrypting your data or securing your users—when it comes to cloud, it always seems to be discussed with caution. We have learned that we are able to secure our cloud-based applications to the same or higher level as our on-premise systems. When being tested on your knowledge of security in AWS, you should remember these key points:

- Always apply permissions with the least privilege approach by only giving the permissions that are necessary to perform a task.
- Prefer applying IAM policies to groups rather than individual users.
- Use roles when automating access to AWS on your EC2 instances, Lambda functions, and so on.
- Remember that access can be granted to other accounts with cross-account roles.
- Remember the limitations of IAM.
- When you see high numbers of users, federation is the correct approach.
- Differentiate between the `AssumeRole` and `AssumeRoleWithWebIdentity` operations.
- You can federate IAM with LDAP, but sometimes a LDAP replica in AWS is the right option.
- Understand encryption in transit and encryption at rest in AWS. Understand which service provides which type of encryption and what protocol or encryption mechanism it uses.

Networking

As networking is essentially a basic component of modern distributed computing and the internet, anyone operating any kind of system in AWS will have to understand networking. You don't need to be a core engineer to be able to work with AWS, but you do need to have some basic understanding of the way networking works. The exam will test your knowledge of AWS networking solutions such as the VPC, subnets, NACLs, Security Groups, internet gateways, VPN gateways, NAT instances, Direct Connect, and VPC peering. However, you should not forget that all of these were initially designed on IPv4, so being able to understand how IPv4 works is crucial. When preparing for the exam, make sure to brush up on the following topics:

- Understanding IP address assignment, DHCP, DNS, name resolution, and routing

- How to design VPCs and the CIDR notation that's used in VPCs, subnets, and security rules
- How to mange subnet security with NACLs and instance security with security groups, allowing and blocking access, stateless NACLs versus stateful security groups, and so on
- Connectivity options in AWS—how to connect to the internet and to on-premise
- Service ceilings for network components
- Remember that VPN automatically encrypts traffic in transit with IPSec

Summary

In this chapter, we have given a brief overview of the seven domains in the AWS Certified SysOps Administrator – Associate exam. This chapter included some recommendations on what to be mindful of when preparing for the exam and what key points to remember when going in to the exam. Before attempting to pass the AWS Certified SysOps Administrator – Associate exam, make sure that you understand the broad range of services that are covered in this exam. Also, make sure that you get some hands on experience with the services as nothing can replace the time and effort spent working with the environment. Once you feel prepared to take on the challenge, take a look at the mock tests that are provided in this book in the next chapter. On the day of the exam, don't forget that you have enough time to read the questions carefully, so take your time and keep calm! Good luck!

Further reading

- **The SysOps Exam Blueprint:** https://aws.amazon.com/certification/certified-sysops-admin-associate/
- **Exam Prep Guide:** https://d1.awsstatic.com/training-and-certification/docs-sysops-associate/AWS%20Certified%20SysOps%20-%20Associate_Exam%20Guide_Sep18.pdf
- **Official Sample Questions:** http://awstrainingandcertification.s3.amazonaws.com/production/AWS_certified_sysops_associate_examsample.pdf

23
Mock Tests

This chapter contains two mock tests that simulate a real AWS Certified SysOps Administrator-Associate certification test with mock questions. This chapter provides an easy way to test your knowledge. Each mock test contains 60 questions. Readers should try to complete a mock test in 90 minutes and achieve a score of 80% or above before attempting to take the AWS Certified SysOps Administrator-Associate certification exam.

Mock test 1

1. You have spun up an EC2 Linux instance with an instance storage root volume. You also attached an EBS for the database. When you stop the instances, what happens to the data on the root volume?

    A. When we stop the instance, the data on the root volume will be deleted.

    B. When we stop the instance, the data on the root volume is copied to the EBS volume.

    C. When we stop the instance, the data on the root volume is automatically saved as an EBS snapshot.

    D. When we stop the instance, the data on the root volume will be available again only after we start the same exact EC2 instance ID.

2. You are running a Linux EC2 instance and need to determine the public IP addresses from the operating system. How can that be done?

    A. Use the AWS CLI to query CloudWatch for the IPAddr metric.

    B. Use the `ifconfig` command in the operating system.

    C. It is not possible to determine the public IP from the operating system, as it is assigned on the router.

    D. Use `curl` to read the local instance metadata.

3. You have created an ELB, an EC2 Auto Scaling cluster, and an ELB health check for the /healthcheck.php page. Due to a traffic increase, your application is scaling out, but all new instances are showing as **unhealthy** in the ELB health check. You don't want to run unhealthy instances in your cluster, but they are not being terminated automatically. You are at your Auto Scaling maximum and need to take action quickly. How can you ensure that any unhealthy EC2 instances are terminated and replaced with healthy ones?

    A. Check the thresholds of the Auto Scaling group health check.

    B. Check the load balancing health check page on the instances.

    C. Raise the health check interval set on the ELB.

    D. Set up a new health check on the ELB with TCP checks.

4. You need to migrate an EC2 Linux instance with a root EBS volume containing a database from one Availability Zone (AZ) to another. What would be the right approach to perform this action?

    A. Shut down the instance. Create a new volume in the other AZ. Specify the EC2 instance's volume as the origin. Start the instance in the new AZ with the new volume.

    B. Create a snapshot of the instance. Use the `c2-migrate-volume` command to move the EBS volume to the other AZ. Start an instance from the copied volume.

    C. Shut down the instance. Create an AMI from the instance. Start a new instance from the AMI in the other AZ.

    D. Shut down the instance. Detach the volume. Attach it to any other EC2 instance in the other AZ.

5. You decide to design a VPC. Which options would *not* be available for your subnets? Choose all that apply:

    A. You will be able to map one subnet to one AZ.

    B. You can assign a CIDR as small as /28 to the subnet.

    C. You don't need routing for the private subnet, as the internet is available by default.

    D. Routing between all subnets in a VPC is enabled by default.

    E. You will be able to map one subnet to two AZs for high availability.

6. You are running a stateless application on one EC2 c5-8xlarge instance. When traffic increases, the application stops responding. You store the state of the application in a DynamoDB table that is always below the provisioned RCUs and WCUs. How could you fix this issue?

    A. Create an ELB. Create an Auto Scaling group that adds another c5-8xlarge instance when the load is high.

    B. The instance needs to be in the same AZ as the DynamoDB table.

    C. Cache the database queries in ElastiCache.

    D. Move the database from DynamoDB to RDS MySQL in a Multi-AZ configuration.

7. You are automating database backup and recovery activities. You would like to use as many AWS-managed solutions as you can, but could use AWS CLI and scripts to do the rest. Identify the task that is best performed by a script:

    A. Regularly creating and rotating EBS snapshots

    B. Regularly creating and rotating RDS snapshots

    C. Regularly detecting and stopping unused or underutilized EC2 instances

    D. Regularly attaching elastic IP addresses to EC2 instances

8. Your physical security system has a video component that produces hundreds of video files on-premises every day with a total size of around 300 GB. The files need to be uploaded to Amazon S3 every night in a fixed time window between 1 a.m. and 5 a.m., but the upload takes over 8 hours. The upload is consuming less than a quarter of the available bandwidth. What needs to be done to make sure the files are uploaded during the time window?

   A. Add a VGW and create a VPN connection to increase your network performance.

   B. Upload the files in parallel to S3.

   C. Compress the files into a single archive – this will reduce the size of the upload and make it run faster.

   D. Use AWS Snowball for this operation on a weekly basis.

9. You need to point your domain's zone apex FQDN (for example, `www.markocloud.com`) to an application sitting behind an ELB. Which option should you choose?

   A. Use an Amazon Route 53 Alias record.

   B. Use an Amazon Route 53 PTR record.

   C. Use an Amazon Route 53 CNAME record.

   D. Use an Amazon Route 53 A record.

10. You need to design a bastion or jump instance. The requirement is that you set up a Windows instance with RDS enabled. Once logged into the instance, you will be able to use PuTTY to SSH to the hosts running in EC2. You need to make sure the instance can be recovered if it fails automatically:

    A. Run two bastion instances, one in each AZ for redundancy.

    B. Run the bastion on an active instance in one AZ and have an AMI ready to boot up in the event of failure.

    C. Configure the bastion instance in an Auto Scaling group. Specify the Auto Scaling group to include multiple AZs, but have a min-size of 1 and max-size of 1.

    D. Configure an ELB in front of a single bastion instance.

11. You are migrating an on-premises application deployed with Chef Automation to AWS. What would be the approach that would have the least management overhead?

    A. Use OpsWorks to deploy the application in a new stack with the existing chef recipes.

    B. Use Elastic Beanstalk's Chef import feature to import the configuration into a new environment.

    C. Deploy a Linux instance and install Chef community on EC2. Import your Chef recipes to the newly deployed Chef server.

    D. Deploy a Linux instance and install Chef community on EC2. Use the AWS CLI to automate the deployment.

12. Which of the following are true regarding Amazon S3? Choose two:

    A. Objects are directly accessible via a URL.

    B. S3 is the perfect data-store for a relational database.

    C. Objects stored in S3 can have unlimited size.

    D. You can store an unlimited number of objects in S3.

    E. Provisioned IOPS is a feature of S3.

13. You are inserting costume metrics into CloudWatch from an EC2 instance. You need to assign permissions to the EC2 instance to be able to write to CloudWatch. Which approach would be correct?

    A. Create an IAM role and assign the role to the instance.

    B. Create an IAM user and inject the user's credentials into the instance metadata.

    C. Create an IAM policy and assign the policy to the instance.

    D. Create an IAM user and use the `/root/.aws/credentials` file to allow the instance to use the correct credentials for CloudWatch.

14. Which AWS allows you to create a daily backup that can be maintained for up to 35 days?

   A. S3 Standard

   B. RDS

   C. EBS

   D. S3 RRS

15. What is an EC2 placement group?

   A. A cluster of Auto Scaling groups that can communicate with high bandwidth and low latency

   B. A cluster of EC2 instances that can communicate with high bandwidth and low latency

   C. A cluster of ELBs that can communicate with high bandwidth and low latency

   D. A cluster of CloudFront edge locations that can communicate with high bandwidth and low latency

16. Your application creates daily DynamoDB tables in multiple AWS regions. You are required to maintain watch over the tables and be able to create a daily report of the total number of throttled requests for your application. What is the correct way to do this?

   A. Use AWS CLI to retrieve metrics from DynamoDB. Pool the data into an CSV file and import the custom metrics into a custom dashboard in CloudWatch.

   B. Use SNMP to retrieve metrics from DynamoDB. Pool the data into your SNMP server, extract the data in a text file, and import the custom metrics into a custom dashboard in CloudWatch.

   C. Tag your DynamoDB tables and use the tag as the dimension for a custom dashboard in CloudWatch.

   D. Attach a CloudWatch agent to DynamoDB and use the agent data as the dimension for a custom dashboard in CloudWatch.

17. You are operating an Auto Scaling chat application in AWS behind a load balancer. Each instance is able to handle the load of approximately 100,000 users. Your application has steadily grown to almost a million users. Your company has secured VC funding and is rolling out a huge marketing campaign in one week's time. You are expecting the application to go viral after this. The marketing projections show that you have so far had about 8% engagement and the marketing has been sent out to the whole US. You estimate that you might need anything up to 300 instances to be able to handle traffic . What should you do to avoid potential service disruptions during the ramp up in traffic?

    A. Make sure to get 300 Elastic IP addresses.

    B. Check the service limits in EC2 and request a limit increase if necessary.

    C. In Auto Scaling group, set a maximum of 300 instances a few minutes prior to the launch of the marketing campaign.

    D. In Auto Scaling group, set a desired number of 300 instances an hour prior to the launch of the marketing campaign.

18. You have a VPC. It has one internet gateway and one ELB. You have created two private and two public subnets in two availability zones. You have an Auto Scaling group of EC2 instances with half the instances in each of the public subnets. You have a MySQL RDS instance deployed in Multi-AZ mode in the private subnets. What else do you need to add to make this architecture highly available?

    A. Nothing.

    B. Attach a second internet gateway to the VPC.

    C. Attach a second Elastic Load Balancer to the Auto Scaling group.

    D. Attach a second Multi-AZ RDS and configure synchronous replication, as Multi-AZ is asynchronous.

19. Your cloud adoption business driver is access to programmable infrastructure. You have been tasked to develop an **Infrastructure as Code (IaC)** strategy for your company that would enable you to deploy the development, test, QA, and production environments from the same Infrastructure as Code document. Which approach addresses this requirement?

   A. Deploy an OpsWorks server into EC2. Use environment tags, such as development and test, to identify the environments and store the IaC document in the tag. Use the OpsWorks server to manage your EC2 instances.

   B. Deploy your servers manually. Use environment tags such as development and test to identify the environment and store the IaC document in the tag. Use the tags to deploy and manage your infrastructure.

   C. Use Elastic Beanstalk. Store the IaC document in Git. Deploy and manage your EC2 instances with Elastic Beanstalk.

   D. Use CloudFormation. Store the IaC document in Git. Deploy and manage your EC2 instances with CloudFormation.

20. Your development team needs to deliver infrastructure for an application that can receive up to millions of messages per second and process them at a regular pace. EC2 will be used to run the application that will process the messages and SQS will be the receiver. You want to ensure your application has sufficient bandwidth to be able to receive the messages and process them as the numbers of messages increase. Which of the following should you do?

   A. Make sure the EC instances are connected behind an Elastic Load Balancer.

   B. Make sure that the EC2 instances are launched with the appropriate network interface attached.

   C. Make sure the instances all have a public IP assigned.

   D. Make sure you launch the instances in an Auto Scaling group and have Auto Scaling triggers configured to match the number of messages in the SQS queue.

21. Your developers are implementing a centralized MySQL database that will be used by all your enterprise applications. Regular analytics jobs are likely to cause the database to become unavailable to other applications due to the complex nature of the analytics jobs. As your data grows, these analytics jobs will start to take more time, increasing the negative effect on the other applications. How do you solve the contention issues between these different workloads on the same data?

    A. Enable Multi-AZ mode on the RDS instance. Point the analytics jobs to the standby DB.

    B. Use ElastiCache to offload the analytics job data. Point the analytics jobs to the ElastiCache.

    C. Create RDS read replicas. Point the analytics jobs to the read replicas.

    D. Run the RDS instance on an x1-16xlarge instance type. Deliver the required centralization from the single database.

22. You are reviewing your company's infrastructure on AWS. While reviewing your web applications behind ELBs, you notice one application that has an Auto Scaling group with 10 instances. All 10 instances are running in the same Availability Zone. What do you need to fix to balance the instances across AZs for high availability?

    A. Modify the ELB AZ attachments. The ELB will auto-balance the instances.

    B. Modify the Auto Scaling group to launch into multiple AZs. Make sure the ELB is set with cross-zone balancing enabled.

    C. Copy your AMI to the other AZ and run a re-balance operation on the Auto Scaling group.

    D. Increase the maximum size of the Auto Scaling Group to 20. This will create 10 more instances in another AZ.

23. You are running an ELB, three EC2 servers, and one MySQL RDS with multiple read replicas and S3 for static files. Your application has started to perform badly. Which CloudWatch metrics would point to the database as the problem? Choose all that apply:

    A. Outstanding I/Os

    B. Write latency

    C. Amount of space used by binary logs

    D. Lag time of read replicas

    E. High average of disk I/Os

24. You have three teams. Each team has one AWS account. You set a monthly budget to each team. What can you do to be aware of the costs and make sure the budget isn't exceeded?

    A. Use AWS Consolidated Billing to get a unified bill.

    B. Use CloudWatch alarms using SNS in each account. Create a notification based on the price and number of instances.

    C. Use CloudWatch billing alerts in each account. Create a notification when the budget amount is spent.

    D. Use CloudWatch billing alerts in each account.
    Create separate notifications at 50%, 75%, and 90% of the budget amount spend.

25. You have a Multi-AZ RDS deployed and the primary RDS instance fails. How can you recover from the failure?

    A. The automatic process of switching the IP of the primary RDS instance is performed on the standby RDS instance, and the traffic resumes as soon as the IP is switched.

    B. You need to manually create a new RDS instance in the standby AZ and resume RDS traffic.

    C. The automatic process that changes the CNAME record from primary to standby and the traffic resumes as soon as the CNAME is switched.

    D. You need to manually reboot the primary RDS instance.

26. You are required to maintain your data across two data centers for 99.99% availability. Your business will start storing data on Amazon S3. How can you ensure the 99.99% uptime requirement is met?

    A. Clone the data among two S3 buckets in different regions, using the CLI.

    B. S3 data is automatically replicated between regions so you don't need to worry.

    C. Clone the data among two S3 buckets in different data centers within the same region using the CLI.

    D. S3 data is automatically replicated between multiple data centers within a region, so you don't need to worry.

27. You are hosting a WordPress site with a forum. The forum sometimes becomes really busy when a hot topic is started and the whole site slows down. You have identified the RDS database as the component that is slowing down your site. What could you do to reduce the load on the site and make sure the site performs well even when the forum is hot? Choose 3 answers:

    A. Use CloudFront to cache the static content in the forum.

    B. Use RDS read replicas for all the read traffic to your database.

    C. Use ElastiCache to cache the most frequently used data.

    D. Use an SQS to queue up the requests for the forum and offload the database.

    E. Use Route 53 health checks to fail over to an S3 bucket with the static content when traffic is high.

28. You are storing session state and caching database queries in a Memcached cluster, deployed via ElastiCache. You notice a high number of **Evictions** and **GetMisses** in the ElastiCache metrics. How can you fix this situation?

    A. Increase the number of nodes in your cluster.

    B. Shrink the number of nodes in your cluster.

    C. Shrink the size of nodes in your cluster.

    D. Increase the size of the nodes in the cluster.

29. You have two EC2 in a VPC in the same AZ in different subnets. You want to confirm that the two instances are able to communicate. How can you confirm the VPC settings are correct? Choose two:

    A. Check that the NACL allows communication between the two subnets.

    B. Check that both instances are of the same type, as they will also have a network adapter in the same zone.

    C. Check the NAT instance and IGW are properly configured.

    D. Check that the Security Groups allow communication between the two instances on the appropriate ports.

30. What feature would provide your EC2 instances with low inter-node latency?

    A. AWS Direct Connect

    B. Placement Groups

    C. VPC private subnets

    D. EC2 Dedicated Instances

31. You have an application on an EC2 instance that is running in the default VPC. The application needs to be PCI compliant and needs to be moved to dedicated hardware. How can this be done in the simplest manner?

    A. Create a dedicated VPC and migrate the instance to the new VPC.

    B. Use the AWS CLI with `ec2-configure-instances` and set the parameter as `dedicated=true`.

    C. Change the properties of the instance and check the box for dedicated tenancy.

    D. Stop the instance, create an AMI, launch a new instance with `tenancy=dedicated`, and terminate the old instance.

32. You have created a VPC with a public subnet, an IGW, and a security group allowing port 22 traffic. You start up a Linux instance with a public IP and try to SSH to it, but you are not able to. The instance is reporting as healthy and should be reachable. What would you check next to try and resolve the issue?

    A. The configuration of a NAT instance

    B. The configuration of the routing table

    C. The configuration of IGW

    D. The configuration of VGW

33. Your application can only work with hardcoded IP addresses and is unable to resolve DNS. You set up an EC2 instance and enter the public IP of the instance in the application. The application works. You test the recovery strategy but discover that each time the instance is stopped or a new instance is created to replace it, a new public IP is assigned to it. How can you set up a static IP so that it can be hardcoded into the application, while also being able to fail over to new instance?

    A. Use an ELB and an Elastic IP. Hardcode the ELB public IP into the application.

    B. Use an ENI and an Elastic IP. Hardcode the ENI elastic IP into the application.

    C. Use an EFS adapter for the hardcoded IP configuration and move it to the failover instance.

    D. This is not possible. The application with the hardcoded IP will need to be rebuilt.

34. Your EC2 windows application in AWS is constantly getting hit by port scans. Your network team has identified the IP address block from where the port scans are coming. No valid traffic has ever come from that IP address block, so you would like to deny access. How can you easily do this in AWS?

    A. Modify the Windows Firewall setting across all EC2 hosts to deny access from the IP address block.

    B. Modify the Windows Firewall settings across all public EC2 hosts to deny access from the IP address block.

C. Modify the access rule to all of the VPC Security Groups to deny access from the IP address block.

D. Modify the Network ACLs associated with all public subnets in the VPC to deny access from the IP address block.

35. You are running web servers in an Auto Scaling group behind an ELB. The web servers store their data in an RDS layer. You would like to understand shared security between you and AWS. What part of security is AWS responsible for?

A. Protect the EC2 instance network with an operating system firewall configuration.

B. Protect the EC2 instance network against IP spoofing or packet sniffing.

C. Protect the EC2 instance network with encryption.

D. Protect the EC2 instance operating system by installing security patches.

36. While automating administration tasks, you have noticed that some AWS services can deliver fully functional services with a built-in setting. Which of these would represent such a service? Choose all that apply:

A. Creating daily EBS backups

B. Creating daily RDS backups

C. Creating daily S3 bucket snapshots

D. Creating daily EC2 snapshots

37. You are implementing a monitoring solution in AZ A that will be pinging EC2 instances with the ICMP protocol across all the subnets in all AZs in the same VPC. How do we enable the monitoring instance to ping the EC2 instances in the most effective manner?

A. This is not possible, as ICMP can not traverse AZs.

B. Put the monitoring instance and the application instances into the same security group. Allow inbound ICMP to the security group from the monitoring instance public IP.

C. Put the monitoring instance and the application instances in separate security groups. Allow inbound ICMP to the application instance security group from the monitoring instance security group.

D. Put the monitoring instance and the application instances in separate security groups. Allow inbound ICMP to the application instance security group and outbound ICMP to the monitoring instance security group.

38. Your e-commerce application requires six servers to run on a daily basis but will be required to scale up to 18 when sales are on. Your application processes payments that may take up to 4 minutes to complete once initiated. What types of instance plan would you recommend to minimize costs while providing high availability?

    A. 9 Reserved Instances and 9 On-Demand Instances

    B. 6 Reserved Instances and 12 On-Demand Instances

    C. 6 Reserved Instances, and 6 On-Demand Instances, and 6 Spot Instances

    D. 3 Reserved Instances, and 3 On-Demand instances, and 12 Spot Instances

39. You are migrating your application to AWS. Your on-premises deployment mode uses Ansible as the configuration management tool. You need to make the transition as simple as possible and deliver a solution with the least management overhead. Which deployment option meets these requirements?

    A. Create a new stack within OpsWorks for Ansible Automation and import the Ansible configuration to the layers of the stack.

    B. Migrate your application to Elastic Beanstalk.

    C. Launch EC2 instances through CloudFormation and then perform configuration management with your Ansible scripts.

    D. Launch and configure an Ansible Server on an EC2 instance and launch the application via the AWS CLI.

40. You need to maintain SSH access into all the EC2 instances due to compliance regulations. Which service would allow you to do this? Choose two:

    A. Amazon Elastic Map Reduce

    B. Elastic Load Balancing

C. AWS Elastic Beanstalk

D. Amazon ElastiCache

E. Amazon Relational Database service

41. You are choosing a schema for the usernames for your organisation. Which would not be a valid IAM username to choose for the schema?

    A. `Marko.cloud`

    B. `Marko@cloud`

    C. `Marko=cloud`

    D. `Marko#cloud`

42. Your EC2 application is designed to perform a high number of read requests to other instances. A monitoring instance maintains a record of all calls and reports a custom metric to CloudWach. A CloudWatch alarm is set up that will trigger if any request fails more than three times within a 30-second period. The alarm notifies your incident response team, but you also need to enable an alarm on the monitoring instance if it becomes unhealthy. Which of the following is a simple way to enable this?

A. Run another monitoring instance that pings the primary monitoring instance and uses SNS to notify your incident response team if the primary monitoring instance fails.

B. Create an EC2 instance status check CloudWatch alarm and notify your incident response team if the monitoring instance fails.

C. Create an EC2 instance CPU usage CloudWatch alarm and notify your incident response team if the monitoring instance goes above the CPU usage threshold.

D. Create an Auto Scaling group of monitoring instances. Record the state of monitoring in a DynamoDB table. If any of the instances fail, the service will survive and the incident response team does not need to deal with this issue at all.

43. You need to design a solution to backup a 1 TB volume that stores about 850 GB of application data. The application server is put in maintenance mode and commits all the writes to disk. The maintenance window is between 1 a.m. and 3 a.m. every night. The backup needs to be completed within that window. The backup needs to be recoverable as a full volume within 1 hour of failure. What would be the simplest way to achieve this?

     A. Take snapshots of the EBS volume during the maintenance window.

     B. Use a third-party backup application to back the volume up to Amazon Glacier.

     C. Back up all data to a single compressed archive on the same volume and store the archive to S3.

     D. Create another 1 TB EBS volume in a second AZ. Attach it to the Amazon EC2 instance, and mirror the two disks.

44. You have an Auto Scaling IIS web application behind a load balancer that delivers news services to users. Whenever a breaking news story is released you start seeing 500 errors in the ELB logs. As soon as the number of connections decreases, the 500 errors go away. What could you do to fix this issue?

     A. 500 errors mean your service is not optimized for the HTTP host type. Install Apache and rewrite your application for Apache.

     B. 500 errors mean your service is overloaded. Increase the maximum site of the Auto Scaling group.

     C. 500 errors are to be dealt with by AWS.

     D. 500 errors can be ignored as the service is still responding to most requests and the errors go away.

45. You need to connect to external networks. Which component of the VPC will allow you to do this? Choose two:

     A. EIP

     B. NAT

     C. IGW

     D. VGW

46. An application is licensed based on a MAC address. You would like to migrate this application to AWS. What approach can you use to be able to use this application in AWS and make sure you don't have to get your license re-issued if the instance fails?

    A. Use an ELB and register the ELB MAC to the license. Route the traffic to multiple backend instances that will verify the license against the ELB MAC.

    B. Use an ENI and register the ENI MAC to the license. If the instance fails, attach the ENI to an instance restored from a backup of the original.

    C. Write a script that changes the MAC in the operating system and apply the script to multiple instances. All of these instances will now be able to respond to requests for the licensed software.

    D. This is not possible on AWS. You will need to ask the provider for a CloudVM license.

47. Your application uses cookies to track sessions. The application has grown and you now need to deploy multiple instances of the application behind an ELB in an Auto Scaling group. You enable sticky sessions on the ELB and deploy the Auto Scaling group. The system works great until, a few weeks in, you notice some servers in the Auto Scaling group are hitting 100% CPU utilization, while others are at almost zero. How can you configure the ELB to properly load balance the requests?

    A. This is the ELB's normal behavior as the sessions from the same user are sent to the same instance.

    B. This is not the ELB's normal behavior. Enable cross-zone load balancing.

    C. This is not the ELB's fault. There must be a leak in your application's code.

    D. This is the ELB's normal behavior. When using cookies, only one AZ can be used. Move the servers that have low utilization to the same AZ as the ones at 100% and the ELB will re-balance.

48. You are taking a snapshot of an EBS volume. What happens during the snapshot process?

    A. The volume cannot be detached from an EC2 instance or attached to an EC2 instance.

    B. The volume can be used in read-only mode.

    C. The volume can be used in read-write mode.

    D. The volume cannot be used until the snapshot completes.

49. You are required to maintain complete separation of duties between different teams so your company decided to create multiple accounts for the development, test, QA, and production teams. Along with these accounts, your company runs a master account for billing and operations. You need to make sure the billing department can easily consolidate costs across all teams. You also need to allow the operations engineers from the master department to gain administrative access to all other accounts:

    A. Use the same credit card on all accounts to aggregate the billing to the credit card. For the operations team members, create a cross-account role in each account and allow the operations team to assume the role to perform maintenance tasks in the other accounts.

    B. Use the same credit card on all accounts to aggregate the billing to the credit card. For the operations team members, create an administrative user in each account and distribute the credentials to the operations team so they can perform maintenance tasks in the other accounts.

    C. Enable consolidated billing for the accounts and aggregate the billing in the master account. For the operations team members, create an administrative user in each account and distribute the credentials to the operations team so they can perform maintenance tasks in the other accounts.

    D. Enable consolidated billing for the accounts and aggregate the billing in the master account. For the operations team members, create a cross-account role in each account and allow the operations team to assume the role to perform maintenance tasks in the other accounts.

50. Which of the following metrics require us to deliver a custom CloudWatch metric in EC2? Select all that apply:

    A. Instance CPU utilization.

    B. Instance memory utilization.

    C. Instance network utilization.

    D. CPU utilization per thread.

    E. Network utilization of an ENI.

51. When designing permissions for users to perform certain tasks, which approach should we be using?

    A. Least effort.

    B. Least privilege.

    C. Best effort.

    D. All policies should be inline.

52. You have identified a need for strengthening the security of your AWS management console access. Which option would allow you to increase the security of your AWS account?

    A. Configure MFA for IAM users.

    B. Create IAM users with full privileges instead of using the root user.

    C. Implement identity federation between a web identity provider (web IdP) and IAM, and use IdP accounts.

    D. Allow management console-access only with access key and secret key ID.

53. CloudWatch custom metrics have some limitations. Which of these would you not be able to record in CloudWatch?

     A. Data transfer on a virtual network adapter on Windows hosts.

     B. Disk usage on C.

     C. Memory utilization of Windows hosts.

     D. CPU utilization of Windows hosts.

     E. All of these can be delivered as custom metrics.

54. You have an application that requires the lowest latency possible between instances. You have spun up five instances in a cluster placement group and the application is working correctly. Now you need to double the size of the group. You try to deploy another five instances, but you are unable to put them in the same cluster placement group. How would you fix this?

     A. Create an Auto Scaling group for the cluster placement group and set the desired number of instances to 10.

     B. Change the cluster placement group desired size setting to 10.

     C. Delete the five instances in the cluster placement group and redeploy with 10 instances.

     D. It is not possible to increase the size of a cluster placement group.

55. Your application uses cookies to store sessions. You now need to create a cluster of instances behind an ELB due to increased volume in your application. You know sticky sessions are an option, but your developers say that they can store the sessions as key:value information in a centralized data-store. What AWS services would be suitable as a sessions storage backend? Choose all that apply:

     A. ElastiCache

     B. SessionCache

     C. DynamoDB

     D. ElastiSearch

     E. Amazon Neptune

56. You have a running instance that has previously been accessible via SSH and HTTP and has suddenly stopped working. No changes to any settings have been performed on EC2 or the network. You verify the security groups, IGW, VPC, and routing tables and see that everything is configured correctly. You look at the EC2 console and see a system status check showing **impaired**. What action would you perform to try and recover the instance?

   A. Stop and start the instance. The operation is likely to fix the *impaired* system status.

   B. Reboot your instance. The operation is likely to fix the *impaired* system status.

   C. Add another dynamic private IP to the instance. The operation is likely to fix the **impaired** system status.

   D. Add another ENI to the instance. The operation is likely to fix the *impaired* system status.

   E. Terminate the instance and redeploy, as this is the only way to fix the *impaired* system status.

57. You are running a hybrid cloud infrastructure with applications that authenticate to LDAP in your on-premises environment via VPN. You are noticing the applications in AWS sometimes time out while authenticating and this is disrupting user's sessions. You need to continue using your LDAP on-premises deployment due to compliance reasons related to your business. How would you go about fixing this issue?

   A. Create a second, independent LDAP directory in AWS and create the users that use the application also in this second LDAP.

   B. Establish a Direct Connect connection alongside your VPN so your applications can authenticate against your existing on-premises LDAP servers faster.

   C. Create a LDAP replica on AWS and configure your application to use the LDAP replica for authentication.

   D. Create a second LDAP domain on AWS and establish a trust relationship between your new and existing domains and use the new domain for authentication.

58. Your application runs in `us-west-1 region`. Recently, an outage caused the application to be unavailable since the whole region was affected. The architects designed a solution with a smaller copy of the application running in `us-west-2 region` to prevent from this kind of outage and have the ability to fail over and scale out the secondary site. The secondary site must always be online and be able to respond to 10% of all requests. Which configuration would achieve that goal?

    A. Route53 record sets with weighted routing policy

    B. Route53 record sets with latency-based routing policy

    C. Auto Scaling with scheduled scaling actions set

    D. Elastic Load Balancing with health checks enabled

59. You have been asked to provide a recommendation on a design for a notification system in AWS. The application needs to be able to receive any number of messages and distribute them across a set of different services that accept requests on different protocols including SMS, email, HTTP, AMQP, JMS, and WebSocket. The solution needs to be unified and be able to deliver messages to systems in AWS and on-premises:

    A. AWS would not be able to support the mix of protocols.

    B. Use SNS to receive messages. Use SQS to distribute them on all the required protocols.

    C. Use SNS to receive messages. Use SQS to deliver the SMS, email, and HTTP and a custom solution for AMQP, JMS, and WebSockets.

    D. Use SNS to receive messages. Use SNS to deliver the SMS, email, and HTTP and a custom solution for AMQP, JMS, and WebSockets.

60. Your company is using S3 for storage of mission critical, sensitive data. A full regional EC2 outage in a separate region raised the question of whether the availability of S3 is enough to comply with the 99.9999% availability you are required to maintain for your data as per your SLA. Your engineers have come back from their research with different answers – which one is correct?

    A. S3 has an availability of 99.999999999%, which is far better than the SLA. No action is required.

B. We would need to implement cross-region bucket replication on the mission-critical data to meet the SLA.

C. S3 has a durability of 99.999999999%. Even if the service is down, the data will survive, so no action is required. We will meet our 99.9999% SLA.

D. We need to create a static website and serve the bucket contents via CloudFront. This will be the cheapest solution and will replicate our bucket across the world via the CloudFront CDN.

Mock test 2

1. Your developers need a simple way to deploy a highly available, auto-scaled web application. What would be the simplest approach with the least management overhead?

    A. Create a VPC with one public subnet for ELB. Create two public subnets for the web servers. Create a private subnet for the database. Deploy the ELB and two EC2 instances in the public subnets and a Multi-AZ RDS instance in the private subnet.

    B. Create a VPC with two public subnets for the web servers and two private subnets for the databases. Deploy the two EC2 instances in the public subnets and a Multi-AZ RDS instance in the private subnets. Direct the traffic to the application via a Route 53 multi-value answer.

    C. Use Elastic Beanstalk to deploy a new application and deploy the code into a new environment.

    D. Use a CloudFormation quick-start template to deploy a new application and deploy the code into a new environment.

2. A private instance is required to update its software from the internet. Which network device would need to be implemented to allow for this?

    A. An ENI

    B. An NAT Gateway

    C. An Internet Gateway

    D. An Virtual Private Gateway

3. You are required to select the appropriate solution for cluster of servers. Each of the servers will require the ability to provide in excess of 100,000 4 KB IOPS from the root volume. Which EC2 option will meet this requirement?

   A. An EBS volume with provisioned IOPS

   B. An instance type with an instance store volume

   C. Any type of EBS optimized instance

   D. A D1 instance type

4. CloudWatch metrics have some limitations. Which of these would you require you to use custom metrics? Choose all that apply:

   A. Disk full percentage of an EBS volume

   B. Disk usage activity of an EC2 instance store volume

   C. Disk usage activity of an EC2 RDS volume

   D. Disk full percentage of an instance store volume

5. A user has created a private S3 bucket where he stores hundreds of files. The user wants to make all objects in the bucket public. How can he configure this with minimal efforts?

   A. Select each object in the management console and make it public.

   B. Use an S3 SDK or AWS CLI script to change permissions for each object.

   C. Apply a bucket policy that makes all objects in the bucket public.

   D. Tag the bucket with `public=true`, which makes all objects in the bucket public.

6. How can we find a particular error that occurred in a MySQL RDS database?

   A. It is not possible to get the log files for MySQL RDS.

   B. Find all the transaction logs from around the time the error happened and query those records to try and recreate the error.

C. The MySQL logs are accessible and searchable directly through the Amazon RDS console.

D. Retrieve the log through ElastiSearch and search for the error.

7. You are operating an Auto Scaling group of EC2 instances. We would like to terminate one instance if the aggregate CPU usage of the Auto Scaling group goes below 20%. How can we achieve this?

A. Set up a notification email using SNS when the CPU utilization is less than 20%. Set the desired capacity to one less whenever you get an email.

B. Use CloudWatch to analyze the data and create a scheduled action to remove the instance when you estimate the usage will be below 20%.

C. Configure CloudWatch to continuously send notifications of CPU usage to SNS. Subscribe a Lambda to the SNS service to determine when the aggregate usage is below 20% and instruct the Lambda to terminate one instance.

D. Configure CloudWatch to send a notification to Auto Scaling when the aggregated CPU utilization is below 20%. Configure an Auto Scaling policy to remove one instance.

8. You need to configure security groups for an application with a HTTP/HTTPS web frontend and a MySQL backend. The IP addressing information is as follows:
   - VPC: `10.10.0.0/16`
   - Private subnet: `10.10.1.0/24`
   - Public subnet: `10.10.0.0/24`

   Which of these entries is not required?

   A. Private security group Source: `10.10.0.0/24`. Action: allow port `80`.

   B. Private security group Source: `10.10.0.0/24`. Action: allow port `3306`.

   C. Public security group Source: `0.0.0.0/0`. Action: allow port `443`.

   D. Public security group Source: `0.0.0.0/0`. Action: allow port `80`.

9. You have designed a CloudFormation script that deploys a MySQL RDS database. The database will be receiving a high amount of data very rapidly after deployment. You must ensure the template is designed in a way that will allow the database to perform at maximum efficiency:

    A. Design the CloudFormation script to attach an S3 volume instead of EBS.

    B. Design the CloudFormation script to deploy a CasandraDB RDS instance instead.

    D. Using a combination of CloudFormation and Python scripting, pre-warm the EBS volumes after the EBS volume has been deployed.

    E. You should not be using CloudFormation. Instead, it would be better to script this using CodeDeploy.

10. What is the durability of S3 RRS?

    A. 99.5%

    B. 99.95%

    C. 99.995%

    D. 99.999999995%

11. You have an Auto Scaling group that runs a web server. The developers are seeing issues in performance and have asked you to deliver logs from the servers. The servers scale in and out frequently and the logs are being lost. How can you design your system to satisfy the request of the developers?

    A. Periodically poll the events on the application via an API and store the results in a local file.

    B. Create a crontab job for the instances that sends the logs to Glacier.

    C. Use the CloudWatch agent to stream the logs into CloudWatch and direct the developers to view the logs in the CloudWatch management console.

    D. Have the developers SSH in daily to extract the logs from the instances.

12. You are running a hybrid environment with a VPN. Your management is considering using a Direct Connect connection instead of a VPN. Which operational aspect would be the most appropriate driver for switching from VPN to AWS Direct Connect?

    A. AWS DirectConnect provides greater redundancy than a VPN connection.

    B. AWS DirectConnect provides greater resiliency than a VPN connection.

    C. AWS DirectConnect provides greater bandwidth than a VPN connection.

    D. AWS DirectConnect provides greater control of network provider selection than a VPN connection.

13. You are exploring encryption for S3 and you are reading up on S3 SSE. What is S3 SSE?

    A. Encryption of data in transit with a private link between the VPC and S3.

    B. Encryption of bucket attributes at rest with a customer-managed encryption key.

    C. Encryption of data at rest with an S3-managed encryption key.

    D. Encryption of attributes in transit. KMS must be used when encryption of all data in transit is required.

14. You are managing a Windows-based .NET application running in Elastic Beanstalk. You need to maintain the application log files due to compliance reasons. The infrastructure will scale in and out and you are afraid of losing the logs. How can you ensure the developers will be able to access only the log files?

    A. Access the logs from the Elastic Beanstalk console.

    B. Enable log file rotation to S3 within the Elastic Beanstalk configuration.

    C. Ask your developers to enable log delivery via the web.config file.

    D. Create a Windows Scheduled task to rotate the log files to S3.

15. You have enabled detailed metrics on all of your ELBs in all of your regions. What would that option do?

    A. Each ELB sends data to the regional CloudWatch endpoint every minute with no additional cost.

B. Each ELB sends data to the regional CloudWatch endpoint every minute at an additional cost.

C. Each ELB sends detailed metrics to one S3 bucket that you specify when enabling the setting.

D. Detailed monitoring is not supported on the ELB.

16. You need to configure routing tables for your VPC. The IP addressing information is as follows:
    - VPC: `10.10.0.0/16`
    - Private subnet: `10.10.1.0/24`
    - Public subnet: `10.10.0.0/24`
      Which entry is required in the main route table to allow the instances to communicate on the internal IP addresses in all subnets?

    A. Destination: `10.100.0.0/24` and Target: VPC

    B. Destination: `10.100.0.0/16` and Target: ALL

    C. Destination: `10.100.0.0/0` and Target: ALL

    D. Destination: `10.100.0.0/16` and Target: Local

17. Your application is running an SQS queue with an Auto Scaling group of consumers on EC2 instances. The group is scaled according to the number of messages in the queue. After a week, you find the group is at maximum with the EC2 instances idling but the number of messages in the queue keeps growing. What would be a possible reason for this situation?

    A. The Auto Scaling group is too small for the number of messages and the messages can not be processed and de-queued.

    B. Try using Kinesis streams instead of SQS.

    C. Messages in the SQS are corrupted and can't be processed and de-queued.

    D. This is the normal operation of SQS. It just takes time to process the messages.

18. You need to choose a service that will allow you to perform daily backups that are kept for 14 days without any management overhead. Which service would allow you to do this? Choose 2 answers:

    A. Amazon S3

    B. Amazon RDS

    C. Amazon EBS

    D. Amazon Redshift

19. You are instructed to deploy a highly available application in EC2. You need to design the application from the ground up. What is the minimum design that will make sure the application is highly available with 99.9% availability?

    A. Create a VPC with a single subnet. Deploy an Auto Scaling group of EC2 instances with a minimum of two instances. Use an ELB to load balance the instances.

    B. Create a VPC with two subnets. Deploy an Auto Scaling group of EC2 instances with a minimum of two instances. Use an ELB for cross-zone load balancing.

    C. Create a VPC with two subnets. Deploy an Auto Scaling group of EC2 instances with a minimum of one instance. Use an ELB for cross-zone load balancing.

    D. Create a VPC with one subnet. Deploy an Auto Scaling group of EC2 instances with a minimum of one instance. Use an ELB for cross-zone load balancing.

20. An application in an Auto Scaling group is misbehaving and the CPU regularly spikes to over 90% with no traffic triggering Auto Scaling. How can you quickly troubleshoot this issue with minimum downtime?

    A. Take a snapshot of your EC2 instance. Delete the Auto Scaling group and the associated EC2 instances. Create a new EC2 instance with your snapshot and then begin troubleshooting. Once you have figured out the cause of the problem, take a new snapshot and use that snapshot as the base AMI for your new Auto Scaling group.

    B. Suspend Auto Scaling. SSH into the EC2 instance and begin trouble shooting. Once you have fixed the problem, resume Auto Scaling.

C. Delete the Auto Scaling group and the associated EC2 instances. Create a new EC2 instance from scratch and reinstall your application. Once you have figured out the cause of the problem, take a new snapshot and use that snapshot as the base AMI for your new Auto Scaling group.

D. Delete Auto Scaling all together and rely on manual scaling based off SNS notifications sent to your SysOps team from the appropriate CloudWatch metric.

21. You are operating a mobile application that has several hundred thousand users. Which authentication solution would allow for distributing data stored in an S3 bucket and provide the highest flexibility to rotate credentials?

A. Use Identity Federation with an identity provider IdP or STS service. Create a role for the federated identities and create an AM policy for the S3 bucket.

B. Distribute IAM users to each client with an IAM policy granting access to the S3 bucket.

C. Create S3 bucket policies with a conditional statement for each client.

D. Create **Access Control Lists** (**ACL**) based on mobile client ID.

22. Your application is running a web server and a database. You are seeing performance decreases in the web responses that are becoming longer and longer. You analyze the setup and see that the database responses are responsible for the slow responses. The more data you have, the slower the response from the database. Which of the following options could speed up performance? Choose 3 answers:

A. Create an RDS read replica and direct database read requests to the replica.

B. Cache database responses in ElastiCache and direct your read requests to ElastiCache.

C. Set up RDS in Multi-AZ and direct database read requests to the standby database.

D. Shard the RDS database into multiple databases and distribute load between shards.

E. Use database responses in CloudFront and direct your read requests to CloudFront.

23. You are required to migrate a single volume instance from one region to another. How can this be done?

    A. Create an AMI from the instance. Create a new instance from the AMI in the other region.

    B. Use the `ec2-migrate-instance` command to move it to another region.

    C. Create a snapshot of the instance. Copy the snapshot to the other region. Create a new instance from the snapshot in the other region.

    D. Create an AMI from the instance. Copy the AMI to the other region. Create a new instance from the new AMI in the other region.

24. You are designing a hybrid environment between your on-premises site and AWS. Your local network has a CIDR of `172.16.0.0/16`. You have created a VPC with the CIDR of `10.100.0.0/16`. Within the VPC, you have a public subnet with a CIDR of `10.100.0.0/24` and a private subnet of `10.100.1.0/24`. You create a VPN gateway with the `vgw-11112222` identifier. Which of the following entries would be valid?

    A. Destination: `10.100.0.0/24` and Target: `vgw-11112222`

    B. Destination: `172.16.0.0/16` and Target: `ALL`

    C. Destination: `172.16.0.0/16` and Target: `vgw-11112222`

    D. Destination: `0.0.0.0/0` and Target: `vgw-11112222`

25. You are using a single multi-homed m5.large NAT instance inside a VPC to allow hosts in the private subnet to communicate with the internet. Lately, updates are not being downloaded to the instances in the private subnet. You decide to monitor the environment during the updates and see that the m5.large instance CPU is being maxed out and some instances can not download the updates. What could you do to fix this? Choose all that apply:

    A. Add another IGW to your VPC and load balance the IGWs.

    B. Change the instance type from m5.large to m5.xlarge.

    C. Implement a Direct Connect link to your on-premises environment and retrieve the updates from on-premises.

    D. Deploy another NAT m5.large instance and add a route table entry that will spread traffic across the two NAT instances.

    E. Point the instances to an ELB rather than an NAT instance. The ELB can scale on demand, so all traffic should pass seamlessly.

26. You have four m5.large EC2 web servers deployed in an Auto Scaling group behind an ALB. You are running a MySQL RDS database with 5,000 Provisioned IOPS. Your application responses are slowing down and you look at the CloudWatch metrics. There is constant 95% CPU utilization on the web servers and only 20% CPU utilization on the RDS. The disk I/Os on the web servers are in the hundreds, while the database disk operations are as high as 2,500. Which two options do you have? Choose all that apply:

    A. Change the instance type to c4.xlarge.

    B. Use Auto Scaling and scale your servers based on CPU utilization.

    C. Increase the database Provisioned IOPS, as the disk operations on the database are where the bottleneck is.

    D. Rewrite your applications to allow for more TCP connections to your web tier. The current application is not optimized and is using too much CPU.

27. You are the SysOps team lead and are trying to increase the security of your operations before the auditing team performs an assessment. What practices should you start using to prepare for the assessment? Choose 2 answers:

    A. Implement a policy for remote administrative access to be performed securely.

B. Implement MFA for privileged team members.

C. Implement a policy to identify which Amazon-published AMIs can be used by your team.

D. Implement Trusted Advisor. Identify and disable all vulnerabilities on your EC2 instances.

28. Your web application operates across the EU and the US. The auditing department identified that the application does not comply with the GDPR. Your developers have designed a registration system where all and new users declare their country of residence. You have discovered that based on their IP, some users seem to be coming from the EU and selecting other countries as their country of residence. How would you enhance the application to allow it to comply with the GDPR in full?

    A. Run a copy of your application in both the US and EU regions. Use Route 53's latency -based routing route traffic to the appropriate region based on the user's origin IP.

    B. Run a copy of your application in both the US and EU regions. Use an ELB with sticky sessions to route traffic to the appropriate region based on the user's origin IP.

    C. Run a copy of your application in both the US and EU regions. Use Route 53's geolocation-based routing to route traffic to the appropriate region based on the user's origin IP.

    D. Run a copy of your application in two AZs in any of the US regions. Use an ELB with sticky sessions to route traffic to the appropriate region based on the user's origin IP.

29. What does the following policy do?

```
{
"Id": "IPBasedPolicy"
"Statement":[
{
"Sid": "IPRange",
"Action": "s3",
"Effect": "Allow",
"Resource": "arn:aws:s3:::imagebucket/*,
"Condition": {
"IPAddress": {
"aws:SourceIP": "10.100.100.0/24"
```

```
},
"NotipAddress": {
"aws:SourceIp": "100.100.100.20/32
}
},
"Principal": {
"AWS": {
"*"
]
}
}
]
}
```

A. Denies any server within the `10.100.100.0` subnet access to the `"imagebucket` bucket

B. Denies the server with the `10.100 100.20` IP access to the `"imagebucket` bucket

C. Allows any server within the `10.100.100.0` subnet except the server with the `10.100.100.20` IP access to the `"imagebucket"` bucket

D. Denies any server within the `10.100.100.0` subnet access to the `"imagebucket"` bucket but allows the server with the `10.100 100.20` IP access to the `"imagebucket` bucket

30. An S3 bucket will serve a static website. The bucket is hosted in Ohio and the the bucket name is `sitefiles`. What is the correct format of the URL that you can use as A CNAME for your website?

    A. `sitefiles.com.s3-website.us-east-2.amazonaws.com`

    B. `sitefiles.s3-website-us-east-2.amazonaws.com`

    C. `s3-us-east-2.amazonaws.com/sitefiles`

    D. `sitefiles.s3-website.us-east-2.amazonaws.com`

31. You have started using S3 as a backup repository for your on-premises infrastructure. You need to back up approximately 150 TB of data to S3. You have a 10 GB internet line that you can use for backing up. The backup needs to be completed in 24 hours. What would be the correct approach to perform this backup?

    A. Establish a VPN with AWS, as the VPN will reduce the data size by 1.5 times.

    B. Upload the files in parallel to S3.

    C. Compress the data into a single archive, upload it to S3, then extract the files in AWS.

    D. Use the AWS Snowball service to order several snowball devices and transfer the data in this manner.

32. You are required to keep track of the performance of your application running across different components of AWS including hundreds of EC2 instances, ELBs, thousands of CS containers, multiple RDS, and DynamoDB databases. What would be the correct approach to creating a simple overview of your application's crucial statistics?

    A. Tag your resources and project the tag name as an attribute in CloudWatch. Create a saved query and use the management console to view the metrics when required with the saved query.

    B. Tag your resources and project the tag name as an attribute in CloudWatch. Create a custom dashboard and use the management console to view the metrics when required in the dashboard.

    C. Tag your resources and project the tag name as an attribute in CloudWatch. Create a CLI query and use the CLI to export the metrics when required with the CLI query.

    D. Tag your resources and project the tag name as an attribute in CloudWatch. The tag can be used directly in the CloudWatch Overview section.

33. You are designing a security group for your web application. The application runs an ELB with the `34.187.12.134` IP, a web server instance group in a `10.200.0.0/24` subnet and a pair of Multi-AZ MySQL RDS instances with sharded data across the pair with the `10.200.100.0/24` subnet. You create a security group for each tier and now need to add the correct rules to the security groups. Which of the following rules would not be required?

    A. Security group - `web-tier`. Source: `34.187.12.134/32`. Port: `80`

    B. Security group - `elb-tier`. Source: `0.0.0.0/0`. Port: `80`

    C. Security group - `rds-tier`. Source: `web-tier`. Port: `3306`

    D. Security group - `web-tier`. Source: `elb-tier`. Port: `80`

34. Which option is not available when configuring the negotiation of client SSL connections on the ELB?

    A. SSL Protocols

    B. Client Order Preference

    C. SSL Ciphers

    D. Server Order Preference

35. If it is possible, identify which of the following options needs to be configured to enable a client to identify a matching cipher in the ELB cipher list when the client requests ELB DNS over SSL?

    A. Cipher Protocol.

    B. Client Configuration Preference.

    C. Server Order Preference.

    D. Load Balancer Preference.

    E. This is not possible.

36. A user has created an SQS FIFO queue. The application has been working great, but the number of messages in the FIFO queue is growing. You determine that the worker servers are mostly idling and are hitting the 300 operations per second limit, and only retrieving 300 messages at a time. The input to the message queue is delivering a much higher number of messages. How can you fix the issue?

    A. Request an operations limit increase by submitting a ticket to AWS.

    B. Use bulk requests in your worker tier.

    C. Reduce the number of incoming messages and purge the queue to catch up with the latest data.

    D. The 300 operations limit is a hard limit. Create a second FIFO queue and distribute the messages across two queues. The FIFO order will be maintained across the queues.

37. You have an application that has predictable performance of approximately 2,500 500-byte write operations per second. You need to select a data store that would be optimal in performance and cost for your application. The solution needs to be highly available and should allow for minimal read performance.

    A. RDS MySQL instance with Multi-AZ

    B. An EC2 instance with a SSD instance store volume

    C. An S3 bucket with 1,250 connections per second provisioned

    D. A DynamoDB table with 2,500 WCUs and a low number of RCUs provisioned

38. You are capturing 5-minute ELB metrics with CloudWatch. For the purpose of analyzing traffic patterns and troubleshooting, you need to also start capturing connection information, such as source IPs. Which option do you need to select to enable the capturing of connection information from your ELB?

    A.Use AWS CloudTrail on the ELB.

    B. Enable access logs on the ELB.

    C. Use the CloudWatch logs agent on the ELB.

    D. Use CloudWatch detailed metrics on the ELB.

39. You are running a hybrid environment with a VPN from AWS to your on-premises location. You have multiple DNS servers on-premises. The on-premises DNS servers are serving internal application DNS records. The internal DNS servers are also able to resolve public FQDN names. The security policy dictates that the internal DNS names should only be resolved within the internal network and not from the public IP ranges. You will be building a public and a private subnet in your VPN that will host an extension to your applications. You need to provide the internal DNS to the EC2 instances that require the DNS names of the internal resources. What would be the appropriate way to allow EC2 to resolve internal resources but not expose the internal DNS to public IPs?

A. This is not possible, as you would be exposing your DNS to public IP space by connecting it to AWS.

B. Use a Route 53 hosted-zone for the internal domain name and replicate the DNS entries from the on-premises DNS.

C. Create a DHCP option set that specifies the domain name server value as the on-premises DNS servers. Replace the default DHCP option set for the VPC with the newly created DHCP option set.

D. Create two DHCP options sets, DHCPSetA and DHCPSetB. Configure DHCPSetA to specify the Amazon-provided DNS server as the domain name server to resolve all internet domain names. Configure DHCPSetB to specify the on-premises DNS server as the domain name server to resolve all internal domain names. Apply both the DHCP options set to the VPC so that both internet domain names and internal domain names can be resolved.

40. You are operating an application using SQS, S3, and EC2. When a file is uploaded to the EC2 web tier it is stored in S3. A message is then created in SQS. The application tier threads the messages and processes the contents of the file. Your application gets hacked over a long weekend and is down for 3 days until you are able to secure it. You want to bring it online, but are worried that the messages received have been lost and the files from the long weekend will not be processed. It this statement correct?

A. Yes, because the default SQS message retention period is only 12 hours.

B. Yes, because the default SQS message retention period is only 1 day.

C. No, because the default SQS message retention period is 4 days.

D. No, because the default SQS message retention period is 14 days.

41. You are running a sports news service that records the information about game scores from across the world 24/7 in real time to a DynamoDB table by game ID. Your users are able to see the scores on the website, but have requested a feature to be notified as soon as a score in a particular game that they subscribe to has changed. What would be an appropriate approach to building this solution?

    A. Subscribe a Lambda function to a DynamoDB stream. Have the Lambda read the changes and send all the changes to an SNS topic that the users can subscribe to. The users can then receive the scores.

    B. Subscribe a Lambda function to a DynamoDB stream. Have the Lambda read the changes and send the changes for each game ID to a corresponding SNS topic that the users can subscribe to. The users can then receive the scores.

    C. Subscribe one SNS topic to each game ID to DynamoDB. When a game ID is updated, a message will automatically be generated that will send the subscribers a notification of the change.

    D. Have the service record the changes in a Kinesis stream. Have the Lambda read the changes in the Kinesis stream and send the changes for each game ID to a corresponding SNS topic that the users can subscribe to. The users can then receive the scores.

42. Which method can be used to prevent an IP address from accessing objects in a public S3 bucket?

    A. Apply a bucket policy on the bucket.

    B. Create a NACL on the VPC of the bucket.

    C. Create an ACL on all objects in the bucket.

    D. Modify the IAM policies of any users from that IP range.

43. You have created a VPC with an **internet gateway** (**IGW**). The VPC has two public and two private subnets each with one subnet per AZ. You have provisioned an ELB and configured it to with cross-zone load balancing. You spin up instances in an Auto Scaling group behind the ELB in both public and the private subnets. You have created a MySQL instance in one private subnet and a read replica for BI purposes in the other subnet. Are there any single points of failure in this design?

    A. There are no single points of failure in this design.

B. You need to create a second IGW to make this highly available.

C. The RDS requires Multi-AZ. Remove the read replica and implement Multi-AZ on the MySQL DB.

D. The RDS requires Multi-AZ. Implement Multi-AZ on the MySQL DB.

44. You are designing a multi-regional web site that can automatically recover from a disaster very quickly with minimum downtime. Which of the following approaches is best?

    A. Use multi-region S3 replication for your buckets.

    B. Use the Pilot Light DR architecture to automatically fail over to a secondary site when the primary site becomes unreachable.

    C. Use a Low Capacity Standby site to automatically fail over to a secondary site when the primary site becomes unreachable.

    D. Use multiple fully functional sites and a Route 53 health checks to automatically fail over to a different site when a site becomes unreachable.

45. You are looking to implement cost oversight of all AWS resources consumed by its departments. The company policy requires each department to be autonomous and have complete control over their environment. Which options would allow you to provide this functionality? Choose two:

    A. Use AWS Consolidated Billing.

    B. Enable IAM cross-account access for all corporate IT administrators.

    C. Use separate VPCs per department within the corporate account.

    D. Use separate accounts per department.

    E. Forward all CloudTrail logs to a centralized billing account.

46. You would like to schedule scaling for your application during work hours. Which of the following parameters is not required in this case?

    A. Desired size

    B. Auto Scaling group name

    C. End time

D. Resource usage threshold for scaling

E. Start time

47. According to shared responsibility, which task does AWS perform to make sure that data does not leak from the AWS environment? Choose all that apply:

    A. AES-256 encryption of data stored on any shared storage device

    B. Decommissioning of storage devices using industry-standard practices

    C. Background virus scans of EBS volumes and EBS snapshots

    D. Replication of data across multiple AWS Regions

    E. Secure wiping of EBS data when an EBS volume is unmounted

48. You are required to extend a highly sensitive application to the cloud. You are required to pass all traffic encrypted through private links. What would be the correct solution for this design?

    A. Deploy a VPN between your on-premises and AWS. This automatically encrypts all the data in transit via IPSec and keeps the data always on private networks.

    B. Deploy a Direct Connect connection between your on-premises and AWS. This automatically encrypts all the data in transit via IPSec and keeps the data always on private links.

    C. Deploy a VPN over a Direct Connect connection between your on-premises and AWS. This automatically encrypts all the data in transit via IPSec and keeps the data always on private links.

    D. It is impossible to keep the data on private links when connecting to AWS.

49. You manage a catalog application where users upload product images for your e-commence website. The users would like to share a link with others to view and comment on the photos. What AWS storage option will offer high availability, high scalability, the lowest cost, and highest reliability to store and share these photos?

    A. Use the instance store on each web server. Replicate the storage using a cluster filesystem.

    B. Use S3 to store the images. Create a system to distribute signed URLs.

C. Use EBS to store the images. Share the EBS among instances of web servers so they can serve the images with signed URLs.

D. Use EFS to store the images. Share the EFS among instances of web servers so they can serve the images with signed URLs.

50. A mission-critical web app with a minimum of eight EC2s and a maximum of 24 instances behind an ELB. The application is running in two AZs in a single region. The app depends on synchronous replication of the database layer to sync the data across all the instances in all the AZs. The application needs to retain full capacity of eight instances even if one availability one goes down. How can the current architecture be improved to ensure this?

A. Deploy a minimum of eight instances in each AZ. This will ensure there is enough capacity at all times.

B. Deploy in three AZs with four instances in each. This will ensure there is enough capacity at all times.

C. Replicate this setup to another region. Use Route 53 round robin and ensure the there are two instances running in each AZ in each region, for a total of eight.

D. Replicate this setup to another region and use the Pilot Light approach to enable disaster recovery if an AZ goes down.

51. You have a global application that needs to share key:value data in a centralized database distributed across regions for HA. What AWS option would be best suited to achieve this?

A. Use one DynamoDB table in one region. All application components should access this one table. Back up the table to a DynamoDB backup to another region for HA and redirect the traffic in case of primary failure.

B. Use one RDS instance in one region. All application components should access this one database. Create a read replica to another region for HA and redirect the traffic in case of primary failure.

C. Create multiple DynamoDB table in multiple regions. Create a global DynamoDB tables by specifying all of the tables you just created. All application components should access the global table.

D. Use an ElastiCache Casandra database cluster distributed across regions. This will enable all the features required.

52. What does the following IAM policy do? Choose all that apply:

```
{
  "Version": "2012-10-17",
  "Statement": [ {
  "Effect": "Allow",
  "Action": [ "s3:Get", "s3:List" ],
  "Resource": "*" },
  { "Effect": "Allow",
  "Action": "s3:PutObject",
  "Resource": "arn:aws:s3:::samplebucket/*" }
  ]
}
```

A. Permission to read all objects from all S3 buckets

B. Permission to write to all objects into the bucket named `"samplebucket"`

C. Permission to deny the listing of all of the objects in the bucket named `"samplebucket"`

D. Permission to read objects from the bucket named `"samplebucket"`

E. Permission to change access rights for the bucket named `"samplebucket"`

53. You run EC2 Instances in an Auto Scaling group behind an ELB. You have been monitoring over the last year, showing that there is no traffic on any day between 1 a.m and 6 a.m. on the servers. The minimum number of servers in the Auto Scaling group is set to two for high availability. How could you optimize the setup to save costs, but also ensure that if any traffic ever comes between 1 a.m and 6 a.m., the site would still provide some kind of valid website response?

A. Create a scheduled scaling event that terminates all the instances at 1 a.m. and brings two instances back at 6 a.m. The ELB will respond with a cached page in the meantime.

B. Create a scheduled scaling event that terminates all the instances at 1 a.m. and brings two instances back at 6 a.m. Create a static S3 website and a Route 53 health check. This will show the static page in the meantime.

C. Create a scheduled scaling event that terminates all the instances at 1 a.m. Create an SQS queue to which the ELB will send requests. Scale according to the queue depth.

D. Create a scheduled scaling event that terminates all the instances at 1 a.m. Create a CPU usage scaling policy that will scale as soon as the ELB CPU usage is above 1%.

54. You are operating a Java application designed with the AWS Java SDK that writes to a DynamoDB backend with 1,000 provisioned write capacity units. The application worked well for over a year. Last week, a developer submitted a ticket to support due to an issue with DynamoDB. When he was testing a new version on the production DynamoDB table, he saw several `"provisionedthroughputexceededexception"` errors come up during his test. You check your application and see that at certain times there are spikes in writes, and approximately 2% of all the daily requests to the backend are receiving the same error. But the application seems to be working properly and no complaints have been received from any of the users. What should you do to avoid losing any data due to this issue?

   A. Increase the size of the WCUs to match the spikes.

   B. Nothing. The SDK automatically retries all the requests that receive this error.

   C. View the performance metrics for provisioned throughput versus consumed throughput in CloudWatch. Determine the times when the spikes occur and provision Spot instances to cache the load during these times.

   D. Implement DAX DynamoDB acceleration to handle the spikes.

55. Which of the following logs are not available in the console for MySQL?

   A. Error Log

   B. Slow Query Log

   C. Transaction Log

   D. General Log

56. You are capturing bulk metric data from weather sensors every hour to your EC2 instance. The metrics are being discarded after 48 hours, but you would like to send the data to CloudWatch to keep them for longer and create graphs of the captured data. How could you do that?

    A. Use the AWS CLI or API to upload the metrics.

    B. Use the AWS Database Migration Tool to import data to CloudWatch.

    C. Download the data from the EC2 instance and use the AWS console to bulk import into CloudWatch.

    D. The weather data is not supported by CloudWatch.

57. You use S3 to store critical data for your company. Everyone requires full access to the S3 buckets. You need to protect against the accidental deletion of critical files in the bucket. Which two options will address this issue? Choose 2 answers:

    A. Enable versioning on S3.

    B. Enable object lifecycle policy to archive data to Glacier every day.

    C. Create a Bucket policy that will change the permissions to read-only permissions at the bucket level.

    D. Configure all the S3 buckets with MFA delete.

58. What are characteristics of Amazon SQS? Choose all that apply:

    A. FIFO queues guarantee ordered delivery.

    B. The maximum size of a message is 512 KB including the metadata (256 KB data + 256 KB metadata).

    C. SQS works in a publisher/subscriber push model.

    D. SQS standard queues have unlimited throughput.

    E. SQS workers can be developed using the Lambda SQS worker CLI.

59. You are looking to update an existing application using EC2 from AMIs, ECS from tasks, Aurora RDS instances, SQS and SNS, ElastiCache, and DynamoDB. You would like to use the blue/green approach. You have deployed your application manually in the past, but now you would like to automate the way new deployments are being delivered. What tool could you choose to achieve this in the simplest way possible?

    A. Deploy your new application with Elastic Beanstalk.

    B. Deploy your new application with CloudFormation.

    C. Deploy your new application with OpsWorks.

    D. Deploy your new application manually according to the design of your current application.

60. You need to analyze the performance of the application behind your ELB. You have enabled ELB logging and are now able to see processing time information. Identify the three processing times you are able to see:

    A. Response processing time

    B. Backend processing time

    C. Database processing time

    D. Frontend processing time

    E. Request processing time

Assessments

Chapter 2 – The Fundamentals of Amazon Web Services

1. IaaS provides VM instances, disk, and networks, while PaaS provides services such as databases and queues.
2. The physical security, securing access to the hypervisor, securing and patching the operating system, securing, configuring and patching the platform.
3. Trade cap-ex for op-ex, use inexpensive compute units on demand, increase the speed of application delivery and agility, matching capacity to demand, ability to go global in minutes.
4. Network, compute, storage, security and identity services, and end user applications.
5. The AWS Management Console, the CLI, and the SDK.
6. An application that's built to run on the cloud (usually on platform and serverless environments).
7. Regions are composed of multiple availability zones, AZs are composed of multiple data centers.
8. No, because a single-availability zone should be considered a fault-isolation environment.

Chapter 3 – Managing AWS Security with Identity and Access Management

1. None. It isn't recommended to keep using the root account for any other case than emergency access to the account.
2. MFA is the procedure of entering multiple authentication factors when logging in – for example, a username will require the user's password and a **Time-based One-time Password** (TOTP) or certificate to authenticate.

3. Set the minimum password length; require at least one uppercase or lowercase character; number or special character; allow users to change their own passwords; enable password expiration after a number of days; prevent the reuse of passwords, enable administrative reset on expired passwords.
4. Users, Groups, Roles, and Policies.
5. Yes.
6. You can't retrieve an existing secret access key. A new key needs to be created.
7. Create a role with the appropriate S3 access and assign the role to the EC2 instance.
8. Use corporate directory federation, STS, and roles to authenticate users within your existing directory and grant them access to AWS resources.
9. False: CloudTrail is now enabled on all accounts by default and provides seven days of data so we can identify the user that deleted the EC2 instance.

Chapter 4 – Networking with Virtual Private Cloud

1. The VPC network and the VPC subnets.
2. A way to determine the network address – in CIDR, IP addresses are described as consisting of two groups of bits in the address: the network address and the host address.
3. Between `/16` and `/28`.
4. Public subnets have a route to the IGW while private subnets don't.
5. IGW for public subnets, NAT gateways for private subnets, VPN and Direct Connect for on-premises.
6. By default, transient traffic isn't supported with VPC peering. To achieve this, a proxy instance could be installed in VPC B, and traffic for VPC C from VPC A would be redirected to the proxy.
7. You didn't allow the ephemeral ports on the outbound policy of the NACL. NACLs are stateless and the return traffic needs to be allowed. Determine the ephemeral ports the instance responds on and allow those in the NACL.

Chapter 5 – Managing Servers on AWS with Elastic Compute Cloud

1. Virtual machine instances, **Amazon Machine Images** (**AMIs**), snapshots.
2. IaaS.
3. Soft limits imposed by AWS depending on the instance type.
4. EBS.
5. Use 2 EBS gp2 volumes that each provide up to 10,000 IOPS and 16 TB. Put the two volumes in a software RAID 0 (striped) configuration to get up to 32 TB.
6. By setting it in a subnet within a VPC.
7. Use an ENI and use the ENI MAC address to apply the license.

Chapter 6 – Handling Server Traffic with Elastic Load Balancing

1. Load balancers operate within a region across one or more availability zones.
2. Application, Network, and Classic Load Balancer.
3. The Network Load Balancer.
4. The Application Load Balancer.
5. None. Load balancers operate within a region.
6. Target Groups.
7. We need to wait for the instances to become healthy before we can browse the address of the load balancer.

Chapter 7 – Understanding Simple Storage Service and Glacier

1. Objects that need to be accessible via HTTP GET and PUT calls.
2. Archives.
3. Eleven nines – 99.999999999% within 24/7/365.

4. We should expect at least 5,500 GET requests, maximum isn't determined.
5. Yes, S3 One-Zone IA and S3 RRS.
6. An index file.
7. We can set a desired number of versions with expiration. By default, all versions are maintained.
8. For training data in machine learning.

Chapter 8 – Understanding Content Distribution with CloudFront

1. A Content Delivery Network.
2. Static and dynamic website data, videos, images, and any cacheable application components.
3. An origin.
4. There is nothing to do, as CloudFront is inherently protected from DDoS.
5. An **Origin Access Identity (OAI)** on CloudFront.
6. Web and RTMP.
7. First, disable it, then wait for the status to change to **deployed**.

Chapter 9 – AWS Storage Options

1. File, Block, and Object storage.
2. NFS v4 and v4.1.
3. EFS doesn't have a published SLA at this point in time.
4. File Gateway, Volume Gateway, Tape Gateway.
5. Cached and Stored volumes.
6. Storage Gateway through the Tape Gateway and Snowmobile.
7. AWS Storage Gateway – I have unlimited time, so why waste money on a Snowball.

Chapter 10 – Working with Route 53 Domain Name System

1. To resolve FQDNs to IPs.
2. Automation, reliability, traffic shaping.
3. Failover routing policy.
4. Geolocation routing policy.
5. TCP health check on port 443.
6. HTTP or HTTPS health check looking for a particular string.
7. Multi-value answer policy.

Chapter 11 – Working with Relational Database Services

1. MySQL, MariaDB, PostgreSQL, Oracle, Microsoft SQL, and Aurora.
2. Read replicas are read-only asynchronous copies, while Multi-AZ has one read-write master and a synchronous slave replica that isn't accessible until failover.
3. Primary instance for writes and replica instance for reads.
4. Snapshots don't affect Aurora's availability.
5. Snapshots can't be restored to an existing cluster.
6. Implement a read replica and point the BI to the read replica.
7. Make the RDS subnet private and specify the EC2 security group as the source in the RDS security group instead of the subnet address.

Chapter 12 – Introduction to ElastiCache

1. Increase performance, increase scalability, decrease database or backend burden, decrease costs.
2. Memcached and Redis.
3. Memcached supports only simple datasets.
4. Implement Memcached caching and move the session state into the cache cluster.
5. Use Memcached to store the write-through data. Point your SQL application straight to the database, as no cache engine supports SQL.

6. Increasing the number of nodes can only be done by adding read replicas, so this isn't possible.
7. Decrease the TTL for your cache accordingly, as stale data is being kept in the cache and delivered to the BI nightly report.

Chapter 13 – Amazon DynamoDB – a NoSQL Database Service

1. False: DynamoDB is addressable via standard HTTP.
2. ACID is fully consistent, while BASE defines eventual consistency.
3. A NoSQL database would be perfect for sessions – it doesn't matter what the application does – it can use SQL on the BI part, but for sessions of NoSQL.
4. C – PUT, R – GET, U – UPDATE, D – DELETE.
5. Tables contain items and items are composed of attributes.
6. 400 KB.
7. Provisioned throughput and on-demand.
8. By dividing 50 MB by 1.5 KB, we get approximately 34.200 items being sent every second to the table – but each item consumes 2 WCUs, meaning we'll need to provision approximately 68.400 WCUs for the table. We're being throttled by the soft limit of 40.000 WCUs per table in the us-west-2 region. We would need to contact AWS to raise the service limit for this table.
9. Create a table with:
    - **Primary key username**: To be able to list users
    - **Sort key date**: So that we can have multiple entries for each student to take the test multiple times
    - **Score as the primary key and username for the sort key for the global secondary index**: To rank users by score

Chapter 14 – Working with Simple Queue Service

1. Standard and FIFO queues.
2. 300 operations per second – up to 3,000 messages with batches of 10.
3. HTTPS.

4. The time the message will be hidden after it was read by a consumer and before it becomes visible in the queue again.

5. `ReceiptHandle` – the unique identifier for the message that was received; `MD5OfBody` – the MD5 sum of the body of the message, used for delivery consistency; and `MessageId` – the identifier of the message in the queue.

6. `ReceiptHandle`.

7. The messages are corrupt and aren't being processed, thus not being deleted before becoming visible again.

8. There's no way to do this: once purged, messages are gone.

Chapter 15 – Handling Messaging with SNS

1. JSON is not a transfer method.
2. Display name.
3. It enhances the SQS distribution model from one-to-one to one-to-many.
4. Email, SMS, mobile notifications.
5. Create a separate notification topic in each region and subscribe each department to that topic. Separate metrics can be collected this way for each topic.
6. If your subscription has been confirmed by the recipient.
7. Disable anonymous access and create a user with a secret key and an access key that will have the permission to only send to this topic. Provide the user to the outside service provider and direct them to use the AWS CLI with the appropriate commands to publish to the topic using the user secret and access key provided.

Chapter 16 – Getting Started with Simple Workflow Service

1. It helps us separate the application processing from the application logic.
2. Decider.
3. False: an actor can be either software or person.
4. False: a task list is populated with actions automatically by SWF.
5. Long polling, they poll for 60 seconds, after which an empty response is received.

6. False: SWF only has regional endpoints.
7. Use roles as temporary keys will be created when workers use a role.

Chapter 17 – Overview of AWS Lambda

1. Amazon Linux.
2. It natively supports Java, Go, PowerShell, Node.js, C#, Python, Ruby, and any other through the runtime API.
3. Any resource where the Lambda can record its response, such as S3 or DynamoDB.
4. Helps with quickly designing invocation triggers, layers, and connecting downstream resources.
5. False: Lambda doesn't have a public endpoint.
6. Provide the appropriate permissions for each bucket in the execution role.
7. Kinesis can't invoke as Lambda works in a pull manner with Kinesis – we need to add the permission to access the Kinesis stream to the Lambda execution role.
8. Implement an API gateway that will proxy the requests to the Lambda function as the Lambda service isn't publicly accessible.

Chapter 18 – Monitoring Resources with Amazon CloudWatch

1. False: namespaces can have any format as long as they follow the namespace rules.
2. True.
3. True.
4. Use the CloudWatch agent to push the EC2 system logs to CloudWatch logs. All CloudWatch logs have an indefinite retention period, but if separate archiving is required, use the AWS CLI to export older logs to S3 and the n life cycle to Glacier.
5. Use tagging on the environment components, then create an alarm and filter the resources with the tag and CPU utilization. Select the EC2 and RDS systems in the results and create the alarm.

6. A current state of a certain metric (for example, the current CPU usage of an instance).

7. Create a query result alarm from the number of delivered and number of failed messages in SNS to reflect the requirement.

8. Create an alarm with a metric that represents the concurrent user number at the performance ceiling of the RDS service (where the database still responds OK). Once the ceiling is reached, an alarm should be sent to SNS where a Lambda service is subscribed. The Lambda has a role with the permission to manage the RDS service. Create a Lambda function that will increase the instance size accordingly to handle the excess traffic. Create another alarm that represents the users numbers going below the threshold, and configure the Lambda function to decrease the instance size when this second alarm is triggered.

Chapter 19 – Understanding Elastic Beanstalk

1. True.
2. True: you can see all the resources that EB creates in the respective parts of the management console.
3. False: we can customize every part of the deployment by using the `.ebextensions` file.
4. A `.zip` or `.war` file of a maximum size of 512 MB.
5. 100 versions.
6. Implement life-cycling with the application's age set to 30 days.
7. Change the instance type in the configuration of the application. The application will be redeployed with the new instance type.
8. Use all-at-once updates. The instances are deleted and new ones are created, which means there are no additional costs incurred by the update process.
9. Use the blue/green approach, as this will allow you to have two production-grade parallel deployments running during the update. If the green environment doesn't perform well, you can instantly switch back to blue, thus maintain up-time throughout.

Chapter 20 – Automation with CloudFormation service

1. A stack.
2. JSON and YAML.
3. Use constraints in the **Parameters** section.
4. Define the LB URL as an output in the **Outputs** section.
5. The deployment is trying to deploy the EC2 and VPC in parallel. Since no VPC exists, the instance creation fails. We can fix this with a **DependsOn** attribute on the EC2 and RDS instances.
6. Create roles for each team with the appropriate permissions for the appropriate resources and allow each team to deploy a stack with the resources that they're responsible for.
7. Determine whether the AWS CLI commands can be written into CloudFormation templates. Store the templates with the code. Provide the location of the templates to the CI server and let the CI server push the template to CloudFormation as a preceding step to the installation of the code on the servers.

Chapter 21 – Cloud Orchestration with OpsWorks

1. False: it also supports on-premise servers.
2. True.
3. Apps.
4. Into layers.
5. Clone the stacks, and name and tag them accordingly.
6. Automate and schedule the deployment of a recipe or module that returns the servers back to compliance.
7. If the CI server support is using the AWS CLI scripts, already-defined is the easiest way. If not, implementing the CLI commands in CloudFormation would be an option. Using OpsWorks would be the most complicated solution in this case, and the infrequent large updates are not the best case for OpsWorks.

Chapter 23 – Mock Test

Answers to Mock Test 1:

Question	Answer(s)	Explanation
Question 1	A	Instance-store data is deleted if an instance is stopped.
Question 2	D	The public IP can be found in the instance metadata.
Question 3	A	The Health check grace period is probably too long.
Question 4	C	You need to create an AMI. The AMI can be deployed into any AZ.
Question 5	C,E	Private subnets have no access to the internet. A subnet can only map to one Availability Zone.
Question 6	A	Not enough power in the application tier. Add another instance.
Question 7	D	A script is needed for creating and rotating RDS snapshots.
Question 8	B	You aren't using all the bandwidth. Upload the files in parallel to S3.
Question 9	A	Alias resource record sets are virtual records that work like CNAME records. But they differ from CNAME records in that they aren't visible to resolvers. Resolvers only see the A record and the resulting IP address of the target record. As such, unlike CNAME records, alias resource record sets are available to configure a zone apex.
Question 10	C	Autoscaling the bastion host will automatically recover it if it fails.
Question 11	A	An OpsWorks stack can be used to deploy existing Chef recopies.
Question 12	A,D	S3 allows you to store virtually unlimited amounts of data as files that are directly accessible via URL.
Question 13	A	A role is the best solution to allow an instance to write to CloudWatch.
Question 14	B	RDS provides a backup as a service solution built in.
Question 15	B	Placement groups enable EC2 instances to interact with each other via high-bandwidth, low-latency connections.
Question 16	C	Tagging and projecting the tag name as a dimension can achieve this.
Question 17	B	Your service limits for the number of instances might need to be increased.
Question 18	A	There is no single point of failure.

Question 19	D	CloudFormation is the right solution that can help you deploy exact copies of different versions of your infrastructure, stage changes into different environments, revert back to previous versions, and identify what versions are running at any particular time.
Question 20	D	Scale the EC2 Auto Scaling group according to the number of messages each EC2 instance can process at a time.
Question 21	C	Read replicas are the perfect solution for analytics jobs.
Question 22	B	The Auto Scaling group is launching in one AZ only. Make sure the ELB has cross-zone LB enabled after you fix the AS group.
Question 23	A,B,E	Outstanding IO, average IO, and write latency will help us determine the performance issue.
Question 24	D	Create multiple notifications so you can take action when each threshold of usage is breached and also project the usage for the whole month.
Question 25	C	RDS Multi-AZ switches the CNAME over to standby when a primary failure is detected automatically.
Question 26	D	S3 data is automatically replicated between multiple data centers and delivers more than 99.99% availability in a region.
Question 27	A,B,C	WordPress stores a lot of data that can be cached both in CloudFront and ElastiCache. Also, using a read replica can relieve the load.
Question 28	D	Evictions and GetMisses are caused due to lack of power. Increase the size of the instance.
Question 29	A, D	Only NACLs and Security Groups can limit communication between instances in the same VPC.
Question 30	B	Placement groups provide the lowest latency between EC2 instances.
Question 31	D	Create a new dedicated tenancy instance.
Question 32	B	Check the routing table is correctly configured with a route to the outside via the IGW.
Question 33	B	An ENI can be used for cases where hardcoded IPs are used.
Question 34	D	NACLs can be easily used to block a whole range of IPs from being allowed into the subnet and are very efficient for this purpose.
Question 35	B	AWS makes sure to not allow spoofing and packet sniffing.
Question 36	B	RDS has a built-in backup solution that allows you to create daily backups.

Question 37	C	With SGs, you only need to define inbound rules as they are state-full.
Question 38	B	You can't use spot instances as the payments can take up to four minutes. Spot instances might get terminated with a two-minute warning, which could mean you would lose transactions.
Question 39	C	There is no service in AWS for Ansible. Simply launch EC2 instances and manage them like you do on-premise servers.
Question 40	A,C	EMR and Elastic Beanstalk allow us to log into the instances.
Question 41	D	# can't be used in IAM usernames.
Question 42	B	The simplest solution is to use an instance-status-check CloudWatch alarm.
Question 43	A	Snapshots of the EBS volume should complete a backup in time.
Question 44	B	Your servers are overloaded if you see 500 errors. increase the number of instances.
Question 45	B,C	Internet gateway for public subnets and NAT gateways for private subnets.
Question 46	B	An ENI is MAC can be used for the license to persist instance failure.
Question 47	A	ELB sticky sessions from the same user are sent to the same instance so the load on the server can be gravely unbalanced.
Question 48	B	An in-progress snapshot isn't affected by ongoing reads and writes to the volume.
Question 49	D	Consolidated billing and cross-account roles are the correct way of doing it.
Question 50	B, D	Memory utilization and thread usage can't be determined by CloudWatch.
Question 51	B	When assigning permissions, always use the least privilege approach.
Question 52	A	MFA will dramatically increase the security of your console access.
Question 53	E	Any metric can be delivered as a custom metric.
Question 54	C	The number of instances in a placement group can only be defined at startup time.
Question 55	A,C	ElastiCache running Memcached or DynamoDB are possible data stores for sessions.
Question 56	A	Stopping and starting an instance is likely to fix the "impaired" system status.

Question 57	C	Use an LDAP replica of your on-premises LDAP to authenticate your AWS resources.
Question 58	A	Weighted routing can be used to send 10% of the traffic to the standby site.
Question 59	D	SNS can receive and deliver HTTP, SMS, and emails while a custom SNS subscriber to the same topic can then further deliver on the other protocols.
Question 60	B	To meet 99.9999% availability, cross-region bucket-replication needs to be used.

Answers to Mock Test 2:

Question	Answer(s)	Explanation
Question 1	C	Elastic Beanstalk is the simplest approach with the least management overhead.
Question 2	B	Use an NAT gateway to connect private instances to the internet.
Question 3	B	Only instance-store volumes provide in excess of 100,000 IOPS.
Question 4	A	CloudWatch can't see into the EC2 instance to determine how much usage is on disk.
Question 5	C	Apply a bucket policy that makes all objects in the bucket public.
Question 6	C	Among other logs, the error log is available in the RDS console.
Question 7	D	CloudWatch needs to notify Auto Scaling. The Auto Scaling policy is executed upon notification.
Question 8	A	Port 80 to the private security group isn't needed.
Question 9	C	Pre-warm the EBS volume to gain the most performance out of the box.
Question 10	B	S3 RRS durability is 99.95%.
Question 11	C	You can stream logs with the CloudWatch agent to CloudWatch Logs.
Question 12	C	Direct Connect can be delivered with a higher bandwidth than VPN.
Question 13	C	SSE is Encryption of data at rest with an S3-managed encryption key.
Question 14	B	Beanstalk supports rotating the logs to S3 and gives developers access to S3.

Question 15	B	Detailed monitoring collects metrics every minute at a cost.
Question 16	D	The local target allows all the subnets to communicate with each other by default.
Question 17	C	Corrupted messages that can't be processed are probably piling up in the queue. You would implement a DLQ for these messages.
Question 18	B,D	RDS and Redshift have the ability to back up the services out of the box.
Question 19	C	For 99.9% availability, running 1 instance is enough, but if an AZ goes down, we need to be able to restore this instance to another AZ, so 2 subnets and ELB are needed.
Question 20	B	You should suspend the Auto Scaling and figure out what's going on.
Question 21	A	Due to the number of users, you'll need to use Identity Federation.
Question 22	A,B,D	Read replicas, cache, or sharding can distribute the load on a database.
Question 23	D	To copy an instance, you'll need to copy the AMI to the other region.
Question 24	C	A route for `172.16.0.0/16` needs to be directed at the VPN gateway.
Question 25	B,D	Increasing the amount of CPU power by resizing the instance or adding more instances will help.
Question 26	A,B	Increasing the amount of CPU power by resizing the instance or adding more instances will help.
Question 27	A,B	C and D don't make sense.
Question 28	C	Geolocation can determine where the clients are coming from and direct them to the correct site.
Question 29	D	The deny statement has `NotipAddress = 100.100.100.20/32` so everyone else will be denied. Explicit denies override explicit allows.
Question 30	D	`sitefiles.s3-website.us-east-2.amazonaws.com`.
Question 31	D	You'll need to use Snowball as there's no way to transfer 150 TB across a 10 Gbit line in less than 24 hours.
Question 32	B	Tag your resources and create a dashboard based on the tag metrics.

Question 33	A	The public IP of the ELB is irrelevant in the security group.
Question 34	B	There's no such thing as a Client Order Preference.
Question 35	C	When configured with the Server Order Preference, the ELB gets to select the first cipher in its list that matches any one of the ciphers in the client's list.
Question 36	B	Bulk requests can fetch 10 messages at a time.
Question 37	D	DynamoDB is the best solution.
Question 38	B	ELB access logs will display connection information from your ELB.
Question 39	C	The onsite DNS can resolve both internal and external addresses. Also, since you can only use one DHCP option, set C is the correct answer.
Question 40	C	The default SQS message-retention period is four days.
Question 41	B	Each game has to have its own topic so that users can subscribe to each game.
Question 42	A	Specify the IP range in the bucket policy.
Question 43	D	MySQl RDS is only highly-available with Multi-AZ. You need to keep the read replica for the BI purposes.
Question 44	D	Route 53 enables automatic failover – all others are manual.
Question 45	A,D	Separate each department into its own account and use consolidated billing.
Question 46	D	We are scaling on a timed basis so resource usage is irrelevant.
Question 47	E	AWS is only responsible for physical disk security.
Question 48	C	Direct Connect makes the link private and the VPN encrypts it.
Question 49	B	S3 is the cheapest, most scalable solution.

Question 50	B	You can't deploy multi-region due to synchronous DB copies. Three AZs with four instances each will allow for a failure of one AZ and still keep eight instances to provide the baseline.
Question 51	C	Global DynamoDB table is the correct solution.
Question 52	A,B	The statement has two allow statements: one that allows listing and reading of all objects in all buckets, and another that allow writing to the `"samplebucket"` bucket.
Question 53	B	Static website with route 53 health check is the only solution that will provide a meaningful response to the restorer.
Question 54	B	The SDK automatically retries all the requests that receive this error.
Question 55	C	General, Error, and Slow Query logs are available in RDS.
Question 56	A	The CLI on the EC2 instance can be used to upload custom metrics.
Question 57	B,D	Both versioning and MFA delete can protect you from accidental object deletion.
Question 58	A,D	The maximum size is 256 KB. SQS works in the producer/consumer pull model. There's no such thing as the Lambda SQS worker CLI.
Question 59	B	CloudFormation would make it simplest to deploy these services.
Question 60	C,D	ELB logs record response, request, and backend processing times.

Other Books You May Enjoy

If you enjoyed this book, you may be interested in these other books by Packt:

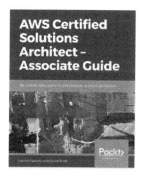

AWS Certified Solutions Architect - Associate Guide
Gabriel Ramirez, Stuart Scott

ISBN: 978-1-78913-066-9

- Explore AWS terminology and identity and access management
- Acquaint yourself with important cloud services and features in categories such as compute, network, storage, and databases
- Define access control to secure AWS resources and set up efficient monitoring
- Back up your database and ensure high availability by understanding all of the database-related services in the AWS Cloud
- Integrate AWS with your applications to meet and exceed non-functional requirements
- Build and deploy cost-effective and highly available applications

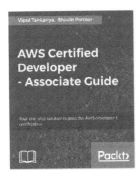

AWS Certified Developer - Associate Guide
Vipul Tankariya, Bhavin Parmar

ISBN: 978-1-78712-562-9

- Create and manage users, groups, and permissions using AWS Identity and Access Management services
- Create a secured Virtual Private Cloud (VPC) with Public and Private Subnets, Network Access Control, and Security groups
- Get started with Elastic Compute Cloud (EC2), launching your first EC2 instance, and working with it
- Handle application traffic with Elastic Load Balancing (ELB) and monitor AWS resources with CloudWatch
- Work with AWS storage services such as Simple Storage Service (S3), Glacier, and CloudFront
- Get acquainted with AWS DynamoDB – a NoSQL database service
- Coordinate work across distributed application components using Simple Workflow Service (SWF)

Leave a review - let other readers know what you think

Please share your thoughts on this book with others by leaving a review on the site that you bought it from. If you purchased the book from Amazon, please leave us an honest review on this book's Amazon page. This is vital so that other potential readers can see and use your unbiased opinion to make purchasing decisions, we can understand what our customers think about our products, and our authors can see your feedback on the title that they have worked with Packt to create. It will only take a few minutes of your time, but is valuable to other potential customers, our authors, and Packt. Thank you!

Index

AWS Storage Gateway 28

T

template analysis
  about 453
  description 453
  mappings 454, 455
  outputs 456
  parameters 454
  resources 455, 456
  version 453
templates, CloudFormation
  AWS Template Format Version 449
  conditions 449
  description 449
  mappings 449
  metadata 449
  outputs 450
  parameters 449
  resources 450
  transform 449
time-to-live (TTL) 207
topics
  creating 343, 344
  deleting 348
  publishing 346, 347
  subscribing to 345
  working with 343
traditional DNS system design
  features 226, 227
Transparent Data Encryption (TDE) 245

U

use cases, Amazon S3 and Glacier
  about 176
  archiving 180
  backup 179
  capabilities, extending of enterprise applications
    179
  data lake for big data 178
  data lakes for machine learning 178
  disaster recovery 180
  serverless hosting 177
  web-scale content delivery 177

use cases, queue
  batch operations example 321
  buffering example 321
  decoupling example 321
  request offloading example 321
use cases, SNS
  application alerts 340
  mobile push notifications 342
  push email 341
  SNS fan-out 338, 339, 340
  system alerts 340
  text messaging 341
user access control 310
user authentication 310
user permissions
  adding, to queue 326, 328
username 294

V

virtual desktop infrastructure (VDI) 30
virtual machine instance
  components 124
Virtual Private Cloud (VPC)
  about 85
  network security 98
  networks, defining 88
  overview 86
  peering connections 97
  private subnets 88
  public subnets 88
  subnets 86, 87
Virtual Private network (VPN) 90
Virtual Tape Library (VTL) 180
virtualization types, EC2 120
Volume Gateway 220
volume web console 130
VPC endpoints 95

W

weighted routing 236
What You See Is What You Get (WYSIWYG)
  design tool 449
write capacity units (WCUs) 304

Made in the USA
Middletown, DE
30 December 2019